HIGH CONCEPT

HIGH CONCEPT

DON SIMPSON
AND THE
HOLLYWOOD
CULTURE OF EXCESS

CHARLES FLEMING

MAIN
STREET
BOOKS

DOUBLEDAY

NEW YORK LONDON TORONTO SYDNEY AUCKLAND

A MAIN STREET BOOK
PUBLISHED BY DOUBLEDAY
a division of Random House, Inc.
1540 Broadway, New York, New York 10036

MAIN STREET BOOKS, DOUBLEDAY, and the portrayal of a building with a tree are
trademarks of Doubleday, a division of Random House, Inc.

High Concept was originally published in hardcover by Doubleday in 1998.
The Main Street Books edition is published by arrangement with Doubleday.

Book design by Brian Mulligan

The Library of Congress has cataloged the Doubleday hardcover edition of this book as
follows:
Fleming, Charles.
High concept: Don Simpson and the Hollywood culture of excess / Charles Fleming.
— 1st ed.
p. cm.
Includes index.
1. Simpson, Don, 1945–1996.   2. Motion picture producers and directors—
United States—Biography.   I. Title.
PN1998.3.S5358F64   1998
791.43′0232′092—dc21
[B]   97-42067
CIP

ISBN 0-385-48695-2

Printed in the United States of America

First Main Street Books Edition: April 1999

1   3   5   7   9   10   8   6   4   2

ACKNOWLEDGMENTS

This book was written under adverse conditions: Don Simpson's family and several of his closest friends opposed the reporting and writing of it. Inquiries and requests for interviews were met with refusals, or silence, from many Simpson acquaintances, colleagues and former employees. Some simply were too depressed or disgusted by Simpson to even discuss him. One former employee said of his time with Simpson, "It was the bleakest period of my life and it almost killed me. I just *can't* go back there." Some of them were silent out of loyalty to Simpson and his family. Others were silent out of fear that they themselves would come under scrutiny. Their peccadilloes and misadventures are chronicled in these pages. Others still were silent for fear of reprisal from the powerful men and women who control their careers. They already occupy the inner circle of hell they deserve. Simpson, who despite everything else was not a coward, would have despised them.

To those who did speak, often at risk to themselves, some under the cloak of anonymity, I am grateful.

I would also like to thank the many, many people whose help, advice, guidance and encouragement made this book possible. Among them are my agent David Vigliano; my book editors Shawn Coyne, Pat Mulcahy and Charlie Conrad; my former editor Peter Bart and current editor Sue

Horton; my colleagues John Connolly, Mark Schwed, Michael Fleming, J. Max Robins, John Brodie, Gordon Dillow, Patrick Goldstein, Richard Natale, Max Alexander, Jeffrey Ressner and Jeffrey Wells; my research assistants Jennifer Fox, Linda Lee, Michelle Perone and Chandler Cook; and my friends Mark Gill, Michael Cieply, Howard Brandy, Dr. Steven Woods, Eric and Jennifer Berkowitz, and Tony De Toro. For the editorial education that enabled me to tackle this project I am indebted to Jeff Silverman, Ray Bennett, Clay Felker, Mike Meyer, Stryker Maguire and Doug Stumpf, and for their unwavering personal support I am indebted to Christopher Hall and Bruce MacKenzie. For their great hospitality I thank Connie and Marty Stone. For two decades of guidance and good advice, I thank my friend A. J. Langguth.

In the writing and researching of this book I received invaluable information and assistance from the many people whose names appear in these pages. I especially want to thank Paul Schrader, Joe Eszterhas, Lynda Obst, Jay McInerney, Steve Roth, Paul Rosenfeld and the film editor Billy Weber, all of whom knew and loved Simpson and were not afraid to say so. I also owe an enormous debt of gratitude to the many journalists who came before I did to some parts of Simpson's story—among them John H. Richardson, Peter Biskind, Shawn Hubler, Chuck Phillips, Maureen Orth, Bernard Weinraub, Nancy Griffin, Kim Masters, Tony Schwartz and Lynn Hirschberg. Their hard work made mine easier, and demonstrates that Hollywood journalism need not be mindless celebrity idolatry.

I could not have written this book without the love and support of my father, mother and stepmother, and my two daughters. I could not write at all were it not for the patience of my wife, Julie Singer—to whom this book is dedicated.

TABLE OF CONTENTS

INTRODUCTION

1

CHAPTER ONE

THE BABY MOGUL

13

CHAPTER TWO

BEVERLY HILLS COP

53

CHAPTER THREE

BAD BOY

79

CHAPTER FOUR

HOLLYWOOD HIGH

111

CHAPTER FIVE

DAYS OF PLUNDER

137

CHAPTER SIX

WRETCHED EXCESS

161

CHAPTER SEVEN

THE PICTURES GOT SMALL

185

CHAPTER EIGHT

DOCTOR'S ORDERS

207

CHAPTER NINE

REHAB

217

CHAPTER TEN

DEATH

237

CHAPTER ELEVEN

AFTERMATH

259

NOTES

277

INDEX

287

It was Monday night at Morton's, and everyone was there. To this famed West Hollywood watering hole, where every Monday night of the year the show business community's leading citizens gathered to dine, do business, gossip and gawk, Hollywood's most powerful men and women had come this wintry 1996 evening to pay their respects to a friend. Sipping Chardonnay or Perrier, Armani-clad in charcoal and black, were Michael Eisner and Michael S. Ovitz. Eisner ran Disney and was at that moment concocting an $18-billion scheme to merge it with CapCities/ABC. Ovitz had been Hollywood's most powerful agent before joining Eisner at Disney, but would soon be evicted from the Magic Kingdom, leaving with a golden parachute valued at more than $100 million. Across the room were the diminutive, casually dressed David Geffen, the billionaire mogul, and Jeffrey Katzenberg, the former Disney *Wunderkind* who had recently teamed with Geffen and filmmaker Steven Spielberg to create the new entertainment giant DreamWorks, after himself failing to achieve the partnership with Eisner that Ovitz was now finding impossible to forge. Barry Diller, the steel-hard executive who had run Paramount and 20th Century-Fox and was now building his own independent entertainment empire, was talking with Joe Roth, who had run Fox's movie division under Diller and now ran Disney's under Eisner. His counterpart at Paramount, the glamorous Sherry Lansing, chatted with Robert Daly, cochairman of Warner Bros., and with Jeff "Ice" Berg, the legendarily tough International Creative Management executive who, in the wake of Ovitz' move to Disney, was now the most powerful agent in the film business.

These were giants. Between them they shared control of the entire entertainment industry, an empire of movies, television shows, records, books, merchandise and theme parks that generated hundreds of billions of dollars a year, and that constituted America's number one export product. The meetings they took, the memos they wrote, the decisions they made every day determined what title was playing at the local Bijou from Kowloon to Kathmandu, what the citizens were watching on television from Rio to Reykjavik, what was playing on radios in Manila and Moscow, what titles Americans were taking home from their Blockbuster and Wherehouse video stores and what characters appeared on the hamburger wrappers when they ate at McDonald's and Burger King. A thumbs-up or thumbs-down from these men and women could make or break a career in an instant. They were here, this Monday night at Morton's, to honor one of their number, surrounded by some of the glittering personalities who helped them sell all that popular entertainment product. The man they were honoring had made many of them rich, many of them powerful and many of them famous.

Warren Beatty was there, as were Michelle Pfeiffer, Don Johnson, Nick Nolte, Richard Dreyfuss, Will Smith and dozens of other celebrities. Producers Dawn Steel and Lynda Obst, each of whom had trained at the honoree's knee and each of whom had written scathingly of what Hollywood can do to humanity, were there, too. Glittery Hollywood hangers-on like Tina Sinatra and Alana Stewart, the former Mrs. George Hamilton, spoke in hushed tones about the guest of honor. Powerhouse attorney Robert Shapiro, who had helped defend O. J. Simpson in his trial for the murders of Nicole Brown and Ron Goldman, nodded with powerhouse attorney Howard Weitzman, who had years before helped defend famed auto manufacturer John DeLorean in his felony cocaine possession case. To their side was private investigator Anthony Pellicano, who had come to Los Angeles to work on the DeLorean case and, finding an entire community of rich and powerful people who needed help skirting the law, never left.

The Melrose Avenue parking lot was filled to capacity with rows of

Mercedes, Jaguar and BMW coupés, their noses pointed out like getaway cars. It was, in the local parlance, an "A-list" gathering. Noting with approval the stellar crowd—and the fact that Morton's was actually closed for this private affair on its most A-list night of the week—talent agent Jim Wiatt whistled and said under his breath, "Wow. Simpson is *hot.*"

Indeed, the guest of honor would have been impressed. But he wasn't there. The guest of honor was Don Simpson, and Don Simpson was dead. This Monday night at Morton's was a memorial service to mark his passing.

His death earlier that January, of sudden heart failure, at the age of fifty-two, had shocked and saddened but not surprised Simpson's friends and colleagues. Although he had been for almost twenty years one of Hollywood's most successful filmmakers—producing, with partner Jerry Bruckheimer, the hit movies *Flashdance, Beverly Hills Cop, Top Gun, Days of Thunder, Crimson Tide, Bad Boys, The Rock* and others—he was also the town's most notoriously excessive bad boy. ("I've been waiting for this call for twenty years," his former boss Michael Eisner said when Simpson's lawyer, Jake Bloom, called to announce his death.) His appetite for illicit sex and illegal drugs was legendary. Like the voluptuaries of ancient Sybaris, and extreme even by the local standards of decadence and depravity, Simpson and his exploits were fabled: his hookers, his hot cars, his drug addiction, his obsessive attention to wardrobe, weight loss and plastic surgery and his fascination with the dark side of life were so continuous they had become commonplace. He was, in the words of screenwriter Joe Eszterhas, "a true American original."[1]

The five-minute video presentation that was the centerpiece to the Morton's gathering mentioned nothing of Simpson's excesses. Instead, as befits a memorial service, the video highlighted Simpson's successes. The lights went down and the room went hushed. Simpson's friends and colleagues watched a montage, created by documentary filmmakers George Zaloom and Les Mayfield, of Simpson moments. Simpson fat, Simpson thin; Simpson bearded, Simpson bare-faced. The childhood Don: in a cowboy costume, in a Cub Scout uniform, a chubby, bespectacled boy cradling a pop gun or swinging a baseball bat. Simpson skiing. Simpson on movie sets and in music studios, under the blare of signature Simpson-Bruckheimer sound track hits like "What a Feeling," "You Take My Breath Away" and "(Highway to the) Danger Zone." Intercut were clips of Simpson-Bruckheimer stars Tom Cruise, Eddie Murphy, Michelle Pfeiffer,

Denzel Washington, Gene Hackman and others. Simpson himself appeared on camera as an interview subject, delivering signature Simpson wisdom in signature Simpson fashion—lightning-fast, without hesitation, without sentiment: "The degree to which you make enough money to feel that you don't need to make any more money is the degree to which you have to deal with something that's pretty interesting. It's called *you*." Or, "Just because you want it and don't have it and you then get it doesn't mean that getting it ain't fun. It *is* fun. You have to be prepared to take it beyond that, however, and be who and what you really are." Or, "There's no such thing as always, and there's no such thing as forever, and there's no such thing as now. My instinct tells me that if there's an is-ness, it always *was* is, and it always will be is, and it ain't gonna be less than or more than." The video concluded with this observation: "I feel like I've been around before. And I feel like I'm gonna be around after . . ."

In a sense, he was. Following Hollywood tradition, Simpson's friends mourned him by placing "tribute" advertisements in the industry trade papers *Daily Variety* and *The Hollywood Reporter*, paying up to $4,000 a page, deifying their lost friend to an almost numinous degree. Paramount, Disney and Warner Bros. bought full-page ads. Jeffrey and Marilyn Katzenberg cited Robert Frost: "I have been one acquainted with the night . . ." Jerry and Linda Bruckheimer wrote "Goodbye, Dear Soulmate." A collection of fourteen Simpson-Bruckheimer assistants pooled their money for a quotation from Shakespeare's *Twelfth Night:* "Be not afraid of greatness." Longtime friend Steve Tisch elevated Simpson even further, citing Jonathan Swift: "When a true genius appears in the world, you may know him by this sign, that the dunces are all in confederacy against him."

The hagiography would continue. Obituaries and appreciations appeared everywhere from the *Los Angeles Times* to the *New York Times*, from *Premiere* and *Screen International* to *Time, People, New York, Buzz, Los Angeles, Playboy* and *Entertainment Weekly.* "Don was an original—the real thing," one friend said. "A philosopher, a poet, an intellect," said another.

As the national magazines took their turns eulogizing, though, Simpson's contradictions became glaring. He was beloved and he was loathed with equal ferocity. A man of intense intelligence and an encyclopedic understanding of film history and the inner workings of the film industry, he was also the cocreator of some of Hollywood's most formulaic, simple-

minded movies. He was outrageously generous to friends and family—
sending his parents on holiday cruises with their friends, paying medical
expenses for one madam who supplied him with prostitutes and helping
another post her bail, putting his younger brother through law school and
paying private school tuition for his niece and nephew—but he was horri-
bly abusive to secretaries and assistants. He was intensely arrogant, but he
was *consumed* by self-doubt and self-loathing. He was a control freak
obsessed with fitness, youth and health, and also a binge eater with a
history of dangerous weight gain and loss, and an out-of-control, seriously
addicted drug user.

He was a carnival of contradictions, a garish, screaming midway of
natural and unnatural impulses, each display a sideshow of excess. Everything he did was done with intensity, total commitment and an admirable
absence of hypocrisy—whether it was browbeating a script through fifteen
writers and thirty-seven drafts until it was a fable made for morons or
beating a hooker until she begged for mercy. And, in Hollywood, he
thrived.

He was, in short, very much a Hollywood fixture. His excesses, his
strengths and weaknesses, his dreams and demons, his enthusiasms and
addictions, personal and professional, were entirely of Hollywood,
uniquely suited to not just the film industry but specifically the film
industry of the 1970s and 1980s. He was so perfect a representation of
what was right with Hollywood, and what was wrong, that he might have
been its mascot.

From the outside, Hollywood is a mass-market fantasy factory responsible for billions of dollars in annual revenue and for America's single
largest export product. It is the creator of our collective imagination, and
perhaps the lasting record of what we are and believe and dream. From the
outside, it is Eldorado to thousands of young people, who every year leave
small towns across the country and travel to Los Angeles dreaming of
becoming the next Tom Cruise or Demi Moore.

From the inside, Hollywood is a shark tank, a place of desperate ambition and greed, a great, grinding soulless machine whose operators have
virtually no idea what they are doing. The most forthright of them admit
that they have no way of anticipating which of their movies—if any—will
succeed at the box office. A star-driven action movie with a script from a
million-dollar Oscar-winning screenwriter, released at the height of the
summer moviegoing season, is as close as Hollywood comes to a can't-

miss proposition—but the movie is often *Last Action Hero* or *Hudson Hawk.* Hollywood is a crapshoot, at best, a place where, screenwriter William Goldman has famously written, the first rule is "Nobody knows nothing."

As a result, the entertainment industry does not require anything of its inside people other than an ability to produce hit movies. It doesn't ask its employees to be intelligent, educated, decent, honorable, fair, good-looking or ethical or ethnical: It only asks that they produce income-generating product.

And, as it does not require intelligence, education, decency, honor or fairness, neither does it reward those qualities. Hollywood is the place where one can overhear dialogue such as this, one morning at the Four Seasons Hotel:

Man #1: "You're lying! You're lying to me!"

Man #2: "Yes, I know. But *hear me out.*"

In Hollywood, so much deviousness is tolerated—expected, even—that objectionable behavior finds no objection. David Geffen brags about steaming open letters in the William Morris Agency mail room, when he was starting out in the entertainment industry, to learn business secrets. In most industries this is called mail fraud, and it is a felony. In Hollywood, this is called ambition, and it is admired. As an industry, Hollywood ignores every kind of personal and professional idiosyncrasy. Vile behavior is not simply excused. It is not noticed. It does not matter.

In this world Simpson thrived as he could not have in any other. He was irrational and unpredictable, and irresponsible in the extreme, but brilliant, often enough, that for a long time none of his peculiarities proved a liability. Among his peers in the movie industry, Simpson was admired for his directness. "Bruckheimer is the one to really watch out for," one veteran industry observer said once. "He'll stab you in the back. Simpson at least will stab you in the chest." That, in Hollywood, is what passes for a compliment.

Simpson was "colorful," at best, and excessive, at worst, to a degree that would have made him an intolerable, unacceptable pariah in other industries. In Hollywood he thrived—because he knew how to work the system and he knew how to create movies that, reviled though they were by the critics, made buckets of money at the box office.

But by the mid-1990s Hollywood was changing. Simpson was, increasingly, an anachronism. When Simpson entered the business, the movie

studios had been self-contained universes run by a small group of powerful men whose personal tastes and personal friendships determined what
movies got made and how and by whom. Many were Simpson's friends,
men who had walked with him on the wild side and who had profited
greatly by his genius. Now most of those men had grown up, as Simpson
had not, and had gotten married and had children and settled down. And
most of them worked for movie companies that were now owned by
enormous conglomerates whose agendas did not always match Hollywood's or its filmmakers', and whose business plans were not informed by
personal relationships with brilliant, undependable filmmakers. A new
brand of film executive, culled from business schools, with M.B.A.'s or law
degrees in hand, was running things. Hands-on producers like Simpson
were becoming powerless. Simpson had seen this coming. "Unfortunately,
most producers today call themselves producers but what they really do is
stay in their offices and make phone calls," Simpson had complained in
1985. "That's why producers have gotten a bad name. They're not filmmakers. They're deal-makers. And they're not developers. They don't
know anything about script. They are businessmen. They are smart with
money. The good producers are self-generators. They come up with the
original ideas. The others go to lunch."[2] Worse, the people running the
corporations that owned the studios misunderstood and mistrusted Hollywood. "A schleppy little vice president in a movie studio makes three
times what a chairman of the board makes in the gypsum business,"
Simpson observed. Executives in other businesses "have a hard time dealing with that. I mean we drive around here in Mercedeses and Ferraris, and
they're driving Volkswagens. They say, those Hollywood guys are living
in these beautiful houses and they have jets and all that stuff." Simpson
didn't think this was unfair—"We are a high-profile, high-glamour, high-
income business," he said. "Nuts and bolts don't make that much
money"[3]—but he also knew that, increasingly, his type of moviemaker
was on its way to extinction. Like the cowboy he pretended to be, with his
hand-tooled boots and his outlaw attitudes, Simpson was seeing his own
personal Old West disappear. The kind of high-concept movie he'd helped
invent would continue to rule release schedules and dominate the Hollywood box office, but his place in the Hollywood food chain had vanished.

Simpson also understood and battled with the truth that the power and
money given a successful Hollywood producer had a potentially self-
destructive cost. He once said that Hollywood crippled its citizenry with

"too much money, too much freedom. It's a town that allows as much eccentricity as you like—as long as you're productive."

Morton's that night was full of eccentrics, some of them very productive indeed. There was the film producer whose idea of a good time was taking a hooker shopping on Rodeo Drive for lingerie—and then wearing it himself while having sex with her. There was the film producer who paid young women substantial sums of money to defecate on him. There was the rock star who hired pairs of young women to have sex while he watched. There was the former studio executive so paranoid and so covetous of his good name that he would only meet hookers at the seediest of motels. There was the husband-and-wife movie producer couple who were among the industry's biggest cocaine users, between them keeping Hollywood's biggest dealers rich. And there around them were their agents, managers, lawyers and colleagues—the executive enablers—who knew all of this, knew it and were amused by it and were paid handsomely to keep it to themselves.

That they were there that night at Morton's was a real testimonial to their affection for Simpson. Many were friends from the old days, when Simpson was a rising star at Paramount—a bright, funny, self-effacing and very effective movie executive with a brilliant eye for character and script structure. Many were friends from Simpson's days as an independent producer, a period in which he cranked out more hits and made more money than any of his peers. Some of them, even, were more recent acquaintances. They knew—as the others did not, as the Hollywood community did not—the real extent of Simpson's drug addictions and sexual depravity.

But even *they* might not have known the real story, because the real story was dark almost beyond knowing.

As autopsy reports and pharmaceutical records would later reveal, Simpson through the summer of 1995, the summer before his death, was on a regimen that included multiple daily injections of Toradol, for pain; Librium, to control his mood swings; Ativan, every six hours, for agitation; Valium, every six hours, for anxiety; Depakote, every six hours, to counter "acute mania"; Thorazine, every four hours, for anxiety; Cogentin, for agitation; Vistaril, every six hours, for anxiety; and lorazepam, every six hours, also for anxiety. He was also taking, in pill and tablet form, additional doses of Valium, plus the pain relievers Vicodin, diphenoxylate, diphenhydramine and Colanadine, plus the medications lithium carbonate, nystatin, Narcan, haloperidol, Promethazine, Benztropine, Unisom, Atarax, Compazine, Xanax, Desyrel, Tigan and phenobarbital. (Simpson's pharmaceutical records for July 1995 show billings of $12,902—from one pharmacy, through one psychiatrist, at a time when Simpson was using at least eight pharmacies and several doctors, receiving medications using the aliases Dan Gordon, Dan Wilson, Don Wilson and Dawn Wilson, in addition to his own name. A law enforcement source who investigated Simpson's pharmaceutical records estimated his monthly prescription medication expenses at more than $60,000. One ten-day period in August 1995 shows Simpson's pharmacy expenses at $38,600.) Police and coroners' documents also show that Simpson was experimenting with prescription doses of morphine, Seconal and gamma hydroxybutyrate, or GHB. These medications were being ingested, autopsy reports would show, in addition to large quantities of alcohol and cocaine.

Excessive doses also have deadly potential. Overuse of Atarax, Benadryl, Compazine, Venlafaxine, Haldol, lithium carbonate, Narcan, Phenergan and Tigan—any *one* of these medications—can cause seizures and convulsions. Overuse of Ativan can lead to confusion, depression, hallucinations and delirium. Among the side effects listed for overdosage of Desyrel are priapism, arrhythmia and "unexplained death." Overdosages of Narcan can cause tachycardia and "cardiac arrest," also a potential risk with abuse of Vistaril. According to the *Physician's Desk Reference*, the sleep aid Unisom, which Simpson had used for years, "should not be taken longer than two weeks [or] concurrent with alcohol or other drugs."[4]

More ominously, Simpson was using heroin. Sometime in 1993 one of Simpson's prostitute friends had introduced him to a heroin dealer who worked under the name Mr. Brownstone. (Heralded in Hollywood song, he is the subject of the Guns N' Roses tune "Mr. Brownstone," a nickname based on the particular brown-hued Mexican heroin the dealer sold.) A frightening character whose eyes burn bright with paranoia, he has long dealt drugs to the record and movie crowd, and even suspects it was his dope the young actor River Phoenix ingested on the night he collapsed and died in front of the Sunset Strip's Viper Room.

Simpson had been a dying man, literally, for at least six months prior to his actual death. Few in the room that night at Morton's knew that. They could easily have rattled off a complete list of Simpson's hit movies, and most had a private Simpson anecdote involving Simpson misbehavior, but few concerned themselves with the degree to which Simpson had corrupted and destroyed himself living those anecdotes and making those movies.

Fewer still knew that, in New York, the mother of Simpson's only apparent blood heir was grieving all on her own.

Victoria Fulton Vicuna, a dark Chilean-born beauty, had been introduced to Simpson at Manhattan's trendy Canal Bar in 1988, at a dinner party attended by Simpson, Bruckheimer, a group of bright young socialites and the novelist Jay McInerney—whose best-seller, *Bright Lights, Big City*, Simpson and Bruckheimer wanted to turn into a movie. (The subsequent screen version was produced by Sydney Pollack and directed by James Bridges.) A twentysomething brunette with an appetite for high times and royalty—she was then involved with the Prince of Lichtenstein—Vicuna began dating Simpson, seeing him when she was in Los Angeles or when he was in New York. Vicuna became pregnant in 1992 and believed Simpson was the father. By then, however, she was involved with another man and was afraid to tell Simpson he had a daughter. When that relationship ended, she contacted Simpson, by telephone and by mail, and gave him the news. Simpson never responded, though he did blurt out to a friend who also knew Vicuna, "You think you've got troubles? Victoria had a baby, and I'm the dad!" Though Vicuna pressed her claim for several more years, Simpson never took or returned her calls, never admitted or denied that he was the father. After his death, and falling on hard times financially herself, Vicuna went to Simpson's brother, Lary, who with his parents grieved that night at Morton's. It would be two years before the family would respond to Vicuna's claims and offer her a financial settlement in the child's name.

Simpson and his partner, Bruckheimer, were once asked to describe their personal and professional differences. Bruckheimer said their differences were most evident in "the way we handle situations. If there's a huge blowup, I'll be sent in to tame the lion, whereas Don will come and shoot him, although he'd decided beforehand that the lion should be left alive. Don comes in and there's blood all over the wall." Simpson immediately countered, with the typical Simpson bravado that was sensitive only to perfecting the pose and the sound bite, "The lion shouldn't have fucked with us."[5]

In the end, Simpson was the lion tamer and the lion he should not have fucked with. His only victim was himself, and there was blood everywhere.

If Simpson can ultimately be seen as representing anything, if his life can be taken as a cautionary tale, the caution is this: Beware a life devoid of negative consequences. Beware what writer Eszterhas described as Simpson's "terminal isolation."[6] Simpson for most of his adult life, thanks in large part to his brilliant conception of the high-concept movie, but also to the indulgences of the industry in which he worked, was able to explore in his personal life the most brutal of excesses with an absolute absence of damage to his professional life. In another industry, his excesses would have resulted in a firing, a suspension, a forced stay in rehab, intervention by his superiors or abandonment by his peers. In another industry, Simpson's behavior would have made him an outcast and ensured his expulsion from the club of the powerful. There would have been negative consequences, and those consequences might have forced him to hit a bottom from which he might have rebounded.

In Hollywood, though, because his movies kept making money, as the tales of his drug use and hooker habit became more and more sordid, Simpson simply became another show business character. "That's just Don," his associates would say, and shake their heads in wonder.

Hollywood fiddled while Simpson burned, and after his final self-immolation, fiddled on.

CHAPTER ONE

THE BABY MOGUL

One spring afternoon in 1981 a visitor checked in at the 5555 Melrose Avenue gates of Paramount Pictures. He was a writer for *The Hollywood Reporter*, the entertainment industry trade paper, and he was there to visit Don Simpson, the young executive who had just been named president of Paramount Productions. A gate guard waved him through and directed him to Paramount's executive building, where offices housed Simpson's bosses—Barry Diller, Paramount Pictures chairman, and Michael Eisner, its president and chief operating officer, and several of Simpson's underlings, among them Jeffrey Katzenberg and Dawn Steel.

The reporter was girded for the worst. The charismatic, burly, bearded Simpson was already a legend in the making, as famous for his snap decisions and his machine-gun patter as he was for his hair-trigger temper. The reporter sat nervously for thirty minutes, until a secretary led him into Simpson's offices—all white, with white linen easy chairs and couches, the walls adorned with Warhol prints of Chairman Mao Tse-tung. One wall was lined with framed copies of Simpson's business cards, chronicling his rise from the bottom to the top of the Paramount executive ranks.

Simpson emerged presently from a back room. He asked the reporter, "What time is it?" The reporter told him it was four o'clock.

"Four o'clock," Simpson repeated. "You know what I like to do at four o'clock? I like to pour myself a big drink, lay out a few lines and abuse a screenwriter. Take a seat."

The reporter watched as Simpson poured four fingers of Macallan Scotch from a cut-glass decanter, cut six lines of cocaine onto a glass-covered side table and serially snorted them into his nose. He took a deep glug of Scotch and dialed the telephone. For the next twenty minutes the reporter listened as Simpson harangued the unfortunate, unidentified screenwriter. "You're the stupidest son of a bitch in Hollywood, you asshole," Simpson shouted between gulps of Scotch. "You're a talentless piece of shit. No one respects you. Everyone knows you're an idiot. You have no fucking future in this business." When he had exhausted his wrath, Simpson hung up the phone and said to the reporter, "So, let's talk about my slate of movies."[1]

Simpson's rise to the president's office had been rapid. He'd come to the studio, to a lowly position, in 1976, and immediately established himself as a sharp mind, a quick study, sure of his opinions and unafraid to voice them. Michael Eisner had named him vice president of creative affairs in early 1977. A year later he was named vice president of production. In 1980 Eisner promoted him to senior vice president of worldwide production. He was part of a young, fast-paced, urgent crowd of senior executives who were changing the way Hollywood did business. Chairman Diller was thirty-seven. Among his chief lieutenants—who would earn the group nickname Killer Dillers—were Eisner, then thirty-six, and Simpson, then thirty-three. (Jeffrey Katzenberg, whose doggedness at Paramount would earn him the nickname the Golden Retriever, had not arrived yet.) Over the next decade these men would transform almost every aspect of life in Hollywood—from the way power was achieved and exercised to every detail of the way movies were conceived, budgeted, cast, filmed, marketed and released. Barely distant over the Hollywood horizon was a monster called high concept. This monster was a supercharged, simpleminded creature, an Aesop's fable on crystal meth, a movie that any producer could pitch in thirty seconds and any audience could understand without even thinking. It was the big-screen equivalent of the popcorn served in the lobby: tasty, devoid of nourishment, free of any resonance. To many critics and entertainment analysts, who credit Simpson with creating it, this is the monster that ate Hollywood.

Simpson's presence on the Paramount lot was, in the first place, unlikely. Five years before, in 1975, he'd come to an interview on a fluke. A pal of his, the Loews hotel heir Steve Tisch—nephew of Larry Tisch, who would later own CBS and Westinghouse—had received a phone call from Richard Sylbert, then head of production for Paramount. He had Tisch in mind for a job on the lot, a job Tisch, who had his eye on movie producing, and who would later make the films *Risky Business*, *Big Business* and *Forrest Gump*, did not want. He turned Sylbert down, but in doing so recommended Simpson for the post. After first apologizing for Simpson's weak résumé and scant movie experience, Tisch told Sylbert, "He's the brightest, most interesting guy I've met here, and he knows everything about Hollywood. You have to meet him." Jerry Bruckheimer, already a friend, lent Simpson a sports coat; Tisch chipped in cash to get Simpson a haircut and gas up his car. Simpson bowled Sylbert over and got the job.[2]

"He had a lot of energy, and he had worked around the business, and he was very rock and roll oriented," Sylbert recalled. "I liked him immediately. He was from Alaska, which meant he could talk about fishing, which meant more to me at the time than movies. We had a meeting and I called [Barry] Diller and said, 'I want to hire this kid.' Diller said, 'Send him down,' and they hit it off and I hired him. You go on instinct, and I just liked him. And he was thrilled to get the job. He came back from Barry's office all lit up."

Employment at Paramount rescued Simpson from a rather aimless existence. For the past several years he had fumbled around Hollywood's lower reaches. He'd originally entered the business in San Francisco, where he'd segued from the advertising agency Jack Wodell & Associates to the marketing department of Warner Bros. For one of his first assignments he'd held a press screening for *Performance*, renting an exhibition space and buying two pounds of marijuana and twenty cases of cheap red wine. ("The movie became the talk of the town," he said later. "Why not? Everybody was loaded.")[3] Warner Bros. brought him in 1972 to its Burbank, California, lot, where he made a strong impression but toiled without distinction. Everyone knew he was smart and ambitious—Sid Ganis, at that time an executive in Warner Bros.' advertising department, would later say, "He was round and bearded and very sharp, and different from most of the kids in the publicity department. He had a presence that put him *out there,* in front of everybody''[4]—but no one knew to what, exactly, his smarts were suited.

No one missed his intensity. "He was just incredibly competitive," recalled Bill Stern, a Warner colleague with whom Simpson shared a Hollywood cottage for a season. "We'd leave for work at the studio at the same time. He'd take the freeway just to get there thirty seconds before me." He did not stay long at Warner Bros. He was fired, and for almost three years had no steady work. It was, as former friend Julia Phillips said, "horrible for him. In this town you absolutely *are* what you do. He was without a job for three years. There is no more embittering experience."[5]

In the interim, Simpson auditioned for acting parts and tried his hand at screenwriting. He and a friend he'd met at the legendary drugstore/coffee shop Schwab's, Paul Bartel, later the celebrated director of offbeat movies like *Eating Raoul* and *Scenes from the Class Struggle in Beverly Hills,* sold only one, the road movie *Cannonball.* Simpson later said, "Within forty-eight hours of pitching [it], I had $6,250 in my jeans! I thought, 'This is it. I'm a star.' "[6] Simpson and Bartel took the movie to the Edinburgh Film Festival, where they shared a hotel room and where Simpson shared some potentially fabricated personal history with his partner. "Don told me he had had homosexual experiences in jail when he was sixteen or so," Bartel later said. "My one real regret is that I didn't have sex with him when I had the opportunity."[7] Simpson later claimed to have demonstrated his heterosexuality, on the same festival tour, to another rising star. He said that, while he and Bartel were attending the Deauville Film Festival, there was a knock at his hotel room door one night. "It was Melanie Griffith, *totally nude,*" Simpson said. "She was only nineteen then—her body, you could bounce quarters off it. So I went to her room and partied till the sun came up. I mean, thank you, God."[8]

By day, "networking" in a rather dilatory fashion, Simpson hung out at the tennis courts in West Hollywood's Plummer Park, playing set after set of men's doubles. He was very competitive, if not naturally skilled. "He was a very good, very aggressive player, because he desperately wanted to win," according to a frequent partner at the time, the actor Peter Cannon. "But he usually lost."[9] (Steve Rasnick, a racquetball teacher and friend, said the same of Simpson's small-court game: "He used to call and say, 'The fat man wants a game.' He had great stamina for a fat guy, but only average speed. What he lacked in skill he compensated for with desire. He was a low B-level player, but he loved the game.")[10] The tennis games were often played for money—a set of singles for ten dollars, a set of doubles for twenty—and the money was important to Simpson, who lived in a small Hollywood apartment and, in a town that attaches great significance to the automobile, was driving a beat-up old BMW. "The tennis money was his eating money," Cannon recalled. "And he hated to lose. He'd get frustrated. When he'd lose, he'd rush up to the net, drop his pants and piss on the net. He'd say, 'I can't take this shit,' and he'd piss on the net." Before games, or after, Simpson and Cannon, sometimes along with other Hollywood hopefuls like the future director Paul Mazursky or the future film producer Craig Baumgarten, would hang out at the International House of Pancakes on La Cienega Boulevard or the House of Pies on Vermont. (Simpson, already a man of prodigious appetite, would according to Cannon sometimes down two entire pies at a sitting.)

He was also part of what might have passed in Hollywood at that time as a "salon" of intellectuals, loosely organized by the husband and wife team of Julia and Michael Phillips. The couple had a home on the beach, at Trancas, where some of the industry's smart set would gather for weekends. Margot Kidder and Katharine Ross, hot off the success of *Butch Cassidy and the Sundance Kid*, were regular guests at the Phillipses' Friday-night-to-Monday-morning parties. So were Ron Howard and Liza Minnelli, then dating. Kidder began dating the director Brian De Palma, who introduced the Phillipses to writer-director Paul Schrader, who brought Simpson into the group. Writer-director John Milius and filmmaker Martin Scorsese were around. Carly Simon was around. There was lots of marijuana and sometimes a cache of coke—like the time the Phillipses financed a group of surfers who smuggled eight kilos of cocaine from Peru.[11]

Simpson would later insist that he was "blindsided"[12] by the job at Paramount, and complained that it had sidetracked him as a screenwriter and condemned him to "ten years in management." In fact, the studio was the perfect proving ground for Simpson's singular genius. For this young executive on the rise, Paramount was paradise.

Studios in the 1970s were relatively lean landscapes. In 1974, when Robert Evans stepped down as head of Paramount, and Barry Diller stepped in, there were only two men running Paramount. Diller and Sylbert's offices were on Canyon Drive in Beverly Hills—not even on the Paramount production lot—a move made at the suggestion of Evans' right-hand executive, Peter Bart. Aside from two development executives and one business affairs officer, Diller and Sylbert were alone, as had been Evans and Bart before them. "We didn't have much of a structure—we just made the decisions and made the movies," Bart remembered. "I went to San Francisco [in 1997] for the twenty-fifth anniversary screening of *The Godfather*, and I bumped into [film director] Phil Kaufman. He'd made *The White Dawn* for us, and we were laughing about the old days. He said, 'All the time I was making that movie, you're the only executive I ever even talked to.' He never met the business affairs guy, or the music department guy, or the legal affairs guy, or the merchandising guy, or any of the other creative executives—because there weren't any. It was just us."[13]

For a while, under Diller, that did not change. "In those days," Sylbert explained, "I was not a 'professional executive.' Most of us weren't. We were people making movies." Paramount was not the machine it would later become; the development roster was almost empty. Sylbert remembered that the exiting Evans had left behind almost nothing. There were two Evans productions in the pipeline, *Marathon Man* and *Black Sunday*. There was a script from Bill Lancaster—Burt's son—called *Bad News Bears*. There was a project that Sylbert optioned his first week on the job, a book that had been collecting shelf dust, called *Looking for Mr. Goodbar*. There were other projects in various stages of discussion, among them the scripts or script material that would later become the films *A River Runs Through It* and *Interview with the Vampire*.

And that was it. Paramount was, at that time, almost a start-up outfit, but one that already had a production lot and a library of films creating revenue. Sylbert had taken a segue into the executive suite in the midst of a career as a production designer, working on such august, and Oscar-worthy, titles as *A Face in the Crowd, Splendor in the Grass, The Manchurian Candidate, The Pawnbroker, Who's Afraid of Virginia Woolf* and *The Graduate*, before coming to Paramount. (After leaving he would earn more Oscar nominations and statuettes for movies like *Chinatown, Shampoo, Reds, The Cotton Club* and *Dick Tracy*.) Now he had a studio to run. Sylbert hired Simpson and turned him loose.

Soon Simpson was creating a mystique and a reputation. He moved fast and he talked fast and he didn't worry about the consequences. The producer Lynda Obst, then a journalist, first met Simpson during the mid-1970s. She was terribly impressed. "He was the coolest, smartest guy I'd ever met—and the fastest," she said. One night, "dazzled" by his intelligence as they talked, she told him, "You are so smart. You could be a magazine editor." Simpson, she remembered, "stared at me like I was from Venus. He said, 'No. I don't want to be the one doing the writing. I want to be the one they're writing *about*.'" Obst was floored. She'd meant it as an enormous compliment. Already, she said, "Simpson knew he was a 'character.' He knew he was the subject. I'd just never met anyone bold enough to say that."[14]

Simpson's blunt, direct manner was applied to work as well. "I'm going to make this really easy for you, and I'm going to make it really hard," Simpson said at the time to a reader—an employee who read and analyzed scripts for the studio and then made recommendations to studio executives, using a printed form to check off boxes marked "recommend," "maybe" and "don't recommend." "There will be, from here on, 'recommend' and 'don't recommend,'" Simpson said. "There will be no more 'maybe.'"[15] Screenwriter Robert Towne, who'd won an Oscar for writing Paramount's *Chinatown* several years earlier, and who went on to become a close Simpson friend and colleague, said, "That sums up Don completely. No more 'maybe.' He wasn't a 'maybe' kind of guy. This town is full of executives who refuse to take a position. They may be smart, but when it comes to judging material, they just don't know. Don knew. He didn't need the 'maybe,' because he always just knew about story."[16] Expanding on the theme, Towne said, "Don had specific ideas on what an audience wanted to feel, when they wanted to feel it and what would be transporting for them. He prided himself on being a member of the audience. He always said, 'I buy my popcorn and watch a movie and want to feel something.'"[17]

Simpson had certainly been busy refining his own "story." He was mythmaking, rewriting his own rather pedestrian childhood until it resembled the Great American Novel—or, since Simpson preferred comic books to actual ones, the Classic Comics version—an almost gothic fairy tale of pain, redemption and resurrection.

He was born Donald Clarence Simpson, on October 29, 1943, at Swedish Hospital in Seattle, Washington. His father, Russell J. Simpson, twenty-six, of Sidney, Iowa, was a mechanic with Boeing; his mother, June Hazel Clark Simpson, also twenty-six, of Cottonwood, South Dakota, was a housewife. Far to the south, Hollywood did not take notice. Headlines for the day indicate business as usual in the wartime film industry: Alan Ladd, then under contract to Paramount, got his army discharge; female members of the Screen Cartoonists Guild were being discharged, too, to make room for returning servicemen who wanted their pen-and-ink jobs back; *Double Indemnity* was in production.[18]

Within two years, the Simpson family would leave their small Seattle home at 1124 27th Avenue for Anchorage, Alaska. There began Simpson's mythmaking.

Alaska, not yet a state, was rough territory, and the Spenard suburb of Anchorage, where the family settled into a small two-bedroom house on unpaved Tugatch Drive (now 36th Street), was a rough neighborhood. (Rough enough that a "Spenard divorce" is the local expression for a man murdering his wife; it's called a trial separation if the wife survives the shooting.)[19] Russell Simpson found work as a driver and mechanic. June kept house. A second son, Lary, was born into their lower-middle-class home. Simpson was, by all accounts but his own, a pleasant, chubby, shy boy, well mannered and on the quiet side. He wasn't as tough as his male classmates at North Star Elementary or, later, West Anchorage High School, for whom fighting in the school parking lot was a daily event, and tended to befriend as many girls as boys. Childhood friends remember a polite "Donny," a good dancer, who didn't smoke or curse, who was fussy about his clothes. In high school, where he was voted "Best Dressed," he showed a dandy's attention to fashion and detail, attending school every day in a jacket and tie. Simpson failed in his campaign to be ninth-grade class president, but he was generally popular. "He was very studious and rather nerdy," his childhood friend Naomi Bowen said years later. "A nice boy."[20]

(Simpson would subsequently exact a peculiar revenge upon the high school classmates who did not take him seriously as a teenager. For his twentieth high school reunion, Simpson flew to Anchorage, hired a helicopter and landed on the football field where the event was being held. He stepped off the chopper, resplendent in a white linen suit and escorted by two Penthouse "Pets" he had hired to accompany him. He walked through the spellbound crowd, just once, greeting old friends, giving everyone an eyeful of what he had become, and then walked back to the helicopter and flew away).[21]

The adult Simpson told a darker story. His parents were religious fundamentalists, devout Southern Baptists who forced him to attend church several times a week and forced upon him the concept of original sin and almost certain damnation. His father, he said, was a brutal man, a caribou-hunting guide who forced the preteen Simpson to hunt and slaughter wild animals with his bare hands. Simpson later told *Rolling Stone* reporter Jeffrey Ressner that "he hunted moose for dinner when he was seven years old."[22] He told *Smart* reporter Debby Bull, "Until I was twelve, there was no grocery store. You didn't go out and buy food—you had to go hunt for it. I started hunting when I was six or seven. We lived on moose burgers and moose steaks. We lived with my grandmother, in the basement of her log cabin, till I was eight. Then we moved to the house my dad built for us by hand."[23] His father was an uptight, upright, highly moral man who neither smoked nor drank, Simpson said, but "was a physical terror with a huge temper. He used to pick me up and throw me against the wall, and as I hit the ground, he'd kick me. I never saw him happy, ever." Expanding, Simpson said, "My mother was brighter than my father. She was really the boss of the family. Very manipulative and very narrow-minded."[24]

He himself "got straight A's and was a star Bible student," Simpson said. "But then along came Little League and sex." After that, he "committed more than a hundred major crimes."[25] In memory, Simpson routinely created a mixed background of religious fervor—"They expected me to be Billy Graham," he said[26]—violent crime and sex. He described himself once as a kid who spent his early teen years "walking around with a Bible in one hand and my libido in the other. It was a lot of fun—go to church three times a week, get on your knees on a concrete floor and thank God for the fact that he didn't kill you that day. [My parents] made it real clear that we were all born evil, nasty, dirty people, and that if we hung on long enough in this life, God would give it all back to us in the next one."[27] Even as a child, he would later say, Simpson knew what religious training was all about. "The way you keep people in line is to scare the shit out of them and tell them the only way they are going to escape this fucking fear is by believing in something *you* know all about. I knew they were full of shit."[28]

So he rebelled. "I was born in Anchorage, Alaska, third generation," he told one interviewer. "I basically lived in the library and stole cars."[29] Simpson in junior high school discovered the opposite sex and books and became, in his own words, "the Baby Face Nelson of Anchorage." He ran afoul of the law and was convicted of four felonies—for grand theft auto, for burglary, for check forging—while still a juvenile. "I got convicted of three felonies, like burglary and writing bad checks," he boasted once to a reporter. "I was elected president of my high school class when I was in jail for my last felony."[30] Or was it college? In an interview published just two months earlier, Simpson said, "My freshman year of college marked the end of the tailspin. I was voted president of my class—but was also in the midst of my third juvenile trial."[31] Representatives of the college Simpson attended say that there are no elections for presidential offices, or any others, at the freshman level.[32]

"He would say he'd been an actor and a hood and a this and that, and I would listen to all these *What's My Line?* vignettes and I would scratch my head," Simpson's Paramount colleague Dawn Steel once said.[33] "It was all about, 'Look at me. Look at me. I'm better than I think I am.' Don . . . was terminally hungry."

Simpson's adolescent adventures, he would later say, came to an abrupt halt. A beastly, terrifying policeman took him aside and undertook his reform. "I was confronted by a cop, the 'Dirty Harry' of our town," Simpson told film director James Toback, while being interviewed for Toback's documentary *The Big Bang.* "This guy was six-four, tattoos all over his body. Got me in a room and kicked the shit out of me. He said, 'Kid, it's real simple. You're gonna turn left or you're gonna turn right. You're either going to be the smartest guy in San Quentin, or you're going to have a life you like.' He really woke me up." In another version of this story, in which an older, frightening mentor takes a "tough love" interest in a troubled young man's life, the older man is a minister to whom Simpson nervously confessed his secret, preteen sexual urges. "I told the truth to Minister Culley," Simpson said. "I said, 'I have these thoughts, I have these feelings . . .' Mind you, I was ten years old. He said, 'If you think about it beyond this moment, God will strike you dead. And if you do anything about it, you will live in hell forever.' At that moment, I said, 'I'm going to play Little League and get laid. This is bullshit.' "[34] In yet another version, Simpson said that a rough, country judge, presiding over a case in which Simpson was charged with a felony, offered the young scofflaw the choice of college or prison—a less likely version of the story, thus one that Simpson rarely used.[35] In still another version, he said his awakening came at a trial: "The same 'Dirty Harry' cop who had arrested me several times convinced the judge to give me one more chance, and all I got was probation until I was twenty-one. We stood on the street outside the courtroom, and he said, 'I stood up for you; now stand up for yourself, or I'll bust your ass for good.' With tears in my eyes, I turned away."[36] He told a subsequent interviewer, "I've had my share of demons. I was a straight-A student until girls and baseball came along. Then I had a confrontation with my minister about some sexual feelings I had towards a lady I met at a prayer meeting. When he told me those thoughts would send me to jail, I knew it was a world of insane people. For the next three or four years, I became a juvenile delinquent and was pretty successful at it."[37]

There is no record of Simpson's gangster life in Anchorage, or any indication that a scary cop, fiery minister or hanging judge ever intervened, or any evidence that he did jail time for a felony or, for that matter, was elected president of his high school class. But Simpson repeatedly told variations of these stories to newspaper and magazine reporters—who almost invariably printed them as told. Childhood friends scoff at them. "Don never got into any kind of a scrap," remembered childhood classmate Bowen. "He didn't even fight in the parking lot like the other boys." "His parents were quiet, hardworking people," remembered Merle Butchar Millar, another childhood friend. "They went to great expense to provide for Don and his brother, when it was difficult for them. They bought him a car. They made sure he went to college—which they had not."[38]

There is one single—and chilling—indication that June Simpson was abusive to her son. A former Simpson assistant recalled an incident: She was on the phone with Mrs. Simpson when her employer came through the room screaming. The assistant put her hand over the phone, but too late. She apologized to Mrs. Simpson but was interrupted. "It's my own fault," Mrs. Simpson said. "I used to put him in the closet for hours when he was bad. Pay no attention to his temper tantrums."[39]

Millar and others dismiss Simpson's recollections of his tough-guy childhood. "Don as Mr. Bad Guy?" Millar asks. "Not at all."

Childhood friends laugh also at Simpson's later posing as an autodidact intellectual obsessed with serious books. They remember a high school kid obsessed with comic books, an obsession Simpson didn't deny. "I used to devour comics like *Sgt. Fury and His Howling Commandos*, he told an interviewer. "I realize my connection to narrative is a function of having lived and breathed adventure novels and TV and comic books when I was growing up." Simpson even recognized the danger in saying that, adding, "I know people will read that and say, 'No wonder [his] movies are the way they are . . .' "[40]

Later, Simpson even created a story to foreshadow his eventual success as a moviemaker. When he was five years old, he said, his mother took him to downtown Anchorage to see *The Greatest Show on Earth*. When the picture ended, with Jimmy Stewart being dragged away by the cops, Simpson flew into a rage and behaved so badly that the theater manager had to intervene. There in the lobby, after being spanked by his mother, Simpson demanded a new ending for the picture. Though the adult Simpson would laugh and refer to this as "my little Rosebud moment"—and say, "I had discovered what I wanted to do for a living. If a movie could have this kind of effect on me, I wanted to do it"—the story was probably fabricated.[41] (Simpson told many variations. In one, he said, "The lights came up and I was crying and I said, 'I'm not leaving till you change the ending.' My mom said, 'It's just a movie.' And I said, 'Not to me.' ")[42] Simpson was only three years old when *The Greatest Show on Earth* was released; he may not have seen the picture until he was a teenager. In other interviews, Simpson said that, at age ten, he was "spellbound" by a double bill of *Rebel Without a Cause* and *Blackboard Jungle*. (He later said, "In my mind, I was Vic Morrow in *Blackboard Jungle* and James Dean in *Rebel Without a Cause*.")[43] He decided, at the Empress Theater in downtown Anchorage, "I wanted to be in movies."[44]

Consciously or not, as he embroidered and improved an ordinary American childhood until it resembled a story worthy of Mark Twain, Simpson was exercising the talent for storytelling that would make him one of the movie industry's most successful producers. A shy, quiet kid who is not very successful with girls, who does not excel in academics or athletics, who has a slight rebellious side that earns him the usual teenage misdemeanor brushes with the law, but who graduates from high school and goes on to an undistinguished career at college, and then succeeds in Hollywood. It's not a very compelling story. How much better to have been the Baby Face Nelson of Anchorage, the rebel without a pause, who haunts the library by day and commits grand theft auto by night, narrowly escaping prison, turned away at the very crossroads of crime and punishment when a stern but loving older man intervenes and shows the good lad the one true way. *That's* a story. High concept is born.

Simpson was also, to a degree, aping those around him. Other men who would thrive during Simpson's rise to power had similarly middle-class backgrounds and overcame them in similar ways, though those ways sometimes bordered on the unethical. Lying about a prep school background, college degrees, military experience, sexual exploits and rich or noble relations has always been a Hollywood habit. Simpson was only carrying it, as he carried everything, to excess.

Others fibbed or fabricated in more traditional ways. David Geffen, who had grown up the poor son of a generally unemployed father and corset-and-brassiere-maker mother, completed high school with a barely passing 66 average and then gave up university after a scant few semesters. Arriving in Los Angeles, and landing a job in the famed William Morris Agency mail room, he learned the tools of agenting: Having lied, to get the Morris job, about graduating from UCLA, Geffen arrived at the agency every morning at dawn to check the mail—convinced that someone, sooner or later, would be informed that he had never even *attended* UCLA. When the inevitable letter from UCLA arrived, he steamed open the envelope and replaced the telltale report with a note he had forged onto stolen UCLA stationery.[45]

The mythmaking was by no means accidental. Like Geffen, who idolized Hollywood legends Louis B. Mayer and Harry Warner, Simpson studied up on early show business moguls like Samuel Goldwyn and Harry Cohn. His friend Steve Tisch, remarking this, once kidded Simpson that he treated these books like "owner's manuals." "Damn right," Simpson replied. "I want to be a legend." Amplifying, Tisch would later say, "Don has this bad-boy image that he's marketed. He's read a lot about old Hollywood. He'd like to immortalize himself and be talked about thirty or forty years from now as one of the great, colorful Hollywood legends."[46]

Simpson's story sold, in part because of his undeniable success as a young executive. In 1978 Simpson was named one of Hollywood's new "Baby Moguls, Hollywood's New Power Elite" by writer Maureen Orth, for *New West* (later *California)* magazine. Simpson, thirty-two, who was then a vice president of production at Paramount, shared the honor with Paula Weinstein, thirty-two, who held a similar title at Fox; Mark Rosenberg, thirty, who held a similar title at Warner Bros.; and Thom Mount, twenty-nine, who held a slightly higher position at Universal. (Orth would also include, in this newly stellar cast, young executives Claire Townsend and Sean Daniel, agent Michael Black and, on their periphery, film directors like Steve Spielberg, Robert Zemeckis, John Landis and Amy Heckerling.) Orth described the four Baby Moguls as "sixties kids who have recently come to power in Hollywood" and accurately predicted that they would "set the tone for the movie industry throughout the 1980s."

The tone reduced directly to "their common cultural experience of growing up in the sixties," Orth wrote, and concluded, "This new breed is young and well-educated. Many of them come from radical backgrounds and are trying to resolve their past with the present. Their sensibility is already starting to have some impact on the way people at the top live in Hollywood, on the films we see and, at a most critical time, on the future morality of the movie business."

The Baby Moguls impressed Orth as workaholics, contradictory to the East Coast perception of Californians as laid-back. And they were entirely different from the older generation of studio executives. "They drink Perrier and some do cocaine on social occasions," Orth wrote. "But mostly they do business—reading scripts, spotting talent, keeping up with everybody else's deals, thinking of artistic packages." Simpson's work ethic particularly impressed her. "From Monday through Friday no alcohol touches these lips," he told Orth. "Then one night a week I give myself a good time—I go out to dinner with somebody I do business with." He stressed a sense of community among the younger generation of show business executives. Using very sixties vernacular, supporting Orth's contention that a sixties mentality pervaded his Hollywood, he said, "I am concerned and care about a lot of people who are in fact my competition. I'm convinced people don't talk to each other the way Thom Mount and I do in business or when we meet socially, because of our shared background in the sixties. We're just straighter. I don't think there's any substantial difference in the way business is conducted, but there's less shucking and jiving. It's not about righteousness. It's about wanting to be cleaner and more direct."

Orth was not spared Simpson's mythmaking. Simpson, she wrote, "is third-generation Alaskan and son of a bush-pilot wilderness guide [and] a Phi Beta Kappa graduate of the University of Oregon. Simpson started out in Hollywood doing market research for films, then wrote scripts. When he was ten, he became so distraught after seeing *The Greatest Show on Earth*—'because Jimmy Stewart, the clown, turned out to be a murderer'—that he refused to go to school for two days. 'I told my mother to tell the theater owner to change the ending . . . And from that point on, I knew I wanted to involve myself with that magical form.'"

Simpson, in fact, did attend and graduate from the University of Oregon, but not with honors—and not, certainly, as a literature major, a fiction he passed off on other journalists.[47]

And Orth's predictions were ultimately not very accurate. Most of her Baby Moguls would not grow to much stature. Simpson aside, his *New West* comrades did not age well. Claire Townsend and Mark Rosenberg died before reaching fifty. Thom Mount, after a dazzling start, became an independent producer. Despite helping create the hit movies *Bull Durham, Tequila Sunrise, Natural Born Killers*, and the critically acclaimed *Death and the Maiden* and *Night Falls on Manhattan*, he was beset by persistent charges of financial improprieties after, critics charged, bamboozling the Japanese corporation MICO-NHK out of several tens of millions of dollars.[48] Mount subsequently filed for Chapter 7 bankruptcy in 1992. Weinstein, with Rosenberg, would go on to produce the successful Jeff Bridges/Michelle Pfeiffer hit *The Fabulous Baker Boys* as well as the far less successful films *Fearless, Flesh and Bone* and *The House of Spirits*, but never achieved the heavy-hitter status Orth expected. Sean Daniel, after leaving the executive suite at Universal Pictures, coproduced almost a dozen small, well-reviewed pictures—among them Richard Linklater's *Dazed and Confused* and Kevin Smith's *Mallrats*—but found box-office success elusive. Only Simpson became a superstar. Orth's editors at *New West* may have been responsible for the poor picks. Orth recalled that both Jeffrey Katzenberg and Mark Canton "were dying to get into the article, but they were deemed unworthy."[49] Both, of course, have had significant success as executives.

Others weren't as easily fooled by Simpson's storytelling. Actor Frank Pesce, who met Bruckheimer in the early 1970s and subsequently became friendly with Simpson—and had small parts in several Simpson-Bruckheimer movies, among them the two *Beverly Hills Cop* pictures and *Top Gun*—recalled that upon his first visit to Simpson's home he saw a set of very expensive golf clubs in the corner. An avid golfer himself, he excitedly asked Simpson, "Do you play?" Simpson said, "Play? I shoot in the 70s." Pesce said later, "He even told me he got a golf scholarship to college. I knew he was full of shit. What a liar! A guy who shoots in the 70s is on the golf course every day, and Simpson was never out there. But that was Simpson. He had to have the most expensive golf clubs in the world, and he had to tell you he shot in the 70s. What a fuckin' liar!"

At least one of Simpson's childhood friends believed that this competitive streak grew out of Simpson's relationship with his younger brother, Lary. J. V. Brown, a friend from high school and college, said, "Lary was better looking, and taller, and very successful with the ladies—which drove Don crazy."[50]

As Simpson was attempting to redefine himself as a human being, his bosses Diller and Eisner were attempting to redefine the entire movie business. Throughout the 1960s and 1970s, moviemaking was primarily done by movie directors. Movie producers, with a few exceptions, were relatively powerless. (And they were the butt of film humor. In the 1970s this was a common joke: "Did you hear about the Polish actress? She slept with a *writer*." Decades before, humorist Fred Allen had described the typical Hollywood producer as "an ulcer with authority" and had defined "associate producer" as "about the only guy in Hollywood who will associate with a producer.")[51] Film executives allowed directors to develop or create material and then funded their attempts to turn material into movies. As a result, the 1960s and 1970s saw the rise of a striking number of talented, if quirky, filmmakers who flourished in this atmosphere. Among the best were Francis Ford Coppola, Martin Scorsese, Robert Altman, Roman Polanski, Peter Bogdanovich, Hal Ashby and Woody Allen—all quirky, independent, offbeat filmmakers who in the 1970s would create some of modern American cinema's best work. From Coppola came the three *Godfather* movies and *The Conversation* and *Apocalypse Now*. From Scorsese, the brilliant *Mean Streets* and *Taxi Driver*. From Polanski, *Rosemary's Baby* and *Chinatown*. From Altman, *M*A*S*H*, *McCabe and Mrs. Miller* and *Nashville*. From Bogdanovich, *The Last Picture Show*. From Ashby, *Harold and Maude*, *The Last Detail* and *Shampoo*. From Allen, *Bananas*, *Take the Money and Run*, *Everything You Always Wanted to Know About Sex*, *Sleeper* and *Annie Hall*.

Many of those were Paramount movies. Many of them were money-losers as well. Diller and Eisner, coming out of television without a film background and without any of the film industry's traditional habits or prejudices, saw no point in perpetuating Paramount's recent award-winning, money-losing practice of leaving film directors in charge of film projects. Following the model they had seen function well in television—a business in which the producer is the true creative power on a show, and the director merely a hired technician—Diller and Eisner began to turn Paramount into a producer's movie studio. In doing so, they would create a world in which people like Simpson would flourish.

By the time Simpson was ready to be an executive, the movie business was ready for him. In 1975, by general agreement, the movie business was changed irrevocably on a single weekend.

The movie *Jaws* was released on June 20, 1975, and, according to Sylbert, then Paramount second-in-command, "Everything changed forever. Suddenly the studios were trying to make something that had never been known before—the summer blockbuster. It changed the level of everything." American audiences had never been exposed to that type of movie, released with that kind of national campaign. Previously, movies were released in selective cities and rolled out gradually around the country. *Jaws* was a wall-to-wall national release, opening in every available theater Universal Pictures could book. It was a national sensation and broke every standing box-office record. The summer blockbuster—the "tentpole" or "event" picture that would become the principal focus of every studio executive in the industry—was born.

So, in essence, was the high-concept movie. Previous executives had attempted to boil down plot and character to easily encapsulated ideas—warning writers and producers not to proceed with anything that couldn't be written down on a single piece of paper or the back of a book of matches. Now it had really been done. *Jaws* was "shark attack." Off the shark's back, subsequent movies would spring to life using the same kind of two- or three-word "pitch." *Alien* was "*Jaws* in a spaceship." *Under Siege* was "*Die Hard* on a boat." Soon, this kind of pitch became industry standard for some executives. The pitchman extraordinaire, producer Robert Kosberg, once walked into the offices at New Line Cinema armed with nothing more than a poster of a snarling dog. His pitch: "Genetic experiments on guard dogs go wrong. It's *Jaws* with paws!" Kosberg unveiled his poster and said, "It's *Man's Best Friend!*" According to Kosberg, New Line executives couldn't get to their checkbooks fast enough.[52]

The search for the next *Jaws* was on. Hollywood in 1978 was vending its wares to a "baby boom" audience, 74 percent of which were between the ages of twelve and twenty-nine. The industry discovered with *Jaws* the first surefire thing to come along in decades—the big, mass-market "popcorn" movie that the kids would go to see time and time again. *Jaws* played all summer long and ultimately grossed $260 million at American theaters and an equally vast amount overseas.

The mandate to find the new *Jaws* was felt strongly at Paramount. Diller had recently installed Eisner as his number two. Under the new regime,

Sylbert said, "It was meetings and meetings and manufacturing stories and manufacturing movies"—a new way of thinking about the moviemaking process. "Until then, we worked with writers on material we believed in," Sylbert said. "Suddenly, it changed. What Eisner brought in was the television mentality, a fodder factory." Former Paramount executive Peter Bart, who would later become a producer and, later still, the executive editor of *Variety* and *Daily Variety*, agreed: "They had both come from television, and so they imposed a television structure. That changed the decision-making process." Said Sylbert, "Eisner said, 'Sometimes we're going to win, and sometimes we're going to lose, but we're going to make a lot of movies, with a lot of laughs in the middle, and nothing too serious. And we're going to make a lot of money.' And he did. Two years later they had *Saturday Night Fever*, and they never looked back."

Ironically, Simpson as an executive had opposed the production of *Saturday Night Fever* from the beginning. Upon reviewing journalist Nik Cohn's first draft of the screenplay, Simpson pronounced it unusable. "According to the late Don Simpson," Cohn later wrote, "my draft script was quite likely the worst in movie history." Simpson called it "the alpha and omega of turkeys."[53]

Diller and Eisner even crafted a playbook for success, called the "MDE Philosophy," which was printed and circulated in January 1982. Though Eisner in that playbook cautioned that "success in the motion picture business is highly prone to complacency and recklessness," he felt he had the game plan for solid success in Hollywood.[54] Among other things, he issued an edict against movies with running times in excess of 100 minutes. "It is so often assumed that Paramount likes to keep its pictures at a running time of 100 minutes because we want to maximize turnover, by having as many shows as possible in any given night. That's simply not the case. It comes down to pleasing the audience. At 100 minutes, people's minds begin to wander. They start worrying about whether or not the dog has been fed. Whether or not they're on their second hour of parking. They start worrying about things other than what is in the movie. In today's kinetic world, we feel it is wise to keep movies at 100 minutes." That was the reigning dictum: Keep the movies light, keep the movies short and keep the movies coming. Eisner put Simpson to work in the fodder factory.

Simpson had proved an effective senior executive, at least at the start. "He was *good,* not great, but good," remembered Barry Diller. "And good is very unusual. He at least had opinions. His take on stuff was good, and he was smart about movies. This doesn't mean he was *right,* but he had good instincts. And he was very willful, and Paramount at that time was a very willful movie division. It was tough."[55]

It was also, as led by Diller, bombastic. Opinions were important; defending them was crucial. To survive, Simpson developed a technique that later became known as the Don Simpson Discount Factor. Coined by his then assistant, Jeffrey Katzenberg, DSDF meant "you would have to make adjustments when he was talking. Say, discount 20 percent on a good day and 80 percent when the bullshit was really flying around."[56] If, for example, Simpson said a certain actor could be hired as cheaply as $750,000; that probably meant his agent had said the actor would not do the role for under $1.5 million. If Simpson said that Sidney Lumet had agreed to direct a movie for him, that probably meant only that Lumet was so far the only director he had thought of to ask. Diller, who was less often exposed to the DSDF, said, "You never knew what was true and what wasn't. And you were always surprised that what you thought was boasting *was* true—like the fact that he could ski well."[57]

According to former Paramount executive Tom Wright, who labored under Simpson, his boss was simply overflowing with ideas, which he kept on paper in his "idea books." The books formed a kind of encyclopedia of high-concept concepts. Sometimes the idea was no more than a title, or three lines of description. Wright said Simpson "had a whole shelf of these notebooks—literally *hundreds* of ideas for movies." Wright and others were most frequently exposed to Simpson's ideas in the form of voluminous memos—transcriptions, usually, of long, rambling tape recordings Simpson made at night and had assistants type up the following morning. "That was one of our jobs, to transcribe his tapes. He'd start at two in the morning and dictate until dawn. Sometimes they were difficult to decipher, but other times they were the most amazing things you can imagine."[58] Katzenberg would later say of Simpson's famed memos, "When Don was writing them, they were gold. He really was laser sharp, and without peer when it came to his skill working with material and being able to pinpoint the things that made a script work."[59]

Sometimes his advice was heeded, sometimes not—as when, two weeks before principal photography was to begin on Walter Hill's *48 Hrs.,* Simpson delivered one of his increasingly routine memos on story and character. One source remembered being in the room when Hill got the memo. "Walter looked at this document for all of two seconds and then dropped it into the trash."[60]

Simpson's marching orders as president of production were clear. He was to oversee production of nine motion pictures through 1981. The titles he inherited were undistinguished, at best, and Simpson knew it. Simpson at first refused the appointment, calling the nine pictures "dogs" and insisting he could not make hits out of any of them. This was not a difficult determination to make: Among the projects he was expected to oversee were *Some Kind of Hero*, a tragicomedy about a returning Vietnam war hero, starring Richard Pryor; *I'm Dancing As Fast As I Can*, a turgid melodrama, starring Jill Clayburgh and based on the Barbara Gordon autobiography, about a woman's addiction to pills and subsequent nervous breakdown; *Partners*, an alleged comedy about two cops, one straight and one gay, that would ultimately star John Hurt and Ryan O'Neal; *Jekyll and Hyde Together Again*, identified as "a wild comedy about a contempo classic of the classic schizoid melodrama," from comedian-screenwriter Jerry Belson; and *White Dog*, a dramatic telling of the relationship between a peaceable woman and a vicious—and racist—attack dog, from director Sam Fuller.

Not only were the pictures undistinguished, they would have to be made under a punishing schedule. Hollywood was facing a potentially crippling strike. The Alliance of Motion Picture and Television Producers—in effect the guild that represents the interests of the major film and television studios—and the Directors Guild of America were at an impasse in contract renewal negotiations. It was widely believed that, within several months, the directors would strike and motion picture production would be frozen. Simpson was told to complete all nine pictures within six months—or Paramount would have no films to release and nothing to put into production for the duration of the strike. Company president Michael Eisner ordered Simpson to begin production on at least six of the films in a single week, between April 14 and April 20, 1981, and announced his intentions to the press. "I don't want to give you the impression that we're the most organized war room thinkers that ever existed, because a lot of things happen just by instinct and chance," Eisner said. "But we have thought this out quite clearly. I personally don't think there's going to be a strike . . . but if there is a strike, and it's a long one, we can easily withstand it." He then went on, jokingly, to "publicly thank" the Directors Guild "for putting the pressure on us to get our act together," and credited his and Diller's television background with giving them the ability to "do great work under a deadline. I really believe that kind of pressure creates quality, not the opposite."[61]

Simpson was daunted, but he made a deal with his boss. There was one project at Paramount about which Simpson felt passionately. Include *An Officer and a Gentleman*, he told Eisner, and he'd take the job and get the production slate done in time. Eisner had no faith in *Officer* and wanted Simpson to concentrate instead on *White Dog*. "Eisner told Don, '*Officer* is a little romantic movie. *White Dog* is *Jaws*,' " said a source on the scene at the time. "But Simpson knew the difference."[62] Simpson understood that the navy milieu, and the rough-and-tumble training scenes, would prove exciting to young males, and that the love story would draw women. And, more important, he felt instinctively that *Officer* was a movie *he* wanted to see—a key ingredient for the movies that, as an independent producer, he would subsequently create to such vast success.

Eisner reluctantly agreed to allow Simpson to proceed with both movies, as part of the overall slate, which included several other titles produced or acquired during Simpson's first year as head of production. In addition to the projects listed above, there were also sequels to *Grease, Friday the 13th, Airplane!* and *Star Trek*. Also on the front burners were the hit *48 Hrs.*, the comedic documentary *It Came from Hollywood* and the very forgettable *Fighting Back, Heidi's Song, The Sea Wolves, The Sender, Lookin' to Get Out* and *Venom*.

Documents from the period also show Simpson obsessing over the project known as *Godfather 3*. Through the spring of 1982, using screenplays and treatments that had been in the works since at least October 1977, Simpson was writing memos and exchanging notes with Eisner and Katzenberg, trying to find a way to turn out a third installment of the celebrated Academy Award–winning series. In one memo, stunning in its clarity, Simpson explained why previous efforts—including story treatments prepared by the series' originator, Mario Puzo—had gone awry, and suggested various ways of getting the story back on track. He insisted that, as *The Godfather* had been essentially the story of Don Corleone, and *The Godfather 2* had been essentially the story of his son Michael Corleone, *Godfather 3* must be the story of Anthony, Michael's son. He suggested that the child has been estranged from his mother, Kay, and has returned to the family, as a graduating naval cadet, to attend Michael Corleone's funeral. Anthony "wants to realize his father's dream of legitimizing the Corleone family enterprises. He's opposed by other dons. Even key members of his family are against him. This modern-day Mafia is a breed apart. The code of Omerta ("silence or death") no longer seems to exist. The organization is full of independent operators with no sense of loyalty—squealers, snitches, informants who can be bought by rival dons and law enforcement alike . . ." The most important interplay must be between family members. "The sons of Corleone are cursed, their lives are an inherited disease, a miasma [that] forces them to commit their fathers' crimes. It is as if crime were contagious—the dead pursuing the living for revenge. Every crime in the house of Corleone is a crime against the filial bond itself," Simpson wrote.[63] Simpson proposed sticking to an earlier-drafted story line, dating from a July 1977 Simpson-to-Eisner memo. As conceived, Anthony brings the Corleone family into an unsteady alliance with the CIA and involves the assassination of foreign political leaders. Simpson at the end of the 1982 memo even attached a list of possible candidates—writers, directors and writer-directors—who he felt could handle the material. Only Jay Presson Allen, who had written Alfred Hitchcock's *Marnie* and Sidney Lumet's *Prince of the City*, made the writers' list. Of the directors, Simpson would only approve Lumet or Alan Pakula. Among writer-directors were, at the top of the list, Francis Ford Coppola, who had directed the first two installments, followed by *Z* director Costa-Gavras, *Taxi Driver* and *Mean Streets* director Martin Scorsese, Simpson's friends Warren Beatty and Michael Mann, TV director James Bridges, *Kramer vs. Kramer*'s Robert Benton and, in a last final suggestion, *The Great Santini* director Lewis John Carlino.

Paramount would spend another eight years getting the third *Godfather* to movie theaters. Simpson, smelling the beginnings of what in the trade is known as development hell, concentrated on *An Officer and a Gentleman*.

Screenwriter Douglas Day Stewart had written *Officer*, largely based upon his own experiences in the navy's officer training school, with John Travolta in mind. A veteran of several produced scripts, Stewart had already enjoyed minor success on a sequel to *The Other Side of the Mountain*, had enjoyed great success with *Blue Lagoon*, a South Seas fairy tale in which teen lovers Brooke Shields and Christopher Atkins discover young love on a deserted island, and had misfired again with Travolta in

The Boy in the Plastic Bubble. Stewart sold *Officer* to producer Jerry
Weintraub, whose intention was to make the movie with folk singer John
Denver in the title role. (Denver was already a national celebrity, having
recorded the hit songs "Rocky Mountain High" and "Sunshine on My
Shoulder.") Weintraub had attempted to set the movie up at Paramount,
through Simpson, who according to Stewart liked the movie—"but not
that much, or at least not enough to make it." So Stewart and Weintraub,
playing a time-honored Hollywood game, sold the movie to Lorimar,
although they had scant evidence that Lorimar actually intended to make
Officer a film. The sale, according to Stewart, aroused Simpson's competitive instincts. "Suddenly he *had* to buy it," Stewart said later. "The
competitive thing was the only way to get through to him."

And it was the "competitive thing" about *Officer*, not surprisingly, that
appealed to Simpson. He told Stewart the movie was "a mentor story," a
"relationship movie" in which the key relationship was that between Zack
Mayo, the wrong-side-of-the-tracks, chip-on-his-shoulder officer candidate, and the steely-eyed gunnery sergeant, Foley, who would whip Mayo
into officer material. (In his imagination, after all, this relationship had
made Simpson a man.) Said Stewart, "Don loved the *mano a mano* stuff.
He never got the love story" between Mayo and the young factory girl,
Paula, with whom he reluctantly becomes enamored.

Early production notes on *Officer* put John Travolta, who'd scored for
Paramount in *Saturday Night Fever, Grease* and, the year before, *Urban
Cowboy*, in the lead. Travolta got close to signing, but bolted, because
Urban Cowboy had driven his asking price too high, according to one
source.[64] Young actors like Kevin Costner, Dennis Quaid and Eric Roberts
(whose sole film credit was on the Paramount movie *King of the Gypsies*)
read for the part. Roberts was offered the role but, according to his agent at
that time, Gary Lucchesi, "He wouldn't say yes. He wanted to do this
after-school [TV] special instead. Simpson called me and said, 'Do you
have any idea the mistake this guy is making?'" Roberts was soon out.
Producer Marty Elfand wanted Richard Gere, who had already made Paramount's *Looking for Mr. Goodbar, Days of Heaven* and *American Gigolo*,
and who fit the part of the inverted, brooding Zack Mayo perfectly. Paramount teamed Gere with director Taylor Hackford, despite initial resistance from the actor, largely because Hackford had a pay-or-play contract
with the studio, which wanted him to start a picture before the impending
directors' strike. According to Hackford, "Gere turned this role down six

or eight times. Eventually Don just *made* him do it." Debra Winger was next on board, hired to play Paula Pokrifki, after initial resistance from Simpson. According to Hackford, the first meeting between Winger and Simpson—despite her success in *Urban Cowboy*—went badly and ended with Simpson telling the actress, "There may be somebody else for this part. I need someone fuckable. You're not fuckable enough for this part."[65] (An actress's fuckability was apparently a key factor in casting at Paramount. During preproduction on *Flashdance*, the choice for leading lady had narrowed to three: Jennifer Beals, who would get the role; Demi Moore, who would later become a star; and Leslie Wing, a model who would go on to play small roles in small movies. Unable to make up his own mind, a frustrated Michael Eisner gathered a group of Teamsters and other studio employees for a viewing of the actress's screen tests. He asked the laborers, "Which one of these girls do you most want to fuck?" They most wanted Beals.)[66] The final bit of casting was a stroke of genius. Hackford and Simpson hired Lou Gossett, Jr.—a fiery black actor who'd spent the previous decade in supporting parts in forgettable movies made for television—for the part of Gunnery Sergeant Foley, a part written with a white actor in mind. The original script called for a "southern white guy," Hackford remembered. "Jack Nicholson was too expensive, and no one else we wanted was available." As producer Elfand recalled, "Mandy Patinkin came out from New York and gave us the best reading I have ever heard. Taylor thought he was 'too ethnic.' " Then Hackford, researching, went to the naval flight school in Pensacola, Florida, and discovered that "all the drill instructors were black. We hired Lou, and didn't change a line of dialogue, and he won the Oscar." (Curiously, Foley is also the name eventually given to the lead character, Axel Foley, in *Beverly Hills Cop*.)

Getting *Officer* made proved far more difficult than getting it green-lit or cast. According to Hackford, Simpson's "creative input" was a terrible nuisance. Every night, often under the influence of cocaine, Simpson would fire new ideas into a tape recorder. His assistants, Ricardo Mestres and David Kirkpatrick, would type up the notes and turn them over to Hackford. All through preproduction, Hackford said, "The script got longer and longer as Simpson made more and more changes. 'This character could really happen!' 'This scene could be wonderful!' He was *too* fucking creative."

And, when *Officer* went before the cameras in Washington State, things got worse. Hackford had begun on a fifty-five-day shoot, having begged for sixty, and found his Washington locations under serious winter weather—"the wettest in history," Hackford would later claim. After two weeks of shooting, Hackford was two days behind. On the set Hackford wasn't getting along with his producer, Martin Elfand, with whom he had a relationship that Elfand freely admits was "acrimonious." Elfand didn't like Hackford, either. He found the director "not very organized, not very disciplined." Elfand recalls Hackford "doing thirty-five takes" on scenes where one or two would have sufficed. ("He had not been through the process before, so he kept shooting while he figured out what he wanted to do," Elfand explained.) Hackford's lack of focus showed up in the work. In Hollywood, executives didn't like his dailies. Simpson called one day to scream at Hackford about a scene he had just shot, a key scene in which Zack visits Paula and her family at their beaten-down, lower-middle-class home. Simpson had seen the dailies and shouted at Hackford, "You don't know what the fuck you're doing! This scene will never cut together. You're fucking it all up!" Hackford stood his ground but within days heard that Paramount was interviewing directors to replace him. Shortly after, Elfand was summoned to the lot and told by Simpson that Hackford would be fired if he fell one single day further behind schedule.

Gossip from the set was fueling the studio's anxiety. According to screenwriter Stewart, Paramount executives were particularly alarmed at reports that Hackford was having an extremely intense and potentially destructive affair with star Winger. "We were shooting a very important scene, the ballroom scene in which Zack and Paula first meet," Stewart recalled later. "There were hundreds of extras. This was an $8-million picture, and this was an important scene. And Winger was late. *Real* late. Elfand took Taylor aside. He said, 'She's late, and you're letting her get away with it because you're sleeping with her. It's irresponsible, and I won't have it.' Taylor took this like a man, and he broke off the affair. Marty managed to keep Taylor's job, but he almost got fired." Actually, according to Elfand, Hackford *was* fired, in the middle of one meeting with Simpson, but by the end of the meeting, Elfand had his director rehired— because, again, of the impending directors' strike. Years later, Elfand said, "We had no time, because of the strike. They couldn't fuck with us that much." Remembered Hackford, "It was an ugly, ugly shoot. But I came back with a film."

Postproduction went smoothly, but not without interference from Simpson. He and Eisner felt the story did not need the scenes scheduled for shooting in the Philippines—scenes that showed a childhood Zack, living with his hard-drinking, whoring navy dad after his mother's early death—that Hackford and Stewart felt explained Zack's character. (After screening the movie for live audiences, Simpson and Eisner were convinced Zack's otherwise largely unsympathetic character needed this backstory, and okayed the extra expense.) Simpson also fought with the filmmakers over the music. Composer Will Jennings had written a song called "(Love Lift Us Up) Where We Belong." Hackford had met Jennifer Warnes, who wanted to do a duet with Joe Cocker. The two singers recorded their memorable ballad, after a rough start. Cocker showed up for the first recording session "so loaded that we couldn't record anything," producer Elfand remembered. "The next night they recorded the song and we knew it was perfect." Simpson disagreed. Simpson hated the song. He told Hackford, "Look, I love the whole movie, but the song is no good. It isn't a hit." Then Eisner saw the film and didn't like the music, either. Hackford and Elfand remembered that Eisner spoke to his friend David Geffen, who had Jennifer Warnes on his music label. Geffen told Eisner, "She was a sweet voice, but she'll never have a hit record, and this definitely isn't it." The following day, Eisner told Hackford that Neil Diamond had seen the movie and had written *his own* theme song for it. Simpson agreed to use the Diamond song, though Hackford insisted it was wrong for his movie. After several more arguments—including one in which Hackford threatened to take his name off the picture—Simpson and Eisner relented. "Up Where We Belong" was a sensation, becoming a number one hit on November 6, 1982, and remaining in the top 40 for the next fifteen weeks in a row. (Simpson never accepted Hackford's decision. He made a hundred-dollar bet with Paramount's resident musical expert, Joel Sill, that the song would never be a hit—and paid up when it was. For years after, according to Hackford, Simpson would shout at him, "It's a rotten fucking song. It should *never* have been a hit.")[67]

Eisner and Simpson crossed swords more seriously over another 1982 release, *Grease 2*. After a preview at Hollywood's famed Cinerama Dome, Eisner turned to his president of production and said, "I can't believe you didn't make the changes I told you to make." According to a colleague at the time, Simpson was "so burnt out that he fucked up" and forgot to insist on editors making Eisner's changes. According to that source, this was the end between the two men.[68]

Even as *Officer* was becoming a hit movie, Simpson's personal excesses were undermining him at Paramount. "Even then he had a lot of personal problems and the drug thing was getting out of control," according to Martin S. Davis, who would later run all of Paramount. Mentor Sylbert remembered, "Don had behaved the way someone does when they want to be an executive forever. He was a team player. He said exactly the right things. There were moments when he'd fly off the handle, and I'd get a complaint from some secretary about his abusive behavior, but that was rare. But the drugs . . . That was getting to be too much. Eisner would not have put up with an executive who wasn't good at the job, and Simpson would not have succeeded if he had not worked well with those guys. But the drugs . . ."

The drugs, coupled with Simpson's rebellious attitude, were becoming evident to his superiors. A corporate retreat to Palm Springs, one source remembered, began badly. Simpson and Katzenberg agreed to race their matching black Porsches to the desert. Simpson, desperate to win, was pulled over by the highway patrol and ticketed for excessive speed. Katzenberg passed him by and got to the hotel first. An hour later Simpson had not shown up for the first meeting. In a back room eighteen Paramount executives, including Diller and Eisner, all in suits or jackets and ties, sat and waited. When Simpson still didn't show, Katzenberg explained that he had seen him getting ticketed on the freeway and said he was sure Don would be along shortly. Minutes later he appeared—wearing jeans and a T-shirt that said "Maui Wowie" on it, coming through the swinging kitchen doors carrying a sloppy cheeseburger. He sat in the one empty chair and, mouth full of food, said, "Sorry I'm late, but I was so fucking hungry I had to eat." According to a source in the room, "Diller's face turned nine shades of crimson." Later in the retreat weekend, when a group was lunching by the swimming pool, Simpson pulled his girlfriend's bathing suit bottom down, in front of several Paramount executives, "and gave her a slap so loud you could hear it across the pool," the source remembered. "Dawn Steel scolded him like he was a naughty boy."[69]

Simpson had been a naughty boy on the lot, too. One source remembered the night when, after a marathon session, Simpson and Katzenberg left their office and found an enormous car, belonging to a visiting Gulf + Western executive, parked in Simpson's spot. He became enraged. He said, "Look at this fucking boat! It looks like a fucking tuna boat. I'll teach that fucking tuna boat captain to park in my space." Simpson kicked in the doors and the fenders. The anecdote was later told with glee by

Katzenberg, who always referred to it as "The Tuna Boat Captain Story."[70] (Katzenberg also liked to tell "The Arctic Training Story." Before Simpson came to Hollywood, when he was working in San Francisco and living in nearby Sausalito, he tried to convince his then-roommate to return with him to Alaska to work on the famed pipeline. They'd make lots of money and set themselves up in business. Simpson insisted this would require a great deal of physical stamina and "arctic training" to get through the long hours and the cold winters. The roommate, who had a cat Simpson hated, refused. One afternoon the roommate returned to their apartment and couldn't find his cat. "What have you done with him?" he asked. Simpson said, "Look in the refrigerator." The roommate opened the refrigerator and found nothing. He opened the freezer, and his cat leapt out. "Why would you *do* something like that?" he shouted. Simpson answered, "Arctic training.")[71]

Worse, Simpson had in less than a year wrecked his car three times while under the influence of drugs and alcohol. Twice he had been sent to rehabilitation facilities. "The feeling was, he'd been warned twice, and if it happened again, there would be a decision made at the highest level," one studio executive at the time remarked.[72]

"It had reached a stage where it had ceased to be his private business," according to Barry Diller, who had found Simpson "smart, eccentric, and a little crazy" during their few years together. But upon perceiving the depth of Simpson's drug habit, he said later, "We were at that point on automatic. That was that. We knew we could not have a head of production whose judgment would allow this to happen. There had been rumors about his drug use. Then, one day, in the private executive dining room, Simpson more or less fell into his soup. It took us one day to decide what to do, and then we acted."

This was vintage Diller, who made no friends, made no apologies and took no prisoners. With Eisner, he was running a no-nonsense studio, a volatile, often explosive film factory. "I tend to like to be in control," Diller said at the time. "I tend to want everything," Eisner rejoined.[73] "We do business a certain way," Diller said. "Do we have fights? Yes. Do we argue our opinions? Yes. Do we differ about dailies? That's all true, but I don't think that makes us arrogant. I think it's our right, our obligation. It *is* our money. Our process is advocacy and yelling."[74] This attitude tended to alienate certain filmmakers—and Diller didn't care. When he originally took over the studio from Bob Evans, Evans came to wish him well. Evans said to Diller, "Congratulations, Barry. I'm going to enjoy working to-gether." Diller replied, "Let's get something straight. We're not working together. You're working for me." He was just as hard on his employees. Simpson remembered an incident in which Diller mandated a meeting, to be run by Eisner, early in their tenure. As Simpson recalled, "We went into a boardroom at nine in the morning. There were maybe eleven people in the room. At the time, we had absolutely nothing good in development, which is the real estate of this business. Eisner said, 'We're going to come up with twenty projects today, even if we have to stay here till midnight. Leave now if you want to, but then don't bother coming back.' Several people looked at him like he was crazy, but by five-thirty we had fifteen projects."[75]

There wasn't room in the fodder factory for an executive with a serious drug problem—especially if that executive's track record, while showing a few hits, also showed so many misses. Diller made the decision without hesitation, sentiment or any real difficulty. His ultimate responsibility was to Paramount's bottom line, and Simpson's excesses were endangering the studio's financial health. Later, Diller said, "Of course we felt sorry for him. We were taking away his prized job, and he had done a good job. Once he was no longer an employee, we thought maybe we could help him continue to be productive."[76] Diller, of course, had no idea just how pro-ductive his fired lieutenant would become. No one had. But many around Simpson were aware that his drug habit was entirely out of control.

It was quite evident, anyway, to some of his friends. Producer Julia Phillips—whose later drug problems would be chronicled in her tell-all autobiography, *You'll Never Eat Lunch in This Town Again*—recalled that Simpson's friends Jim Wiatt and Jim Berkus, both agents at ICM, came to her individually in 1982 to discuss getting help for Simpson. "It was blow," Phillips said, "and it was bad. We talked about the whole issue of giving up drugs, of Don giving up drugs. Wiatt said, 'Maybe you ought to talk to Simpson,' but it was hopeless. No one could talk to him about that."

At the annual ShoWest convention in Las Vegas, in February 1983, where the nation's movie theater owners mingle with the major studios' executives and preview the movies to come that year, the signs of Simp-son's impending demise were evident. "After *Officer* was out, we went to ShoWest," director Hackford remembered. "I was named Director of the Year. Richard [Gere] was Actor of the Year. But up on the dais, Simpson was in Siberia. Richard made a point of thanking Don—he called him 'the man who made me do this picture'—but it was clear to everyone that Don was *out*. We all thought, 'He'll become a producer, and he'll fail.' "

One afternoon in the spring of 1983, weeks after the ShoWest debacle, Simpson was summoned to Michael Eisner's office and told he was to step down as president of production. As was then and is today Hollywood custom, he was offered a producer's deal, with offices on the lot. "They made him a producer because it was 'less corporate,'" recalled friend Lynda Obst. "That was the euphemism." Devastated though he was at the firing, he accepted. As a bonus, Eisner steered Simpson toward several promising projects, among them a screenplay from a first-time writer called Tom Hedley. The screenplay was called *Flashdance.*

Though he would make a hit of it, Simpson never recovered from the shock of being fired. According to his colleague of the time, Dawn Steel, "Don went into a very deep depression at that point. I had numbers of meetings with him and Joe Eszterhas on the call box, 'cause I couldn't get him to come out of his house. So even then it was a pattern for Don to hide."[77]

And he never forgave Diller for firing him. More than a decade later, drinking and under the influence, he groused to an acquaintance, "They fired me on a fucking morals charge! They had executives buggering boys in the backseats of their Porsches, and they fired *me* on a fucking *morals* charge!"[78]

Simpson had met Jerry Bruckheimer almost a decade earlier, at an industry screening of the 1973 Jamaican reggae picture *The Harder They Come;* they were introduced by Bruckheimer's wife, Bonnie, who had known Simpson from his Warner Bros. days. The two men had remained friendly and even shared a house—in 1974, when Bruckheimer and his wife separated, Bruckheimer moved from his Laurel Canyon house to live in Simpson's Laurel Canyon house, on Horseshoe Canyon. After shacking up, the two men continued to do business separately. Both thrived, which surprised Bonnie Bruckheimer, who'd found Simpson "smart, funny, clever, well regarded, but not very ambitious. I remember him taking naps at work at Warner Bros." She also thought he was excessive. He had an enormous collection of pornographic videos, for one thing. For another, at the Horseshoe Canyon house, there were constant parties, filled with girls and drugs. "It was a real bachelor pad," Bonnie Bruckheimer recalled. "There were always girls around. These were both bright guys, and they attracted a lot of girls. And *everybody* was doing drugs then."[79] She had some doubts about Simpson's future, but felt her ex-husband, who did not share Don's excesses, would certainly succeed.

Jerry Bruckheimer, a Detroit native who'd left a successful photography and advertising career there to pursue bigger dreams in Hollywood, had already had several successes as a film producer. In 1972 he'd helped make Fox's *The Culpepper Cattle Company*. In 1975 he'd teamed with George Pappas to remake the noir classic *Farewell My Lovely*. In 1980, while at Paramount, Bruckheimer had hit big with the moody *American Gigolo*, a success that came under Simpson's watch at the studio.

Simpson knew he needed a partner, if he was to make movies, for he himself knew little about the process by which they were made. In mid-1983, with *Flashdance* in production, he and Bruckheimer announced their partnership, under rather unfavorable circumstances. Simpson had been a brash executive, a buyer whose job was to say no as often and as bluntly as necessary. Now he was another hat-in-hand seller, and many of those whom he'd offended at Paramount were hoping he would fail as a producer. Simpson himself exuded his characteristic braggadocio, telling a *Los Angeles Times* reporter, "If we can't be the Ted Williams of movie producers, why produce movies?" He and Bruckheimer set to work on *Flashdance*.

The two men were as different as night and day—Simpson the night, Bruckheimer the day. Where the burly, barrel-chested Simpson was brash and pugnacious, the slight, slender Bruckheimer was politic and cautious. Simpson admired and coveted friendships with the "creative" side of the business—the writers and directors. Bruckheimer was more suited to dealing with producers and line producers—the nuts-and-bolts men and women who actually made the movies happen. Throughout their career, Simpson would be the big-idea guy, the dreamer; Bruckheimer would be the man who made Simpson's dreams into reality. "At the onset, I was the 'verbal,' Jerry was the 'look,' " Simpson once said. "If we were painting by numbers, I'd look at the big frame while Jerry filled in all the blanks."[80]

The producer-friendly Paramount was the perfect home for them, too. They were take-charge guys who refused to cede power to directors or stars. "We're not only hands-on but feet-on," Simpson said. "We don't take a passive role in any shape or form. Some directors who shall remain nameless do regard movies as an extension of their internal emotional landscape, but Jerry and I decide on the movie we want to make. We then hire an all-star team who can implement the vision. I don't believe in the *auteur* theory. The movie is the *auteur*. It tells us what it needs to be. We're here to serve the movie as mistress. No one person, director or writer, is above the call of the final result."[81]

As would be most Simpson-Bruckheimer projects, *Flashdance* was achingly simpleminded, a high-concept fairy tale cued to modern sensibilities. Jennifer Beals played Alex, an eighteen-year-old Pittsburgh welder—"a girl's gotta pay the bills,"[82] she explains—who dreams of becoming a ballet dancer and who, in the absence of achieving her dream, by night performs erotic routines at a blue-collar workingman's bar called Mawby's. As would be the case with most of the future Simpson-Bruckheimer heroes, Alex appears to have no parents, relying instead on an older mentor—in *Days of Thunder*, the veteran car designer named Harry; in *Flashdance*, an elderly danseuse named Hannah—for support and guidance. Alex falls in love with an unlikely target, the man who runs the company for whom she welds, and achieves her against-all-odds ambition, in this case acceptance to a tony dance academy. As in many Simpson-Bruckheimer movies, the story begins with a sunrise, signifying the new day, the fresh start and the impending opportunity, and ends with a freeze-frame, signifying permanence and perfection of the story's denouement. "Simpson had this very strong conviction that to have a hit movie, the central character, before triumphing—and he *had* to triumph—must first be reduced, psychologically, and almost destroyed, before the comeback," said screenwriter Joe Eszterhas, who wrote the final version of *Flashdance*. "He called it 'the pits.' 'You gotta live down in the pits,' he'd always say."[83]

Through it all—sometimes pumping up the action, sometimes saving the illogical story from becoming too apparently preposterous—is a thundering musical score. (Production designer Richard Sylbert, who first hired Simpson as a Paramount executive, said, "All their movies were rock and roll, MTV videos, and that was all Don's doing. It's 'rock and roll in a steel mill,' or 'rock and roll in a jet airplane,' or 'rock and roll in a race car.' That was a very commercial instinct.") As Simpson and Bruckheimer would do with their next film, *Beverly Hills Cop*, which made a hit song out of Glenn Frey's "The Heat Is On," and as Simpson had done with his previous film, *An Officer and a Gentleman*, which made a hit song out of the

Joe Cocker/Jennifer Warnes duet, "Up Where We Belong," they would here make hits from the *Flashdance* songs "What a Feeling," by Irene Cara, and "She's a Maniac," by Michael Sembello.

Simpson may have been the first producer in Hollywood to understand the power that the nascent MTV would become. He was certainly the first to properly exploit it. "MTV became a huge selling point for [Simpson's] movies," according to Barry London, a Paramount distribution-department executive at the time. "His movies grew up with MTV and became a new way to get the movie to the consumer. We were supplying a video channel, which was just starting up, with fresh programming. And every time the song played, it was like a free commercial. Paramount cut the videos, and MTV played 'em. Don really got this."[84]

"Maniac" hit the charts on July 2, 1983, at number one and stayed on the charts sixteen weeks. Cara's "Flashdance . . . What a Feeling" was released April 16, 1983. It was a number one song for six weeks and stayed in the top 40 for twenty weeks.

"Don went on to make a series of sound tracks in search of movies," said early colleague Julia Phillips. "And then everyone fell all over themselves trying to take credit for this piece of shit—as if it were actually a good movie!"[85] Credits would ultimately go to Lynda Obst, who'd originally developed the material; to Peter Guber and Jon Peters, who'd owned the material prior to Paramount's involvement; to Simpson and Bruckheimer; and to Tom Jacobson, who had been unit production manager on Bruckheimer's *Cat People* and *American Gigolo* and who was asked by Bruckheimer to come aboard *Flashdance*.[86]

As they would in most of their movies, Simpson and Bruckheimer with *Flashdance* would ask audiences to sit through wooden acting and woodenly delivered speeches of significance—repeated serially for audience members too unsophisticated to get it the first time around. The message here is "follow your dream," made evident by Alex's determination to enter the dance academy, by her friend Jennie's drive to become a star ice-skater and by Jennie's boyfriend Richie's struggle to succeed as a stand-up comic. "Don't you understand?" Alex's boss asks her. "You give up your dream, you die." Indeed, the first words of Cara's anthemic "What a Feeling" are "First, when there's nothing, but a slow moving dream."

This was anything but accidental. Story notes exchanged between Simpson, Paramount executives, director Adrian Lyne and screenwriters Tom Hedley and Joe Eszterhas demonstrate a like-minded obsession with hammering the message home. They also demonstrate a curious awareness that the *Flashdance* story and characters bordered on the ludicrous. In note after note, the creative minds involved stressed the importance of keeping *Flashdance* just this side of absurdity.

In his first documented remarks on the screenplay, director Lyne objected first to the offhand way in which Hedley introduces the idea that his heroine and her friends "are girls doing men's jobs . . . not to comment on it seems wrong really. Taking for granted that girls bang nails and drill bits of wood . . . will get a laugh when you don't want it." He objects to the appearance of a gang of bikers as "the final cliché." He derides the dialogue—"pretty revolting, I think," at one point, and "awful, cliché stuff" at another—and the banality of the characters: "They're like Boy Scouts or something." After one scene, he concludes, "This dialogue really is pretty horrendous." Summing up, he writes, "I think the screenplay takes itself deathly serious, but unfortunately it's often unintentionally funny. The characters are really hackneyed, and it's tough to care or get involved with anybody." But, he believes, "Raven [later changed to Alex] has enormous possibilities, however, too often in the screenplay she is hooker-like and gross." Lyne remained convinced of the cinematic power of "flashdancing" and the cinematic potential of the dance sequences, especially if, he writes, the movie were shot "in the way [director Bob] Fosse did in *All That Jazz*," moving "in and out of reality, and I have itemized scenes that could be 'fantasy' musical sequences." His one abiding concern was his central character. In Hedley's original screenplay she is, Lyne felt, a tramp who goes too easily into bed, too often, with the wrong people. That could be fixed. "If we can combine her aggressive sexuality on the one hand with an ingenuous and childlike quality on the other," Lyne ultimately decided, "we are a long way towards making this an exciting movie."[87]

Simpson had earlier determined that *Flashdance* had real problems but believed that it could be salvaged into a hit movie. In April 1982 Simpson prepared a thirteen-page story memo to convince his Paramount colleagues that "this screenplay can become the compelling and entertaining movie we all envision."[88] In language that seems borrowed from self-help best-sellers, Simpson wrote, "Like many modern women, [Alex] is torn between the need to be totally independent and the desire to find security and affection in an intimate relationship with another human being. She disdains those who would try to define her identity or limit her dreams and aspirations . . . By day, she works a manual labor job while secretly yearning for a better way to exercise her independence. By night, she becomes a provocative, alluring 'flashdancer,' an eccentric creature who glories in the spotlight."

But there were script problems. (He would later say, of the project's genesis, "We bought a script that was awful, a soap opera—a tawdry comic book of sex, alcohol and stupidity. We only kept the title and idea that the girl would become a dancer. I came up with a seventeen-page outline and we hired writers to work with it.")[89] Simpson felt Alex's desire to become a ballet dancer was "inaccessible to a general audience." (He suggested she simply desire "an education.") The love triangle in the screenplay was "clichéd and out of place." (He suggested they eliminate one leg of the triangle.) He felt that the inclusion of the gay character Howard, Alex's best friend, was unworkable. (He suggested—perhaps saying more about his own life than anything else—that "it is a rare occurrence in modern cinema for a straight man and woman to simply have a platonic relationship. It would be an original touch to make Howard one of [Alex's] closest friends without consummating it sexually." The character was, in the end, simply eliminated.) Most important, though, for all his concern about the details of Alex's life, job, friendships and background, Simpson knew that *Flashdance* would succeed only on the strength of its simplistic message and its visual impact. "If we have done our job, we have established [Alex] as a blindingly unique and talented person, a combination of street-bright, tough and gutsy, but also extremely vulnerable and truly good as a human being. We have given the audience a feel for the art of flashdance within the believable milieu of the hard-hat blue-collar bar. Finally, we have ended the picture on an incredibly high up-beat note . . . This is [Alex's] film. Our memory of her earthy sensuality, her savvy and courage, should not easily fade. Even as the lights come on in the theater, the image of her moving, moving, must remain burned into our minds."

Simpson worked through the spring with screenwriter Hedley, while Lyne hesitated to commit as director. *(Flashdance's* first producer, Lynda Obst, would recall that Dawn Steel, who succeeded Simpson as head of production, asked Lyne to direct *eight times* before he finally agreed.)[90] As late as June, though, he remained thoroughly frustrated with their progress. He sent a copy of the script to a friend, screenwriter David Freeman, asking for help on several key plot points. Referring to his and Hedley's efforts as "the worst forms of cliché," the note asked Freeman how they were to identify Alex's "dream," how to show she is approaching it and how to cheer for her as she does. It concluded, "How the fuck do you end this picture with a bang so the audience knows that our heroine succeeds, which, of course, is the conundrum—just what the fuck is her definition of success?"

The answer to that question, and others, came in the form of Joe Eszterhas, who was eventually hired to rework the entire movie. His relationship with the producers started off on a bad note. In late 1979, when Simpson was still a Paramount executive, Eszterhas was invited to the studio to discuss turning his book *Nark*, about abusive narcotics agents, into a movie. Eszterhas recalled his first meeting with Simpson, held in his Paramount office, attended by several of Simpson's junior production people. As they talked through some story ideas, Simpson got up from his desk and began pacing around, "declaiming, shooting out ideas," Eszterhas remembered. Then Eszterhas, getting excited, got up and started pacing around, too, and declaiming and shooting out ideas. After a while, he ran out of ideas and sat down in Simpson's chair, behind Simpson's desk. The room went silent. Simpson said, "Excuse me. What the *fuck* are you doing, sitting in my fucking chair?" Eszterhas replied, "It's a nice chair, and I'm very comfortable sitting in it. Would you like me to get up?" Simpson roared with laughter and said, "I knew I was going to like you, motherfucker."

Nark never turned into a movie. But in 1981 Eszterhas heard from Simpson again. His then agent at ICM, Simpson's friend Jim Wiatt, called to say they wanted Eszterhas for a rewrite on *Flashdance*. Eszterhas took a meeting, and listened to Simpson's ideas, and concluded that what he wanted was not a rewrite but a completely new script. "They wanted to keep the title and the basic concept, but they hated the Tom Hedley script," Eszterhas later said. "I told Wiatt, 'I'll do it, but I want to be paid the same as if I were writing an original.' My rate in those days was about $275,000, for an original, so Wiatt told Simpson that's what I had to be paid. Simpson was furious. He told Wiatt, 'Fuck that! Fuck that greedy fucking bastard.' But two weeks later I was hired."[91]

Eszterhas spent the next two months hammering out the basic *Flashdance* story. He'd have long meetings at Paramount, where Simpson had recently been ejected from the executive offices and was now a producer, fighting with the studio over his termination package. Simpson never attended the meetings. Eszterhas would sit with new president of production Dawn Steel, Bruckheimer and other executives. Simpson would attend the meeting via speakerphone, calling in from his house—running the meetings, disembodied, by telephone. When Eszterhas had finished his first draft, he later remembered, he sent it from his Marin County home in Northern California and waited for a response. Simpson called to say the screenplay was "terrific" and that he liked it very much. But shortly after, Eszterhas received a forty-eight-page memo from Simpson, criticizing the screenplay and challenging many plot points and character issues. Eszterhas responded with his own memo, a twenty-five-page rejoinder, answering all of Simpson's challenges and telling Simpson why *his* ideas were no good. Eventually, after many more notes and many more drafts, *Flashdance* was ready for production.

Almost. Lyne, three weeks before principal photography was to begin, conceived a new idea about the character's motivation, if not her definition of success. He called for a powwow with Simpson, Bruckheimer and Eszterhas. He told them the character's *real* backstory was that she had been sexually molested by her father, at the age of eight. Eszterhas balked. He told Lyne, "This movie is a powder puff. It's a fairy tale with music. You put in something heavy like that, it will sink the entire story." Lyne was adamant. Over three days, meeting in a garish suite in Las Vegas—while Simpson lolled in a Jacuzzi, drinking gin, smoking cigars and presiding over the argument—Lyne and Eszterhas went back and forth over this point. Eszterhas finally became so irritated with Lyne that he walked out of the meeting, checked out of his room and flew back to his home in Marin. Lyne, according to Eszterhas, was stunned. "Why did he leave?" he asked Simpson. Simpson told him, "When the gorilla shits in your face, you leave the room." Eszterhas eventually won the argument.[92]

Even as they worked out final story details, there was disagreement between the producers and the Paramount executives over what, exactly, their movie was to be. "Don and Dawn Steel fought ferociously for *Flashdance*," a studio employee of the time said—but they disagreed on what *Flashdance* was. "Dawn thought it should be about the fashion industry and that the ending should be a fashion show. Don knew it had to be this blue-collar worker who dreams of dancing ballet."

Once that was secured, Paramount sent Jerry Bruckheimer and screenwriter Eszterhas to Toronto to scout for color in the "flashdance" bars where the action would take place. They returned downhearted and reported to Steel. "I have terrible news, but I also have some good news,"

Eszterhas said. "The terrible news is, there *are* no 'flashdance' bars. They don't exist." Steel was aghast, and asked for the good news. Eszterhas smiled and said, "The good news is, we can just make it up!"

The final story and character points were hammered out in a marathon ten-hour meeting days before cameras were to roll. Simpson, Steel, Eszterhas, Bruckheimer, director Lyne and Lyne's assistant, Casey Silver, finished the brainstorming at midnight.

It was an ambitious combination—a film sensitive to women's dreams and ambitions but flashing enough hard-body skin to keep men tuned in— and it worked. Lyne's dance and workout sequences achieved the heretofore unthinkable: They made exercise erotic, made sweat suits and sweat itself sexy and laid the groundwork for what would become a national obsession with physical fitness, publicly displayed muscle tone and Capezio dance wear. (If the exercise empires that would explode in the 1990s were looking for a template, this was it: throbbing music, writhing, fit, barely clad bodies and athletic dance.) The songs became number one singles, one after the other. *Flashdance* opened in theaters on April 15, 1983, but was only a hit in New York and Los Angeles. But the music kept the film alive. As Barry London, by then head of distribution for Paramount, remembered, "We opened the film in April and it went all the way to September. The music kept it hot. It seemed like there was a new hit song [released to support the movie] every week!"

The musical nature of the film wasn't lost on reviewers, who took *Flashdance* to task for its general emptiness. "Watching *Flashdance* is pretty much like looking at MTV for ninety-six minutes," *Variety*'s review said, describing the movie as "virtually plotless, thin on characterization and socially laughable." *US* magazine said, "*Flashdance* the movie is a hokey vehicle that's not nearly as exciting as 'Flashdance' the music." In the *New Yorker*, Pauline Kael was vicious: "For this picture the producers have put together a prime collection of rumps: girls' rumps, but small and muscular and round, like boys'. The picture is a lulling, narcotizing musical; the whole damn thing throbs. It's soft-core porn with an inspirational message, and it may be the most calculating, platinum-hearted movie I've ever seen."

Nor was its emptiness lost on Paramount employees. Just after production on the film was complete, the entire story department was brought in for a screening. According to one reader in the department, the now-retired John Boswell, "As it was unreeling, there were glances going around the room. *What is this piece of shit?* Then the lights went up, and [the executives in charge] said, 'Well, what do you think?' I said I thought it was *appalling*. They said, 'Okay, but what did you think about the humor in it?' We were all stunned. The *humor?* There wasn't any humor."[93] According to another source, Eisner remained convinced that the movie would never succeed. "Eisner thought *Flashdance* was going to be the anchor around Don's neck that would take him to the bottom of the sea. He thought it was a joke."[94]

Boswell wasn't surprised at the vapidity of *Flashdance*, because he had labored in Paramount's story department during Simpson's executive reign—and found Simpson sorely lacking in movie intelligence. Boswell recalled helping the studio develop a musical, in the late 1970s. He read a piece of material and recommended it to Simpson, saying, "This piece of material is really *42nd Street*. It's really a remake of the old movie." Simpson responded, "What movie? What's it called?" "I couldn't believe my ears," Boswell said. "The name of the movie is *42nd Street!*"

Despite the critics, and although it was never a number one movie, *Flashdance* would ultimately earn $95 million at North American box offices, bringing Paramount its number two picture of the year behind *Terms of Endearment*.

Simpson and Bruckheimer were set. And Simpson had stunned his detractors. "Everyone at Paramount wanted Don to fail, and before the movie was released, the marketing people said, 'This is a ludicrous movie. Simpson is going to eat it,' " a studio source remarked.[95] "Simpson felt he had to be a star, and he had gone for the ultimate commercial formula. Then the marketing people tested the movie, and it tested through the roof. They *had* to go out and sell it. It wasn't a good movie, but it was a hit, and Don had desperately needed a hit."

But the movie did not sit well with Simpson's family. After the movie opened, screenwriter Eszterhas said, Simpson received a Bible from his mother. In it was a note: "If you read and study this book, you will never make another movie like that again."[96]

Leaving his Paramount executive post, Simpson had not left much behind. The veteran executive Ned Tanen, who returned to Paramount in Simpson's wake, would complain later that Simpson's development skills as head of production had not resulted in much actual development. Tanen arrived to find virtually nothing worth producing. "What did he leave me? He left me *King David,* which was Richard Gere in a fucking toga, and *Compromising Positions*"—a weak comedy that would star Susan Sarandon and Raul Julia—"and *D.A.R.Y.L.,*" a comedy about a childless couple that adopts a little boy who turns out to be a robot. "He left nothing behind," Tanen griped.

Almost nothing. There was also *Beverly Hills Cop.*

CHAPTER TWO

BEVERLY HILLS COP

One spring afternoon in 1977 the screenwriter Danilo Bach got a telephone call from a young development executive at Paramount Pictures named Don Simpson. Simpson wanted a meeting. Warner Bros. had recently overpaid for a Bach project called *Horse Opera*, and, though the movie wasn't moving into production, Bach was a hot property.

The project Simpson wanted to discuss was not. Sitting in a Paramount office opposite Simpson and Michael Eisner, Bach listened as Simpson pitched him a rather uninspired story. A Los Angeles policeman, an East L.A. cop from the wrong side of the tracks, gets transferred to Beverly Hills. The end. Simpson seemed excited about the project and told Bach the movie would have elements of Clint Eastwood's cop thriller *Dirty Harry*, elements of Warren Beatty's social satire *Shampoo* and elements of Roman Polanski's film noir *Chinatown*. However, Bach recalled, "There was no story. There was just this vague idea about a cop who turns Beverly Hills upside down."[1] Bach closed the meeting, telling Simpson he didn't think he could do much with the idea, but promising to think about it. Two weeks later, growing restless with the absence of forward motion on his Warner Bros. *Horse Opera* project, he called Simpson back and asked for a second meeting.

This time Bach did the pitching. It was just before lunchtime at Paramount as he sat down, again, with Simpson and Eisner. He told them the story of a badass policeman from a decaying East Coast city, a rough street cop who comes to Beverly Hills to investigate a murder and take down a villainous killer. Simpson and Eisner got increasingly excited, particularly about the role of the villain, a smooth-operating Beverly Hills magnate. Eisner finally jumped up from his chair and shouted at Bach, "I love it! The guy you're describing is the guy I'm having lunch with! Go and write the screenplay—don't even bother with an outline. I love this!" Eisner left the room. *Beverly Hills Cop* was born.[2]

Two weeks later Bach and his attorney, Barry Hirsch, received a letter from Bach's agent, Bob Bookman. Attached was a two-page memo from Don Simpson, identifying "an original story idea" about a project called *Beverly Hills Cop*. It outlined for Bach the movie Simpson and Eisner wanted him to write—vague and unoriginal though the "original story idea" was. It was high in concept, but short on details.

"A tough, hard-bitten cop from the wrong side of Los Angeles is transferred temporarily to a case with the Beverly Hills Police Department," the memo read. "He's a loner who doesn't talk much, slow to boil, but then—watch out. Quick and sure with a gun. His habits of independence have gotten him into trouble many times with the department in the past."

The unnamed officer "has covered gang wars in the barrios, shoot-outs with drug traffickers, armed robberies in the ghetto. Now he suddenly finds himself in the richest suburb of the United States—a kind of Camelot, with gilded castles and money-green lawns, a Valhalla for rich, rich people . . . This is where the legends go home at night to take off their makeup." The city boasts a police department whose skills are limited to helping "drunk millionaires find their way safely home to Roxbury Drive or Tower Road late at night."

Beyond that, there wasn't much story. "Whatever the case our hero is assigned to," the memo continued, giving no indication what that case might be, "it requires his special brand of toughness. He finds himself a maverick working with soft cops who go by regulations and have too much respect for money and fame." That the hero would find himself in a bad Beverly Hills situation—and ultimately triumph—is not in doubt, though the "original story idea" suggested neither what the situation would be, nor how the hero would triumph. The memo closed with a mixed metaphor of Goldwynian perfection: "The way the case unfolds brings out our hero's style: he's going to kick rich ass, and he's not going to put on kid gloves to do it."

From that limited document Bach took his guidance and wrote his screenplay, an original that he called *Beverly Drive*. Though Bach would later concede that "it wasn't much of a comedy," and differed widely from the eventual hit movie, many of the key elements were contained in his first draft. It opens in Pittsburgh with the brutal murder of a petty thief named Leon Schecter. Schecter is a friend of a Pittsburgh detective, a Sergeant Elly Axel—described in Bach's original as "an exposed raw nerve, an intense younger man born with no discernible advantages except the scars of survival." Axel takes Schecter's murder investigation to Beverly Hills, where he focuses his attention on an evil, wealthy tycoon, named Dalgleish, under the watchful eye of a straight-arrow Beverly Hills police lieutenant named Bogomil. There's a woman in jeopardy, an innocent named Jolie who's tied in with Dalgleish. The drama concludes with a shoot-out at Dalgleish's Beverly Hills estate, and Dalgleish's death, and a thank-you from Beverly Hills' straight-arrow cop: "Twenty-five years I've washed their dirty linen," Bogomil says. "I guess it's about time somebody cleaned house."

"They told me at the time it was the best original they had ever commissioned at the studio," Bach remembered. "What they responded to was the villain of the piece, which was really Beverly Hills itself—a corrupt personal service community [full of] Dr. Feel-Goods, drugs, women, all the privileges that insulate people and ultimately bring havoc on other people's lives. Don said, 'My God, you hit all the points. You went after every one of these cultural institutions.' Ironically, of course, Don's entire life was made up of those same 'privileges,' those same 'institutions.'"

Simpson prided himself on having an instinctive ability to recognize and perfect great plots and great characters. He would later boast that *Beverly Hills Cop* went through thirty-seven different drafts, and eleven different writers, before it was made into a movie. ("Script is king with us," he told *Interview* magazine in 1985.) After Bach had done two or three passes, Simpson hired new writers. Over the years, as the project languished, as Simpson lost his Paramount job and then redeemed himself as a producer on *Flashdance*, Simpson and Bruckheimer hired William Wittliff (who'd written the western *Barbarosa*) and Vincent Patrick (who wrote *The Pope of Greenwich Village*). In 1983, though, the producers met and hired Daniel Petrie, Jr., a new writer who put into *Beverly Hills Cop*, as it was now officially called, the requisite comic touch.

In Petrie's screenplay, which he completed for Simpson and Bruckheimer in July 1984, Elly Axel has become Axel Elly. He's now a Detroit cop, ostensibly because Simpson and Bruckheimer had already done a film in Pittsburgh, with *Flashdance*, and Detroit was, anyway, Bruckheimer's hometown. Axel is still a brash, young, devil-may-care detective, and he still finds himself in Beverly Hills investigating a murder—though now the dead man, Schecter, has become a boyhood friend. The woman in jeopardy, Jolie, is now Jeannette, and she's the dead man's sister. The evil Beverly Hills magnate is now called—alarmingly, for this writer—Fleming. The dead Schecter used to work for Fleming and may have brought about his own murder by stealing from his employer.

Most important, though, Axel is funny. When he can't get a source to cooperate, he threatens, "Give me the number or I'll come over there and give your balls a haircut." When two undercover Beverly Hills cops stake out his hotel room, he has the hotel deliver club sandwiches and Lite beers to their unmarked sedan. When Jeannette makes him wear a suit that he thinks is ugly, she tells him, "It's Perry Ellis!" He responds, "I don't care if it's Perry fucking *Mason*. I look like a queer baboon."

The script attracted the attention of Mickey Rourke, and rewrites were ordered to customize the part for him—until he lost interest and chose instead to star in MGM/UA's *The Pope of Greenwich Village*. Then Sylvester Stallone got interested and took over the rewriting process himself, removing all the script's humor and turning *Cop* back into a standard action movie.[3] ("They offered me the rewrite when it was nothing more than Sylvester Stallone and an exotic gun—which was pretty ridiculous," remembered screenwriter Chip Proser, who would later write Simpson and Bruckheimer's *Top Gun*.)[4] Director Martin Brest, whom Paramount had just fired off the set of *WarGames*, needed a project. Producer Joel Silver, Brest's friend, got his lawyer, Jake Bloom, who was also Stallone's lawyer, and who would later be Simpson's lawyer, to convince Stallone to meet with Brest.[5] Brest survived the meeting and stayed on the project; Stallone dropped out, ostensibly to concentrate on his next picture, the catastrophic *Rhinestone*. (Simpson would later tell friends a story—impossible to corroborate—about how he finally got Stallone off the project and got the project back on track. He and Stallone had a mutual interest in "youth treatments," and Simpson knew of a Swiss doctor who was experimenting with injections of a sheep hormone that increased tumescence. Simpson managed to get Stallone's name "put at the top of the list," Simpson boasted to a friend, for an appointment with the very exclusive doctor.[6] Stallone flew to Switzerland. Simpson, if this story is to be believed, proceeded on *Beverly Hills Cop* without him.) Eddie Murphy—still hot from Paramount's hits *48 Hrs.* and *Trading Places*—was cast for the lead character, now known as Axel Foley. Though there was subsequent argument between Simpson and Jeffrey Katzenberg over who'd originally conceived of casting Murphy—and, ultimately, between Simpson and Michael Eisner over who'd conceived the original story—by the time *Beverly Hills Cop* opened, it did not matter.

Indeed, it was something of a success before it opened. By the time *BHC* was ready to be shown for Paramount executives, Diller and Eisner had left the lot—Diller to 20th Century-Fox, Eisner to the Walt Disney Company. Frank Mancuso, who had run Paramount's distribution operations for years, had been installed by CEO Martin Davis as the new head of the studio. Jeffrey Katzenberg was waiting for him when Mancuso arrived one fall afternoon. He ordered a screening, the following morning, of *BHC*, which the studio had planned to open at Christmas. Mancuso and Katzenberg sat down, side by side, just in front of Simpson and Bruckheimer, for a 1:00 P.M. viewing of the movie. When it was over, Mancuso turned to Simpson and—in what was his first decision as head of the studio—said, "This is going to be as big as *Ghostbusters*. Let's commit right now to a sequel."[7]

The movie was an instant sensation when it opened on December 7, 1984. Frank Pesce, an actor who plays a role in the opening sequence, as Axel Foley tries to foil a truck heist, was in the audience on the Paramount lot for the first big "industry" screening. "By the end of the first scene, it was obvious this was a huge hit," Pesce recalled. "I drove up to Simpson's house afterwards to tell him. He was so nervous, he stayed home, locked up in his house."[8]

Reviews were mixed. *The Hollywood Reporter* wrote admiringly of "the wry, character conscious direction of Martin Brest, who coaxes a silver-bullet performance from star Eddie Murphy." The *Los Angeles Times'* Michael Wilmington said the movie was "the sort of slick and sleek, unabashed high-style Hollywood entertainment that seduces you in spite of yourself. The plot may be formula, the intent may be narrow, but still the movie sparkles with intelligence." Less convinced, the *Los Angeles Herald Examiner*'s Peter Rainer said, "*Beverly Hills Cop* isn't terrible, and there are felicitous touches and surprising character-actor turns all the way through it. But if you eliminate Murphy, all you have is a tricked-up TV cop series episode."

Beverly Hills Cop earned $15.2 million its opening weekend, on just 1,532 screens—a huge amount, compared to later blockbuster debuts, when many big films opened on 2,500 to 3,000 screens and got similar grosses. The movie would ultimately earn $235 million in domestic ticket sales alone, to be the top-grossing R-rated movie ever released. (*Beverly Hills Cop 2* grossed $160 million domestically, and *Beverly Hills Cop 3* $74 million. All in all, ancillary markets included, the series returned over $1 billion to Paramount.)[9]

More than simply making a hit, Simpson had helped popularize a brand-new style of movie. With *Beverly Hills Cop*, the "action-comedy," created two years earlier with the Eddie Murphy hit *48 Hrs.*, became a genre. It would spawn, in addition to sequels to both those titles, the vastly successful *Lethal Weapon* and *Die Hard* series as well as the less success-ful, but endless, stream of *Last Boy Scout*, *Last Action Hero*, *Ford Fairlane*, *Bird on a Wire*, *Tango and Cash*, *Hudson Hawk*, *Demolition Man*, *Striking Distance*, *True Lies* and far too many failed, direct-to-video "buddy action movie" titles to name. These were all aggressive, profane, noisy movies in which the audience was asked to witness scenes of graphic physical violence interspersed with moments of wisecracking, slapsticky humor—and respond positively to both. The genre created entire careers for otherwise useless actors like Jim Belushi, with movies like *The Princi-pal*, *Red Heat* and 1997's *Gang Related*, and Patrick Swayze, with movies like *Roadhouse*, and gave Whoopi Goldberg, following her Oscar-nomi-nated debut performance in *The Color Purple*, a run of wretched 1980s action-comedies like *Jumpin' Jack Flash*, *Burglar* and *Fatal Beauty*.

Audiences embraced this new style of movie, and the genre would revive the careers of Arnold Schwarzenegger and Sylvester Stallone and make international box-office stars out of Mel Gibson and Bruce Willis.

Years after the fact, Eisner and Simpson were still bickering over *Cop*. In 1985, Eisner, taking the high road on both *Cop* and the earlier *Flash-dance*, said, "These films . . . were all Paramount projects we gave to Simpson and Bruckheimer. They wouldn't have *worked* without Don and Jerry, but the idea that they developed *Flashdance* and *Beverly Hills Cop* by themselves is ridiculous." Still, Eisner said, "I love that Don takes credit for everything, because it just shows what a great appetite he has."[10] Simpson, five years later, disputed the story that Eisner had originally conceived *Cop* after himself being stopped by a Beverly Hills policeman, while driving a borrowed, beat-up station wagon, on a traffic violation. "The trail of paperwork began four years before Michael got stopped by Beverly Hills police," Simpson insisted. "Michael is the best, the single most creative executive alive, but he's also given to hyperbole. It pains me if he forgets what happened."[11]

There were grumblings elsewhere, too. Joel Silver insisted the whole idea for the movie was outright theft, a crime he explained in a roundabout way that says volumes about the way modern studio movies are conceived and produced.

Silver bore Simpson no grudge. Indeed, he credits much of his early success as a producer to help he received from Simpson at Paramount, when Silver was working for producer Larry Gordon. "Don allowed me to be more than just Larry's shadow," the fast-talking, manic Silver would say later. "And he *made 48 Hrs.* happen. Paramount had a commitment to Nick Nolte. They'd paid him $1.5 million for two pictures. The first one was *North Dallas Forty*. Paramount had just a little time to exercise their option on the second picture. We had developed *48 Hrs.* for Burt Reynolds and Richard Pryor" at another studio. (In an earlier incarnation it had been a Stallone project at United Artists.) "Since there was nothing at Paramount for Nolte, Don asked me, 'Couldn't you do *48 Hrs.* here, with Nolte? Bring in Nick, bring in Walter [Hill, the film director] and since it's an interracial movie, get Gregory Hines.' Hines wasn't available. But Walter's girlfriend was [then talent agent] Hildy Gottlieb, and she represented Eddie Murphy. Eisner and Larry [Gordon] didn't know Eddie, but Don did, and he had the clout to get him hired. Later, when Don was fired, Katzenberg took his place. Katzenberg's first act of business was to fire Eddie, three weeks into shooting. I told him, 'You're a fucking idiot!' We fought over it. By the time we finished the movie, they all hated it so much that they committed all their theaters instead to *Airplane 2*. This was the first starring appearance of the biggest star of the 1980s. And they wanted to fire him.'"[12]

But *Beverly Hills Cop*, Silver insists, was still stolen from him and Gordon. Silver identifies a scene from *48 Hrs.* in which Murphy's character, Reggie Hammond, stuns a group of rednecks into silence with the line

"I'm your worst nightmare—a nigger with a badge." Silver would later lament, "*Beverly Hills Cop* was pretty great, but it was really just *48 Hrs.* without Nick Nolte. All they did was steal Reggie Hammond."

Simpson did not steal anything for his next picture, *Top Gun*. He simply bought it.

One afternoon in 1983, as Bruckheimer would later remember, he and Simpson were at their Paramount office.[13] They shared a desk, a long, customized oval in the shape of an elongated letter "C." The two executives could face each other at the center of the "C," or could sit at the center of it and face out to negotiate with visitors. This particular afternoon, as most afternoons, Simpson was on the phone. Bruckheimer was reading a magazine and came upon a photograph of fighter jets. He said to himself, "It looks like *Star Wars* on earth." He jumped up and ran to Simpson's end of the desk and started jabbing his finger at an article in the middle of the current issue of *California* magazine. Simpson read the title on the article, upside down, as he continued his phone conversation. He wasn't interested. "I went, 'Forget it,' because I thought it was a western," he told *Interview* in 1985, when *Top Gun* was in production. Then, after reading the entire article, Simpson realized his mistake. He told his partner, "Let's buy this immediately." *Top Gun*, the movie, was born.

Simpson had been fascinated by guns since childhood. His father hunted. He himself was photographed as a child waving toy pistols, cradling a BB gun and a child's target-shooting rifle. As he grew older, he would tell stories of boyhood shooting expeditions with his father, hunting caribou and Kodiak bear. When he could afford serious weapons, he indulged this interest. He delighted in showing off his collection and, when possible, frightening people with his weaponry.

Adrian Kizyma was an electrician Simpson hired to wire his house. The first day he arrived there, Kizyma parked in the driveway and started walking to the house. "All of a sudden this black Porsche comes roaring up behind me," Kizyma remembered. "This guy jumps out holding a gun and shouts at me, 'Who the fuck are you?' I said to him, 'I am your electrician, and if you want anything done right here, put down that fucking gun and stop talking that way to me.' He never talked to me that way again. But another time I was working, he came downstairs and shined this red light onto my forehead. He said, 'Whatta you think of *that*?' It was an Uzi submachine gun with a laser scope. He thought it was funny."[14] On another occasion, a Simpson assistant recalled, the screenwriter Warren Skaaren arrived at Simpson's house to discuss the work he was doing on *Top Gun*. He found Simpson downstairs "in his underwear, waving an Uzi and screaming about some guy on his roof," the assistant said. The late Skaaren, she recalled, "was terrified. I'm going to work for *this?*"[15] Chip Proser, another *Top Gun* writer whom Skaaren was being asked to rewrite, had a similar introduction. "I was at the house, and he took out these two guns. One was a 9mm, and one was an Uzi. The Uzi has a thirty-round clip. This one was full of dumdum [or hollow point] bullets, and it had a laser scope on it. Simpson pulled the clip to show me the bullets and then started waving the thing around. He'd point it at something and say, 'Whatever that light shines on, you're fucking dead.' So I said, 'Lemme see that,' and took it away from him. I put the clip back in, and he started to panic. He said, 'Take it easy. You don't know where the safety is.' I said, 'Sure I do,' and—click!—I released off *both* safeties. Simpson went white," Proser said, and did not calm down until after the screenwriter had left his house. "That's *his* worst nightmare," Proser said, borrowing the phrase from *48 Hrs*. "A screenwriter with a gun!"[16]

Other writers had similar experiences. At their first meeting together, Simpson and Larry Ferguson, the writer who would ultimately write *Beverly Hills Cop 2*, sat in Simpson's Paramount office. On the desk was a 9mm automatic pistol. Ferguson, a rough-hewn writer who grew up on an Oregon ranch in circumstances roughly parallel to Simpson's Alaska childhood, and who like Simpson had graduated from the University of Oregon, had recently been hired by Paramount to pen their *Presidio*. (Like many Hollywood writers, Ferguson has an unusual writing "style." On deadline, he calls in a secretary, strips off his clothing and dictates scenes while chugging a bottle of Wild Turkey. When asked about this, Ferguson said, "Hey, you do what you need to do.")[17] Ferguson had heard the Simpson stories before getting the call. Two days before the meeting, he ran into director Marty Brest, who'd filmed *Beverly Hills Cop*, and asked Brest for advice. "Wear a fucking bulletproof vest" was Brest's only comment. But Ferguson was determined not to be intimidated. While they talked about *BHC2*, Ferguson calmly removed the pistol from Simpson's desk and slowly fieldstripped the weapon. "[Simpson] was a powerfully built guy, and he'd get in your face. I decided to show him I knew what a gun was, so I took it apart in front of him. Neither of us said a word about it. I just tore it down, while we talked, and then put it back together. When I was done, Don said, 'We want to be in business with you.' I said, 'Okay.' He said, 'That's it? Isn't there anything else you want to ask me?' I said, 'Yeah. There's one thing. Why does everyone think you're such an asshole? You don't seem like such an asshole to me.' I thought I'd never hear from him again, but a short time later he called me and said, 'You're on. We want you to do *Beverly Hills Cop 2.*' I told him I was already assigned to *Presidio.* He said, 'Fuck that. You're working for me now.' I was impressed. I was talking to a guy who had the clout to order me off one Paramount project and put me on another. And it was all because I knew how to fieldstrip a 9mm automatic.''[18]

The guns didn't impress everyone. The writer Ted Mann, who knew Simpson well in the late 1970s and early 1980s, recalled, ''Don always wanted to show me his Uzi, his Colt Commander, his .45. One day in his office he whipped this gun out at me. I took one look at it and said, 'It's not real. This is a replica.' He said, 'Yeah, but you shoulda seen the look on this fuckin' guy when I shoved it under his chin and told him to get outa my face!' I said, 'Don? Are you nuts? What if he had been carrying a *real* gun?' He just laughed at me.''[19]

The posing was part of Simpson's autobiography, conceived over the years and continually updated. In 1989, as part of the documentary film *The Big Bang,* Simpson posed as tough guy for his friend the director James Toback. Dressed in black boots, a black turtleneck and black leather jacket, Simpson glared at the camera and said, ''I would kill someone with absolutely no compunction. If they transgressed me, if someone threatened my life, and they were going to kill me? *Next.* They're gone.'' Asked if killing, even in self-defense, could ever be justified, Simpson replied, ''I have seen people killed, and I've seen them killed in the act of self-defense—not by me, but by someone else. It was justified. And you know what? That's showbiz.''

Never mind that, in *The Big Bang,* Simpson as tough guy is entirely upstaged by another interview subject, Tony Sirico—a real tough guy. It was part of Simpson's act. ''Don desperately wanted to be *street,*'' said his friend the actor Frank Pesce. ''He wanted to be tough. Guns were part of that.'' When Simpson heard that Pesce and some friends were going to participate in a weekend of ''paintball'' war games, Pesce said, ''Don was like a little kid. 'Can *I* go? Can *I* go?' '' Pesce arrived at the Malibu war games site Saturday morning to find Simpson completely outfitted for battle. "Most guys would just show up and rent the paint guns," Pesce said. "Not Don. A week before, he'd gone out and bought all top-of-the-line equipment—guns, clothing, the works. He showed up looking like General Patton. And the funny thing was, he was horrible. *Horrible.* He was always the first guy to get killed. He had *zero* street smarts. I was like, 'What? You got killed *again?*' "[20]

Simpson, in his desperate attempt to fit in and in his childish playacting, was acting out a common fantasy. As the 1980s dawned, it would turn into a local obsession. Simpson himself did not belong to a gun club. In that, among his peers, he was a relative rarity. A 1991 account of the rising popularity of guns in Hollywood—cheekily titled, *Gunfight at the I'm OK, You're OK Corral*—focused on the Beverly Hills Gun Club and prominently featured names like Eddie Murphy, Sylvester Stallone, Sean Penn, Emilio Estevez, Charlie Sheen, Mickey Rourke and rocker/gun activist Ted Nugent.[21] (Murphy was, of course, the star of *Beverly Hills Cop*, in the part originally written for Rourke and subsequently rewritten for Stallone; the Gun Club itself was used for scenes in *Beverly Hills Cop 2*, as the shooting gallery where Murphy's onscreen nemesis Brigitte Nielsen was employed.) A 1992 gathering of shooting enthusiasts in Hollywood brought out such tough-guy actors as Charlton Heston, Robert Conrad, Richard Crenna, Chuck Norris, Paul Sorvino, Jamison Parker, Brian Dennehy, Robert Stack, Andrew Stevens and Jan-Michael Vincent.[22] Guns were chic, and, where chic was concerned, Simpson was always roaming somewhere along the cutting edge.

In 1984, though, Simpson had his sights on a bigger gun. It was called *Top Gun.*

Having bought the film rights to the *California* story about the naval flight school, Simpson and Bruckheimer hired the writing team of Jim Cash and Jack Epps to make their magazine article a movie. They had already, though, approached other writers and been turned down. One who passed on the project was Chip Proser. The Boston native had spent ten years writing a movie called *Interface*, which he'd sold to Francis Ford Coppola. Coppola had in turn sold it to Paramount, for $1 million, when during the production of his film *One from the Heart* he'd run short of money. As Proser recalled, the threat of a writers' strike had forced Paramount to move quickly on several script purchases—including his. They hoped to get a group of movies into production, with completed scripts, before the writers' strike prohibited hiring anyone to rewrite scenes under the studios' legal agreements with the Writers Guild of America. But Paramount's top executives were horrified to discover what they'd really bought in *Interface:* It was a movie written, and to be filmed, entirely in "POV." There was no leading man or leading lady; the lead character was, in essence, the lens of the camera, watching from the point of view of the hero as the action unfolded before him. Proser recalled that in his first and last *Interface* meeting with Simpson, the Paramount head of production had banged his fist repeatedly on his desk, shouting, "This studio is never going to make a POV movie! Never!" Proser pounded the table back and shouted, "Fine! Give it back to me!"[23]

Simpson was impressed with Proser's hard-nosed reaction—as he invariably was with anyone who did not crumble beneath his bullying wrath. He brought Proser back for a meeting shortly after he and Bruckheimer had optioned the *Top Gun* magazine article, and pitched him the story. As when he pitched Danilo Bach on *Beverly Hills Cop*, though, Simpson had only a concept. "It was two guys in leather jackets and sunglasses standing in front of the biggest, fastest fucking airplane you ever saw in your life," according to Proser. "Don said, 'This is it. This is the concept.' But it wasn't even a concept. It was just an image." Still angry at Paramount's refusal to release *Interface,* Proser turned down the job, saying, "I am not working for Paramount. Period."[24]

Simpson did not like rejection. He assigned the project to Cash and Epps, who turned in their first draft in May 1984. (Simpson would later boast of "going through eleven writers" on the project before getting it right.) In this *Top Gun*, Pete Mitchell is Maverick, described by the screenwriters as possessing "the supreme arrogance of the fighter pilot: poise, confidence and a refusal to recognize failure or fear." Josh Bradshaw is Goose—"angular, hawk-nosed and straight out of Alabama." Woody Calloway is Wolfman, "a spontaneous extrovert with linebacker shoulders." Dave Boudrea is Hollywood, "a perfectly groomed, extremely handsome man of poise and charm." Introduced early, while the four heroes report for Top Gun fighter pilot school in San Diego, is the inevitable movie nemesis, in this instance Iceman. There are also the girls, in this case Kirsten and Julie Lindstrom, sisters who, rather like the characters played by Debra Winger and Lisa Eilbacher in *An Officer and a Gentleman,* frequent the bars that surround the military base, hunting among the recruits for officer-husband material. Maverick will have a reckless romance with Kirsten, a romance whose real passion and permanence are evident only to the audience.

For the Top Gun pilot trainees, the mission is to survive several weeks of intense aerial combat training, learn to become "the first line of this country's defense, the tip of the spear," compete against other pilots and vie for the coveted "Top Gun trophy," which will guarantee that flier a coveted spot as a Top Gun flight instructor.

Maverick, like the young driver Cole Trickle in Simpson and Bruckheimer's *Days of Thunder* and like Zack Mayo in Simpson's earlier *An Officer and a Gentleman*, has a missing, miscreant father. Like Trickle and Mayo, he's a loner who plays by his own rules—much as Simpson himself did. Like Trickle and Mayo *and* Simpson, he is both admired and admonished for this. In an early flying mission, Maverick takes on the undefeated veteran flight instructor Viper, flies brilliantly and loses. Viper tells him afterward, "That was the best flying I've seen since Nam. Twenty years experience, and I pulled out every trick I've ever had, but you stayed right there on my ass. You're a great flier. You fly cowboy style—reckless, wild, out of formation half the time. You've got great instincts, but no discipline. I said you're a great flier—I didn't say you were a smart one. With your talent, you could have a brilliant career. Instead, you buck the system and do everything the hard way."

As in *Days of Thunder* and *Officer*, and as in the fictional accounts Simpson gave of his own early life, much of the dramatic tension in *Top Gun* will stem from this relationship: A gruff but loving older man will square off with the young maverick, who ultimately, in order to succeed, must open himself to the older man and ask for help.

He needs it soon. On a mission against imaginary MiGs, Maverick is assigned "military lead." There is a midair collision during the flight. Maverick and his partner Goose bail out of their burning F-14. Goose does not survive the crash. Maverick is not held accountable, but—exactly like *Thunder*'s Trickle—he loses his nerve and, after the crash, cannot regain his competitive edge. Like Trickle, he feels his life slipping away from him. "The only thing I ever cared about scares the shit out of me now," he says. Maverick leaves flight school but is talked back to the base by Kirsten. As did Harry (Robert Duvall) in *Thunder*, as did Gunnery Sergeant Foley (Lou Gossett, Jr.) in *An Officer and a Gentleman*, Maverick's mentor, Viper, stands by his young charge, who does indeed buckle and beg for help. "Send me out on that Alpha Strike, Skipper," he asks. "You've got to give me a chance to get over this." Viper agrees, and offers to partner him on the air strike. Maverick performs heroically, and he and the other recruits defeat the veteran instructors. At graduation ceremonies, however, it is Iceman, not Maverick, who wins the Top Gun trophy. But Maverick has been made a man: He is shipped to an aircraft carrier, where he leads an air battle against real, North Korean MiGs. Wolfman dies in the battle, but Maverick defeats the Koreans. Maverick is injured, and returned to Top Gun to become a flight instructor and to be reunited with his love, Kirsten.

Simpson was unsatisfied with Cash and Epps' first several passes at the script, and returned to Proser, through his agent. The agent advised Proser to take the project—because Simpson and Bruckheimer were offering $30,000 a week, for a proposed three-week, top-to-bottom rewrite. Proser took the Cash and Epps screenplay and reworked it, changing several characters, eliminating others, using his own flying research to bring more verisimilitude to the air battle sequences. (Cash and Epps in several scenes had pilots announcing they were "going ballistic," to indicate they were going to top speed. "Going ballistic," in fact, means the pilot is flying too fast to control his aircraft.) He turned in his draft and was told to wait by the phone—Mr. Simpson would be reading it and delivering his notes directly.

Proser reworked Cash and Epps significantly. Maverick is still a reckless maverick, though his name is now Evan Mitchell. He is sent to Top Gun school only after another flier destined for San Diego panics in the air and is sent home. Looking very much like Richard Gere in *Officer* and Tom Cruise in *Days of Thunder*, Maverick makes his appearance blasting up on a large motorcycle, behind aviator glasses. His mentor is still Viper. The nemesis Iceman has become Ice, and Viper pits the two fliers against each other, literally and metaphorically, early in the script—Maverick is the hot-blooded cowboy, and Ice is the cold-blooded textbook. Kirsten the aerobics instructor has become civilian flight instructor Charlotte Blackwood, or Charlie, a Ph.D. in astrophysics. She and Maverick meet-cute in the officers' club; the following morning, they meet again in the officers' training room. (This change was entirely intentional. Dawn Steel, then the Paramount executive in charge of the *Top Gun* project, felt Maverick's love interest character was "such a bimbo," remembered writer Proser, and refused to green-light the project until something had been done with her.

By making her an astrophysicist working at the Top Gun school, Proser reasoned, he could accomplish two things: satisfy Steel's desire to make her more intelligent, and give the character a reason to be physically close to Maverick and to understand his passion for flying.)[25]

The plot itself did not change much. Maverick impresses his superior early on as a brilliant but difficult flier. Maverick's pal Goose is killed in an exercise, and Maverick is implicated in his death. (A fiery shipboard crash sequence aboard an aircraft carrier was scrapped when the navy objected.) Maverick is cleared of blame but cannot fly properly after the accident. He tries to leave flight school, but Charlie talks him back. Maverick again goes to Viper to plead for help, and Viper stands by him. In the ultimate battle, though, this time Maverick comes to Ice's rescue, downing two MiGs to Ice's one and saving Ice's life. Maverick wins the Top Gun competition and is given his spot as an instructor at the Top Gun school in San Diego— where he is reunited with an adoring Charlie.

Proser completed his script in April 1985. He waited for Simpson's reaction, enjoying what he called his "dream employment week." He waited by the telephone Monday, then Tuesday, then Wednesday, then Thursday, and then Friday, without hearing from Simpson. (One afternoon one of Simpson's assistants called Proser and found the line busy, and was horrified at the prospect of her boss needing Proser on the phone and being unable to get through. The following day Proser had a second line installed—the Simpson line, he called it—and went back to waiting.) He was paid $30,000 that week, for sitting at home watching the phone not ring.

But then it did. His agent told him, "He's read the script, and it's not good news. Call him." Proser did, and was told by an assistant that Simpson had written a critique of the script. Proser asked to have it sent over by fax.

It was *really* not good news. Proser recalled that Simpson's reaction was "horrible. He hated everything. I called him on the phone, and I said, 'You're brilliant. I've read your notes, and they're absolutely brilliant. You are right about everything. The characters suck. The pilots *are* egocentric assholes. The girl *is* a moron. The dialogue *is* fucking terrible.' " Simpson seemed to like hearing all this, so Proser continued. "I said, 'Mr. Simpson, *my* script is the one in the *blue* cover! You read the wrong one!' " Simpson had evidently gone back and reread the Cash and Epps script he had earlier rejected, and had written new script notes critiquing it. Proser was rehired for a fourth week, after Simpson and Bruckheimer read *his* rewrite. They kept him on for an additional five weeks, until the production start date was nearing. Bruckheimer called and said, "We've got a budget problem, and we're running out of money. We have to adjust your salary down to $5,000 a week." Proser responded, "Fine. Go find yourself a $5,000-a-week writer." Simpson and Bruckheimer brought in the late Warren Skaaren. Preproduction resumed.

It was clear to Proser that Simpson's involvement with cocaine had already reached severe levels. During his first three-week writing assignment, he said, Simpson never once came to the Paramount offices in Hollywood. He refused to take meetings. He refused, in fact, to leave his house. According to Proser and several other sources, Simpson believed that the Mafia had ordered a hit on him. He was barricaded inside his Cherokee Avenue house and would not come out. One afternoon Proser demanded a visit. He found a surveillance camera posted over the wall separating the driveway from the street, a second surveillance camera over the driveway and parking area, and a third surveillance camera over the front door. Inside the house were monitors where Simpson could watch anyone approaching his house. Also inside was "an armory" of weapons, Proser recalled, and evidence of considerable drug use. Proser found Simpson, dressed all in black, in his study, surrounded by walls of audio equipment, also colored all black. "He was coked out of his mind," Proser said. "His eyes were like little fucking BBs—little pinpoints." Simpson wasn't making much sense. At one point he ran excitedly from the room and returned with a piece of paper. "Check this out," he told Proser. The piece of paper was an uncashed check, for $2 million, for his services on *Flashdance*. Later that day, Simpson showed Proser his "pack of cards," as Proser put it. It was a stack of Polaroid photographs, each depicting a naked woman, each taken in Simpson's Paramount office. "He didn't say much about them," Proser remembered. "It was just like, 'Do you think I can get these girls to take their clothes off if they think they can get a part in my movie?' And of course he could."[26]

On another occasion, Proser arrived to find a "big blond guy" whom Simpson identified as his "bodyguard." Proser had heard the rumors about the "guys from Las Vegas" who'd ordered the Mafia hit. "Simpson," he recalled, "was incredibly paranoid. He thought we were all against him. He thought [the film's director] Tony Scott and I were trying to take his movie away from him." That, in turn, made Proser and Scott paranoid. They started taking their own "story meetings" in Santa Monica, so that none of Simpson's friends would see them talking in Hollywood restaurants. On subsequent days, Proser recalled, he would try to take "story meetings" from the Paramount offices, as he, Bruckheimer and director Tony Scott each sat with a phone extension. One conversation began with a barely audible Simpson saying, "So how are all my little Jews in the office today?"[27]

When he was in the office itself, Simpson continued his use of cocaine. As one former assistant said, "He was split between the cocaine and the alcohol. At 4:00 P.M., he'd start on the twenty-five-year-old Macallan. He'd be so loaded he could hardly walk. Then at 5:00 or so, he'd start on the cocaine. He'd spend the whole afternoon in and out of the bathroom."[28]

Proser left the project angry with Simpson, angry with Bruckheimer and still angry at Paramount. Years later he would sum up his feelings about Simpson. "The thing is, he was incredibly intelligent. There was always this thing of one-upmanship, but you could *talk* to him. He was aware of the weaknesses in his movies, but he did have this amazing ability to find the through-line that made his movies accessible to an IQ of 100. He came along at a time when there wasn't a lot of testosterone being pumped through the system—and he and his movies had a lot of it."

Ned Tanen, hired to run Paramount after Barry Diller had left the studio for 20th Century-Fox, and Michael Eisner and Jeffrey Katzenberg had gone to take over Disney, remembered that Simpson and Bruckheimer requested a meeting the very day he took office. Tanen, who'd been around the Hollywood block several times already, was a tough, no-nonsense executive—a point he was eager to make to Paramount's hotshot producers. When they arrived in his office, Tanen sat them down and said, "I'm not Michael Eisner. I don't take any shit. Just tell me the truth, and we'll get along fine. If you lie to me, I'll fucking bury you."[29]

Simpson and Bruckheimer had come to plead with Tanen to reverse a decision Eisner had made before leaving, according to Tanen. "They had this project they loved, that Eisner had put into turnaround," Tanen said, using the standard Hollywood term for a project that has been developed and deemed unworthy, and is now up for sale. Frank Mancuso, a Paramount veteran who had just moved to the West Coast to become chairman of Paramount Pictures, recalled that the material had not yet been picked up by another studio, though it was available. Mancuso said that he and Tanen received a request for a meeting with Simpson and Bruckheimer almost immediately upon Mancuso's arrival on the lot. They wanted to talk about something called *Top Gun*. According to Mancuso, "They said, 'There's this thing that Michael and Jeffrey put in turnaround. Let's get it back.' " Mancuso and Tanen agreed to consider their request and to review the material. "I read their material and called them back forty-five minutes later. I said, 'The budget isn't right. You say you can make this movie for $15.5 million. I think it's more like $16.5 million. Figure the budget out.' " Three nights later Tanen received a phone call from Simpson, at his house. Simpson said, "Can I come see you at the house?" Tanen answered, "I never do business at home. But come over at eight if you have to."

Hours later Simpson and Bruckheimer arrived, "with this bedraggled-looking guy who'd just got off a plane," Tanen remembered. "He was shabby, dirty, exhausted-looking. He said hello and sat down and immediately fell asleep. Don and Jerry and I talked about him for forty-five minutes, and we talked about the movie. This guy finally woke up, and I said, 'Congratulations. You've got a movie. Go and make it.' " The bedraggled traveler was British commercial director Tony Scott, who was about to get his first feature assignment. Tanen laughed, later, about how the project stumbled into production, saying, "I turned out to be right on the budget, and the movie turned out to be *Top Gun*. It was our biggest picture of the year."[30]

Making *Top Gun* required the approval of the navy and the cooperation of the navy's Top Gun school in San Diego. That came in the form of Pete Pettigrew, a retired two-star admiral in the navy reserve, who had been a flight instructor and at the time was attached to the flight school. He was hired as technical adviser to the *Top Gun* production. Early in preproduction, Pettigrew met with screenwriters Cash and Epps, with Simpson and Bruckheimer, and with Tom Cruise, who was interested in *Top Gun* but had not committed himself to the role. At their first meeting, Cruise, who had just finished shooting *Legend* and still wore his hair shoulder-length, expressed his concerns. Primarily, Pettigrew recalled, Cruise did not want *Top Gun* to be a movie about killing. He wanted to know about the "locker room" scenes and the locker room facilities at the Top Gun school, because, according to Pettigrew, Cruise felt that's where a lot of the action should take place. "He wanted to make this look like a sporting event, not about warmongering but about competition and excellence," Pettigrew said. Pettigrew expressed his doubts: The school at San Diego did not encourage competition; the Top Gun trophy was entirely Cash and Epps' creation. Further, Pettigrew had objected to most of the flying sequences, telling Bruckheimer, "This kind of stuff hasn't been done for thirty years." Bruckheimer told him not to worry: "Mom and Pop in Oklahoma don't know that, and we're making this movie for Mom and Pop in Oklahoma," he said. To Pettigrew's concerns over the locker room scenes, Simpson was blunter. When Cruise left the room, Simpson told Pettigrew, "Look, we're paying one million bucks to get him. We need to see some flesh."[31]

According to a former Cruise assistant, the actor needed to see some cash. He was considering several projects that appeared to interest him more than *Top Gun*, but the price for *Top Gun* kept going up—until it hit $1 million. "Don was nonstop" in his negotiations, the assistant said. "He *had* to get Tom Cruise, but Tom didn't want to do it. He thought it was *Flashdance* in the sky. But Don wouldn't give up, and he kept raising the ante." A final meeting was set, but on the appointed day Cruise's agent, CAA's Paula Wagner, was out of town. The meeting was set to take place in Simpson and Bruckheimer's Paramount offices. Cruise called the assistant in a panic. "I can't go over there," he said. "They'll devour me. Let's set up the meeting at CAA." The assistant called Simpson to announce the change, and Simpson lost his temper. "This fucking meeting is at Paramount," he shouted. "Get me Ovitz!" The final negotiations for Cruise's role took place at Paramount, with the powerful Ovitz representing his relatively new young client, Cruise. The deal was made.[32]

Pettigrew yielded on the locker room, as he was later to yield on much more. After Cash and Epps had completed their work, and Proser had rewritten it, and production had begun with Skaaren in attendance, Simpson and Skaaren rewrote scenes every night. Often Pettigrew would not know what was being shot until he showed up to observe, and he would then find that scenes he'd approved had disappeared. The scene in which Charlie, the bar babe, is revealed as Charlotte Blackwood, the astrophysicist, was supposed to take place in the flight school's dark, wood-paneled classroom. Pettigrew arrived to find the location had been changed to an airplane hangar with flimsy plastic chairs. Some Top Gun instructors dropped by to watch the filming, as Kelly McGillis, playing Blackwood, addresses her students while they ogle her legs. One instructor asked Pettigrew what the scene was doing in a hangar. "I'm just trying to keep them from turning *Top Gun* into a musical," Pettigrew replied.

Pettigrew would later agree that most of Simpson and Bruckheimer's changes added drama to the story. "Most of the decisions they made, made the movie better than reality," he said. "They just knew how to make it work." Other scenes, Pettigrew later agreed, also stretched reality and made for better drama. More than 100,000 feet of air sequences had been shot by second-unit camera crews, over water, before director Tony Scott began filming. When he did, he staged air sequences over land, and below altitudes at which trainees were allowed to fly. Ultimately, Pettigrew felt, any real pilot viewing the flying sequences would laugh at their lack of verisimilitude—but audiences would respond enthusiastically.

One afternoon Pettigrew thought he discovered the Simpson-Bruckheimer secret. Shooting was six days a week, and very intense. Simpson impressed Pettigrew as "brilliant, the ideas guy." But most days Simpson was not in attendance. Most of the shooting found Bruckheimer wandering the set, or wandering the boardwalk near the set. Often Pettigrew would see Bruckheimer standing on the boardwalk, looking at the teenage boys and girls sprawled sunbathing on the sand. On one of these occasions he said to Bruckheimer, "I see. What you're doing is trying to get inside the heads of these teenyboppers and figure out what they want to see." Bruckheimer seemed honestly surprised. "Oh, no," he replied. "You've got it backwards. Don and I *dictate* what they want to see."[33]

With Cruise on board and the Charlotte Blackwood character corrected, casting proceeded. Cruise had appeared earlier in *Endless Love* and *Taps* and had made a splash with the 1983 film *Risky Business,* but then had appeared in the flat *All the Right Moves* and in 1985 had filmed the flop *Legend,* helmed by *Top Gun* director Tony Scott's brother Ridley. Kelly McGillis, who would play Blackwood, had done Paramount's *Witness* the year before and was riding a crest of good reviews but uncertain box-office potential. For the part of Ice, Simpson and Bruckheimer cast Val Kilmer, a fine-looking young actor who had appeared in the spoof *Top Secret!* and the failed *Real Genius.* Other key parts would go to an array of gifted but as yet uncelebrated talent. Meg Ryan was four years away from appearing in *When Harry Met Sally . . . ,* which would make her a star. Tim

Robbins was three years away from making *Bull Durham*. Anthony Edwards was a promising actor still looking for a breakout hit. Tom Skerritt, Adrian Pasdar and Rick Rossovich filled out the cast. A personal trainer was hired to spend three weeks getting Cruise appropriately toned for his part, and production began in San Diego.

Paramount needed a hit. Its strongest movie the year before had been *Witness*, which Harrison Ford and a taut script had turned into a $65-million picture. But its top-earning picture behind *Witness* had been the witless *Summer Rental*, which earned only $23 million. (Ten additional titles failed to earn even $20 million.) Paramount had been the number one studio in 1978, when it controlled an overpowering 24 percent of market share. By 1983 that had fallen to 14 percent, and by 1985 to 10 percent—on a par with the fumbling Columbia Pictures and far behind the industry leader, Warner Bros., which controlled 18 percent.[34] The most promising pictures on its 1986 release schedule were a fourth installment of the studio's *Star Trek* series, a sixth installment of its *Friday the 13th* series, a John Hughes comedy called *Pretty in Pink*, a high school comedy called *Ferris Beuller's Day Off*, starring the relatively unknown Matthew Broderick, an action-comedy from Australia, called *"Crocodile" Dundee*, starring the wholly unknown Paul Hogan, and the high-expectation return of Eddie Murphy in *The Golden Child*.

Simpson and Bruckheimer needed a hit, too. Early in 1985 Paramount had sweetened the Simpson-Bruckheimer deal, extended it for four years, beating out bids entered by Simpson's former colleagues Barry Diller, now at Fox, and Michael Eisner, now at Disney. By late 1985, with *Top Gun* well under way, Simpson began stoking the publicity machinery, pumping himself up for the movie's release, preparing to make himself a star.

Newsweek featured Simpson and Bruckheimer in a piece called "The Producer Is King Again," in May of 1985, calling their movies "high-concept notions with a high-tech gloss." (An accompanying photograph shows the two producers seated on a Paramount back lot bench. Bruckheimer wears a white shirt and tie, Simpson a white turtleneck; both men wear black suits and beards, and face the camera unfriendly and unsmiling.) Simpson and Bruckheimer were both honing their public image, buying with money the little they hadn't earned in Hollywood respect. They purchased matching jet-black Ferraris and matching jet-black Mustang convertibles. They had their houses redesigned by the trendy Westside architect Don Umamoto until they matched, too. They even hired matching, identical twin secretaries, Beth and Debbie Cahn. "It was so sick!" said an employee of the day. "They're the most successful producers in Hollywood, and they're driving identical cars and abusing identical twin secretaries! It was sick!"[35] Simpson, anyway, was shameless. Interviewed by *Interview* in September 1985, Simpson was cocky, already getting too big for producer's britches. "I'm getting really tired of producing," he said. "Jerry is not. That's why I want Jerry to produce *my* movies—he has the temperament of a producer. I want to do it all."[36] (Writer Douglas Day Stewart, calling Simpson "a frustrated artist," agreed, saying, "Bruckheimer is a filmmaker's producer but Don does want to be a director. His ego has to go in that direction.")[37]

Indeed, Simpson did little to "produce" *Top Gun*, leaving that chore to Bruckheimer. He was rarely on the set. He spent part of the spring in a rehabilitation facility, trying to drop his cocaine habit.

When he was on the set, though, it was a party. Technical consultant Pettigrew recalled director Scott "auditioning" young actresses, after all the *Top Gun* parts had been cast.[38] According to one assistant, Scott, who was then dating actress Brigitte Nielsen—who'd starred opposite Schwarzenegger in *Red Sonja* and opposite Stallone in *Cobra*—had already started his "boobs and Bulgari" relationships with women he fancied. He'd pay for a breast augmentation surgery, then shower them with jewels from the Beverly Hills Bulgari showroom.[39] Former assistants recalled Simpson arriving in San Diego, high on cocaine, driving a rented black Chevrolet Trans Am—and, on more than one occasion, crashing it in the parking lot as he made his speeding arrival. According to Pettigrew, the high point on the shoot was the celebration, in August, of Cruise's birthday, at the North Island Officers Club. "Kelly had brought this girlfriend down from Los Angeles," Pettigrew remembered. "She was big and had a deep voice, and they were dancing by the pool." Remembered one assistant, "It was insane! Don and the Daves [Dave Robertson and Dave Thorne] had brought in all these chicks from the beach. Tom had his girls there, and Kelly had her girl there. She's doing the entire navy, plus has her lesbian girlfriend coming down on the weekend from Los Angeles! Tony had his girls with the huge boobs, plus Brigitte was there. It was insane."[40] Every Friday, director Scott said, was like a wrap party. This one culminated at the officers club pool. McGillis stripped naked and jumped into the water. Her costars, and some of the pilots working on *Top Gun*, decided to throw Simpson and Bruckheimer in with her. (Bruckheimer agreed to be thrown in, but asked to take off his expensive cowboy boots first.) Simpson resisted, hanging on to a metal railing and fighting off the young *Gun* actors until they relented. The pilots, though, would not relent. Five of them fought at Simpson until they got him loose and threw him into the pool. He sank to the bottom, having been too embarrassed to tell anyone that he could not swim.[41]

Simpson was having increasing trouble staying afloat with the press as well. Through the end of *Top Gun* production he continued to court the media. Buoyed by the *Newsweek* and *Interview* pieces, and over the saner Bruckheimer's objections, Simpson agreed to be profiled by *Esquire*'s Lynn Hirschberg, a crafty, low-key reporter with a keen eye for the telling detail. In Simpson she found many—mostly from Simpson's own boasting about his membership in what he called "the club," the small group of hyperpowerful men who were running Hollywood.

"People want me," Simpson told Hirschberg. "They may hate me, but they want me. *That's* being a member of the club. And without that, you might as well be dead." Simpson identified the members: "First, there's Jeff Katzenberg. He used to be my assistant. Now he's head of production at Disney. Next: Craig Baumgarten. He used to be an executive V.P. at Columbia, until they found out he starred in a porno film. Now he's a president at Lorimar. Jeff Berg, who calls me the Werewolf. And Jim Wiatt, who I call Jumbo—they're both agents at ICM. David Geffen, one of the smartest men anywhere. Larry Gordon, who used to be at Paramount. He thinks he invented me. He's head of production at Fox. Michael Mann, who wants me to direct an episode of *Miami Vice*, which he produces. Steve Tisch, another old friend, who coproduced *Risky Business*. And more and more and more and more."[42]

Hirschberg watched Simpson in action—calling friend Steve Roth "a prick" in one phone conversation, screaming "Crank me up!" at his assistant, badgering a writer from *Newsweek* for not including his name in an Eddie Murphy cover story and asking, "Who do I have killed at *Newsweek?*" He shared with Hirschberg his thoughts on possible directors for his next project, saying about Steven Spielberg, "I'm surprised for a smart Jew he's as white-bread as he is." Simpson slagged Douglas Day Stewart, who'd written *An Officer and a Gentleman* and then written and directed Simpson and Bruckheimer's failed *Thief of Hearts,* saying, "Doug Day Stewart is a man with nice hair. He should probably stick to writing." Of Warren Beatty, Simpson said, "If I was a girl, I'd sleep with him. My

Levi's wouldn't hold me when I saw *Splendor in the Grass*." He took on Michael Eisner, saying, "Michael Eisner lied. He told two outright lies in newspaper articles. He had nothing to do with *Beverly Hills Cop*, and he said twice that the movie was his idea. It was *my* idea. I invented it." A month later Simpson and Hirschberg are together again, speeding toward Morton's in his Ferrari. Inside the restaurant, he is seated near Eisner, Gordon and other members of the club. Bruckheimer joins them. Katzenberg drops by. Eisner does, too, and challenges Simpson on the *Beverly Hills Cop* question, making Simpson so nervous that he leaves the table and hides in the rest room.

Simpson was invariably incautious with reporters, unusual in an industry that has become increasingly mistrustful of the press. Even among working reporters who covered the studios to which Simpson and Bruckheimer were attached, Simpson was surprisingly unguarded. Simpson joked with a reporter writing a piece about Disney that its film division head, Jeffrey Katzenberg, and his wife, Marilyn, had had twins "because that way he only had to fuck her once."[43] Even in off-the-record conversations, with reporters whom he should not have trusted, Simpson could not keep his opinions to himself. "Don had an addiction to the truth," journalist John H. Richardson said. "The truth kept jumping into his mouth."[44]

Days later, Simpson opened up to Hirschberg again, on the subject of women, saying, "I'm no good at subtlety between men and women. I read subtext at business meetings perfectly, but when it comes to men and women—they could have a sign over their heads saying, 'I will do the following,' and I couldn't read it. It's just unfathomable to me. That's why I have this." Simpson took out his American Express gold card. "I flash this and say, 'Do you like me?' " Later, watching MTV with Hirschberg, Simpson stared at a girl in a short skirt dancing over the screen. "I like her," he said. "She's trashy. I like trash. I *am* trash."

The *Esquire* piece was a devastating portrait, and Simpson was devastated. He would later tell friends that Hirschberg's article was the single worst event of his adult life, that he remained depressed for five years after its publication. His personal publicity campaign had backfired entirely. According to Peggy Siegal, Simpson's publicist at the time, "It really blew up in his face. It haunted him for years."[45]

Outwardly, it would not matter. *Top Gun* opened on May 16, 1986. Tom Cruise was a sensation, as were the Ray Ban sunglasses he and the other fighter pilots wore. The Giorgio Morodor/Tom Whitlock song "Take

My Breath Away" was a number one hit and would win an Oscar the following March.

Reviewers were not kind. *New York* magazine's David Denby called the movie "a gleaming techno-dream of clean-limbed young studs blasting evil out of the air," in a review that otherwise belittled director Scott's achievements. *Variety* called it "revved-up but empty." The *New York Times'* Vincent Canby called it "a truly absurd movie." *Box Office* called it "fast-paced, loud and very irritating." *Orange Coast* magazine's Marc Weinberg said, "The film reeks of rock videos: flashy visuals, jump cut editing, a pounding rock score and practically no story whatsoever." *Los Angeles* magazine's reviewer said that "the production team of Don Simpson and Jerry Bruckheimer makes great two-hour commercials . . . and with *Top Gun* they give us the most expensive, most opulent Navy recruiting film ever made." *Box Office* concluded, "With their track record, Simpson and Bruckheimer can afford to laugh off critics who dismiss the partners' movies as stylish fluff."

They had the box-office receipts, too, to divert criticism. *Top Gun* would ultimately earn $176 million in the United States alone—and become the top-grossing movie of the year. Simpson and Bruckheimer had become, unofficially, the most successful movie producers in Hollywood. Frank Mancuso, their boss at Paramount, said, "The Don and Jerry show was *the* show in town. Their movies had almost all made $100 million—which was unheard-of at that time."[46] On the same ShoWest dais in Las Vegas where, in 1983, Simpson had been banished from the Paramount executive lineup, Simpson and Bruckheimer would shortly be named Producers of the Year, for the second year in a row, by the National Association of Theater Owners. The movie itself was awarded a People's Choice Award for "favorite motion picture." (Visitors to Simpson's home knew, from framed artwork on the walls, that *Beverly Hills Cop* had been given the same award and that the National Association of Theater Owners had voted *Cop* Picture of the Year.) The Hollywood Foreign Press Association, which distributes the Golden Globe Awards, had in 1984 called *Cop* the Best Motion Picture in its "musical or comedy" category, as the previous year they had given the same award to *Flashdance*. In 1988 the Video Software Dealers Association would give its top honor to Paramount Home Video, for *Top Gun*.

The movie was enough of a sensation that it was even spoofed in the 1994 Gen-X angst-comedy *Sleep with Me*. In that film, which chronicles a love triangle between stars Eric Stoltz, Meg Tilly and Craig Sheffer, the writer-director Quentin Tarantino makes a cameo appearance as a party guest. In an amusing aside, he explains what film critic Leonard Maltin, reviewing *Sleep with Me,* called a "unique theory about the subtext of *Top Gun.*"

Insisting that *Top Gun* was the "best script ever written in the history of Hollywood," oozing a video shop clerk's obsession appropriate to Tarantino's own retail background, the Tarantino character said, "It is the story of a man's struggle with his own homosexuality. You've got Maverick. He's on the *edge,* man. He's right on the fuckin' line. And you've got Ice Man and all his crew. They're *gay.* They represent the gay man. And they're saying, 'Come! Go the gay way! Go the *gay way!*' [Kelly McGillis] is heterosexuality. She's saying, 'No, no, no, no. Go the *normal* way. Play by the rules and go the normal way.' And they're saying, 'No! Go the gay way! *Be* the gay way, go for the gay way!' That's what's going on, throughout that whole movie."

Top Gun had entered the popular imagination. Simpson had honors, riches and near total dominance of Hollywood. He had it all. He wanted more.

CHAPTER THREE

BAD BOY

In 1985 Simpson was introduced to Elizabeth Adams. "Alex" Adams was a short, pudgy, plug-ugly woman who, widowed, broke and, tireless in her pursuit of money, had abandoned the flower business that had been her trade and entered the netherworld of high-class prostitution. From 1971 to 1992 she had become Hollywood's leading procurer. It is not clear who introduced her to Simpson, but in many respects he did not need an introduction. He was young, powerful, energetic and amusing, and he fulfilled both of Alex's requirements for client status: He had money and a prodigious appetite for hookers.

Alex herself was an unlikely candidate for the job. Born in 1933 to a German American father and Spanish Philippine mother, Adams grew up privileged and overprotected in Manila's posh Makati district. At the advent of the Second World War her mother moved the family to San Francisco; Adams later relocated to Los Angeles. After a failed marriage and a brief career as a florist, Adams in 1971 purchased a client list and a stable of five "girls," and entered the prostitution business, reasoning, at the time, "In the Philippines, prostitution was wide open. It was part of our social life."[1]

It was a get-rich-quick scheme, and it worked: By 1972 Adams had quit the flower business and become a full-time madam. By 1977 she controlled a substantial percentage of the entertainment industry's high-end prostitution business. Adams began "trading up" in the real estate market, moving from Beverly Hills to Malibu and back to Beverly Hills, settling eventually into a gracious estate down the street from the Bel Air Hotel on Stone Canyon Road—adjacent to the home Simpson was subsequently to occupy. In time she dubbed her home Casa Pussy and herself Madam Alex. She relocated to 1654 North Doheny Drive, high above the Sunset Strip, an elegant house—staffed by Filipino maids, decorated with Dalis and Picassos—that famously stank of cat urine. Operating from the enormous Dutch antique bed in her bedroom, surrounded by George, Georgina, Harry Handsome, Fatima and her other felines, fueled by a two-gram-a-day cocaine habit and spending virtually every waking moment working four telephone lines—gossiping with friends, making appointments with clients, barking orders at her employees—Alex ran a stable of 200 to 250 girls, supplying the movie industry's rich and famous men with young, fit and willing fantasy women. On any given night, twenty-five to thirty-five of Alex's girls were on duty, earning $1,000 to $1,500 per john—or higher, if the client had special interests—for each session worked at exclusive Bel Air, Beverly Hills and Brentwood homes and hotels.[2] Alex got rich, and, under the protection of police contacts with whom she traded tips for a tacit license to do business, thrived.

Simpson was a good client—he once jokingly referred to himself as Beverly Hills Cock—and a good friend. He was a good gossip and would trade dirt with Alex in late-night phone sessions. At holidays, he and Alex exchanged gifts: She'd send Simpson a girl, on the house, or an expensive bauble from Tiffany or David Orgell; Simpson would send Alex cash, sometimes as much as $10,000. Alex would show off the expensive flower arrangements Simpson liked to send her. By the early 1980s Simpson was using three to five of Alex's girls a week.[3]

"Don didn't date. He *fucked*," recalled Susan Panetz, who worked for Simpson and Bruckheimer in 1983 and 1984. "The girls were professionals. They came in at ten o'clock and they were out by two."[4] As Simpson himself once said, "When you meet a lady and she says, 'Would you like to make love?' well, the first thing I like to do is fuck—not make love."[5]

This was not entirely new for Simpson. Childhood friends say Simpson lost his virginity, in Alaska, with a prostitute. As was the custom of the day, Simpson and some friends had gone to Anchorage's poor side of town, known as Chester Flats, for their first taste of sex. Anchorage was a conservative, working-class town, and in the late 1950s, as Simpson came of age, eons away from the dawning of the free love era, sex was illicit. An unmarried mother in his high school class was an enormous scandal, recalled childhood friends, several of whom said that Simpson and boys of his age were forced to go to Chester Flats to learn the hard-core facts of life. "Don and the boys he hung out with all would go down to Chester Flats for girls," said Naomi Bowen. "It was the black section of town and the boys would go there for prostitutes."[6]

Nor was Madam Alex's profession anomalous. Hookers in Hollywood were as much a part of the local scene as moguls and movie premieres. As the forward to *You'll Never Make Love in This Town Again* stated, "exploiting women's bodies is a booming business" in Southern California.[7] Prostitution, though illegal, was simply another service industry, like photocopying or flower delivery, that fed the entertainment business. For as long as there had been Hollywood, there had been Hollywood executives for whom professional sex was a matter of course.

Outsiders find this an oddity. Why, with so many beautiful starlets around, would an attractive, able-bodied young executive bother with a prostitute? Why, with so many young, hungry actress wanna-bes about, with the casting couch such a time-honored institution, would any successful Hollywood producer require the professional service of a hooker? The answer, most sources agreed, is simple: Hiring a hooker is easier than picking up a girl, involves fewer complications and takes less time. A hooker isn't going to get pregnant and show up with paternity suit papers in hand. A hooker isn't going to interfere with your business dealings. A hooker isn't going to file for palimony payments. A hooker—or most hookers, anyway—aren't going to think you're a pervert, no matter what perversion you suggest in bed, and they won't embarrass you by gossiping about it afterward. And, with a hooker, *you* are in control—or, at least, that is the commonly accepted fiction.

On a more elemental level, the professional call girl is a stand-in for the woman who, prior to success in Hollywood, a Hollywood powerhouse could not get. "There are a lot of men who had real issues with women in high school, and who can now buy the women they couldn't *touch* in high school," observed Lynda Obst, who was aware of Simpson's predilection for prostitutes. "They prove to themselves that they are now the men who can get the women they could never get before."[8] The screenwriter Joe Eszterhas, who had worked with Simpson on *Flashdance* and enjoyed numerous evenings on the town with him, said, "Don was your typical smart, overweight, nerdy kid in high school. He never got over that."[9] As producer Joel Silver put it, "It's the real *Revenge of the Nerds*. Most of these guys were short, fat, ugly kids who couldn't get laid in high school. Now they're in control, and they're going to make everyone in the world pay for what the world did to them."[10]

One of Alex's other key clients explained the psychology of the men who patronized Alex: "You have an important position, which is vastly overpaid, and you are adulated, and surrounded by people who are constantly at your beck and call. Your whole life is about control. You *have* control, in every situation—except in your private life. You may ask a girl out, and she may say no, or she may not want to go to the restaurant you want to go to, or she may not want to sleep with you. This way, you get everything you want—they go out, they take their clothes off when you want them to, they fuck you and then they leave."[11]

"You don't pay them to come," Simpson once observed, using, advertently or not, a double entendre. "You pay them to *leave*."[12] Asked once to explain his sexual "transgressions," Simpson said, "They're not transgressions. They're transfusions."[13]

Besides, as Simpson himself rather disingenuously said, on the job sex wasn't that easy to obtain—and the casting couch was nothing but myth. "I'm the kind of guy, you would look at me and think, I would fuck anything that walks," he said. "And it is true. I will. But [the casting couch] is such horseshit that my partner and I laugh about it all the time. I have never gotten laid less than while in the movie business. There are a lot of fringe people in this business who claim to be producers or whatever, and it does go on there. They are taking advantage of people. And the people who are being taken advantage of aren't that bright. But anybody who thinks they can fuck their way into this business is an idiot."[14]

Simpson, moreover, said on many occasions that he hated dating. He was shy about meeting women and asking them out. "I had a secretary who had this incredible crush on him," remembered friend Joel Silver, who one night arranged for the secretary to stay late so that she and Simpson could meet. "She was in my office. I went over to Don's office and told him about her. He said, 'I don't know what to do. What do I do?' He didn't even want to talk to her. I said, 'Just go in. She's waiting to talk to you.' Well, she waited there all night. He never did go in."[15]

The film producer Michael London once traveled to New York with Simpson and Jerry Bruckheimer, shortly after he'd joined their company as a development executive. They'd scheduled a night on the town, and London was looking forward to seeing the legendary Simpson in action. The three men dressed, got a limousine and went downtown to attend a party being thrown by a major New York modeling agency. That meant, Simpson promised, girls. Beautiful girls. As London remembered it, "We got there, and Jerry went straight to the bar and started talking to this woman. Don went to a sofa, in the back of the room, and sat down alone. After a while, we left Jerry at the bar with the woman and split." London told Simpson he was disappointed to discover that a big night on the town with Don Simpson was so dull. "Well," Simpson responded, "now you know what I really am. Jerry will ask nine women to sleep with him, and nine will turn him down in a row. The tenth woman says yes, and he goes home with her. Me, I ask one girl to go out with me, and she says no, and I want to go put my head in the oven." Later, London said, "Simpson told me he hung out with hookers because he couldn't bear to risk rejection."[16]

Actor Frank Pesce, who often visited the Sunset Strip nightclub Carlos 'n' Charlie's with Simpson, told a similar story. He and Simpson were friends in the late 1970s with Bruckheimer, who was already the successful producer of *American Gigolo*. Bruckheimer had a splashy bachelor pad in Laurel Canyon. Simpson hadn't found his place at Paramount yet, and Pesce was barely surviving on work as an extra, so they used Bruckheimer as date bait. At Carlos 'n' Charlie's, Pesce would spot a pair of attractive women and say to Simpson, "I'll tell 'em we're going to Jerry's house, and see if they want to come." Pesce would then approach the women and try to impress them with an invitation to the house of the movie producer who made *American Gigolo*. "Nine times out of ten they'd go for it," Pesce recalled. "But then every once in a while they'd say no. I'd walk back to the table, and Simpson would say, 'What happened?' I'd tell him, 'They don't want to go.' And he'd be crushed. He'd say, 'Oh, man. That's *horrible*. How can you stand that?' I'd already be looking for someone else to ask, and he'd want to fuckin' go home. I'd tell him, 'Hey, you miss one bus, you wait for the next one.' He'd say to me, 'I could never do that. I'd want to kill myself.' "[17]

More poignantly, screenwriter Eszterhas said, Simpson was nervous even when the women were hired professionals. He recalled an evening when he, Simpson and Bruckheimer were in New York, at Bruckheimer's loft. They were in town doing research for a *Flashdance* sequel and had planned to go out nightclubbing. But Simpson wanted a date and offered to call a friend who ran an escort service. He said, "Let me call this guy I know and get him to send over some girls." Over the next half hour, as they waited for the women to arrive, Eszterhas said, "Simpson guzzled a quarter bottle of gin. It was pure nerves. He was like a little kid, waiting for his date to show up."[18]

On another occasion, three weeks before *Flashdance* was to begin production, the film's director, Adrian Lyne, had a sudden change of heart about his central character. He called for a conference. Simpson suggested that the film's creative team go to Las Vegas, there to hold some meetings and, with a casting director, look for dancers to put in the movie. Everyone had a suite, at Caesars Palace. Simpson's had a Jacuzzi in the living room. Every day, for several hours, Simpson, Bruckheimer and Eszterhas would talk—while Simpson sat in the Jacuzzi, smoking a cigar and drinking Tanqueray. Every afternoon girls in bikinis would be paraded through the suite. On their final night in town Simpson arranged a party, Eszterhas recalled, to be attended by the four men and "forty of the most beautiful dancers you have ever seen in your life." There was a surfeit of champagne and booze. One especially beautiful dancer singled Simpson out and went for him. "I watched this for about a half an hour," Eszterhas later said. "This girl was all over Don. She's dying to get into the movie, and she obviously knew who he was. There's nothing this woman isn't going to do. She's sitting in his lap. And, in the most earnest way imaginable, Don is telling her the story of his life—like it was the most important thing in the world, at that moment, that she know everything about him. Like he was *wooing* her."[19]

One of Simpson's friends from the period, the actress Greta Blackburn, remembered a skiing trip she and then-husband Gary Woods made with Simpson to Aspen. Joking around between runs, Simpson took his lift pass and pretended to paste it on his forehead. He said, "What you need to do is stick your platinum card in here, and then every chick knows you've got the money to buy them what they want so they'll sleep with you," Blackburn later said. "Simpson described his idea of the perfect date: You get the girl a limousine, and you give her the platinum card, and you stock the limo with the champagne and the cocaine and whatever they want, and you send them shopping on Rodeo Drive. By the time they get back, you're done. All the 'dating' shit is out of the way, and you can get on with it. With the sex."[20]

Journalist John Richardson once asked Simpson to explain his weakness for hookers, especially for watching two hookers perform sex acts for him. Simpson responded, "It's not a weakness. It's an *interest*."[21] The journalist Tony Schwartz, who had met Simpson in 1983 while writing about the movie business for *New York* magazine, said that, during that time, Simpson made his *interests* abundantly clear—even boasted about how many women he had used. "I would go and hang out at the house," Schwartz recalled. "Simpson would take out his Polaroids and describe them to me, as if he were describing a sport. He called it his 'entertainment.' He would talk to me about sex and hookers and that whole life. He'd describe the women and what he'd done with them." What was depicted in the Polaroids? "Nothing that unusual," Schwartz said. "Girls having sex with each other. Girls beating each other up. Girls peeing on each other. You know, stuff like that."[22]

My own experience with Simpson is telling, on several counts. One night we met for a drink at the Bel Air Hotel, hard by Simpson's Stone Canyon house. I had to be at the hotel for a press conference being thrown by *Penthouse* magazine, at which the magazine's editors were going to display the first of a series of *Penthouse* interactive CD-ROMS. Simpson asked to attend the party with me. He said, "They're all hookers, you know. All the *Penthouse* girls are hookers." Simpson proceeded to regale me with stories about the centerfold girls and mentioned one in particular, a very tall, strikingly beautiful brunette named Julie. He'd met her the year before, at a New Year's Eve party on the Hawaiian island of Kauai, and hired her for the night. "It cost me $5,000," Simpson said. "And it was worth every cent."

We subsequently walked across the sedate grounds of the Bel Air, to the conference room where the *Penthouse* people were holding court. The door was opened for us by a very tall, strikingly beautiful brunette. She greeted me and then turned to my companion. "Don!" she trilled. "My God! I haven't seen you since, what, Hawaii? New Year's Eve!"

Over more cocktails, Simpson became more loquacious. He told the group around him that, during a recent flight on American Airlines, a stewardess had ordered him to either put away or have taken away a copy of *Penthouse* that he was reading during the flight. He said he had screamed so loudly about his freedom of speech rights that the stewardess threatened to have him arrested. (Simpson on another occasion made this rather improbable story more preposterous, by insisting it was a copy of *Playboy* that had so upset the stewardess.)

Later that night, after Simpson had consumed many, many drinks—and had impressed the other journalists with outrageous stories of Hollywood misbehavior—Simpson asked me to drive him home. When we got to the gates outside his house, he said, "Come on in and have a drink. I'll call Julie and get her to bring a friend. My treat." I reminded Simpson I was a married man and left him there at the gate.

Years later, after Simpson's death, I met Julie, who worked under the name Julie Strain, an actress who had since married and changed her name. She'd been getting regular work in B movies and by taking off her clothes for soft-core video presentations from the *Playboy* empire. I told her Simpson's New Year's Eve story, which shocked her. "I was there that night with my boyfriend," Julie said. "Simpson humiliated me badly. I told him I was going out with this guy"—a wealthy young Hollywood player. "Simpson said to me, 'You're the third girl this week that's said *that.*' It turned out he was telling the truth. This guy was horrible. But Simpson's lying about being with me. It's true that most of the girls in the magazine *are* hookers, or strippers, which is really the same thing. Simpson may have had a lot of action with them, but he didn't have any with me."[23]

Simpson would sometimes take his hookers on dates and introduce them to friends—but never as hookers. "He literally told me a hooker he was with was a neurosurgeon," said Obst, who'd been the original producer on *Flashdance* and from the late 1970s to the mid-1980s was an unabashed Simpson friend and admirer. "He introduced her to me—she was wearing this outrageous jumpsuit—and he told me, literally, that she was a neurosurgeon *and* that she was a decathlete training for the Olympics! He tended to Pygmalionize his hookers. He would always tell me, when he introduced a girl to me, that she was an astrophysicist or an anthropologist. He was clearly galvanized by tits and ass, but he also had this idea that the women had to be smart. He was very attracted to smart women."[24]

Heidi Fleiss, to whom Simpson would later turn for service as Fleiss began taking away Madam Alex's key employees and clients, believed Simpson's ineptitude with women dated from his high school days. "He told me he was obese, and I think probably in school the girls would go,

'Ooooh, it's Don,' and make fun of him," Fleiss said. "When he came to Hollywood, he lost weight, got cosmetic surgery, became a millionaire, and all the girls went, 'Oh, it's Don, the babe.' Inside, he still remembered the girls abusing him."[25]

Another Madam Alex client was the producer Robert Evans, who as a Paramount executive had overseen the production of classics like *Chinatown* and *Rosemary's Baby*, and who as an independent producer had been in charge of the failed Francis Ford Coppola debacle *The Cotton Club*. He had fallen from Hollywood grace when one of *The Cotton Club* producers, a New Yorker named Roy Radin, turned up dead. Evans was never named as a suspect, but the eventual testimony regarding his relationship with Radin's killers—one of whom had been Evans' girlfriend and cocaine supplier—sent Evans into hiding for almost a decade. Producer Steve Roth was another client. His own drug habit, and his involvement in the motion picture debacle that would be Columbia Pictures' *Last Action Hero*, would eventually evict him from the motion picture business altogether. Producer Jon Peters, who with partner Peter Guber had helped produce *Flashdance*, and who after a string of movie hits would later help dismantle Sony Pictures Entertainment before being banished from the lot, was also a client. So was a man who would be close to Peters' fall from grace—a pugnacious, oily photographer-turned-film producer, the Hungarian-born Ivan Nagy, who would take his own fall from grace at the side of Heidi Fleiss.[26]

According to Roth, Simpson's Cherokee Avenue home, from the early eighties on, was *the* place to get women. "The girls, all the 'ho's, all went there. It was where you went to hook up with chicks."[27] The bare, bleak, hypermodern home, done in cold patterns of rock and steel, was where Simpson pals Bruckheimer, Roth, Steve Tisch, Jim Berkus, Craig Baumgarten, Jim Wiatt and others would hang out on weekends. The screenwriter Paul Schrader—who wrote *American Gigolo* for Bruckheimer—was around. Paul Jasmine, the composer, was around. It was a fast, loose group, and girls and drugs were staples. "In the beginning," Roth said, "we were so hot and so rich and there was nothing but cocaine and hookers and millions of laughs."[28]

Simpson did not limit his sexual exploits to professionals. For a time he dated a shy, very bright young woman named Enid Hertz. He dated a film editor, Priscilla Nedd, who later married the film producer David Friendly. He dated Susan Lentini, a petite, bright brunette. He dated Melissa

Prophet, who subsequently married Craig Baumgarten. And he dated, or at least had sex with, a variety of women who were simply hungry for some connection to Hollywood power.

"We were in New York together when he was auditioning girls for the *Flashdance* TV show" (a project that never made it to the airwaves), recalled a former Simpson crony, the film and television writer Ted Mann. "The hallway [outside Simpson's hotel suite] was *lined* with these girls." Simpson would bring each girl in for her "audition," Mann said. "Every thirty minutes or so, Simpson would come out, combing his wet hair. I'd say, 'How was the last one?' and he'd say, 'Not bad. Next!' This went on for an entire day."[29]

The B-movie actress Jewel Shepard had a similar "audition," reading for Simpson while he watched from a couch. After a few minutes Simpson said, "Okay, do you want to do some coke, or would you like to fuck me?" Shepard said, "Excuse me?" Simpson said, "What part of it did you not understand?" Simpson then took Shepard into a bathroom, where he showed her a container of cocaine, and said, "We could either discuss this nicely and you could probably get a part, or you could go through the charade of reading for it."[30]

There were also the women sometimes known as MAWs—"model, actress, whatever"—and sometimes known as half-a-hookers, that occupy a certain stratum of the entertainment industry. One source described these women as "girls that depend on other people to give them money, but it's not like, 'If you fuck me, I want twenty dollars.' It's like, 'I want my rent paid.' "[31]

In time, though, as Simpson's sexual interests tended almost exclusively toward experiments in bondage, domination and sadism, hookers were his only connection with sexual pleasure.

Ivan Nagy is a craggy, worn, troubled man who chain-smokes cigarettes and chain-drinks diet soda. He lives in a Century City condominium that today is littered with the detritus of his new business—a soft-core CD-ROM business that specializes in titles like *Beverly Hills Models* and *Totally Nude Gymnastics*. Though Nagy insists that he never procured girls for anyone—and certainly did not deserve the pandering charges brought against him in 1993, and ultimately dropped, by the Beverly Hills cops—his company is called MacDaddy Entertainment. (MacDaddy is a street slang expression for "pimp.") The business is thriving, but Nagy is not. It is late in 1996, and his former girlfriend, the notorious "Hollywood Madam" Heidi Fleiss, is about to be convicted on pandering charges, having already been convicted on tax evasion charges, and she is awaiting sentencing. Nagy has been getting strange phone calls. So have his friends. In a voice worn ragged by cigarettes and anxiety, Nagy says he is increasingly concerned that Heidi, as she awaits sentencing, will attempt to cut a deal with the prosecutor's office, and that cutting a deal will mean ratting Nagy out. He insists there is nothing legitimate she can throw the cops— that he never procured women, never dealt drugs, did anything illegal at all. (He did plead no contest, in 1991, to bookmaking charges and was convicted.) He was never, he says, anything more than a man in love with the troubled Heidi Fleiss. Despite their ugly falling-out, Nagy still has snapshots of Heidi everywhere on his condo walls. He fires up another Camel 100 and sighs as he talks about her.

They met in 1989. (Nagy already knew Simpson, whom he'd met in the late 1970s at the home of Paul Monash. Simpson was a Paramount executive; Nagy was directing movies-of-the-week for Paramount TV, cheesy entertainments like *Mind over Murder* and *Midnight Lace*. At Monash's house he and Simpson played what Nagy calls network tennis, a variation on the game in which "you return everything, softly, and 'network' with the more powerful players." Simpson at the time was boasting about his upcoming role in *Days of Thunder*, telling Nagy that he was going to act full-time and be more famous than anyone else in Hollywood.) Nagy was already a Madam Alex client, one of the favored ones who got invited to Thanksgiving dinner and who were welcome to drop in and chat with the short, obese Alex as she lay in bed surrounded by her cats and telephones.

Nagy and Alex had met, by accident, through one of Alex's girls, whom Nagy had met at a New Year's Eve party in 1985 and begun to date. Eventually they were living together at Nagy's Marina Del Rey apartment. But she kept strange hours; she'd get phone calls late at night and have to go out. After a while she admitted to Nagy that she "worked for this madam." Nagy asked for an introduction. Several years later, when he and Alex had become friends, the situation repeated itself. He told Alex one night that he'd met a girl and fallen in love. Her name was Heidi. Alex cackled, Nagy remembered, in a particularly unpleasant way. "You idiot!" she laughed. "Heidi works for *me*."[32]

Madam Alex herself told a different version of the story when she was interviewed by British filmmaker Nick Broomfield, for his 1996 documentary *Heidi Fleiss, Hollywood Madam*. She insisted that Nagy brought Fleiss to her house and "sold her to me for $450." Confronted with this while being interviewed in his apartment, Nagy had waved his arms around at the paintings lining the walls and said to Broomfield, "Look around! Do I need $500? I mean, come on. It's an insanity!"[33] Former Los Angeles Police Department Detective Jim Wakefield told Broomfield that he believed Nagy "was pulling the strings. He in fact took information from Madam Alex, on who the johns were, added information that he'd developed. He was basically orchestrating [Heidi's] network."[34]

Heidi Fleiss was one of three daughters born to Paul Fleiss, a popular Westside pediatrician who raised his girls in the Hollywood Hills suburb known as Los Feliz. Heidi, though bright, was a high school dropout with an early drug habit and a thing for older men. When she was still a teenager, she hooked up with the high-flying international financier Bernie Kornfeld, who, conveniently for Heidi, had a thing for younger women. (He gave Heidi a Rolls-Royce Corniche and $1 million in cash for her twenty-first birthday, sources have said.) Heidi moved into Kornfeld's massive Beverly Hills estate and began a tempestuous years-long love affair that was just ending when she met Nagy. Nagy was older and European, like Kornfeld. He had money, and a yacht, and could be charming. Soon Nagy had convinced Alex to stop sending Heidi out on "dates." Soon after, he and Heidi were living together. Soon after that, Heidi went into business for herself. Madam Alex was aging and unwell and had legal problems. Heidi poached many of her best girls, and many of her best clients, and set herself up in a Hollywood Hills home, above the Sunset Strip, that her father purchased from actor Michael Douglas—using Heidi's money, clumsily laundered in a way that would not escape the attention of Internal Revenue Service investigators years later. (There is no indication that Douglas, though a confessed "sex addict" who had undergone professional treatment for his addiction, ever had business dealings with Heidi herself.)

Heidi's business plan, according to Nagy, was simple, and employed several tricks she'd learned from her mentor, Madam Alex. For one thing, according to retired Detective Wakefield, Heidi and Ivan had possession of Madam Alex's "black book" of clients. In 1992 Alex had reason to believe she was going to be indicted on pandering charges, and she was making preparations to leave the country, Wakefield says. "That's how it was possible for Ivan and Heidi to get started. Alex was going to leave the country, or she was going to prison. That enabled them to be started."[35]

Moreover, both Heidi and Alex had relationships with men who were "strategically placed," Nagy says, at nightclubs. Sometimes it was the bartender, sometimes the bouncer, sometimes the owner. (One of Heidi's best friends was Victoria Sellers, whose stepfather, Lou Adler, is the music business impresario who owns the Sunset Strip nightclubs the Roxy and On the Roxx. She is the daughter of Britt Ekland and the late Peter Sellers; her previous stepfather was Rod Stewart.) Heidi and Alex would pay these men to produce willing girls for them. Sometimes Heidi would pick out the girls herself. With Sellers or another friend, at nightclubs like Roxbury or Vertigo, Heidi would approach a group of attractive young women. She'd say, "Hey, we're giving this party for Billy Idol," or, "There's this party for Mick Jagger," or, "There's a birthday party for Charlie Sheen." According to Nagy, Heidi was very straight with the young prospects. "She'd just flat out tell them, 'I'm a madam,' " Nagy said. "She'd ask if they were interested in working. If they said yes, she'd follow up with a phone call. If they said maybe, she'd follow up with a phone call. Heidi understood that, sooner or later, all of these girls would need money. They all liked to hang out, and most of them didn't work and didn't have any talents or skills. Hanging out is expensive, and you can't hang out all night, especially if you're doing drugs, and then go to a real job in the morning. Heidi knew that sooner or later these girls would need some money and, if they had her phone number, the phone would ring. 'I lost my job.' 'I got a DUI.' 'I'm in Greece and the guy I was with took off with all the money.' 'I can't pay my phone bill.' They'd all call, sooner or later."[36]

As Alex Adams said, "Face it, the kind of girl who wants to become a hooker is a bad girl. These girls were lazy and greedy and, above all, wanted something for nothing."[37]

One former prostitute amplifies that. Heidi, she says, capitalized on the hunger of young Hollywood women trying to make it in the entertainment industry. "Heidi and people like her use that ploy," said Liza Greer. "If you go on this trick, you'll make $10,000, *plus* you'll meet Don Simpson, and he can put you in his next movie."[38] Several of Heidi's girls did, in fact, get bit parts in Simpson's movies.

Nagy believes, though, that Heidi herself became sufficiently celebrated to attract women on her own. "Heidi was like this rock star, with a big house in the Hills," Nagy says. "She was a star."

She was also, though, a junkie who was loudmouthed about her success and increasingly indiscreet. "What took Madam Alex ten years to do, I did in one year," she boasted to a reporter at the time of Alex's death.[39] But unlike Alex before her, Heidi had no relationship with the Los Angeles Police Department.

Fred Clapp worked in the LAPD's vice squads for twenty-two years. He was eventually in charge of administrative vice, and his beat was high-class call girls and their madams. A smiling, affable man with clear blue eyes and thinning pale hair, Clapp has since retired from the force and runs security for MCA-Universal. In the 1980s he ran Madam Alex. As a younger cop, Clapp had been promised by his LAPD mentor that, when he retired, Clapp would inherit Madam Alex as his snitch. The introduction never happened. Clapp attempted to create the relationship himself. "I door-knocked her," Clapp remembers, "but she wouldn't cooperate. So I put a case on her."[40] Clapp's case led to Alex Adams' first conviction for pandering, in 1982. For years, she'd been protected by her handlers on the force, with whom she exchanged inside dope on other criminals for her own safety. After Clapp allowed her to plea down the pandering charge, that became their relationship, until Adams' retirement from the business in 1990. Clapp would visit Adams at home; she'd offer him gifts—money, jewelry, a girl—which he would decline. Then they'd get down to business. Adams supplied Clapp with enough information to make dozens of arrests. He, in turn, allowed her to keep doing business. "She was my informant, but she wasn't untouchable," Clapp says. "But if you know someone's talking to a cop, you back off." The madams and their "high-line" girls weren't that big a priority to law enforcement, which according to Clapp during the 1980s was concentrating more on escort services and "out-call" services. (Among other things, Clapp says, they are easier to prosecute: You make the call, get the girl, use a credit card and follow the paper. With a madam, proving pimping or pandering is harder, because you have to follow the money from the john to the girl to the madam and establish direct links along the line.) According to Clapp, Alex had among her clientele some of Southern California's richest and most powerful men—among them members of the Saudi royal family and ranking officers of the movie studios. Don Simpson was a good client to Alex, and a good friend. "She liked Simpson, and he liked her," Clapp recalls. "Simpson even paid her hospital bills when she was dying. All I knew was that he was a customer of hers and of [competing madam] Cathy Black. To anyone who had any girls, he was a client. Alex talked about him freely, because she knew we wouldn't do anything about it." She also talked about Robert Evans, whom Clapp calls "the biggest whoremonger in Hollywood." Her principal competition, Clapp says, came from Janice Flannery, Lauralei Hart and the husband-and-wife team of Cathy and Joe Black—all of whom, in his career, Clapp says he arrested and saw convicted. (He arrested Flannery, personally, in 1982.)[41]

They all had helpers. Clapp calls Ivan Nagy "a pimp" and "a con artist." "He was absolutely Heidi's pimp," Clapp says. "No question about it. That's exactly what he was, and is."[42]

In 1992, when LAPD Police Chief Daryl Gates was ousted, the old police regime began to crumble, and the new regime had new priorities. Alex Adams was out of business, and most likely would not return—because the new LAPD handler she inherited, after Clapp had moved further up in the police ranks, had labeled her "a snitch." Most of her girls had lit out after that, many of them running to Heidi, who, Clapp and others say, set up shop with Nagy.[43]

For a while, no one on the police force paid attention. Madams are always somewhat elusive, from a legal standpoint, even though their activities are well known to the police. As Detective Wakefield explains, "Pimping and pandering cases are difficult to prove. The money has to be directly traced to the pimp. Most of the pimps like to 'try on the merchandise' before they put the girls into service. That limits your options with undercover officers."[44]

But Heidi was boastful, and loud, and she was getting sloppy. According to LAPD Captain Glenn Ackerman, "Heidi was brought down by her own big mouth."[45] In June 1993 Fleiss was set up in a sting operation. An undercover cop posing as a visiting Japanese businessman had Heidi deliver several girls and several grams of cocaine to a Beverly Hills hotel. Heidi's girls, and later Heidi, were placed under arrest. After a series of trials that led to 1996 convictions on tax evasion and pimping and pandering charges, Heidi was ultimately sentenced to almost a decade in a California prison.

According to Nagy, Heidi's relationship with Simpson, as Alex's before that, was close professionally and personally. Like Alex, Heidi liked to gossip. Like Simpson, she did drugs and liked to stay on the phone late at night. There would be periodic spats, especially as the time of her arrest approached, as when Heidi began objecting to the sorts of sexual acts Simpson asked her girls to perform. Heidi herself has said the objections concerned the girls' safety: "I had a rule that said if I wouldn't do it, I couldn't, in all fairness, ask my girls to do it."[46] Nagy has said it was simply a question of money: "Heidi wasn't concerned about the girls. She was only concerned about money. She was concerned about elevating the fee for certain kinds of activity. That pissed Don off. She wanted more money, and he didn't want to pay." One or two of these disagreements got out of hand, when Heidi cut Simpson off and refused to send him any more girls. Simpson apparently believed that another Heidi confidant, Robert Evans, was behind this. One night Evans called Heidi in a state of panic. "Don called and is threatening to kill both of us!" he told her. "He thinks it's my fault you don't send the girls. You've got to calm him down! I think he's got a gun!"[47] Sometimes Simpson would bring his friend Anthony Pellicano, a private detective known around Hollywood's underworld as having a talent for pushing the envelope on investigation and law enforcement, into the mix. Once, according to Nagy, Simpson sent Pellicano to Heidi's house to settle an argument. Pellicano tried to frighten Heidi, asking her menacingly, "Do you know who you're fucking with?" Heidi wasn't spooked. "What the fuck do I care?" she shouted at Pellicano. "What are you gonna do—shoot me? Fuck you." Other times, Pellicano would meet more cordially with Heidi; money would exchange hands; her business dealings with Simpson, and their friendship, would be restored.

Simpson had met Pellicano in the 1980s, and by late in that decade was relying on the private detective for all manner of personal services. For this, Pellicano was the perfect employee. A middle-aged self-styled "forensics expert" with swank offices on the western end of the Sunset Strip, Pellicano is tough-talking, Italian-and-proud-of-it. His office features piped-in operatic arias. He introduces himself to visitors by shrugging at the music and saying, apropos of nothing, "What can I tell you? I'm Sicilian."[48] (One Christmas, reminding clients why they'd hired him in the past or should in the future, Pellicano sent as holiday presents small ceramic paperweights—a regulation-size baseball set on a crude base where resided the words SOMETIMES . . . YOU JUST HAVE TO PLAY HARDBALL. PELLICANO INVESTIGATIVE AGENCY LTD.[49]) Pellicano carries a Louisville Slugger in the trunk of his black Lexus—perhaps the same bat with which he claimed to have once beaten a bad guy on behalf of a client.[50]

Pellicano had come to California to help investigate matters on behalf of accused cocaine dealer John DeLorean, after leaving his home of Chicago under a bad cloud; he'd resigned under pressure from the Illinois Law Enforcement Commission when reports linked him to the underworld.[51]

In Hollywood Pellicano found plenty of business, from celebrities in trouble who didn't blink at his $25,000 retainer. Pellicano investigated on behalf of Michael Jackson, when he was accused of child molestation; Kevin Costner, when a woman sold details of her eleven-year-long love affair with the actor; Roseanne, when she wanted to find the daughter she put up for adoption; and Simpson, when former Simpson-Bruckheimer secretary Monica Harmon sued the producers for sexual harassment and a battery of other charges.

Pellicano impressed Simpson. "You always want to be on the right side of Anthony Pellicano," he once said. And Pellicano impressed himself— and bragged about his exploits and his business practices. "Anybody who wants to malign one of my clients, I dig into their pasts," Pellicano told a journalist. "So they gotta take the same heat that they dish out." He added that his job was to make people "remember why they're afraid of the dark."[52]

It is not exactly clear where Pellicano's relationship with Simpson started and ended, but Pellicano clearly felt a kinship with his sometime client. "I love him like a brother, and I will do anything necessary to protect him," he once said.[53]

Nagy probably knows more about the high-stakes prostitution game in Los Angeles than anyone besides Heidi Fleiss and the late Madam Alex. He insists that he never pimped and that his 1993 arrest on pandering charges, along with three accused prostitutes, was simply harassment. (Alex Adams called Nagy "the biggest pimp in Hollywood" in 1995.)[54] But he knows the players the way a talent agent knows his clients or a head-master his students. Perusing a list of girls removed from Simpson's office by a former assistant, Nagy talks fondly of each as her name comes up. "Jeannelle was a girl Don saw near the end. She got girls for him after Heidi was gone. Sasha was another madam he used. Peggy was one of Heidi's girls. Penny was this very pretty Orange County girl who worked for Alex and then Heidi. She's married now. Uschi, now, that was a beautiful girl. She disappeared. Karen was nice, too. She had an *almost* promising acting career. She got some decent movies in the early eighties, but she never got past that. Charisse. Tracy. Clarissa. Debra. Lauren, she was very good friends with Michelle. All Heidi's girls."[55]

Nagy, from his long and close associations with Alex and Heidi, also knows a lot about their clients. Melissa Prophet, he says, was a "house girl" for international financier Adnan Kashoggi, procuring women for him while living in his home, a statement echoed by former *Playboy* model Cathy St. George, who was friendly with Prophet in the late 1980s,[56] and by film executive Paul Rosenfeld, who knew Prophet through the man she would later marry, longtime Simpson friend Craig Baumgarten. Producer Joel Silver knew Prophet well, too, but was not actually a customer, though Melissa would set him up on dates. Producer Robert Evans actually went into business with Prophet, when, at the tender age of twenty-five, Prophet attempted to help Evans raise money for his failed film *The Cotton Club*.[57]

Producer Evans, during his hibernation period in the 1980s, didn't have enough steady cash to be a steady customer, but according to Nagy he helped Heidi find new clients, so Heidi always sent him girls. Alexandra Datig, a former Heidi and Alex girl, remembered that Heidi told her, "He's not going to pay you, but just go. He's really nice, and you'll have fun." Datig did, many times. Usually, there was no sex involved, and the evening consisted chiefly of sharing drugs. Evans, Datig said, was particularly fond of a smoked form of cocaine that Datig called cocoa puffs. Datig would pinch the end off a cigarette, remove the filter, replace it with the stiff, rolled-up end of a matchbook cover, then shake half of the tobacco out. She would then snort a line of cocaine into the cigarette and slowly "melt" the cocaine, over a candle, into the remaining tobacco. She'd then light the cocoa puff for Evans to smoke.[58]

Bonnie Bradigan, who would later gain some measure of fame as the dominatrix in Simpson's home video feature *Bonnie Beats Mary*, was the steady professional "girlfriend" of some of Hollywood's top players. Simpson introduced her to his director friend Tony Scott. She was later with Robert Evans. Jon Peters, Nagy says, was a "great customer" while he was cohead of Sony Pictures Entertainment, often calling to buy girls for actors whom he was trying to lure into multipicture deals at Sony.

With Heidi's sentencing, Nagy and his friends stop getting strange phone calls. The former high-flying playboy stops worrying and goes back to running MacDaddy. There are orders to fill, product to license. Nagy lights another cigarette. He's still in love with Heidi, he says.

Simpson's sexual predilections eventually became the stuff of literature, in a public humiliation that just barely preceded his death. In the fall of 1995 a Beverly Hills publishing company called Dove Books, which had recently hit big with a book by Faye Resnick, a close friend of the late Nicole Brown Simpson, published *You'll Never Make Love in This Town Again.* (The title was a takeoff on former film producer Julia Phillips' 1991 Hollywood tell-all, *You'll Never Eat Lunch in This Town Again.*) In the Dove book, a hooker named Tiffany recounted several episodes in which Simpson indulged his burgeoning passion for S&M bondage games.

Describing Simpson as "handsome . . . in a rugged sort of way," Tiffany liked the fact that the film producer had "a flat stomach, a very sexy belly button, and a sexy hair line that goes from his chest to his navel. The tight blue jeans that he wore were obviously chosen for the way they flatter his masculinity." Simpson began their first meeting by showing Tiffany a videotape, in which Simpson "interviewed" one actress after another and "ended up having sex with them." A final tape was more serious, Tiffany wrote. "It involved a dominatrix dressed in black leather who was torturing a beautiful young girl. Both women were prostitutes, but what Don and the dominatrix did to this girl should have gotten them both thrown in prison. She was bound and tortured, tied up in bondage apparel, including a large rubber ball strapped to the girl's mouth so she couldn't scream. She was then led to the bathroom. The dominatrix, a prostitute I recognized named Patricia Colombo, forced the girl to lean over the toilet. With her head dunked in the water, the girl was told to drink. At the same time, the dominatrix had a black, twelve-inch dildo strapped to her body. She fucked the girl with it, and also put another specially designed tool up the girl's ass. Don Simpson, meanwhile, was standing over the toilet pissing into the bowl as the girl drank."[59]

On a different occasion Simpson had Tiffany and the dominatrix Colombo at the Stone Canyon house and, Tiffany said, "something possessed him to call Heidi for a third girl. When the third girl arrived, she took one look at Patricia—dressed in patent leather boots that came up to her mid-thigh, a leather studded bustier, whip and mask—and swallowed hard. Don took this innocent-looking girl upstairs to the bedroom and before too long we could hear her screaming. About an hour later, the young girl came downstairs in tears, obviously shaken up. Don paid her the thousand dollars and told her to leave. He told us that he had 'turned her out'— beaten her, screwed her, and introduced her to S&M for the first time. It gave Don a good deal of pleasure to take a naive young girl and do this to her.''[60]

In real life, Tiffany is the tall, blond, blue-eyed former hooker named Alexandra Datig. Swiss-born, and poorly educated there and in Southern California, Datig met Simpson in February 1992. She had fallen into prostitution in the traditional way. Broke, sharing a Westchester apartment with two friends, she needed money and did not know how else to get it. ''All I knew was I was in a bad spot, and I needed money,'' Datig says frankly. ''I felt this was the best and easiest and fastest way to get ahead. And I was excited by the whole 'call girl' thing—meet the cool guys, make the money and have fun. I was *proud* of it.''[61]

She had already heard about Simpson from her roommate Rachel, whose friend Afifa had spent many evenings at the producer's Stone Canyon house. Rachel had introduced Datig to Madam Alex, who soon had her turning tricks. She heard Simpson's name periodically. Afifa had laughed talking about him, saying, ''All he wants to do is talk all night. He's on cocaine, and he's crazy.''

So Datig was not alarmed when, one night at ten o'clock, her friend Rachel called and told her she had a date with Simpson. Datig was in her pajamas, in bed. Rachel said, ''Be there at ten-thirty. You'll get $1,000, and all you have to do is talk.'' Datig dressed hurriedly in green tights and a green jacket over a frilly shirt and platform shoes. She was surprised, upon arriving, to find Simpson such a handsome man, and told him so. He thanked her for the compliment and brought her into the living room. His house assistant, Todd Marrero, brought a fresh bottle of Cristal champagne from the kitchen, poured Datig a glass and prepared a Chivas Regal on the rocks for Simpson, who took out a cocaine grinder and a Swiss Army knife and began cutting lines of cocaine onto a coffee table. For an hour or more, as Afifa had presaged, they simply talked. Simpson gradually wound the conversation around to sex and began talking about people's ''unusual'' sexual habits, Datig recalls. She told him, ''Hey, I don't care what people *do*. Whatever it is, it could be interesting.'' Simpson's face, Datig said, ''just lit up. He said, 'Let's go upstairs.' '' After more cocaine and Cristal and Chivas, Datig and Simpson got undressed, and for the next several hours "lounged around, naked, talking, just fooling around," Datig said. "There was no sex—well, there was no penetration. It was just fun."

At the end of their meeting, when dawn was drawing near, Simpson said he wanted to see Datig again—that he would call Madam Alex and ask for her specifically. Several nights later he did.

As before, Marrero brought out a fresh bottle of Cristal, while Simpson sipped Chivas and snorted lines of cocaine. Again he invited Datig upstairs, to his large, dark bedroom. There Simpson sat Datig on the bed and mashed a button, and a television set rose silently out of the mahogany desk before them. "I want to show you something," he said. The television monitor began to play an amateur video, featuring a black dominatrix being "serviced" by several men. "Lick my shoe!" the dominatrix commanded. "Suck the heel of my shoe!" That video was followed by another, in which a prostitute Datig recognized as Patricia Colombo "dominated" a prostitute Datig knew as Michelle. In that video Colombo penetrated Michelle's vagina with a twelve-inch strap-on dildo, while violating her anally with a smaller, handheld plastic penis. In a third video Colombo mounted the prostitute Afifa with a large strap-on dildo while forcing her head into a toilet bowl. Barely within frame, Simpson could be seen urinating into the bowl, onto Afifa's partially submerged head.

Datig took the videos as a challenge. She told Simpson, "You know, this is really serious stuff." To herself she said, "I'm intimidated that he has someone in his life who can do this. But I can *outdo* it." Simpson said to her, "Isn't this shit great? You've got to meet Patricia." Datig agreed. Powered by the champagne, the cocaine and a few hits of Mandrax, she accepted the challenge. She said to Simpson, "Fine. You're not going to fuck me. All we do is talk, and then you show me some pictures. Why am I here?" Simpson grinned and said, "You've got to meet Patricia." They fell asleep on Simpson's bed. The following day, waking around four in the afternoon, Simpson gave Datig a thousand dollars and told her to expect his call.

It came the following night. Datig arrived around eleven-thirty. Patricia Colombo was already there—and Datig was instantly intimidated. Colombo was almost six feet tall, in her early thirties, and she was very black and very built, 180 pounds of powerful muscle. After a brief introduction and a brief stare-down, Datig said, it was clear that there was a problem: Neither she nor Colombo was going to be submissive to the other. Mar-

rero arrived with Cristal; Simpson prepared lines. For about an hour the
three talked. No one made a move. After midnight Simpson rang Madam
Alex and said, "I need you to send over a 'dom,' now." By the time the
new girl walked through the door, an hour later, Datig and Colombo had
reached an agreement: Whoever she was, she was going to be dominated—
badly. When Marrero led a young, pale redhead into the living room,
Datig winked at Colombo and said, "Let's go."

They took the redhead upstairs and began rifling through Simpson's
impressive collection of "gear." In a closet were leather boots in many
sizes, dog collars with metal studs, strap-on belts fitted with dildos large
and small, handcuffs, gags, masks with zippers over the eyes and mouths,
rubber skirts, nipple clamps, paddles, whips, belts and hats—lots of hats,
especially the kind of "police" hat Simpson favored, a leather one with a
patent-leather bill. Datig and Colombo dressed the redhead in a rubber
skirt that barely covered her genitals, and put a leash and collar on her.
They made the redhead crawl to Simpson's bedroom, yelling at her to
"bark like a dog." Colombo penetrated the redhead's vagina from behind
with a strap-on dildo while Simpson paddled her bottom. After a while,
Datig and Colombo switched places. Simpson grew increasingly bored. He
finally said, "This is bullshit. Somebody has got to turn that girl out, and
you aren't doing it." He left the room, irritated and went downstairs. A
short time later he paid all three women and sent them home.

Datig, again, felt challenged. For a while, she didn't see Simpson. She
had moved, and switched allegiance from Madam Alex to Heidi Fleiss, and
initiated some new rules. She told Fleiss, "No show business people, no
music business people and no one local." She turned tricks for Fleiss on a
strictly East Coast basis, flying to New York for rendezvous with Fleiss'
out-of-town clients. In the meantime, Datig had introduced another of her
roommates, Shannon, to Simpson, who immediately paid for Shannon to
get breast enlargement surgery. When they spoke again, Simpson issued
Datig a challenge. He said, "Find me a fucking *freak*, Alex. Find me
someone who's fun."

A few weeks later Datig did. She phoned Simpson and said, "I have
what you need." They set a date for the weekend. The "freak" Datig had
in mind was a woman named Michelle, a tall, thin, large-breasted crystal
methedrine addict with frizzy hair and bright blue eyes. Michelle was an
unwed mother with a child at home and a reputation for rough stuff.
Among her regular clients was a New York businessman who paid Fleiss

$50,000 a weekend for sending him four girls at a time, girls he would brutalize so severely that Michelle complained to Datig of being unable to "sit down for a week" afterward. Datig promised Michelle $1,000 and told her the time and place.

When Datig arrived, she remembered, Simpson was snorting cocaine and talking with a top ICM agent. The two men were drinking and paging through photographs of Don's "girls," selections from a vast collection of Polaroids Simpson kept in a dresser by his bed. A woman introduced to Datig as the agent's fiancée was also there; the two were on their way to the airport for a flight to Hawaii. Simpson was in a good mood, teasing the agent, when the fiancée got up to go to the bathroom, saying, "I'm going to fuck her for you. That's my wedding present." After a while, more guests arrived. There was one of Hollywood's most successful TV producers. There was a Burbank plastic surgeon who'd also become a close Simpson friend. The agent and his fiancée left around the time that Michelle arrived. Patricia Colombo arrived shortly after. Michelle stripped and introduced herself to the audience, saying, "I'm a spank monster," and then demonstrated her ability to tie her vaginal lips into a knot. Simpson was not impressed. Datig recalls that Simpson, dressed "like an animal trainer" in jeans, T-shirt and a police cap, ordered everyone upstairs to the bedroom.

There, for the next hour, Colombo "dominated" Michelle, the black hooker penetrating the white hooker with a twelve-inch strap-on dildo, from behind, while the white hooker serially placed four "pussy clamps" to her vaginal lips. Unfortunately, Datig said, Michelle "was loving every minute of it" and refused to play the proper "submissive" role. "It was like Michelle was dominating Patricia," she said, "and not the other way around." Patricia was sweating so heavily that she requested a towel. Michelle showed no sign of exhaustion, but kept calling for more. The male members of the audience were drinking, taking half-hits of Mandrax and taking turns beating Michelle with paddles and whips. But still the unsubmissive hooker called for more. Datig, who had spent much of the hour videotaping the two prostitutes, finally saw her moment. She dragged Michelle and Colombo into the bathroom and said, "This is over. And I'm going to finish it." She took Colombo's strap-on dildo and dressed herself in thigh-high leather boots, a rubber miniskirt, a policeman's hat, reflecting sunglasses and surgical gloves. She took Michelle back into the bedroom, placed her on her hands and knees and began furiously assaulting her from behind with the dildo. Within fifteen minutes Michelle achieved either ecstasy or exhaustion and passed out on the floor. A triumphant Datig said to Simpson, "*There*, asshole."

The party wound down. The plastic surgeon, who had passed out sometime during the show, roused himself and, according to Datig, began performing cunnilingus on the just-revived Michelle. Colombo and Datig cleaned up and put on white robes. Near dawn, everyone went home. It would be Datig's last successful "date" with Simpson. A week later she returned to the house with Michelle for another session. This time Michelle demanded more money from Simpson, who smelled a shakedown. He and Datig argued, and she left the house, Simpson standing in the doorway shouting, "Get out and stay the fuck out of my house." It would be nearly a year before the two met again—a year in which Datig heard, repeatedly, that Simpson intended to kill her.

Bonnie Bradigan walks into a West Hollywood restaurant looking exactly like the exotic dancer/professional stripper that she is—tall, blue-eyed, big-breasted, badly dressed in a too-tight peach-colored dress and too-tall heels, and pawing at an unruly mane of hair colored somewhere between red and magenta. She sits unsteadily and orders a Tanqueray and tonic.[62]

Bradigan grew up in Buffalo, New York, interested in the arts and ultimately attending the State University of New York there and graduating with an M.F.A. degree in theater arts. She moved west to Los Angeles, intending to continue her arts education at UCLA and find work as an actress-comedienne.

That never happened. Money grew scarce. Soon Bradigan was taking her M.F.A.-related theater arts skills, which included dance, and applying them as a stripper, working for companies like Escorts Unlimited and Elegance Unlimited, dancing at bachelor parties. One time it was a Super Bowl Sunday party, where she worked as a topless waitress for a local businessman. Other times it was a Japanese client who needed three women to accompany him to a business dinner and a client who wanted six strippers to dance at a party, one at a time, all night long. It was the mid-1980s. Drugs were around. Soon Bradigan was using speed to keep her energy level up.[63]

By 1985 Bradigan had become friendly with several of Simpson's acquaintances. She'd met fellow New Yorker Frank Pesce, an aspiring actor who had worked with Simpson on *Beverly Hills Cop*. She'd met John La Rocca, the modeling agent who had represented Michelle Pfeiffer and Demi Moore. (La Rocca told her to get a nose job, saying, "Get your nose fixed—Michelle's career didn't take off until she got hers done," Bradigan said.) She'd met Shep Gordon, the film and music producer, and bon vivant, who would later make an appearance in the Hollywood hooker tell-all *You'll Never Make Love in This Town Again*. She'd met Madam Alex, Hollywood's reigning procurer-to-the-stars, and done several jobs for her. According to retired Los Angeles Police Department vice chief Fred Clapp, "Bonnie Bradigan worked for Alex as a high-line call girl."[64]

In April 1985 her friend Pesce said, "I want you to meet this friend of mine. He's a producer, the guy who made *Flashdance*." Bradigan was thrilled: *Flashdance* was her favorite movie. Pesce said his name was Don Simpson. That rang a bell. Bradigan remembered reading his name in a recent copy of *Playgirl* magazine, in which Simpson was identified—along with Robert Evans, Jon Peters, Warren Beatty, John Davis, Daniel Melnick and others—as one of Los Angeles' ten most eligible bachelors.[65] Together she and Pesce drove up Coldwater Canyon to Simpson's house on Cherokee Avenue.

Simpson was hot stuff in 1985. He'd hit with *Flashdance* in 1983, and the following year had hit again with *Beverly Hills Cop*. In addition to his inclusion in the *Playgirl* article, he was being profiled for *Esquire* by journalist Lynn Hirschberg. He was becoming a celebrity. And he liked to party.

That first night, Bradigan recalled, she began by asking Simpson for his autograph. He liked that. "His ego puffed up," Bradigan said. And she was immediately drawn to Simpson physically. She found him "a little heavy-set, with a salt-and-pepper beard and black hair. He wasn't polished-looking, or genteel. He had this wild, Alaska-looking thing—wild and natural." While Simpson conducted business on the phone and showed Bradigan around the house, she and Pesce drank and talked. She told Pesce, "This is wonderful. I *need* a wealthier boyfriend." That first night, Bradigan stayed until three or four o'clock in the morning, "drinking and, you know, playing around." There was lots of cocaine, which Simpson dug into hungrily, using the tip of a Swiss Army knife to maneuver the powder from a baggie to his nose. Two days later Simpson called her and said, "Come on over." She stayed several days.

Over the next year, Simpson would see Bradigan often. He bought her things—especially lingerie. One night he said, "Here's $800. Buy something sexy." She bought a black leather outfit from Trashy Lingerie, on La Cienega. Another time Simpson gave her $3,000 for several outfits—a "white wedding fantasy" getup and more black leather. Simpson would take Polaroid pictures of her, and she of him. They started experimenting with various mild S&M fantasies—at his suggestion, Bradigan recalled, she wore a chastity belt, and they played spanking games—that led to more serious stuff. Simpson got a post office box and was soon subscribing to magazines so hard-core that, Bradigan believed, they were illegal.

Increasingly, S&M became the focus of their sexual relations, and Bradigan became increasingly part of Simpson's life. She remembers trying to help him work out a story line for *Beverly Hills Cop 2* and trying to figure out a way to do a remake of the 1969 sociosexual study *Bob & Carol & Ted & Alice.* "I was his sex slave, and he was my mentor," Bradigan says. Simpson tried to get her an agent and sent her out for various acting jobs—which she didn't get, she said, because that was before she had her breast augmentation surgery, and "they always wanted girls with big tits." She and Simpson had sex, but they also had fun. He was a lively lover, and he made her laugh. One night they pretended to be animals in bed—literally. "He said, 'Bonnie Baboon, meet Donald Chimp-son,' " Bradigan says. She even appeared in subsequent press coverage of Simpson's difficulties with former assistant Monica Harmon. She pulls out a clipping from *Spy* magazine and points to a line where it says, "Mr. Simpson, your slut is on line three." "That was *me*," Bradigan says. "I was his slut on line three."[66]

Bradigan had made $1,000 to $1,500 working for Madam Alex. Simpson, she says, wasn't paying her for their time together. But he offered her money for other things. One night in late 1985 he made her a proposition: He'd pay her $1,000 to strip for his friend Tony Scott, at his bachelor party. She agreed. "I was his present to Tony," she says. At that party and two subsequent ones Simpson hosted, Bradigan says, she met many of Simpson's friends. The producer Steve Roth was there, as were Simpson's friends Steve Tisch, the producer, and Jim Wiatt, the ICM agent. Michael Eisner attended one of the parties. Jerry Bruckheimer attended all of them. In January 1986, Bradigan says, Simpson said, "Don't you want to have a good agent? Then meet mine," and introduced her to Wiatt. Wiatt promised to help Bradigan with her career. Shortly after, Bradigan got a chance to help Wiatt, instead. "Don said to me, 'I love you, but I want you to keep Wiatt company for me.' " Simpson gave her $1,000 for the favor. Shortly after, at another party, Simpson hired another woman, a former *Penthouse* cover girl named Angela Giovanni, to dance with Bonnie. "They were getting ready to do *Top Gun*, so all those guys were there—Tony Scott, Jerry Bruckheimer, Wiatt and Don," Bradigan said. "It was wild. Angela ended up with Jerry."

On other occasions Simpson would bring in more than one girl for himself. Bradigan wasn't jealous. "Sometimes a man needs to reaffirm his sexuality," she says.

By 1988 Simpson was getting interested in other things. He had been watching Scott direct and had grilled him on the finer points of camera work. After *Top Gun*, Simpson was talking about reinventing himself as a director. Bradigan told him, "Direct *me!*" and Simpson said he would. He had two Paramount assistants deliver video cameras and lighting equipment to the house. Simpson, who'd brought a prostitute named Mary to the house, too, then "recruited" the assistants, and got them to undress and have sex with the two women while he filmed the whole thing. Bradigan, who says she was on her second bottle of champagne before the camera rolled, remembers the event as nothing but a big laugh—designed, she says, to "take Don's mind off his problems with the Mafia."

Simpson had told her that he had "insulted" some woman at a party and that she had turned out to be connected to the mob. He had been told that her boyfriend had ordered Simpson killed, and he believed that his life was in danger. He slept with a loaded, semiautomatic Uzi in his headboard, Bradigan says, and had several bodyguards on the property. He seemed obsessed with security, and Bradigan thought the video would provide a healthy distraction. "It was all my idea," she says today. "I loved him, and I thought it would take his mind off the Mafia."

Bradigan spent two weeks at the house with Simpson in 1988, around the time, she remembers, that *Top Gun* was opening. But she'd also been spending time with other men. Frank Pesce introduced her to a top action movie star, and, she says, she later had a "wild three-way" evening of sex with him and a supermodel covergirl. (She remembers having heard that the action star had problems maintaining an erection and that he had undergone some sort of surgical procedure to help him with the problem. She jokingly asked him if his penis was, in fact, all his. "This is me!" he'd said, and showed her the member in question. "Don't you see? This is all me!'') That connection led to an audition for a part in the action star's next movie, but she did not get the part. Over the next several years she would do soft-core pornographic films—with titles like *Tunnel of Love, The Pleasure Dome* and *Liaisons*—that appeared on the Playboy Channel. She found she got more work after her breast implant surgeries, although, unlike her costar in *Tunnel of Love,* Ginger Allen, she would not continue into the world of hard-core films and videos. (Allen would later become Ginger Lynn Allen, a star in the adult film world, and would subsequently be romantically linked with actor Charlie Sheen.)

Within time, Bradigan saw less and less of Simpson, and soon she was back to her former occupation—stripping at bachelor parties, having one-night-stand sex with strangers. According to Clapp, she was one of the many Alex Adams girls who defected to Heidi Fleiss in 1991, after sloppy police work put the word on the street that their employer was a police informer. ''When Alex got busted in 1991, she was exposed as a snitch, and all her girls left—Bonnie included. She went to work for Heidi.''[67]

Now Bradigan is back to stripping. Her interest in speed continues. She gets misty when she talks about Simpson now. ''I was in love with Don,'' she says convincingly. ''I'm still in love with him. I believed we would end up together. I thought we'd have another twenty-five years to enjoy together. I still can't believe he's gone.''

Simpson was not the only Hollywood celebrity embarrassed by Tiffany's confessions or by her *You'll Never Make Love in This Town Again* coauthors, Robin Greer, Liza Greer and Linda Hammond. (The rumor immediately following Simpson's death was that *You'll Never Make Love in This Town Again* was the book he was reading, on the toilet, when his heart stopped beating. In fact, he was reading a new biography of the filmmaker Oliver Stone.) Among those caught in the hookers' spotlight were actors Jack Nicholson, Warren Beatty, Don Johnson, Charlie Sheen, Gary Busey, Matt Dillon, John Ritter, James Caan, Dennis Hopper and Timothy Hutton; musicians George Harrison, Rod Stewart, David Crosby, Billy Idol, Don Henley and Glenn Frey; and other notables like Adnan Kashoggi, restaurateur George Santo Pietro and football great—and O. J. Simpson pal—Marcus Allen. Producer Robert Evans was given extended treatment, as Liza recounted being taken to Evans' Beverly Hills home, by Tiffany, when Liza was just sixteen years old. Tiffany had made an assignation with Evans, who seemed delighted when she appeared with a younger friend. After drinks, cocaine, Quaaludes and small talk in Evans' famous screening room, the two women were led to Evans' bedroom. There Evans directed the action, Liza wrote, giving instructions like, "Tiffany, you touch Liza there" and "Lisa, you lick Tiffany there." Suddenly, Liza wrote, Evans said, "Tiffany, would you please piss on me?" Tiffany complied. Evans later presented her with "a large sum of cash" and "a fee for having brought me along," Liza said. (Alexandra Datig, or Tiffany, would say much later, "I adore Evans. He taught me everything I know about loyalty.")

Other celebrities from the books would stay in the headlines. Charlie Sheen was brought to the stand to testify during Heidi Fleiss' tax evasion trial. When asked if it was true he'd spent more than $50,000 on Heidi's services, Sheen grinned and said, "It does add up, doesn't it?" (Sheen's hooker expenditures—including the detail that he liked young blond women to dress up like cheerleaders—were reported widely enough that Sheen even became the butt of a joke on the Academy Awards broadcast. Host Whoopi Goldberg, addressing the more than 1 billion Oscar viewers, reviewing the list of Best Actress nominees for the 1995 films *Leaving Las Vegas*, *Mighty Aphrodite* and *Casino*, said, "Elizabeth Shue played a hooker. Mira Sorvino played a hooker. Sharon Stone played a hooker. How many times did Charlie Sheen get to vote?") Jack Nicholson was charged with beating up a prostitute after she'd had the temerity to insist on being paid for the sex she'd given him. (The Los Angeles city attorney's office declined to prosecute the complaint.)[68] Charlie Sheen was charged with beating his girlfriend and threatening to kill her if she told anyone why she'd needed seven stitches to close a cut on her lip. James Caan checked into rehab. Gary Busey went into rehab. Actress Pamela Bach— the actress who is married to *Baywatch* beefcake David Hasselhoff—was identified as a former Madam Alex girl by a former drug dealer named Rayce Newman, who had once counted Don Simpson among his best customers. David Crosby lost his liver to drink and drugs and required a transplant. All were victims, one way or another, of their own excess. Heidi Fleiss went off to jail, and had the dubious honor of a porno movie being based on her life. *Heidi Does Hollywood*—which featured "plenty of sex to satisfy all kinds of hard-core fans," a catalog promised—was available for the curious in early 1995.

Liza Greer cleaned up, got past her addiction to free-base cocaine and left the game. She would later say that she "felt bad" about naming names in her *You'll Never* tell-all. But, she reasoned, so what? "A lot of these people hurt me," the husky, mannish blonde said in November 1996. "What about me? What about my family? These people weren't that nice to me, either."[69]

Datig subsequently exacted her revenge on Simpson and Hollywood. After her falling-out with Simpson, she became friendly with Keith Zslomsowitch, the manager of a Brentwood restaurant named Mezzaluna, which would subsequently become famous as the place of employment for Ronald Goldman and the location of Nicole Brown Simpson's last supper. Leaving Zslomsowitch's apartment one night, she was pulled over by undercover policemen who knew her identity and had an arrest warrant on $7,000 in outstanding moving violations and parking tickets. Datig was sent to jail and was soon telling police investigating prostitution and drugs in Hollywood everything she knew about the madam and her clients. (She even drew a map of Don Simpson's home for the cops, who wanted to know in what rooms and in what drawers he kept his narcotics.) Datig was scared: She kept hearing, from friends, that both Heidi and Simpson wanted her dead. She complained to her friend Robert Evans. She complained to Jack Nicholson, whom she met at a party thrown for music impresario Rick Rubin. She complained to former Eagles drummer Don Henley, whom she'd met on the call girl circle. Henley told her, "Relax. Simpson wants to kill *everybody*. It's old news." But still she stayed close to Simpson's circle. She flew in a private jet to Aspen with Simpson's plastic surgeon pal, and slept with him there during the Christmas holidays, in 1993, reasoning. "If I was with him it would reduce the chances of Simpson killing me." While on that trip, she got closer to one of Simpson's personal assistants, having sex with him in Jerry Bruckheimer's Jeep Cherokee and subsequently falling in love with him. She continued her affair with him after their return to Aspen. She only saw Simpson once more, on a New Year's Eve, at a party. She looked across the room at him and burst into tears. Simpson crossed to her and said, in a low, conspiratorial voice, "You and I are going to have a very long talk, Alexandra."[70]

Alexandra Datig, today, is clean and free of her drug habit. She has taken up screenwriting, teaches riding and trains horses for a living.

Bonnie Bradigan is, today, a lot sadder and a little heavier. Upon hearing of Simpson's death, she says, she started drinking vodka and ended up gaining twenty pounds. She works bachelor parties for a living—two in a night, some weekend nights. She finds it hard to believe that Simpson is really gone, and has written notes to the coroner asking him to "rescind" Simpson's certificate of death. She snorts speed to get by.

And prostitution thrives—a fact that might bring Simpson some pleasure. "There weren't many things Don believed in," observed a friend, the screenwriter Larry Ferguson, whom Simpson had hired to work on *Beverly Hills Cop 2*. "Don didn't have many causes. But he actually did believe in the legalization of prostitution. Wherever Don is today, right now, I hope he's enjoying himself. I hope there's prostitutes there."[71]

CHAPTER FOUR

HOLLYWOOD HIGH

Avoiding narcotics in Hollywood in the 1980s was as difficult as avoiding the Southern California sun. Drugs were everywhere, and cocaine was king, the champagne of recreational stimulants. Demand and supply rose dramatically in the early part of the decade, as price fell and availability increased. According to the National Household Survey, the number of occasional users of cocaine rose between 1974 and 1985 from 5.4 million to 22.2 million. Frequent users increased fivefold over the same period. The number of high school students who used cocaine over the same period doubled.[1] By another barometer, cocaine usage was rising at a staggering rate: Emergency room treatments for cocaine-related medical problems increased 200 percent between 1981 and 1985. The rate of cocaine-induced deaths tripled over the same period.[2] The appearance of cocaine at Hollywood parties was as common as chips and guacamole a decade before.

The social uses of cocaine were myriad: It was a terrific icebreaker, an instant pick-me-up and a great come-on. *Everything* went better with coke. It stimulated conversation and intellectual activity, and increased sexual appetite and prowess. It didn't leave telltale odors or next-day hangovers. It wasn't passé, like marijuana or martinis, and it wasn't deadly, like heroin. It was portable and easy to hide. Ingesting it required no "kit," no special equipment. And, as an added bonus, it was just expensive enough that the *hoi polloi* couldn't afford it. Like other staples of the upscale 1980s—the health club membership, the record company jacket, the BMW or Mercedes, the club bouncer who knew your name—cocaine was a status symbol that said its user was young, hip and alive. "It was the ultimate drug for the times, and the ultimate metaphor for the period," said novelist Jay McInerney, whose *Bright Lights, Big City*, among other works, chronicled yuppie cocaine use in the 1980s. "It was the perfect consumer product—the more you get, the more you want. And it was *fun.*"[3]

It was also the ultimate high—and the ultimate metaphor—for movies Simpson wanted to make. Like a good cocaine high, Simpson's movies blasted from moment to moment, each scene and stunt and joke a jolt of adrenaline, until the viewer, like the user, was giddy with sensory overstimulation. There was nothing tangible left when it was over, in either case, and not much memory of what had passed—just the happy, visceral sensation of having had a good time.

Coke was everywhere you wanted to be, too. At trendy restaurants, nightclubs, bars or private parties, any reasonably attentive person could locate cocaine in any reasonably private location—usually the bathroom. "It was impossible to take a piss," remembered producer Joel Silver, a non-drug user who found cocaine's pan-evidence irritating. "There were six people in every bathroom at every party and in every nightclub in town. You'd have to *pretend* you wanted to do drugs just to get into the bathroom."[4]

Simpson wasn't pretending. He fully embraced drugs in the 1980s, turning what had been an aggressively pursued recreational habit into a full-scale addiction. "Don was in trouble with drugs before *anybody* was in trouble with drugs," observed Simpson's longtime friend actor Gary Woods.[5]

In the beginning, for Simpson, as for many users, cocaine was fun. In Hollywood, hanging out with Steve Roth, or in New York, hanging out with McInerney, it was about having a good time. On a typical evening out in Manhattan, McInerney said, he and Simpson would dine, get high and then spend the rest of the night hitting the hot nightclubs. "It was drinking, doing drugs and looking at women—all night long," McInerney said. "Don was enormously entertaining, and we were both rising 'bad boys,' and the idea was to have fun. New York was my town, and I was showing him the fun." McInerney organized the evenings and kept the supply of drugs coming. "It was my role to show Don what was happening, and the places you wanted to go were the places where drugs were always available."[6]

In Hollywood, Simpson already knew where those places were.

"J.R." is a tall, lanky man who wears his dark brown hair in a long ponytail and describes himself as "sort of English Jewish looking, a real music industry type."[7] He resembles the actor Keith Carradine, and he's a cocaine dealer. Now semiretired, J.R. was the coke king of the Sunset Strip in the late 1980s. Simpson was a client.

J.R. had come to Los Angeles intending to hit big as a guitar player. He was good, but he wasn't good enough to distinguish himself among the thousands of other guitar players who'd come to town with the same dream. Many of them got work playing casuals at weddings and bar mitzvahs, playing lounge music at Holiday Inns, doing session work in recording studios or teaching music to younger guitar players whose dreams had not yet yielded to reality. J.R. was broke and had an expensive speed habit when a friend loaned him some cash, gave him a pager and a client list and sent him to work selling drugs.

J.R. had a good head for business and a keen interest in avoiding arrest. He put the two together to form an ingenious sales stratagem. Every afternoon of the week he would meet up with "Frank," a homeless man he'd befriended after a sidewalk encounter. J.R. would give Frank a collection of "bindles," cocaine wrapped in plastic or in glossy magazine paper folded, origami style, into small packets. The bindles came in different sizes and were priced at different rates. Frank would pack twenty-dollar bindles in one pocket, fifty-dollar bindles in another, hundred-dollar bindles in another. Frank took his work seriously and stayed in character: He never bathed, never washed his hair or clothing, and before starting work would assiduously urinate on himself to intensify his homeless-person odor. After sundown Frank would make his way by public bus to the Sunset Strip, where he would park himself on the curb outside the Rainbow Bar & Grill, the famed music industry watering hole.

By 9:00 P.M. J.R. would be at his usual table inside. Working the room with him would be two or three of his "girls," usually music industry groupies who supported their drug habit by helping J.R. deliver the goods. J.R. would sit sipping champagne. A client would drop by his table to ask if J.R. could hook him up. J.R. would tell the client, "Talk to one of my girls," and send the client away from the table. A girl would presently come to J.R.'s table and say, "He needs a fifty." J.R. would tell the girl to get the money. He would then wander outside to the Rainbow parking lot, check for police presence and then stroll out to the curb. He would pretend to make a phone call on the public telephone there. When he was finished, the homeless Frank would ask him for money. J.R. would shout at him loudly, saying, "Fuck off," or "Get a life, you piece of shit," and then give him fifty cents. While passing the money, J.R. would in return be given a fifty-dollar bindle—or a twenty-dollar bindle if he'd given Frank a quarter, or a hundred-dollar bindle if he'd given Frank a dollar bill. J.R. would then walk the fifty feet back into the club and hand the bindle to his girl, who would later give him the cash.

It was a fine system. J.R. himself would only be in possession of drugs for the time it took him to walk from the curb into the club, and he would only be in possession of a small amount. His girls did the actual transaction. The homeless Frank, who looked, acted and smelled the part of a harmless street bum—and who was therefore unlikely to be searched by even the most dedicated policeman—carried all the inventory. J.R. often turned $5,000 in sales in a single night.

His bulk drug business was pretty good, too. Through connections in Texas and New Orleans, J.R. would buy large quantities of cocaine. Through a car shipping business that formed the front for his drug import business, he would have Louisiana associates stuff automobiles with drugs and then ship the cars to Los Angeles. J.R. would pick up the cars, unload the drugs and bill the customer shipping charges on the car. For reasons J.R. cannot explain, his front was never exposed and he himself was never busted. He came close, one night at the Rainbow, when a friend told him the cops were outside looking for a guy with long brown hair who wore a beret and a long black leather trench coat—J.R.'s signature nighttime attire. J.R. dashed into a bathroom, where he found a guy in a ratty leather jacket. He complimented the man on the jacket and then proposed that they switch. The man agreed. J.R. said, "There's this crazy chick here, chasing me. I need to ditch her. I'll trade jackets with you if you'll just put on my coat, walk out to the sidewalk, then turn left. There's $1,000 in cash in the pocket, and that's yours, too, if you'll just do that." The man happily agreed. They switched coats and the man swaggered out of the Rainbow. J.R. waited at the door, watching until the cops noticed the man in the long black leather coat. When they approached him, J.R. dashed across the parking lot and hid in the back of his friend Al the Limo Guy's limousine. The last thing he saw before crawling into the trunk was the unhappy new owner of his trench coat crumpling to the sidewalk as six cops with billy clubs worked him over.

In the early days most of J.R.'s customers were from the music industry. One night a friend named Gina asked if he'd sell $100 worth of cocaine to two friends sitting in a limo outside the Rainbow. The friends were a vastly successful pop siren and her comedienne companion. J.R. went outside and was introduced to them and sat in the back of the limo for a half hour as the two women went through a gram. Then he sold them three more grams and watched as they snorted at that before driving off into the night. Vince Neil, of Mötley Crüe, was a steady customer—but an irritant. Neil would call J.R. and ask him to deliver a gram to the recording studio where, usually in the company of several half-naked women, he and the band were working. A half hour later he'd call back, wanting an eighth of an ounce. He'd then call again for another gram. A frustrated J.R. would plead with him, "Why don't you just buy a whole ounce, so I don't have to keep coming back?" Neil would scream, "Just bring me the fucking stuff—I'll give you an extra $250." Sometimes the entire Guns N' Roses group would sit at the main "Kings Table" at the Rainbow, making steady purchases all night long. Members of the Allman Brothers and Van Halen would stop by. J.R. felt like a celebrity and found that, soon, what was hip in the music industry was becoming hip in the film and TV industries as well.

He sold dope to Kelsey Grammer at the Vampire Room. He dealt to Charlie Sheen, who mostly bought $200 to $300 at a time, at the Rainbow, or at another club J.R. worked called Roxbury. Billy Idol would make his purchases at the Rainbow, a gram at a time, gram after gram, until the early morning hours. At the Viper Club, J.R. would sit at the "Dragon Table" and wait for customers to approach him. River Phoenix bought cocaine, which he mixed with Valium and Xanax.

J.R. wasn't Phoenix's only supplier. A dealer who goes by the name Nicky sold Phoenix speed several times in the years before the young actor died on the sidewalk outside the Viper Room. One night, in fact, four years before that tragedy, Phoenix nearly died in Nicky's apartment. The dealer remembered that Phoenix had stopped by to score some speed. He shot up while Nicky and a friend watched. In a scene stolen from Quentin Tarantino's *Pulp Fiction*, Phoenix overdosed, passing out and, Nicky recalled, "going totally code blue." Nicky and his friend were experienced drug users, though. "We knew what to do," the dealer said. "We packed his genitals in ice and got his heart beating again. When he came to, he said, 'I was gone, wasn't I?' He *knew*, man." An hour later, fully recovered, Phoenix said to Nicky, "I hope you guys would have done the right thing and thrown me in a Dumpster if I hadn't come out of it."

Don Simpson had out-of-town dealers as well and knew where to go for the highest-quality rocket fuel in other cities. In New York, according to a close friend from the early 1980s, he stumbled onto a blow monkey's dream. His regular dealer was about to be busted, so she took a recent Colombian shipment and hid it in a closet in her parents' apartment on the Lower East Side. Then she got busted. She told her mother, "There's something valuable in the closet. If you ever need money, you can sell it." When the family ultimately did need money, her mother went for the cocaine. What she failed to realize was that it was almost pure cocaine and had not yet been "cut" for street sales. For a while, Simpson and his friend got pure, full-strength cocaine at bargain-basement prices.[8]

In Los Angeles J.R. wasn't Simpson's only dealer. J.R.'s principal Sunset Strip competition was Rayce Newman.

Newman was a tall, pale, rangy kid from Ventura, California, who in 1980 had come south to Los Angeles to enter the big-time drug dealing business. He was eighteen years old and had gotten regular bit work as an actor before he discovered cocaine. He'd developed a habit and discovered that dealing drugs was the best way to satisfy it. After dealing out of a Ventura nightclub called Garfield's, he got fired. A high school friend named Belinda invited him down to Los Angeles, where she was hooking for Madam Alex. Soon Newman was escorting Belinda to parties and meeting her clients. One night they attended a wrap party for a movie called *Transylvania 6-500*, starring Jeff Goldblum and Ed Begley Jr., held at a nightclub called Tramps. A producer named Jonathan Axelrod took Rayce into the bathroom for a hit of coke—low-quality coke, as it happened. Newman returned the favor, and Axelrod liked his cocaine better. The pair wound up spending two days at Axelrod's house, partying until the drugs ran out. By the time he left, everyone at the party had Newman's telephone number, and his career as a Hollywood cocaine dealer was on.[9]

Newman met Don Simpson at a party thrown by music impresario Richard Perry, at the Sunset Plaza house Perry had bought from Ronald and Nancy Reagan. There were music business people like Don Henley and Rod Stewart, and music mogul-turned-movie producer Ted Field, and movie producer Joel Silver. After the introduction, Simpson and Newman would meet on the Strip circuit, at Tramps, Voila, Carlos 'n' Charlie's, Helena's and Vertigo.[10]

Newman had a rhythm for the circuit. On Monday night he'd be at the China Club on Beverly, where he'd do drugs with Simpson, Henley, Stephen Stills and others, in the downstairs bathroom. On Tuesday night it was Roxbury, where there was a convenient walk-in closet off the kitchen. Wednesday night was Bar One, at the westernmost end of the Strip, where there was a convenient upstairs office. Thursday night was Stringfellows, on Rodeo Drive, in Beverly Hills. Friday night was the big night of the week, and Newman would serially work Vertigo, Carlos 'n' Charlie's and Roxbury. Simpson would usually buy a gram at a time, or sometimes an eighth of an ounce. He'd often ask Newman, "Can I owe you?" but he was always good for the money. Newman would sometimes drop off cocaine at Simpson's house or at the studio—once actually pretending to deliver a script, which he deposited on a silver tray in front of Simpson and several Paramount executives while Simpson conducted a business meeting. After 1991, Newman recalled, Simpson stopped making the circuit and became more of a stay-at-home user who didn't socialize.[11]

But Newman was very social, and he was having fun. Unlike J.R., he partied with the clients. He'd snort cocaine with Charlie Sheen, who'd return the favor by phoning Heidi Fleiss and having girls sent over for both of them. He and Robert Downey Jr. and Julian Lennon would rent a suite at the Mondrian Hotel and stay high for three or four days at a time, snorting or freebasing cocaine. (Newman seemed to specialize in second generations of Hollywood talent. On other occasions he partied with Lou Rawls Jr., Marvin Gaye Jr. and Chad McQueen.) Downey Jr. stopped by Newman's apartment on Burton Way, the day after he had come out of his first extended stay in rehab. He knocked on the door, came inside and said, "Can I just get a line?" Newman replied, "Man, you just got out of rehab!" "I know," Downey said, "but it's just a line. One line won't hurt." Two hours later the two men were smoking cocaine and watching television—actually watching Downey's appearance, taped that afternoon, on *The Tonight Show*, where Downey discussed his newfound sobriety.[12]

J.R. hung around with bigger actors, too. While Jack Nicholson was playing the part of the Joker in *Batman*, he and Newman and producer

Robert Evans, a longtime Nicholson pal, would hire hookers and stay up all night doing drugs. Nicholson, Newman recalled, would come straight from the set to Evans' house, stay high all night and then go straight back to Warner Bros. the following morning. ("Nothing is as funny as seeing Jack do lines," Newman said. "Watching him put the bill or straw up to his nose and snort always reminds me of the scene in *The Shining* where he breaks through the door and says, 'Here's Johnny!' ")[13] One night at Roxbury, Newman partied with Bobby Brown, Julian Lennon and George Hamilton, and was introduced to Eddie Murphy. (Murphy never did drugs, and told Newman, "I don't care what *you* do, but don't ever bring drugs into my house." Murphy would thereafter always stop at Newman's table to say hello.) Newman partied at Sylvester Stallone's house, after his hooker friend Belinda began sleeping with the star.[14] Other nights he would meet O.J. and Nicole, with Marcus Allen of the Raiders. He met Rick James. He got high with Princess Stephanie of Monaco and Rob Lowe. "The one thing that everyone had in common," Newman said, "was the drugs. Everyone was doing drugs."

One winter he got an emergency call and was asked to make a delivery of a large quantity of cocaine to a party taking place that night in Aspen, Colorado. It was Christmas Eve, 1984. The party was an annual event being thrown by Don Simpson and Jerry Bruckheimer. (Newman only met Bruckheimer once after that night, when, in 1987, he had to leave a Beverly Hills party to score more drugs and discovered that his car was blocked by a black Porsche. High, and impatient, he decided to steal the Porsche, make his run and return it. When he got back to the party the host screamed at him, "You stole Jerry Bruckheimer's car, you asshole." Newman laughed and went back inside with the drugs.)[15] Newman packed a large popcorn bag with cocaine and flew that night to Aspen.

He found a virtual who's-who of chic Hollywood. The minute he arrived he was dragged into a bathroom by Nicholson. Don Henley was next. Then Michael Douglas. George Hamilton was there. Mickey Rourke and Don Johnson were there with Melanie Griffith, then Johnson's wife. ("Don and Melanie were so damn wasted at that party," Newman said, "that they didn't remember me" when they met weeks later, back in Los Angeles, at Bar One.)[16] Jean-Claude Van Damme was there. After he'd "partied out" Nicholson and the other celebrities, Newman went off to the Paradise Club, then Aspen's hottest nightspot, and partied some more before flying back, the same night, to Los Angeles.[17]

It was a glamorous life, and Newman played it out until it almost killed him. By 1991 his six-foot-three frame had shrunk to 137 pounds. He was living with musician Rick James, who would shortly after be arrested for imprisoning, torturing and sexually abusing a young woman in the room where Newman had slept—crimes for which James would ultimately serve time in a federal prison. James' freebase cocaine habit had driven him into a $12,000 debt to Newman, who had been his dealer for years. Newman was broke, so he moved into James' Mulholland Terrace house to cut his costs and work down James' debt. For a while, this was fine. James was on a $25,000-a-month allowance from his managers. On payday he and Newman would have drugs delivered and stay up smoking cocaine for six days straight. Then they'd take Halcion and sleep for two days. "And then we'd start over, until the money was all gone," Newman said. Late one night James came into Newman's bedroom and started rooting around in his closet. When Newman woke, James was cleaning a freebase pipe—with shaking, junkie hands. He cleaned the pipe with rubbing alcohol and then cooked the cocaine and then tried to light the pipe. But he had spilled rubbing alcohol on his bathrobe, and as he lit the pipe he also lit himself on fire. Newman leapt from the bed and knocked James to the floor and put out the flames. James stood up and left the room, his bathrobe smoldering, still trying to light the pipe, as if nothing had happened. Newman hit bottom. Newman called his friend Herbie Hancock and begged for help. Hancock helped Newman get out of Los Angeles and back to his family in Florida. (Newman later made several calls to Don Simpson, who had many times, over the years, said to Newman, "If you ever want to clean up, come to me. I'll help you." Now, clean but needing work, Newman found Simpson would neither take nor return his calls.) Newman has been drug-free since and now makes his home in Arkansas.[18] He wrote of his exploits in the 1994 book *The Hollywood Connection*.

J.R.'s bottoming-out took a different form. He got out of the drug business the day after the murders of Ronald Goldman and Nicole Brown Simpson—a crime in which he was nearly implicated.

In addition to chance meetings with O. J. and Nicole Brown Simpson, J.R. had already brushed up against another player in the future Simpson murder story. One night in 1991, outside a club called the Coconut Teaser, when Ice-T was performing, J.R. made some sales and left the club to find his limousine waiting outside. A young woman named Faye Resnick was sitting inside it. They shared a few lines of cocaine. Then Resnick asked him to give her a gram. J.R. said, "How about a blow for that blow?" Resnick seemed shocked and said, "I'm not a prostitute." J.R. answered, "That's a gram, and that's the deal." And, J.R. remembered later, "The next thing you know, she's got a gram and I'm getting a blow job in the limo."[19]

On the night of June 12, 1994, as J.R. remembered it, he was in his motel room watching the basketball play-offs. At about 8:30 his pager buzzed: 777. J.R. claims he packed a bindle and walked to the Burger King. He arrived at 8:45 and found O. J. Simpson's Bentley in the parking lot. Kato Kaelin was driving; O.J. was sitting in the passenger seat. J.R. found Kaelin "very sketched out"—nervous, jumpy. J.R. opened the back door and sat, as Kaelin gave him a hundred-dollar bill and J.R. passed him a gram of speed. Kaelin immediately removed a mirror from his pocket and cut out a line of speed and snorted it. He then passed the mirror to O.J., who shot a nervous glance into the backseat and said, "What the *fuck*, Kato?" Kato laughed nervously and said, "J.R., man, why don't you get us some burgers?" J.R. left the two men in the parking lot. He came back ten minutes later. Simpson was wiping his eyes and nose on a handkerchief and looked stoned. J.R. gave Kaelin the bag of hamburgers and left for his motel room.

The following morning he heard the news about the murders on Bundy Drive, and he panicked. "It was a double murder, and it was O.J., and there were drugs involved," J.R. said later. "I freaked out. My prints were in that Bentley and probably in the Bronco. I thought, 'I gotta get the fuck outta here.' I called a friend in Florida and the next day booked a flight. Then I thought that was too expensive, so I went Amtrak. I didn't contact anyone in Los Angeles for a month. Later I heard O.J. say. 'We went out to McDonald's.' I thought I was fucked for sure."

A panicky J.R. attempted to clear his name, and to cash in on his new celebrity-adjacent status by selling his story to the press. Rumors about O.J. and Kato making a drug run on the night of the murders began to surface. J.R. submitted to polygraph tests for at least one tabloid newspaper. In time, scattered reports made the mainstream media. One report held that an unidentified drug dealer, reportedly in hiding in Florida, had "sold Simpson $100 worth of crystal methamphetamine two hours before the murders." Kaelin himself later insisted to Barbara Walters that he and Simpson did not buy drugs on the night of the killings, and stuck to his

HIGH CONCEPT: With *Flashdance* and *Beverly Hills Cop* behind him, Simpson took to the skies in 1986 with *Top Gun*. It would put Tom Cruise, here with Simpson, Bruckheimer and costar Kelly McGillis, on target for stardom, and make Simpson and Bruckheimer the most successful producers of the year. EVERETT COLLECTION

MAKING MR. MURPHY: A year after *Top Gun*, Simpson and Bruckheimer hit big again with their *Beverly Hills Cop* sequel, which defied logic and outearned its predecessor, catapulting star Eddie Murphy into the pantheon of highly paid actors. EVERETT COLLECTION

DAYS OF PLUNDER: The creative team behind *Days of Thunder* spent late 1989 and early 1990 spending buckets of Paramount money creating a failed motion picture. The writing was already on the wall when star Cruise, coproducer Bruckheimer, writer Robert Towne, Simpson and director Tony Scott (*r. to l.*) posed here in Daytona, Florida. Simpson wears one of two tailor-made racing suits, for a *Thunder* acting part that almost disappeared. EVERETT COLLECTION

MR. LONELY: Simpson spent the late 1980s looking for love in all the wrong places, courting Madams Alex and Heidi, hiring their girls and running personal ads in local magazines. Those answering the ads got copies of this photograph— Don at his handsome best.

VANITY FARE: Simpson spent a small fortune and much of his prodigious energy fighting his weight, enduring plastic surgery and buying a wardrobe to suit his wobbly self-esteem. Seen here in 1993, he is temporarily ahead of the game. *OUTLINE*

BAD BOY: Less than two years later, at a premiere party with partner Jerry Bruckheimer for 1995's *Bad Boys*, Simpson is sliding badly. He has told friends that only by staying out of Hollywood can he maintain his sanity, but friends note he is back in town permanently, and back to his bad-boy habits. FITZROY BARRETT, GLOBE PHOTOS, INC.

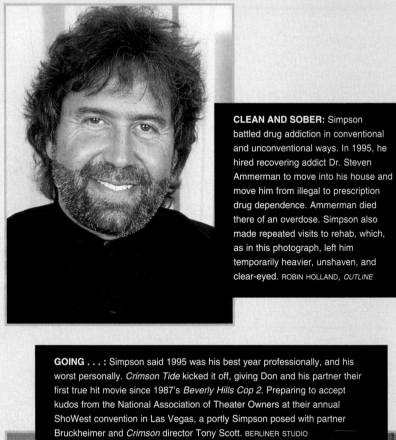

CLEAN AND SOBER: Simpson battled drug addiction in conventional and unconventional ways. In 1995, he hired recovering addict Dr. Steven Ammerman to move into his house and move him from illegal to prescription drug dependence. Ammerman died there of an overdose. Simpson also made repeated visits to rehab, which, as in this photograph, left him temporarily heavier, unshaven, and clear-eyed. ROBIN HOLLAND, *OUTLINE*

GOING . . . : Simpson said 1995 was his best year professionally, and his worst personally. *Crimson Tide* kicked it off, giving Don and his partner their first true hit movie since 1987's *Beverly Hills Cop 2*. Preparing to accept kudos from the National Association of Theater Owners at their annual ShoWest convention in Las Vegas, a portly Simpson posed with partner Bruckheimer and *Crimson* director Tony Scott. BERLINER STUDIO

GOING . . . : *Crimson Tide* hit big in mid-1995, and was followed by two more hits, *Bad Boys* and *Dangerous Minds*. Simpson and Bruckheimer, seen here with their *Bad Boys* executive at Columbia, Barry Josephson, and husband-and-wife actors Bruce Willis and Demi Moore, were the temporary toast of Las Vegas. BERLINER STUDIO

The super producers chatted also with Michael Eisner, who'd let the hit *Bad Boys* go to Columbia, but who would score with *Crimson Tide* and *Dangerous Minds*. Less than a year later Eisner would say, "I've been waiting for this call for twenty years," when informed of Simpson's death. BERLINER STUDIO

GOING . . . : As he had done twelve years earlier with *Beverly Hills Cop*, Simpson took a script written for a white actor and turned it into a hit with a black cast. Simpson, radiating pride and prescription drugs, beamed at the 1995 *Bad Boys* premiere, shaded with costars Martin Lawrence and Will Smith.
BERLINER STUDIO

GONE: Simpson's onetime protégé, Jeffrey Katzenberg, poses at his former boss's memorial service, on a Monday night at Morton's, with *Dangerous Minds* star Michelle Pfeiffer (BERLINER STUDIO) and longtime Simpson pal Steve Tisch (BERLINER STUDIO). Katzenberg had recently left Disney, where he lured Simpson and Bruckheimer post-Paramount, to form DreamWorks with another longtime Simpson acquaintance, David Geffen, and Steven Spielberg, whom Simpson had once described as "really white bread, for a Jew."

BRUCKHEIMER UNBOUND: Simpson's best friend and producing partner for almost fifteen years, Jerry Bruckheimer took the podium to eulogize his lost friend at the Morton's memorial service in January 1996, only two weeks after Simpson's death. Declining to share his reminiscences with the press, Bruckheimer said, "I will protect him in death as I protected him in life." ERIC CHARBONNEAU/BERLINER STUDIO

THE END: Simpson's last publicity tour was in support of *Crimson Tide*, the 1995 submarine thriller that would announce his return to superstar producer status. Less than a year after its release, well before subsequent hits *The Rock* and *Con Air* made it to movie theaters, Simpson made his date with untimely death. E. J. CAMP, *OUTLINE*

story about buying a quick dinner. "No Burger King," he said. "We went to McDonald's."

J.R., now thirty, subsequently returned to Los Angeles, but not to dealing drugs.

For Don Simpson, drugs were still fun, part of his forever-young, do-or-die, bad-boy image. He delighted in taunting his "straight" friends. Once, on a trip to the Toronto Film Festival, he and friend Steve Roth teased agent Michael Ovitz—tossing a vial of cocaine back and forth, doing lines and then tossing the vial to Ovitz, who did not do drugs and was horrified to be around people who did. Roth kept trying to get a snapshot of Ovitz holding the cocaine, but Ovitz would hot-potato the vial back to Simpson each time it was tossed to him.[20]

Among friends straight or not, Simpson was entirely open about his affection for drugs. Paul Schrader, who wrote the Academy Award–winning *Taxi Driver* and *Raging Bull*, and directed movies like *American Gigolo*, *Cat People* (both produced by Simpson's partner, Bruckheimer), *Patty Hearst* and *The Comfort of Strangers*, was a close Simpson friend from his days as a Paramount executive, where Simpson was responsible for *American Gigolo*. He and Simpson were part of a group Schrader referred to as "that whole Scarfiotti circle," a social set that swirled around the famed production designer Ferdinando Scarfiotti, who had created the look for award-winning films like *The Conformist* and *Last Tango in Paris*, and who in Hollywood had created the enigmatic, erotic looks for *Cat People* and *American Gigolo*. Regular set members were producers Sean Daniel, Mark Rosenberg, Paula Weinstein and Howard Rosenman, film executives Barry Diller and Thom Mount, music mogul David Geffen, composer Paul Jasmine and others.

"It was a very glamorous, hip world," according to Schrader, "and those were very cokey times."[21] He and Simpson, who both came from strict religious backgrounds, were the kind of people who "would get very stoned and sit around talking about God. After several hours, Don and I would be the only people left in the room," Schrader said. One night Schrader and Simpson left a party, because Simpson wanted to show off his new Porsche. They sat in the front seat, snorting lines of cocaine. "All of a sudden," Schrader said, "it was five hours later. We went back inside and no one was there. For five hours we had talked—serious, deep stuff about aesthetics and morality and ideas about God—and to this day I have no memory of what we actually *talked* about. It was one of those college dorm sorts of conversations which, even if they are sort of jejune, are not that easy to find in Los Angeles." Producer Lynda Obst, a friend to both men, said, "That was the best Los Angeles had to offer—Simpson and Schrader holding court."

Obst recalled that it was during these legendary all-nighters that Simpson began to create, in Obst's memory, what was to become the "high-concept movie"—what Obst calls Simpson's one real contribution to the world of cinema. "Don *did* create this," Obst said. "He created the three-act structure that we all use, the one that Robert McKee and Syd Field use and take credit for. Don made up this logarithm. There is the hot first act with an exciting incident, and the second act with the crisis and the dark bad moments in which our hero is challenged, and the third act with the triumphant moment and the redemption and the freeze-frame ending. Don created the framework for the high-concept movie."[22]

It goes almost without saying that Simpson was running on an almost perpetual cocaine high while he created that framework. A host of Simpson assistants, colleagues and friends recalled that within Simpson's late-night, coke-fueled, tape-recorded "memos" were the seeds of his real brilliance. The memos themselves were rambling and unfocused, but within their manic maelstrom were always bits and pieces of true genius, the crystallized flakes of story and character that would ultimately turn into blockbuster movies.

Simpson's Porsche would feature heavily in a similar episode that eventually made print. In his 1986 short fiction collection *A Hollywood Education: Tales of Movie Dreams and Easy Money*, writer David Freeman barely disguised Simpson in a story called "The Burning Porsche."

In the story, Freeman tells of "Teddy," a movie business hotshot who had left his native South America for Hollywood "carrying a change of clothes and three pounds of creamy, flaked Bolivian cocaine." He'd studied briefly at UCLA, sold some cocaine and gotten hooked up with Hollywood executives with a taste for the Bolivian powder. He'd parlayed those relationships into a studio executive slot, until "the corporate bosses in New York got wind of his nocturnal activities" and fired him. So Teddy became a producer, "took a script called *City Boy* off the shelf, hired four writers, and started dictating changes. *[City Boy]* grossed $65 million and Teddy never looked back."

As the story opens, the narrator and Teddy are attending a bachelor party for a friend, eating at the legendary Beverly Hills Chinese restaurant Mr. Chow's. Teddy "was hot enough to burn," at that stage of his career, and his life was "like a fevered movie dream. The man was breathing hits and wrapping Porsches around trees. He'd wreck one, stagger away, and order another. He'd gone through five of the damn things. Live hard, live fast, make millions." He was also doing a lot of cocaine. Through the evening at Mr. Chow's, Teddy "kept jumping up to go to the bathroom. After the fifth trip to the loo in two hours, he had white dust dribbling from his nostrils." Everyone else was ready to go home by eleven, but "Teddy boy . . . however, was ready for more." He and the narrator went outside Mr. Chow's and sat in Teddy's black Porsche, talking deals and Hollywood.[23]

"Teddy kept the engine running and the cocaine coming," Freeman wrote. "Despite his altered state, the discussion was pertinent—casting, directors, budget, script problems. He talked fast all the time, and when he was on coke, his words rushed out, blurred but not confused. Watching him shovel the stuff into his nose made me feel as if I was watching the scene from across the street. The more loaded Teddy got, the farther away I felt."

The two men sat for hours, snorting cocaine, rambling on about Hollywood. The narrator was working on a script set against the backdrop of life on a daily newspaper. Teddy analyzed it for him: "He's sixteen. She's twenty. Her father's the publisher of a newspaper and he's a copy boy or delivery boy. Why does it have to be a newspaper, anyway? Nobody cares about that shit. Fuck this movie. I want to do one about dope. Put it on a marijuana farm. Two thousand cannibas sativa plants in Oregon and the National Guard comes down with choppers and flame-throwers. Search and seize. Scorch the earth and nuke the dopers. Your boy rises up, organizes the kids, and offs the Guard. Put in the romance if you want. I don't give a shit."

In an earlier conversation, Teddy had told the narrator how to run his life and, at the same time, how to write screenplays that would electrify American audiences. "Start fast and hard and loud and then stay that way," he said. "Don't let up for two hours. Story problem? Character logic? Fuck it. Turn up the music and dance. I know what America wants."

"What does the country want, Teddy? Educate me."

"Sex. Loud music. Hot clothes. Drugs. Fast cars. Did I say sex? We'll open two movies. Side by side. One's called *Sex, Drugs and Death,* the other's called *Mom and Dad Go for a Walk.* Now, where you going to put your money, white boy? You do movies about milking the cow. I'll do ones about fucking and getting loaded. See you at the finish line."

Later, after four o'clock in the morning, Teddy and the narrator part. An hour later, the narrator learns, Teddy was speeding his Porsche through Encino, "doing ninety down Balboa Boulevard. He clipped six parked cars, bounced off a telephone pole, and went through the display window of a lighting store. His Porsche flipped over, bounced off a wall, and slammed into a display of floor lamps and chandeliers, all of which were as lit up as Teddy was. Ripping through all that wiring set the shop on fire. The car burned too, just like in the movies. There were drugs and alcohol in his system and a lot of second- and third-degree burns on his body. The police arrested him and took him to the Sherman Oaks Burn Center."

Freeman captured a real incident accurately. According to Rusty Cook, the custom car designer who worked on Simpson's automobiles, the Encino accident happened just as Freeman described it. And, as Freeman wrote, it was only one of many. On one occasion Simpson and Bruckheimer were racing their Mustangs, and Simpson lost control of his car and "wound up in someone's front yard. He tore the suspension right off the car."[24] Cook bought that Mustang for parts. Simpson would routinely "hit curbs too fast and tear the front bumper off" of his older-style Ferrari 308, Cook said. In another San Fernando Valley accident, Cook recalled, "Simpson was doing one-hundred-plus down Reseda Boulevard and made a right turn onto Ventura. He didn't make it. He spun out and went over the curb and took out a fire hydrant. The car filled with water, and the water damage totaled it. The car went right to the salvage yard, and Don walked away from the accident before the police got there."

For Simpson the accidents were only about money. One of his assistants was saddled with the duty of "settling" his moving violations. Most cost $1,000 to fix, until, at one point, Simpson had racked up so many that not even his skillful lawyer could get one removed from his record. The assistant relayed the lawyer's message that Simpson would have to go to court and answer the charges. Simpson fired the assistant and found a new lawyer.[25]

Simpson was obsessed with his automobiles. He'd buy expensive Porsches and then have them customized to one-of-a-kind perfection. William Stoeffel, of Hollywood's Coach Craft, routinely put a "fender flare" job on Simpson's new Porsches, a procedure that added about $8,000 to the $40,000 cost of the car. Then he'd add special tires and wheels, for another $6,000. Stoeffel put a customized stereo system into Simpson's Ferrari 328, a car that sold for $120,000. When Stoeffel didn't or couldn't do Simpson's repairs or customizing quickly enough, Stoeffel recalled, Simpson would take his work elsewhere, and Stoeffel wouldn't see him for six months. Then he'd return, often with a friend, like director Michael Mann, who had bought a similar car and wanted Stoeffel to similarly customize it.

Simpson's automobile enthusiasms often approached mania. Cook remembered that, when Ferrari of Italy designed its first all-black Testarossa, Simpson became obsessed with being the first to own one in California. He dispatched an assistant, with a $100,000 cashier's check, to San Diego, where the new Ferraris were being off-loaded for sale in the southwestern United States. The assistant drove down, predawn, to be on hand when the San Diego warehouse opened at 6:00 A.M. He traded the check for the sports car. Simpson became, as he would later brag to all his friends, the first man in California to own an all-black Testarossa. "This was very important to him," said Cook, who worked on the Ferrari many times. Never mind that, within an hour, several other Californians owned black Testarossas. Simpson owned the *first* one.[26]

And sometimes Simpson's car antics brought him trouble.

Cathy St. George, the model and *Playboy* centerfold, is a California blonde with the classic centerfold physique—petite, slim-hipped, slender and large-breasted. (According to the Miss August 1982 "Playmate Data Sheet," this Leo-Virgo was 34-22-34, carried 102 pounds on her 5'4" frame and listed among her "turn-ons" Manhattan, British accents, massages and credit cards. Her favorite sports were "the ones you play indoors."[27]) Though subsequently sober and free of substance addiction, in the 1980s she was a regular on the New York and Hollywood party circuits. Visiting Los Angeles from New York for the Fourth of July weekend, in 1986, she was invited by her friend Melissa Prophet to attend a Malibu beach party. She drove out in the company of her friend Ava Fabian, another local beauty who had herself graced the *Playboy* centerfold pages in August 1986 and made a cover appearance in April 1987. (Favorite turn-ons for the 36-24-34 Fabian, a 5'7" brunette, were "men in uniforms, whipped cream massages, flowers . . ."[28] Drug dealer Rayce Newman, in his confessional, refers to Ava as "my favorite centerfold friend."[29] He and Fabian were acquainted the way Newman was acquainted with most people: He sold her dope. "Ava loved to snort her coke," Newman wrote. "She got very quiet when she was high, unlike most people who you can't get to shut the fuck up."[30]) St. George was a little leery of Prophet, whom she knew as "one of the biggest madams in L.A. at that time," and of the fast crowd she moved in. But she was bored, and lonely: Her boyfriend was in New York, and she herself was recovering from minor surgery. After some urging, she agreed to join Fabian.

The house belonged to film executive and producer Craig Baumgarten, who was married but dating Prophet. He moved in pretty fast circles, too, having been expelled from the Columbia Pictures executive ranks after his bosses discovered he'd starred in a pornographic movie he was producing in an earlier professional incarnation.[31] According to one source, Baumgarten had taken his position in front of the camera when his leading man became incapable of maintaining an erection.[32] Simpson, without mentioning the latter details, exposed Baumgarten to further ridicule when, while being interviewed for the 1985 profile in *Esquire* magazine, told reporter Lynn Hirschberg, "He used to be an executive V.P. at Columbia until they found out he starred in a porno movie"—taking Baumgarten's humiliation to the national level.[33]

St. George and Fabian arrived to find the small party in full swing. "There was tons of coke and tons of champagne," she said, "and it was obvious that [the other revelers] had been up all night."[34] The producer Steve Roth was there, along with Jerry Bruckheimer, Don Simpson, Prophet and several other women St. George did not know. Simpson stopped her minutes after she'd come through the door. He said, "When you came in, I thought you were pretty cute. What did you think of me?" St. George answered, "I was kind of looking to see who was here. I actually didn't notice you." Simpson muttered, "What a bitch," and walked away laughing. By midafternoon everyone was "very high," St. George recalled. Simpson had cornered her again, this time because he'd overheard her say she was renting a house temporarily from Robin Leach, host of the then-popular TV show *Lifestyles of the Rich and Famous*. Simpson demanded an introduction and begged St. George to tell him how he could arrange to be featured on the show. "He went on and on, really to excess," St. George remembered. "But then *everything* was to excess, with the coke and the champagne and all."

Sometime in the late afternoon the phone rang, and a panic went through the house: Baumgarten's wife was on her way. Melissa Prophet dashed outside and drove away. Fabian got into an argument with Simpson, who proposed sex to her and flew into a rage when she declined. Words and blows were exchanged. Fabian followed Prophet out the door and drove away, abandoning St. George. Simpson asked her where she needed to go and then suggested he drive her home: Her home on Tulis Drive was only blocks from his place on Cherokee Lane, near the top of Coldwater Canyon, high above Beverly Hills. She agreed.

Once inside Simpson's car, a vintage, restored Corvette, St. George realized Simpson was "very fucked up." He was still raging about Fabian not wanting to have sex with him. He told St. George, "Ava was for *me*, man. She's a centerfold, and everyone knows a centerfold is only good for one thing—fucking and sucking." St. George was relieved to realize Simpson didn't know that she, too, had been a centerfold. But she was alarmed at Simpson's obvious inability to handle his 'Vette. When she asked him if he was okay to drive, he told her he'd taken two Mandrax and admitted he was having trouble driving. "I thought he was going to kill me," St. George said.

He didn't, but a few blocks from St. George's house Simpson lost control of the car and rammed it into the side of a house. "His car was literally stuck into the side of this wall," St. George said. Soon the owner was outside, threatening to call the cops. Simpson panicked. He grabbed St. George and made her walk with him up the street to his house. St. George, coming down from the cocaine and champagne, staggered into Simpson's backyard and fell asleep in a lawn chair. It was dark when she awoke. Inside, she found Simpson and Prophet snorting coke. St. George split.

The following day, while sitting poolside with friends, St. George telephoned Simpson to make sure he'd survived the wild night. In low, uneven tones, Simpson told her, "You should probably leave town." Why? she asked. "I've told everyone you were driving my car. You're gonna have to take the heat for the accident." Simpson claimed that he had asked Prophet and another girlfriend to give police a "positive identification" of

St. George as the person who had stolen his car the night before and crashed it. When St. George protested—asking, "Why should I go to jail for you? I don't even *know* you"—Simpson became threatening. "You leave town now, or I'll have someone hurt you. I *know* people." St. George just laughed at him and said, "Oh, yeah? My dad *pays* the people you know."

It was only a gag, but it set Simpson up for real trouble. St. George's father was, in fact, a man who manufactured and installed swimming pools.

But St. George's boyfriend was a different story.

Alphonse Persico, known in mob circles as "Little Allie Boy" Persico, was at the time of the incident beginning a twelve-year sentence in a New York prison for his involvement in the criminal activities of the Colombo crime family.[35] His uncle Carmine "Junior" Persico—known as Snake to his enemies—had just been sentenced to thirty-nine years in prison for racketeering.[36] Allie Boy's father, Alphonse "Big Allie Boy" Persico, upon his death in 1989 was described as "a convicted murderer with a forty-year history of arrests,"[37] most of them resulting from crimes committed as he rose through the Colombo family to finally achieve the number two position there. Though St. George insists that she did not even tell Little Allie Boy about the incident at the time, Simpson was telling *everyone* that he'd gotten on the wrong side of the Colombo crime family. ("Such a drama queen," St. George would say later.)[38] Word went around Little Italy, and then Los Angeles, that a film producer named Don Simpson had threatened the life of Little Allie Boy Persico's girl.

Within several days Simpson was visited at home by two Italians. They told him that St. George's boyfriend had ordered a hit and that Simpson was "a dead man."[39] They offered to try to make good with the Colombo family and the Persicos, but they told Simpson it would cost a lot of money. According to St. George, who found the shakedown hysterically funny, the Italians extorted $250,000 from Simpson over the next two years. "It was so stupid," St. George would say years later, laughing at the whole incident. "If he'd offered me $20,000, I would have clammed up."

(St. George's friend Fabian has scary connections, too. In the early 1990s she hooked up with John Scotto, a New Yorker with a shady past and a family history of mob ties—his father, Anthony Scotto, was a former president of the International Longshoremen's Association and "reputed to have mob ties."[40] Though son John reportedly "determined to leave his old pursuits and family connections behind,"[41] he was convicted in 1993 of attempting to bribe an agent of the California Alcoholic Beverage Control office and sentenced to prison. The conviction stemmed from Scotto's attempt to get a liquor license for the trendy West Hollywood nightclub, called Ava's, that he'd purchased in his girlfriend's name and at which she and Scotto entertained a broad spectrum of New York wise guys and Hollywood heavyweights—among them Simpson. This would not have come as a total surprise to regular readers of *Playboy*. In her August 1986 centerfold appearance, the pillow-breasted Fabian listed the Roaring Twenties as her favorite era and included gangsters and Duesenbergs among her favorite aspects of that decade.[42] Among Fabian's other Hollywood conquests was, by his own admission, agent John Burnham.)[43]

St. George's only other brush with Simpson came several years later. She was at a friend's house and found herself playing Trivial Pursuit with Tom Cruise, who had just achieved superstar status with *Top Gun*. When St. George asked him if that wasn't a Don Simpson movie, Cruise laughed and said, "No. That guy was in rehab the whole time we were making *Top Gun*."

She would have another brush, however, with the ugly side of Hollywood. Visiting Los Angeles several years after her night with Simpson, and hard up for money, she got a call from a friend. A photographer named Vince Conti had contacted St. George's agent. There was going to be a photo shoot in Las Vegas, for a Ron Rico rum advertisement. Conti needed three girls to fly to Vegas for a test shot. He'd pay each of them $500 to make the test shot and would pay $2,000 to whichever model got the job. St. George's agent told her, "Conti's got a reputation. If it's at all strange when you get up there, just get out and go home." St. George decided to take her chances.

That was the wrong move. Conti did indeed have a reputation. According to court records and Heidi Fleiss' former lover, photographer-producer Ivan Nagy, Conti's usual employment in Hollywood was procuring women.[44] He'd had a regular role on the TV series *Kojak*. Conti, who has worked for producer Robert Evans, was in 1993 sent to prison on a felony pandering conviction, Nagy said.[45] In what must surely be the only instance on which the two men would agree, Nagy's statements are echoed by former LAPD vice chief Fred Clapp. "Vince Conti used to catch girls and turn them on to madams, for a fee. That's how he made his living. He'd meet a girl in a club and then introduce her to Cathy Black or Alex Adams."[46]

Conti had more than a photo shoot in mind for the three women who traveled to Las Vegas. St. George met the other two on the flight up. Both had been centerfolds, and both were beautifully dressed. They explained that they were to have dinner that night at the Dunes hotel. St. George was instantly suspicious. The Dunes was owned by the wealthy playboy Adnan Kashoggi—for whom, she knew, Melissa Prophet used to procure women. The two women told her that it was Kashoggi, indeed, with whom they were to have dinner. St. George refused to go: She was coming down with the flu, she said, and she wasn't interested in meeting Kashoggi. She went directly to her room at the Dunes and went to bed.

Hours later, there was a knock at the door, which she opened to find Kashoggi and two of his associates. St. George was not intimidated. She told the billionaire, "Look, if you wanted to party, that's fine. But not with me. And you shouldn't have lied about the photo shoot. You should never lie about work."

Kashoggi, St. George said, was aghast and apologized immediately. He told her, "I had no idea that's how Conti got you here." Concerned, too, about St. George's flu, Kashoggi had the house doctor come upstairs for a medical examination. He placed $500, in cash, beside the bed. When St. George protested, Kashoggi said, "No. I want to." St. George got up early the following morning and flew back to Los Angeles. She never worked with Conti again, but she learned a lesson. "The photo agencies all treat their supermodels like superstars, but they all sell their younger models to their friends," she said. (Ex-cop Clapp once had an informant among Alex Adams' employees, and one of the jobs that girl did was for Kashoggi. Clapp said his informant had told him Kashoggi was "a complete gentleman, really a pretty decent guy.")[47]

St. George decided, among other things, it was time to change agents. Later, she changed careers altogether and began working as a makeup artist. Among her first assignments was doing the makeup for Ava Fabian's return appearance on the cover of *Playboy*.

And she never saw Simpson again, although his name would come up. Every time she bumped into her friend Barry Beckerman, the producer, he would tell her how much fun he had razzing Simpson on the Paramount lot. "You'd better watch out," Beckerman would tell Simpson. "I heard that Cathy's boyfriend got out early. You're in deep shit."

Simpson took this seriously enough, friends would later remember, that he bought several weapons for the house, improved its security system and hired some muscle—in the form of Vic Manni, a bodyguard who wanted to become an actor. Simpson helped him do that, giving him roles in *Top Gun, Beverly Hills Cop 2* and *Bad Boys*.[48]

For Freeman "The Burning Porsche" also caught, perfectly, the excited, magic, manic tone of Simpson's voice—a fact not lost on Simpson. Long after the book's publication, when he had not seen or spoken with Simpson for several years, Freeman received a phone call from Jerry Bruckheimer. "Don's got this idea. Come on over." Freeman met with Simpson and Bruckheimer at their Paramount offices. The two men faced him from behind their huge C-shaped desk—placing Freeman, as so many before him, in the uncomfortable position of being unable to look at both men at a time, as both men stared at him. Simpson's idea, Freeman recalled, "was about two cops who are brothers, and the girl who comes between them. There wasn't much detail." Still, they agreed to hire Freeman and go forward.

At the end of the meeting Freeman said, "I'm still waiting. Finally I reached over to shake his hand, but then he wouldn't let go. He said, 'About that story . . . What is this South America shit? You *know* I'm from Alaska." Simpson held Freeman's gaze a moment longer. "But you got the fucking voice *just right*." Freeman counted this among the highest compliments his writing had ever earned him. Simpson never mentioned the story again.

"The Burning Porsche" was not Simpson's only appearance in Hollywood fiction. The journalist and novelist John H. Richardson used Simpson as a model for the character of Jennings West[49] in Richardson's brilliantly observed *The Vipers' Club*.

Richardson's novel, initially serialized in *Premiere* magazine under the name "The Blue Screen," is a Hollywood murder mystery. It follows the misadventures of Peter, an East Coast preppie who has come west and found employment as the personal assistant to the colorful film producer Max Fischer. (Fischer is based, by Richardson's own account, almost entirely on the colorful film producer Joel Silver, to whom the novel is dedicated.) Peter is in love with Tracy, the daughter of a film producer who resembles real-life film producer Larry Gordon. Tracy is raped and beaten in the opening stages of the novel, and her best friend is subsequently found murdered. Peter and Fischer are both implicated. Clearing his name—which also involves a private investigator, named Dogosta, who very much resembles real-life Hollywood investigator Anthony Pellicano—takes Peter through the nether reaches of Beverly Hills, Bel Air and the movie business, and into the world of Jennings West.

"West always had plenty of women around, all of them so very congenial," Richardson wrote. "Some were upscale hookers, some genuine party girls attracted to the money and glamour, and some were young actresses taking charge of their careers. They were all in their twenties, all 'model quality.' "[50] West is assisted in procuring the "model quality" women by Madame Meursault, a character with more than a passing resemblance to Alex Adams, whose exploits Richardson had chronicled, with help from Simpson, for *Premiere*. (In the novel, Meursault offers Peter a freebie, asking, "Wouldn't you like to try one of my creatures? I can give you the house discount." Richardson said that Madam Alex made a similar offer, which he declined, when he interviewed her. "She just said, 'Would you like to take one of these girls?' I was on assignment, and I was married, and I didn't want to give a sleazebag like Madam Alex anything on me," Richardson said later.)[51]

The murder investigation ultimately alienates Peter from his explosive, temperamental employer, who in one of the novel's most amusing passages fires him. "The second message was curt. 'It's ten P.M. Call me now.' The third was informative: 'I'm in a forgiving mood and you better call me soon. We have to discuss.' After that the messages started getting less friendly. 'I *told* you to pick up your messages every hour, asshole. Just because I fired you doesn't mean you can go *out of touch.*' 'It's two. You're fired *again.*' 'It's two twenty. Don't use me on your resume, pal.' " The messages conclude after dawn the next day, having run all night. "At 7:12: 'You're *over*. You hear me? *Over*. Terminated, finished, *extinct*. The next time I see you, you're going to be asking me if I *want a cocktail before dinner*. Will I have *the baked potato or the rice?*' "

(Silver, in real life, once by his own account lambasted a colleague in the same fashion, screaming down a phone line, "Repeat after me: Would you like that in a pump or a flat? Because when I get through with you *you'll be selling ladies' shoes!''*[52] Another rendition of this diatribe also appeared in the amusing film *Swimming with Sharks.* Its writer-director, George Huang, declined to say on whom he based this incident.)

Richardson said, of the Jennings West character, ''Yeah, Jennings was the 'Don' character in the novel. I borrowed a line [from Simpson] for the novel, where Max Fischer [leaving a party at West's house] says, 'What I don't understand is why these sleazy bastards like whores so much. I mean, why pay for it? All the women in Hollywood are whores already.' ''[53]

Richardson, who was fond of Simpson, found him a useful source. He was also sympathetic, to a degree, to Simpson's attitudes about sex and sexuality. ''I feel that over the last twenty years male sexuality has been put down,'' Richardson said. ''The idea of 'you have only one thing on your mind' has carried over into feminism, and the culture at large, and normal male lust and horniness has become criminalized. For Don, this was an area in which he wouldn't take any shit. He wasn't going to accept any put-downs about his sexuality. I felt a kinship with that. For all his drug derangement, he was *adamant* about not being full of shit.''

Even as Simpson was reveling in the nightlife, burning Porsches and brain cells with cocaine and booze and throwing his money and his heart at hookers, there were indications that he hungered for something more meaningful and lasting. From the depths of his shyness—a timid emotional reticence that relegated his romantic conquests to hookers and forced him, even with professionals, to blanket his libido and his personality with protective layers of drugs and alcohol—came a voice crying out for a real connection. The voice spoke in the form of a series of ''personal ads'' in local newspapers and magazines. Like many of his schemes, this one also backfired and embarrassed him in the press.

On March 2, 1993, under the rubric Dish, *Daily Variety* correspondent Claudia Eller reported that an amusing personals ad had appeared in *Los Angeles* magazine's ''Matchmaker Matchmaker'' section in January. She quoted heavily from the ad, in which a ''wealthy Hollywood bad boy''—which Eller identified as a ''big clue'' to the author of the ad—described himself as a ''sexy, wealthy, 40s, 5'10", 165-pound filmmaker of numbers of blockbusters.'' He said he was looking for ''a partner in crime, social, sexual psychological crime. NOTHING illegal. Everything ETHICAL. Must be an artist/outlaw at heart.'' The big words continued: ''I am PRO romance, truth, adventure, art, ethics and sex . . . which leads me to, women. I'm tired of the club scene and have never, nor will ever trade my professional status/access for social or physical favors. However, I am very generous. I am ANTI 'group think' of any kind, including morals, political correctness, white picket fence dreams of eternal marital bliss, or the idea that humans are NATURALLY monogamous.[54]

"The woman I'm interested in sharing my mind/body with must be daring, bright, witty, curious (very), ambitious, independent, stylish (very) and an artist/intellectual/outlaw not unlike myself. She should be between 20 and 30 and extraordinarily good looking/beautiful/sexy (race not important). (On a 1 to 10 scale, a 12 at least.) My terms are non-negotiable.

"If the tone of terms of this ad anger you (yes, exterior appearances are crucial), don't waste my time or yours by writing to convince me how arrogant/selfish or wrong I am. You either GET IT or YOU DON'T."[55]

Without naming Simpson, Eller speculated as to the identity of this "artist/outlaw." "We can think of only one Hollywood hotshot with the chutzpah" to take out such an ad. Eller phoned her unnamed candidate, whom, off the record, and never in print, she subsequently identified as Simpson. The candidate responded coyly, "Well, it's very well written. And if anyone calls you or wants to send photos, pass them on to me."[56]

Word circulated that the man in question was indeed Simpson, an assertion he vigorously denied. "Like I need to run a fucking personal ad?" he protested at the time.[57] But the story stuck. It aggravated Simpson deeply, and for years he would raise the issue and remind reporters of the rumors, in order to deny them.

At least one young woman was intrigued by Simpson's bravado. Sarah (not her real name) wrote to Simpson in care of the magazine, introducing herself and expressing her interest, but declining to send the photograph that Simpson's ad requested. Simpson responded at once, on a handwritten card, in his usual staccato tone of voice. "Nice letter," he wrote, and then chastised Sarah for omitting the photo. "Look, a guy like me is honest about looks . . . they are *critical*. I have no need for new friends, etc., since I spend time keeping people *out* of my life. I'm single, not looking for relationships or marriage . . . just adventure. However, I'll take a shot. The enclosed info speaks for itself."[58]

Simpson enclosed a photo of himself, lean and tanned, with a scruffy

Miami Vice–style stubble, as he flexed for the camera. "Here's my *package*," the accompanying note read. "Call me."

Sarah did, but most of her contact with Simpson was by mail. In his notes Simpson invariably returned to his original theme—that he was looking for "adventure," not romance—and often sent along a book or magazine article he thought would interest his correspondent. He generally name-dropped, too. "Been on the road with young Tom Cruise," he wrote at one point. "Working on our race car movie." In another note he said, "Been traveling and crazed on the Tom Cruise movie," and later wrote, "Just got back to town after wrapping *Thunder*."[59]

In each of the notes Simpson promised that he and Sarah would get together as soon as he was back in town, but they never did. Sarah grew confused by this and finally sent a note asking, directly, why they had never met in person. Simpson wrote back: "One: I've been making a movie and etc. Two: I am into *sex* . . . yup. And my concern became that you were too straight and I don't value straight or traditional values. If I'm wrong, let me know." (More than a decade earlier Simpson had said exactly the same thing to Tova Laiter, when the two met on a blind date. "He told me right up front that he wanted a companion who was sexually adventurous," Laiter recalled later. "A woman who was willing to explore everything sexually. He didn't want the white picket fence.")[60] Simpson wasn't wrong about Sarah, but she responded angrily. "I told him that I liked fucking, too, but that I would choose who I fucked—and it wasn't going to be him," Sarah said later. Simpson wrote back, apologizing, saying, "I truly meant it in a quasi-joking manner. It obviously did not translate well." Simpson followed the note with fresh flowers. Sarah did not write again.

The brush-off unnerved Simpson. He had already warned Sarah, in an early note, "I'm a known public figure, so discretion is a must." Now he was evidently worried that this "straight" girl would blow his cover. After they stopped corresponding, Simpson would periodically call Sarah's office—keeping tabs, checking to see if she still worked there. Finally, many months later, Sarah was introduced to Simpson in person, at a screening. "He was incredibly uncomfortable," Sarah said, "like he couldn't get away fast enough. He apologized again, and ran away."

Years later, having left the entertainment industry and reinvented herself in another career, Sarah would only shake her head and say, "Pretty sad, isn't it? He had everything, and he had nothing."[61]

CHAPTER FIVE

DAYS OF PLUNDER

Late one evening in January 1990, Simpson called a friend from Paradise Raceway in Daytona Beach, Florida. He and Jerry Bruckheimer were halfway through filming *Days of Thunder*, a roaring tale of race cars and redemption that starred Tom Cruise, Nicole Kidman and Robert Duvall. From an original script by Robert Towne, an old Simpson crony who'd won an Oscar for *Chinatown*, and an original story concept from Towne and Cruise, and under the direction of another Simpson crony, Tony Scott, who'd shot Simpson and Bruckheimer's *Top Gun*, *Days of Thunder* was meant to be Paramount Pictures' biggest summer movie. Going in, it looked to have all the elements of a huge hit. Midway through production, though, bad news from the set was filtering back to Hollywood: Cost overruns were pushing the budget through the roof; the dailies looked terrible; Cruise wasn't happy with the script, which was being rewritten nightly; the production, and the producers, were out of control. To the friend in Los Angeles, who asked if the rumors were true, Simpson laughed and said, "Are you kidding? I'm having the time of my fucking *life.*"

In fact, *Days of Thunder* would ruin his life and derail his professional career as a moviemaker for a full five years. Simpson had taken the high-concept movie and run with it, producing an unprecedented string of hit films. But success had gone to his head. His hit movies had made him a celebrity in behind-the-scenes Hollywood. Around the studios he was a demigod—insane and unpredictable but with an instinct for success that gave him the reputation as a Midas with an unfailing touch. By 1990, though, he had confused his celebrity with stardom. He didn't simply want to employ Tom Cruise; he wanted to *be* Tom Cruise, or to be *bigger* than Tom Cruise. In attempting to become that, he lost sight and lost his grasp of the very things that created his success. He forgot about character and story and script and made a mess of his movie. In the process he would destroy his relationship with the studio that had been his home for more than ten years.

Going into *Thunder,* after fifteen years in the movie business and seven as a movie producer, Simpson was at a career high. With *Flashdance, Beverly Hills Cop, Top Gun* and *Beverly Hills Cop 2* behind him, he and Bruckheimer had achieved unparalleled Hollywood power. In 1985 Paramount executives had won the wooing for Simpson and Bruckheimer, signing them to a lucrative four-year deal at the studio, beating out competing offers from ex-Paramount executives Barry Diller, now at Fox, and Michael Eisner, now at Disney. Months before, they had signed a deal with Paramount so unprecedented, and so unusually lucrative, that they were able to force the studio to purchase full-page advertisements in the *New York Times,* the *Wall Street Journal,* the *Washington Post,* the *Los Angeles Times* and Hollywood's two trade papers, to announce a "visionary alliance."

It had not been an easy deal to reach, partially because Simpson was demanding contract details and language that no right-thinking studio head would ever deliver. According to Lance Young, who was at that time a senior production executive at Paramount, Simpson and Bruckheimer were seeking an overhead deal of "unprecedented" size. They wanted Paramount to pay for two development executives, two assistants each, two secretaries each, new offices, new cars and funds for constructing home screening rooms; and they wanted Paramount to grant them unfettered license to draw cash against their producing fees—all at a cost Young estimated at over $3 million a year.[1] Worse, Simpson wanted it stated *in the contract* that he would also direct and star in future movies. Even worse, he wanted these future movies to be "artistic" movies. "This was a huge roadblock," Young recalled. "Don was burned out on making these big movies. He didn't want to make *Top Gun* again. He wanted artistic projects, and he wanted to be a director and he wanted to be an actor—and he wanted all that to be in the deal." Said a former Simpson employee, the producer Michael London, "He wanted to make *Driving Miss Daisy,*" the movie that, while Simpson toiled in Florida, had just received nine Oscar nominations and was number one at the box office.

Another studio, or Paramount at another time, would have ended the negotiations there and told Simpson and Bruckheimer to leave the lot. Paramount couldn't, though. *Days of Thunder* was under way, and the studio was desperate to have it for their summer release schedule.

Under the terms of the deal, as announced on February 1, 1990, Simpson and Bruckheimer were promised a production fund of $300 million, over five years, to make five pictures. *Any* five pictures. They were not required to submit scripts or budgets to Paramount for approval, or to ask for director approval or cast approval. They just had to make the movies.

Advertisements that ran in leading papers said:

> From the premise to the premiere. From the first draft to the last detail. From the first shot to the millionth cassette. Don Simpson and Jerry Bruckheimer are total filmmakers. It began with the landmark blockbuster FLASHDANCE. Then came three of the biggest hits of all time: BEVERLY HILLS COP, TOP GUN and BEVERLY HILLS COP 2. And from these: 2 Academy Awards. 10 Academy Award Nominations. 14 Top Ten Songs. 4 #1 Soundtrack Albums. 4 #1 Songs. 4 Multi-Platinum Albums. 4 #1 Videos. Paramount Pictures is pleased and proud to announce a new five-year alliance with Don Simpson and Jerry Bruckheimer as they enter a new era of producing and directing at the studio they call home.

Asked to amplify, Simpson boasted, "It's simple. They put up the money, we put up the talent and we meet at the theater."[2]

That, anyway, was Simpson's version. It wasn't the truth, and the lie, so publicly spoken, caused immediate damage.

In New York, at Paramount's headquarters, Paramount CEO Martin S. Davis burned with rage at Simpson's cockiness. In Hollywood, at the Melrose Avenue studio, Paramount executives fretted. But in Florida, on the *Thunder* set, Simpson glowed. In the wake of his "visionary alliance" deal, *Thunder* had begun production at a budget of $40 million—$7 million of it, according to former Paramount production executive Lance

Young, paid in salary to Cruise. By now the budget had ballooned to $70 million. But Simpson, who had turned Cruise into a bona fide movie star with *Top Gun*, which had also made his *Thunder* director, Tony Scott, a Hollywood power, seemed unperturbed. The *Thunder* location was a permanent party. By day, from his suites at the Daytona Beach Marriott, Simpson would dispatch two assistants, Dave (known as Dave the Rave) Robertson and Dave (known as Baby Dave) Thorne, to area beaches, to ask attractive young women if they wanted to attend a party for Tom Cruise. By night the women would join Simpson, Bruckheimer, Cruise, Towne and Scott for dinner and after-hours discotheque dancing. One night the crew rented an entire bowling alley and threw a party. Another night a local Daytona Beach discotheque called the Palace was closed down for a party, where rapper Tone Loc performed. The booze and the cocaine—kept in steady supply by the two Daves—were plentiful. "One morning I found three *bags* of cocaine stuck behind a cushion on the sofa," one assistant remembered. "He'd been pounding on my door at 4:00 A.M., yelling at me to come and party."[3]

The girls came and were rewarded. Simpson kept a production office closet at the Marriott full of Donna Karan dresses, wrapped in plastic and organized by size, to give to the ones he liked. He had another entire room redesigned to hold his own vast wardrobe. He'd spent $400,000 of Paramount's money turning two hotel suites into a private gym and installing an enormous music system. After rising late—"basically, he would sleep all day," a source on the set remembered[4]—while Bruckheimer oversaw the actual production of the movie, Simpson would work out every day on equipment specially ordered from a list supplied by muscular movie star Arnold Schwarzenegger. If work went on too late or there was work left to be done at the end of the day, says a *Thunder* source, Don would laugh and say, " 'Jerry, I can't do that. It's six-thirty. I have to clean up and get dressed and I have a date at seven-thirty. I can't *be* there. *You* do it.' And Jerry would always do it." ("Jerry is a workaholic," says a friend of the two men. "Don hated to work. He'd be the first to tell you. I remember sitting in his office one night, and it was seven o'clock, and the TV was on. *Magnum, P.I.* came on, and you could see Don's whole body relax. He said, 'I love this.' I said, 'What?' He said, '*Magnum, P.I.* is on. That means it's seven o'clock. That means no more phone calls.' ")[5] *Thunder* star Cruise later said, "Don attended script meetings, but he wasn't on the set a lot. Jerry was always there when you needed to get it done."[6]

For a while, Simpson was even enjoying a relationship that bordered on the ordinary. While casting *Thunder* in Los Angeles, he'd met a North Carolina–born actress named Donna Wilson. He'd liked her and begun dating her, and, with Towne, had written into the script a part for her. It wasn't a large part—that of a "pit girl" at the racetrack—but it was sufficient to get her to North Carolina for the first five weeks of shooting and then move her to Florida. This raised eyebrows among the crew: "She's a pit babe and she has one line, and she's on the set for fifty-four days?" wondered one. According to that source, though, the relationship soured. "The drug use freaked her out, and it affected Don's ability to, you know, perform." Wilson eventually began dating *Thunder* director Tony Scott, whom she subsequently married.

Even better than the sex and romance, maybe even better than the drugs and money, Simpson was with *Thunder* achieving a lifelong dream. Leaving his native Alaska for college at Eugene's University of Oregon years before, Simpson had told his high school buddy Carl Brady Jr., "I'm going to Hollywood to be a movie star."[7] Now, in Florida, he was about to do just that. He and Towne had written into the *Thunder* script a part for "Aldo Bennedetti," a veteran race car driver, and Simpson was to make his motion picture debut playing the role. He'd worked hard to look the part. He was down to a lean, muscled 170 pounds. ("We were in Charlotte, North Carolina," where production began, recalled an editor on the movie. "It was the coldest winter in a hundred years. I'd be walking back to the hotel from the editing room at ten at night. It was eighteen degrees. Don would be outside, working out.")[8] He'd had collagen implants in his chin and cheeks, giving his previously broad, flat face a new, angular definition. He was deeply tanned; and he fit handsomely into the two pairs of tailor-made racing leathers he wore on his infrequent visits to the set—one blindingly white, one pitch-black, both emblazoned with a bright red stitched panel advertising Goody's headache powders, a red that matched the stripped-down, NASCAR-style number 34 Chevrolet Lumina he'd drive in the racing scenes.

Simpson did not especially admire actors—indeed, during this period he sneeringly referred to his star Cruise as "the Audie Murphy of the 1990s" to a journalist[9]—but he envied them, and he wanted to be one himself. In 1988 he'd auditioned for a part in the melodrama *Beaches*, according to its producer, Bonnie Bruckheimer, the ex-wife of Simpson's partner. "We were casting male parts, and Jerry called me and said, 'Don really wants to read for you,' " Bruckheimer said. "I brought him into a casting session with [director] Garry Marshall. He was surprisingly good."[10] But he didn't get the part. He told people he'd appeared in an uncredited sequence, as a tough hombre, in the 1988 film *Young Guns.* But he had not. According to *Guns* producer Paul Schiff, it was actually Cruise who made the uncredited appearance.[11] (Cruise had come to the set to visit his friend Emilio Estevez, was herded into makeup and wardrobe and then was filmed in a scene in which he gets shot.) Simpson would later tell people that he'd appeared in almost every movie he and Bruckheimer made together—although there is no record of any on-screen appearance in any of them except *Days of Thunder.* This was his big break, and he was taking it seriously.

Simpson was sitting on top of a guaranteed box-office monster, and he wasn't shy about letting his competitors know. Memorial Day marked *Thunder's* release date. It would open against Disney's big-budget *Dick Tracy*, a vanity project directed by and starring Warren Beatty. Beatty was a friend, and a nearby Bel Air neighbor, and Disney's film division was run by Jeffrey Katzenberg, formerly Simpson's assistant at Paramount. Taunting Katzenberg, Simpson sent a fax: "You can't escape the *Thunder!*" Katzenberg faxed back: "You won't believe how big my *Dick* is!"[12] Simpson had T-shirts made for the cast and crew that read, "Don't Fuck with the Thunder."

Thunder at the script stage was almost mind-numbingly simple. Robert Duvall is Harry Hogge, a veteran race car builder who, the season before, has lost his best friend in a Daytona car crash for which he himself may have been responsible. Cruise is Cole Trickle, a cocky young driver whose previous racing career ended when his no-good father defrauded Cruise and his car's investors. Trickle—whose name may have been suggested by veteran NASCAR driver Dick Trickle—is an immediate racing sensation and immediately locked into mortal on-track combat with Rowdy Burns, played by Michael Rooker. Their racing rivalry ends in a fiery crash. Rowdy and Cole are badly injured; they are treated for head injuries by fetching brain surgeon Dr. Claire Lewicki, played by Nicole Kidman. Cole recovers, but loses his driving privileges and begins an uneasy romance with Claire. Rowdy does not recover and so turns his car over to Cole for one last try at Daytona. Cole is traumatized by his accident, though, and has lost his competitive edge. He must overcome his inner demons—and assuage Harry's certain belief that he will lose another beloved driver in another fiery crash—to win. And, of course, he does. Cole beats back his terror, drives bravely, takes the checkered flag, gets the girl and finds a new father in Harry. Lacing through the thundering racing action was music from Jeff Beck, Joan Jett and the team of Elton John and Bernie Taupin. There were excellent character parts for Randy Quaid, as the unscrupulous but ultimately loyal used car dealer who invests in Cole's career, and Cary Elwes, as the cocky younger driver who replaces Rowdy Burns as Cole's racing nemesis. There was the tall, luminous, red-maned Kidman, brand-new to American audiences (or those who missed the Australian thriller *Dead Calm* the year before) and on her way to becoming Tom Cruise's wife. There was the putative excitement of stock car racing and the Daytona 500, described in the film several times as "the Super Bowl of motor racing events." And there was Simpson's own role as Aldo Bennedetti, "the perennial contender from Reading, Pennsylvania."

And then there was the script, by all accounts incomplete when shooting started. Former executive Young remembered that the studio was "desperate for a summer movie. We knew the script wasn't ready, but we needed a movie for Memorial Day. We needed to work off this tremendous overhead we were paying Don and Jerry. We had a window [of availability] on Tom Cruise. Suddenly we all felt more fondly about the script."

When production and editing ended, the script was still painfully pedestrian and full of howlingly unlikely moments. Duvall's Harry actually has two separate scenes in which he speaks aloud, in prayerlike reverence, to the car he is building. There is a scene in which Cruise is given a "surprise" victory gift—a costumed "state trooper" who is actually a prostitute procured for his pleasure—meant to support Cruise's post-accident belief that Dr. Lewicki is not a surgeon but just another floozy the boys have hired for him. Quaid is called upon to utter the line, in disgust over Cruise's on-track antics, "We end up looking like a monkey fucking a football out there!" Significant lines—"I won't make a fool of you, Harry," and to describe intentional on-track collisions, "We're just rubbing. Rubbing is racing!"—are repeated tiresomely, as are portentous declarations of personal ethic: "I can tell you what I don't want to be—and that's a fraud," Cole tells Claire, and says, "I'm more afraid of being nothing than I am of being hurt."

Outwardly, however, *Thunder* was "Top Gun 2." Simpson and Bruckheimer had assembled Cruise and Scott, added pal Towne and were once again making a big noisy boys' movie with their favorite boys around them. (According to production executive Young, bringing Towne aboard had sealed the Simpson-Bruckheimer deal to produce. "Don told us, 'I will only do this movie if I can get Towne.' His deal was triggered on that.") There were key differences, though. *Top Gun* had been filmed for a frugal $19 million, when the average studio film cost only $17 million. *Thunder,* even if it had held its original budget of $40 million, cost double the studio average; at $70 million it cost more than triple.

Privately, midway through production, Simpson's enthusiasm was waning. *Thunder* was a mess. It wasn't just the soaring budget, though that was a growing problem. The producers were using a fleet of thirty "stock cars," most of them modified Chevrolets, to film the racing sequences. They cost $100,000 each to outfit, but they weren't NASCAR quality and they didn't come with teams of qualified stock car mechanics. "They broke down constantly," Gary Lucchesi, head of production at the time, recalls. "That meant delays, and that meant money." Half the fleet, at any given time, was in the shop. When they were on the track, too, there were problems. One afternoon a car spun out of control and ran into a bank of cameras, an accident that cost a long delay and $40,000 in camera equipment. There were also weather problems, as rain caused days of delay. Having begun production without a fully completed script, Cruise and the others were being fed new pages every morning and new lines even as they worked. For a while, Cruise read new lines off the dashboard of his speeding stock car, until keeping his eyes off the road caused him to crash. After that, Cruise listened to new lines as Towne dictated through a headset. All of this, of course, meant further expensive delays. "The movie was a disaster while we were shooting," said a source from the set. "It was taking so long, and we weren't getting it. We didn't finish shooting principal [photography] until May, and we were supposed to release the movie in May, and we still weren't finished. We had shot up to the end of the race, but we didn't have the end of the race. We actually didn't have a scene of a car crossing the finish line!"[13]

Alarmed at the rising cost of production, Paramount sent executive Young to the Charlotte, North Carolina, set to visit with the producers and force the production accountants to open the books. "I was sent down to exercise control," Young says, "but there was nothing to be done. The studio was committed to the release date, and that meant we had no leverage. We couldn't tell them to stop, because we were locked onto the release date. The key to this entire business is knowing when you do and when you do not have leverage—and your only leverage, ever, is to say,

'No. We are not making this movie.' We had no leverage." As for the
soaring budget, Young said, "The cost of flying in hookers was the least of
it. We're talking about *millions* of dollars being spent. Don and Jerry
didn't even try to hide it. They said, 'Look, we got three crews shooting
simultaneously. We have four teams of editors working. What do you
want from us?' "

More personally, though, Simpson was worried about his acting scenes.
According to film editor Billy Weber, who'd begun his relationship with
Simpson and Bruckheimer on *Beverly Hills Cop* and was on-set for the
duration of the *Thunder* production, Simpson simply couldn't act. The
dailies, Weber says, "were painful. It was clear to Tony [Scott] and to
Towne *and* to Don that his scenes just weren't working. It was just bad.
The way Tony shot it was bad—and that may have been intentional. It was
unusable."

According to another source on the set, it was star Cruise who eventually objected to Simpson's scenes—although Cruise would later say that
the idea of Simpson acting in the film was *his*, not Simpson's. One morning midway through production, already well behind schedule, Cruise was
delivered new script pages, rewritten the night before by Towne, for a
scene that a character named Aldo was supposed to perform opposite
Robert Duvall. (Aldo's dialogue was meant to bring some comic relief to
an otherwise heavy scene, in which a humbled Cole Trickle must admit to
veteran Harry that he does not understand racing cars and cannot win
races without Harry's help—for which, in his pride, he is loath to ask.)
Cruise wasn't familiar with Aldo and asked director Scott who it was. "It's
Don," he was told. Cruise read the scene—four pages of dialogue and
action between Aldo and Duvall—and objected. "We're so far behind, and
we're going to waste an entire day for nothing," he said. Scott felt he could
not tell Simpson the scene had to be cut, so Cruise volunteered. He walked
to Simpson's trailer, where the wanna-be actor had been in makeup for
two hours, preparing for his big debut. According to the source, Simpson
immediately sensed Cruise's discomfort with the scene—without asking
where the discomfort lay. He said, "Is it a shitty scene? It *is* a shitty scene!
It sucks. I *hate* this fucking scene! Get rid of it!" "He made a big display of
this," said the source, "running from his trailer and collaring some second
assistant director or something and shouting at him, 'Get rid of this shitty
fucking scene! Now!' "

Ultimately, Simpson's role as Aldo Bennedetti would be cut down to fleeting seconds on-screen, with only a single spoken line. (As Cole prepares his comeback, a leather-suited Aldo says to an ESPN "interviewer," "I'm glad he's well enough to come back, and I hope I beat him, at the same time.") And it was Weber who had to deliver the bad news. "I was the one who had to go to his office, and close the door, and say, 'You're only going to be in this movie *this much*,'" recalls Weber. "He said, 'Why?' I said, 'You come to the cutting room with me. I will close the door and lock it. *You* look at the footage. You come downstairs, and look at it, and just tell me: Anything you want in, I'll put in.' Because I *knew* he would never put anything in the movie that was bad. And he looked at it and said, 'I'm fucked.' So he was in the movie this tiny bit. The best stuff he had, Cruise wouldn't allow to be in the movie. He said it took away from the focus of the bar scene."

Simpson was demoralized. One afternoon Weber found him sitting with his head in his hands. "We're fucked," he moaned. "We're *fucked*. There's no story here. We barely have a first act, and then we don't have anything after that."

Thunder was born of Tom Cruise's desire to do a racing movie. The actor told *Rolling Stone* magazine's Jeffrey Ressner—for a story tied to the movie's July 1990 release—that the idea came to him while he and Paul Newman were doing practice laps at Daytona, after the two finished filming director Martin Scorsese's *The Color of Money*. Cruise, high on the speed and the course's sharply banked turns, said out loud, "I'm going to make a movie about this!"

Veteran film executive Ned Tanen, who had run Universal and Paramount at stages in his career, takes credit for planting the race car idea in Cruise's mind. Himself an avid sports car nut, Tanen kept a vintage Porsche—a car so highly tuned that it burned aircraft fuel instead of regular gasoline—in a hangar at Santa Monica Airport. He'd take the car out, predawn, on Sunday mornings and fly through the streets until the sound of police sirens warned him back to the hangar. One morning he invited Cruise along for a ride, while Cruise was preparing for his part in *Top Gun*. "He just fell in love with racing," Tanen recalled. "That was the beginning of *Days of Thunder*."

Paramount had already put two racing movies into development. Donald Stewart, who had written the Academy Award–winning script for the movie *Missing* and who for Paramount would go on to write *The Hunt for Red October*, *Patriot Games* and *Clear and Present Danger*, was writing a stock car script. Eric Hughes, who had written *Against All Odds* and cowritten *White Nights*, was working on a Formula One racing script. Having heard that Cruise was interested in making a race car movie, and wanting to land a project for a Simpson and Bruckheimer movie, Tanen took his lieutenant, Lance Young, aside and said, "I think we can convince Don and Jerry to do this movie."[14] He was correct.

Billed in early discussions as *Top Gun on Wheels* or, simply, *Top Car*, it would do with the NASCAR racing circuit what *Top Gun* had done with the navy's flight training school in San Diego. Paramount chairman Frank Mancuso would later say, "It *sounded* like it had all the elements of a hit, and all the elements that were perfect for Don and Jerry. It has action, romance, music and speed. When Tom Cruise signed on, and then Tony Scott, it had all the makings of a commercial success." For Mancuso, it was like the continuation of the Simpson-Bruckheimer franchise. "There was *Top Cop, Top Gun* and now *Top Car*. We felt very comfortable with it."

Cruise was represented at the time by Creative Artists Agency's Paula Wagner, who also represented screenwriter Towne. Cruise had written a crude story outline and then hired veteran screenwriter Douglas Day Stewart, the writer of *An Officer and a Gentleman* and the writer-director of *Thief of Hearts*, to polish it. After a pitch to Ned Tanen, the project was officially in development. Warren Skaaren, who had written segments of *Top Gun*, was hired to script. After seven drafts, from sheer exhaustion and impatience with Cruise's demands, he gave up. Wagner, meanwhile, came to Simpson-Bruckheimer, who were looking for another movie to do with Cruise and director Scott. Cruise, in turn, wooed writer Towne— who, conversely, had unsuccessfully wooed Cruise to take the lead in his film *Rush*—by taking him to the racetrack at Watkins Glen, New York. Towne liked what he saw and told the actor, "I get it, Cruise. This is fantastic." Towne went to work. Paramount needed a big "tentpole" picture for summer 1990. *Thunder* got the green light.

Even then, some Paramount executives were worried. In production meetings and marketing meetings, they expressed their concern over the story and the script. Sid Ganis, then copresident of Paramount, recalls one meeting, held days before the movie was due to start shooting, at which Simpson was asked hard questions about the budget. "He was up against it," Ganis would say later. "And he starts screaming. 'Fuck you! Fuck *all* of you! You don't know what you're talking about. You *never* know what you're talking about. So fuck you!' And he walks out. I was shocked by it.

I mean, I'm the head of the studio!'' As production rolled on, and costs mounted and the budget skyrocketed out of control, Ganis knew he should visit the set. He *always* visited his sets—but the building acrimony from Simpson kept him away. A more sympathetic Barry London said, ''There was a lot of concern about the budget, because it was getting very expensive. The studio was trying to hold the cost of the film down, and [Simpson and Bruckheimer] were trying to make the best film they could make with the material they had—and that costs money. Believe me, we had *many* discussions about how much overbudget the movie was going . . .''

Lesser filmmakers, or milder filmmakers, would have quailed. Simpson and Bruckheimer did not. Editor Weber says, ''Don and Jerry were never panicked. It wasn't their style. Their agenda was only, 'How do we make this the best movie possible?' They knew that the script had problems. Don said to me, the first week of shooting, 'I don't know why we're out here. The first act works. Nothing else works. What are we even *doing* here?' Don was smart about scripts, but Tom [Cruise] wanted to do the movie, really badly. That made it happen.'' For reviewers and the entertainment press, Simpson and writer Towne issued statements explaining their *Thunder* intentions. ''It is a film about the difference between courage and bravery,'' Simpson explained. ''We hoped to create a very powerful story of personal growth,'' Towne said, adding that the film's story ''becomes the struggle of a driver to replace his belief in his own infallibility with the courage of a man who recognizes that even if some things are beyond his control he must go on to face them if he is to race, to win, to live his life.''

Their comments were either too little or too late. Audiences didn't buy it. Early test screenings of the movie in Los Angeles confirmed Simpson's suspicions that the movie's third act, especially, didn't pay off. ''There was a predictability about the second half of the movie,'' production head Lucchesi would say later. The ''cards,'' the industry term for the forms filled out by ''test'' or ''preview'' audiences, were ''very bad,'' Lucchesi said. ''It's like you're doing *Ben-Hur*, and you've got five chariot races. How do you make the last two interesting, when you know Charlton Heston is going to live? The problem was inherent in the script. There wasn't a climax that was unique or thrilling, and it ultimately wasn't satisfying.''

In an attempt to correct that, the cast and crew reassembled for reshoots. They filmed a finish-line ending, with Cruise's Cole triumphant.

They also shot new footage of Cruise recovering from his injuries, attempting to demonstrate why winning meant so much to him and to show how he learned "the difference between bravery and courage." When those reshoots could not be completed in a day, Simpson brought the producer hammer onto director Scott's head, telling him he had to finish that night. Scott, enraged, threatened to walk off the picture. The scenes were shot.

The exposition didn't help. Sid Ganis would later say, "*Days* was so difficult, so painful, all the way. There was almost no story, and there was no ending. It was just cars, going around a racetrack. We shouldn't have started without a script." Ganis knew the movie wouldn't perform up to either expectation or budget. Simpson and Bruckheimer, Lucchesi thought, knew it, too. "Don and Jerry had been around a long time. They knew what was up. They knew what was coming, and there was nothing you could do about it. We threw as much money as we could at it." Paramount delayed the opening of the movie from the planned Memorial Day date, pushing it back to June 29, spending vast quantities on television advertisements to pump up opening-weekend receipts. "We tried to buy the opening, and we succeeded."

They could not convince critics, though. Reviews for *Thunder* were almost universally bad. *New York* magazine's David Denby was savage, assaulting not just *Thunder* but Cruise's other movies, *Top Gun, The Color of Money* and *Cocktail*, as well. "He is Cute and he's Great At Something (flying, racing, playing pool, mixing drinks)," Denby wrote. "But he's also Cocky, and he Shows Off. He is Reckless, Callow, Stupid. He is Out For Himself, and he Goes Too Far. He must Mature. He becomes the very soul of maturing. But it isn't easy. There is a Crisis. He is Alone, Confused, Crestfallen. He seeks a Father Figure . . ." Denby concluded: "As in every Simpson and Bruckheimer production, the movie hypes itself." The *New York Times'* Janet Maslin said, "The typical scene . . . is one that has screeching brakes, pounding drums, roaring engines, crashing fenders and someone shouting at the top of his lungs." *Box Office* called it "a minor film with major pretensions." The *Los Angeles Times'* Jack Matthews called it "a pastiche of cliches and antiquated myths." Only *Daily Variety's* Todd McCarthy and the *Washington Post's* Hal Hinson seemed to like *Thunder*. McCarthy wrote that the movie "has all the elements of a can't-miss summer box office firecracker: thrilling racing footage, as many Cruise close-ups as any starstruck fan could want, canny Robert Towne

dialog for adult viewers and another indelible Robert Duvall performance." Hinson, while observing that Cruise "as an actor, has tremendous
limitations," noted that *Thunder* was similar enough to *Top Gun* to "almost qualify as a sequel." "If *Top Gun* was a stylish bimbo of a movie, all
cleavage, white teeth and aerodynamic flash," Hinson wrote, "then *Days
of Thunder* is its paradoxical twin—a bimbo with brains."

Better reviews might have helped. After an opening weekend of $15.4
million—comparing unfavorably to rival Katzenberg's *Dick Tracy*, which
opened two weekends before at $22.5 million—and a second weekend of
$10.7 million, *Thunder* began to sink. Despite the presence of Cruise, and a
huge marketing push, it limped to just $82.7 million in ticket sales.

It wasn't only the film's poor performance that undid it, nor was it the
budget. In addition to *Thunder* and *Dick Tracy*—which would ultimately
outearn *Thunder* by almost $20 million—the 1990 Hollywood release
schedule was littered with expensive movies. *The Hunt for Red October,
Die Hard 2, Total Recall, Kindergarten Cop, Another 48 Hrs.* and *Bird on
a Wire* were released the same year, and all featured the same kinetic
combination of big budgets, big stars—Alec Baldwin, Bruce Willis, Arnold
Schwarzenegger, Eddie Murphy and Mel Gibson—and big action. The
irony: The top-earning 1990 movies were two kiddie comedies, *Home
Alone* and *Teenage Mutant Ninja Turtles;* two wildly fantastical romances,
Ghost and *Pretty Woman;* and an unlikely historical epic, *Dances with
Wolves.* Paramount counted its *Ghost* receipts golden and penciled out
profitably on *The Hunt for Red October* but had overspent and misfired
badly on *Thunder* and *Another 48 Hrs.* and had fizzled on two highly
anticipated sequels, *The Godfather 3* and *The Two Jakes,* the studio's second chapter to *Chinatown.* Richard Gere had stiffed in *Internal Affairs,* as
had Dennis Hopper in *Flashback,* Dudley Moore in *Crazy People,* Paul
"Crocodile Dundee" Hogan in *Almost an Angel,* Gene Wilder in *Funny
About Love,* Winona Ryder in *Welcome Home, Roxy Carmichael* and
Andy Garcia and Robert Duvall in *A Show of Force.* With *Ghost* and its
$217 million in domestic receipts, not a terrible year. Without *Ghost,* a
catastrophe.

"Paramount at that time was terrified of bad publicity, and they had no
ability to control these guys," Lucchesi said. "Don and Jerry had insisted
on those 'visionary alliance' ads, and the studio went along. They were at
the point where they could ask for anything and get it, so they had started
thinking up really weird things to ask for." Among those things: Simpson

had wanted Paramount to build them offices in New York, to get closer to the publishing world and thus closer to nascent book and magazine projects that had movie possibilities. Paramount had refused. "After *Days of Thunder*," Lucchesi said, "the relationship was going downhill fast."

For Mancuso, the entire "visionary alliance" episode was an embarrassment. "The 'visionary alliance' stuff was important to the talent, and we felt that we had to make the deal. In retrospect, it was a mistake. So was Don's desire to explain the deal—that all he and Jerry needed from us was our money. This was as annoying to [CEO Martin] Davis as it was to me. It was a richer deal for them personally than most deals, but it was nothing more than *a deal*. Don's statements were not factual. The deal consisted of a certain amount of money for a certain number of pictures that all had to proceed through normal channels."

Days of Thunder proved conclusively that Simpson did not have the chops to become a movie star. So he did the next best thing: He began acting like one. This, again, backfired and left him humiliated by the press.

On July 11, 1989, the *Los Angeles Times* entertainment industry reporter Michael Cieply had broken a story about a sexual harassment lawsuit filed against Simpson by a Paramount secretary named Monica Harmon. Harmon had worked under Simpson and Bruckheimer for twenty-one months in 1986 and 1987. In her civil lawsuit, filed in Los Angeles County Court on October 12, 1988, and asking $5 million in damages, Harmon alleged that Simpson had forced her to witness illegal drug use in his Paramount offices, forced her to schedule rendezvous with prostitutes, exposed her to pornographic films played on videocassette in his office and subjected her to several other kinds of physical and mental abuse.

Harmon had originally come to work at Paramount in early 1986 and soon found herself assigned to the Simpson-Bruckheimer production offices, and the target of Simpson's special tirades, which she outlined in her legal complaint. Simpson had shouted at her for putting regular milk, not nonfat milk, in his coffee—"trying to get him fat," he had screamed. He "used cocaine in his office," in the company of partner Bruckheimer and with Richard Tienken, Eddie Murphy's manager and an executive producer of *Beverly Hills Cop 2*. He "left a pile of cocaine in his office and in his office bathroom and ordered [Harmon] to clean it up before it was discovered by others." Simpson had "maintained lists of girls he used as prostitutes and required [Harmon] to keep and update these lists." He "required [Harmon] to schedule his appointments with some of the prostitutes." Simpson "played pornographic videocassettes in the office." And, "as a condition of [Harmon's] employment, [she] was required to read lurid and pornographic material." Simpson on a regular basis had called Harmon things like "dumb shit," "garbage brain" and "stupid bitch," as in, "You fucked up again, you stupid bitch. You cannot do anything right." Simpson had further reduced her to a state in which she could not sleep and suffered headaches, muscular tension and stress.

Other Simpson-Bruckheimer employees would later confirm most of Harmon's charges. Abuse was commonplace. "There was always one girl in the bathroom crying," said a former assistant. "The abuse was constant, and Monica got her share of it."[15] Simpson's tirades were inspired by surprisingly small details. If he was on holiday in Hawaii and woke up hungry in the middle of the night, according to one assistant, he would not call room service; he would wake up an assistant in Los Angeles or New York and make *her* place the order. If his food hadn't come fast enough, he'd throw it on the hallway floor when it arrived. Assistants were fired for bringing Simpson his coffee with cream in it when he was dieting, or for bringing coffee without nonfat cream in it when he was not. Assistants were fired for overtoasting the bagels Simpson ate with mustard spread on them, or for buying the bagels anywhere but the chain I 'n' Joy, or for buying any kind of mustard but the preferred French's brand. "If his bagel was toasted too much, he'd have a heart attack," a former assistant recalled. "If you got the wrong kind of mustard, you were dead. It had to be a whole-wheat bagel toasted with mustard—and it had to be French's. If someone *ate* one of his bagels, there was panic . . ."[16]

At the Regency Hotel in New York, Simpson once lambasted an entire housekeeping staff after they had returned a pair of black jeans to his room—pressed and starched, not fluffed and folded. "I asked for fluff and fold! How dare you! *Fluff and fold!*" he screamed.[17] On another occasion, when he had chartered a jet to take several friends on a fishing expedition, he chewed out the secretary who had booked the flight—because, on the return trip, the plane had encountered so much cloud cover that it could not immediately land. "He called and screamed at me about cloud cover," the secretary recalled. "Like I could do anything about that!"[18] On yet another business trip, he screamed at a secretary because the limousine she'd ordered for a New York outing had a less than pristine interior. "He said, 'You should have checked it out,' " the recipient of his abuse said.

During that same visit to New York, an assistant remembered, Simpson got upset because the window in his hotel room didn't open. "So he just threw a chair through it," she said. "He could not open the window, so he just threw a chair through it. We'd have to check out of his hotels for him, because he was too impatient, so we'd just pay for this stuff."[19] His assistants' clairvoyance must be international: He once screamed at a secretary who'd had the foresight to book Simpson an appointment at a Hong Kong health club when he was there for a film opening, but not the foresight to know that towels are not provided in Hong Kong health clubs.[20] And sometimes there were extravagant demands for extravagant services ordered on a whim—as the time Simpson, after attending a Giorgio Armani showing in Italy, suddenly felt a need for his *own* Armani sweater. He had an assistant drive to his home, pick up and pack his sweater and have it rushed to him in Rome, at a cost far exceeding the price of a new sweater at the Armani showroom, a sweater he could have owned instantly.[21]

Simpson fired his longtime personal publicist, New York's Peggy Siegal, over a similar incident. He was planning to attend the Deauville Film Festival in France, and he gave Siegal instructions: "He wanted to be rushed, upon arriving at customs, by a mob of screaming fans," Siegal said. "Well, I didn't know how to do that." Days later, laughing on the telephone with a mutual friend, the producer Larry Gordon, Siegal retold the story. It got back to Simpson, and he fired the publicist for bad-mouthing him.[22]

Otherwise, Simpson seemed to feel no embarrassment over these tirades. Nor did he make any evident attempt to hide his sexual predilections. "Don was Caligula," an assistant added. "Everyone knew he used hookers. He had a whole section of his Rolodex marked 'Girls.' They'd come to the office the next day, and Monica [Harmon] would have to pay them. This was common knowledge. His tastes were very special, and he was into S&M."[23]

One day, during the editing on *Top Gun*, several assistants were in the office with film editors Billy Weber and Chris Lebenzon. One assistant found a videocassette on Simpson's desk, labeled *Sue Beats Mary* and *Bonnie Beats Mary*. Curious, the assistant ran the video while the editors and the other assistants watched.

In the twenty-minute video one prostitute heavily outfitted in S&M gear abused another. As the scene moved from the bedroom to the bathroom—both recognizable to the assistants from Simpson's Cherokee Ave-

nue home—Simpson's voice gradually became audible, as he gave orders
to the girls between the *zzzzzp* sound of a Polaroid camera. Both Dave
"Baby Dave" Thorne and Dave "the Rave" Robertson were in the film as
well, though Baby Dave was barely eighteen years old at the time. The
production value was quite low. In the background, one assistant remembered, was playing the radio jingle from the Thrifty drugstore chain:
"Every day's a savings day, at Thrifty . . ."

Simpson-Bruckheimer and Paramount brought heavy muscle down on
Monica Harmon. Rather than, for fear of public humiliation, simply buy
Harmon's silence, they began an investigation to undermine her character,
if not her accusations. Simpson hired the legendarily rough litigator Ber-
tram Fields, of Greenberg, Glusker, Fields, Claman & Machtinger, to prepare a countersuit against Harmon, eventually filing a $5-million libel suit
against her. Simpson then hired Anthony Pellicano—the private investigator who had originally come to Los Angeles to help get accused cocaine
trafficker and famed automobile manufacturer John DeLorean off the
hook—to trash Harmon's reputation.

Pellicano flew to Minnesota and located a former Paramount employee
named Patrick Winberg. Winberg would later tell Fields, in depositions,
that Harmon was a regular cocaine user to whom Winberg had delivered
half a gram of the powdered drug on an almost daily basis; that Harmon
had snorted cocaine more than a hundred times in his presence, at Simpson-Bruckheimer and elsewhere; that Harmon had given him stolen
merchandise from Simpson-Bruckheimer films—leather jackets, caps,
T-shirts; and that Harmon had routinely hired limousines and used a
messenger service on Simpson-Bruckheimer's bill for her personal use. It
was later revealed that Pellicano had loaned Winberg $4,000 and overpaid
substantially for meals and expenses he incurred for the three days he
supplied information to Pellicano and Fields.[24]

Most of Harmon's accusations—and ultimately her entire suit—were
dismissed in court. But even Harmon coworkers who found her difficult
don't dispute the truth of her accusations against Simpson. "The charges
were all true," said an assistant who worked alongside Harmon.[25] "They
just turned the victim into the criminal." Harmon was offered settlements
of various sizes, but, wanting justice, refused them. In the end, Simpson-
Bruckheimer agreed to drop their countersuit if Harmon would go away
and remain silent. To this day, she has never spoken publicly about her
humiliation. Simpson and Bruckheimer were vindicated.

That wasn't enough to mollify Paramount or to end their embarrassment over Simpson's shenanigans. Paramount wanted change. They
started looking to shake Simpson-Bruckheimer loose. It is a Hollywood
cliché that "you are only as good as your last picture." Had *Days of
Thunder* been a hit, Simpson and Bruckheimer's future at Paramount
might have been secure. But it had not, and Simpson's behavior over the
Harmon suit and over the "visionary alliance" deal had unsettled the
studio. In combination, the details were professionally lethal.

"Our deal required the production of a certain number of films, and it
became evident that it wasn't going to happen," Mancuso would say
later.[26] "The behavior just became impossible. We couldn't manage them
anymore, and that was a problem. If you continued to tolerate the behavior, you couldn't preserve the structure of the studio. Somewhere along
the line you have to say 'stop.' We came to the conclusion that we would
be better off without them."

"After *Days*, Paramount wanted out of the deal," Lucchesi recalled. "It
was all very political. The decision from New York was, corporately, they
were making us look bad, like *we* were out of control. The 'visionary
alliance' thing did them in, and the bad publicity on *Days*, and then the
poor box-office performance. It was like, 'you let these guys look more
important than you, and then the movie doesn't perform.' Getting rid of
Simpson-Bruckheimer was a way of showing Wall Street we were in
control." Barry London, a decades-long Paramount veteran who had recently risen from head of distribution to cohead of the studio, said, "Simpson felt the film was a failure, and didn't live up to his own expectations.
He became negative, belligerent, angry. Seven years of great relationship
changed almost overnight. He and Jerry had been such a success with the
Beverly Hills Cop movies and *Top Gun*. But the 'visionary alliance' thing
put them in a whole new area. When *Days of Thunder* didn't perform, it
was over."[27]

Studio relations do not, however, end that easily. Simpson-Bruckheimer had a host of projects in development for Paramount—among
them another buddy action-comedy that would ultimately become *Bad
Boys*—and they still had years to go on their "visionary alliance" contract.
But Martin Davis began to put pressure on studio head Frank Mancuso to
move Simpson-Bruckheimer off the lot. One of the pressure points was
Beverly Hills Cop 3.

The sequel had remained in active development for years. In the fall of

1987 Simpson got excited about a piece of material from a writer named Michael Alan Eddy—a period gangster movie about the life of Bugsy Siegel. He'd tried to buy the script, but it went to 20th Century-Fox. So he had one of his creative executives, Michael London, contact Eddy about writing *Cop 3*. At first, Eddy refused, having heard that both Simpson and his *Cop* star, Eddie Murphy, were "difficult." When he agreed to finally meet with Simpson and Bruckheimer, he liked what he heard. *Cop 3* was going to take place in London, as Axel Foley chases down an international killer and, as a fish out of water in Jolly Olde England, rubs shoulders with Scotland Yard detectives just as he had the Beverly Hills Police Department in the first two movies. Comic relief was to be supplied by the bumbling John Cleese, with whom Foley would be partnered as he solves the crime. For the next year, Eddy worked at the story line and the script, getting intermittent input from Simpson—intermittent but not always consistent. "We'd have a meeting, ideas would go around, and I'd leave with the intention of pursuing a certain plotline," Eddy said. "At the next meeting an assistant would always say, 'Let me go in first and remind them what they told you at the last meeting—because they will have forgotten.' "[28] Or, worse, they'd have changed their minds. "Don gave me a book on these two London gangsters, identical twin brothers who were really nuts. He thought we could base a good villain on these guys. When I came back for the next meeting, he was surprised. He said, 'That's not what I want you to do and that's not what I said and that's not what we're doing.' It was an incredible waste of time." Near the end of his year's labors, Eddy arrived at Simpson's office to discuss new developments. He'd created an excuse for getting Foley to London in the first place: A notorious gangster is captured in Detroit, and the London authorities arrange to have him extradited to stand trial there. The ultimately fatal job of escorting the gangster falls to Foley's best friend on the Detroit Police Department, the character played by Paul Reiser in the first two films. Michael London objected before the meeting started. "He said, 'Don't do that. They love the Reiser character. If you lose him, you'll lose the [screenwriting] gig.' I said, 'No, the movie is Eddie [Murphy] and a great villain. That is the franchise—not bringing back Paul Reiser.' " Then the meeting began, and, undaunted, Eddy told Simpson his idea. Halfway through, Simpson abruptly raised his hand for silence. He said, "That's brilliant. Put it on paper, and bring it back to me, and that's where we'll go." Axel Foley was off to London.

Its star, Eddie Murphy, had since the first *Cop* made the flop *Best Defense* and the hit *The Golden Child*. Since *Cop 2* he had done well with *Eddie Murphy Raw* and *Coming to America*, scored mildly with the sequel *Another 48 Hrs.* and flopped in his directorial debut, *Harlem Nights*. He needed a hit as badly as Simpson and Bruckheimer. For the next four years, working first with Eddy and subsequently with at least seven other writers, they tried to make story sense out of draft after draft of Foley's adventures. (The extradited-gangster story line was ultimately rejected, Eddy recalled, because it was too similar to the story line for Michael Douglas' *Black Rain*, also a Paramount movie, in which a Japanese yakuza is arrested in New York and extradited to Tokyo with resulting mayhem. *Black Rain* had a green light, and *Cop 3* didn't. Simpson pulled the plug on the London idea.)

By 1990 Simpson and Bruckheimer were resisting making the sequel, and refused to pay for it out of their $300-million "visionary alliance" fund, but eventually agreed to do *Cop 3* from a script by Steven De Souza, then a hot commodity, having penned the successful action movies *48 Hrs.*, *Commando*, *Die Hard* and *Die Hard 2*. But the deal Paramount proposed, and the budget, a mere $25 million, were impossible. Mancuso, for one, was not sure there was enough life left in the franchise to justify spending more. "We had a sense of concern about how much do you spend for the third in a series. We weren't sure there was still an audience for the series, and we saw the law of diminishing returns at work. This wasn't like *Star Trek*, or the James Bond movies, or the Indiana Jones movies. This was just a Detroit cop who winds up in Beverly Hills with a couple of friends. We didn't think we should spend more on the third one than we had on the first or the second."[29] Especially if it was set in New York, a famously expensive location.

As Lucchesi recalled, "To do *Cop 3* in New York, with all that action, with Eddie getting paid $8 million and Don and Jerry getting $6 million each, for a budget of $25 million, was ridiculous. To ask it was insulting."[30]

Simpson himself called it "the politest 'fuck you' in movie history."[31] There would be a less polite "fuck you" shortly. Paramount, reviewing the receipts from *Days of Thunder*, made a request. Simpson and Bruckheimer had each been paid $9 million for producing *Thunder*. The movie had not performed. Paramount's chief, Mancuso, asked the producers to return $1 million of their fees, each, to help the studio correct its feeble *Thunder* balance sheet.

"It was despicable to renege on the deal," production executive Lance Young said. "That's not the way the industry works. Yes, it was a rich deal and, yes, they were impossible to deal with. And people here didn't think they were prolific enough, and didn't generate *Days of Thunder* on their own anyway. But forcing them to hold to that release date was suicide— and that was Frank's decision, not theirs. They never got the chance to make a good movie. Frank felt that their development was shit, and that we were never going to get anything good out of them, and that the only person who could reason with them—the only person they respected— was Ned Tanen. And Ned was leaving the studio."[32]

So, ultimately, were Simpson and Bruckheimer. They refused to return any of Paramount's money. The relationship was dead. The two producers started shopping for a new home. They found it in the unlikeliest of places. Their old colleagues from Paramount, Michael Eisner and Jeffrey Katzenberg, were now running Disney—but were bringing to the studio a new frugality entirely out of step with the kind of big-ticket, big-event pictures on which Simpson and Bruckheimer had built their reputations and made fortunes for Paramount and themselves. On January 18, 1991, a trade story in *Daily Variety* read, "Simpson-Bruckheimer Sign with Disney on 5-Year Non-Exclusive Basis." The three-page press release that Simpson and Bruckheimer created to herald their move indicated a great relief at escaping Paramount—so great, in fact, that the release, while enumerating the many hits they'd made there, did not even mention *Days of Thunder.*

And Paramount pressed its *Cop 3* campaign. Despite Simpson-Bruckheimer's new relationship with Disney, they were to be offered first crack at the sequel. They ultimately refused: Trade paper headlines on October 7, 1991, announced "Simpson-Bruckheimer Won't Do BHCop III." Desperate for a summer hit for 1993, Paramount had Simpson's agent and longtime pal Jim Wiatt take the *Cop 3* project to Joel Silver, then working on the Warner Bros. lot. Silver brought together two of the film's key elements—star Murphy and screenwriter Steven De Souza—with Murphy's *Trading Places* and *Coming to America* director, John Landis. Paramount's expectations proved too high for even the high-powered Silver. "Paramount said we need it at this budget, and we need it for summer," Silver later said. "I said, 'It cannot be done.' And it couldn't. Mace Neufeld and Bob Rehme [successful producers responsible for Paramount's earlier *Necessary Roughness* and *Patriot Games*, and later *Clear and Present*

Danger] did it, but not in New York, and not for a full year later." *Beverly Hills Cop 3* was ultimately released in 1994.

By then, Simpson and Bruckheimer were on the lot, if not on a roll, at Disney. It would have been possible for the producers to bunker down at Paramount, and probably, despite the studio's recalcitrance, make their movies. But that meant a chilly internal exile, and that wasn't Simpson's style. As he said at the time to a journalist, "I didn't come here from fucking Alaska to wind up jerking off in some office on the back lot"[33]—a fate he'd avoided for the second time in a decade, since, in 1983, Paramount had fired him as president of production. Simpson was, after all, and despite himself, not a loser. He liked to tell people he'd come up hard, in the hard-core Alaskan hinterlands, and wasn't about to be beaten by Hollywood. He welcomed adversity. "I'm a survivor," he told the *Los Angeles Times* in 1984. "I love sports because I'm a total competitor. I love head-to-head combat. Battle is a joy to me. But I've never in my life cheated in a sport. I believe unequivocally in ethics. I will not lie, cheat or steal. I'll do what I have to do to get the job done within ethical boundaries. On the other hand, I'll slit someone's wrist or throat in two seconds if they screw with me."[34]

It was tough talk, but Hollywood was a tough town. For Simpson, it would get a lot tougher.

CHAPTER SIX

WRETCHED EXCESS

"Take a look at *that*," Simpson told a visitor to his Stone Canyon home in February 1987. "I just had it framed."

To the wall of his dark study, as he pulled a vial of cocaine out of a desk drawer and began shaping the white powder into lines, Simpson directed his visitor's gaze. There on the wall was a framed photocopy of a check, from Paramount Pictures Corporation, made out in Simpson's name. The check was for $1,063,161. On the wall below it was an earlier check, from the previous October, for $1,000,000. On the wall below that was a still earlier check, for $2,013,115. The checks were partial payment for Simpson's work at Paramount on *Top Gun* and *Beverly Hills Cop*.

"Not too fucking shabby, eh?" Simpson said.[1] In case you didn't know, here was the evidence: Simpson was a very, very successful movie producer.

The checks were just a fraction of what Simpson had earned from his Paramount movies. One studio source estimated that the six movies he and partner Jerry Bruckheimer made for the Melrose Avenue studio had earned Simpson more than $40 million between 1983 and 1990.[2]

The 1980s had been good to Simpson, as they had to Hollywood and much of the rest of the country. As Wall Street burned ever hotter, making billions of dollars and household names out of individuals and companies like Michael Milken, Ivan Boesky and Drexel Burnham Lambert, Hollywood flamed. More movies were making more money than ever before, and the high-concept blockbuster had become the centerpiece to every studio. No one knew the high-concept blockbuster like Simpson and Bruckheimer. Hollywood paid them handsomely for their work and made them both rich men.

All around them friends and former colleagues were getting rich, too. Simpson's former mentor Barry Diller had left Paramount Pictures to become chairman and CEO of 20th Century-Fox, from which, in 1992, he would depart with an estimated $150 million in severance money. His former boss Michael Eisner had left Paramount at the same time, to run Disney, where he was earning a salary estimated at near $10 million and picking up stock options that would run his annual benefits to over $70 million. His former assistant Jeffrey Katzenberg, who had joined Eisner at Disney, was doing well, too, enjoying annual benefits roughly a third of Eisner's—not bad when a third means close to $25 million a year. And his friend David Geffen was doing even better, having parlayed a brilliant ear for pop music and pop stars, and a brilliant eye for investment, into a $1-billion portfolio.

Big bucks impressed Simpson. He might have been happy with his lot in life, and with his millions, but he compared himself to men far richer and found his lot in life wanting. "Don was in awe of guys like Michael Eisner, who, creatively, is a big, stupid lunk," a friend of Simpson's said. "Don was far brighter, but he had tremendous respect for these guys who had a lot of money—even when *he* had a lot of money. He was always talking about how smart Eisner was, by how much money he had, by how good he was at business. I'd say, 'Yeah, but he's a moron.' Don was very blue-collar, in essence, a real working-class guy. He never got over that."[3] Said another friend, the screenwriter Louis Garfinkle, who'd cowritten *The Deer Hunter* and for years tried to get a project going with Simpson, "He always felt intellectually inferior to guys like Eisner and Katzenberg—which was ridiculous, because he was really much brighter than either of them."[4]

Simpson framed his paychecks. Others demonstrated their newfound wealth in different ways. Diller eschewed the public limelight and lived in a tasteful, modest home in Coldwater Canyon. Katzenberg and Eisner made fat donations to charities but didn't boast about their salaries. Geffen did, about his wealth, once screaming at a reporter, "I'm a billionaire! I'm a fucking *billionaire!* I don't fucking work for anyone!"—when that reporter asked Geffen about rumors he might go into a business partnership with Diller.[5]

But Simpson wanted to do more than just show visitors his pay stubs. He wanted to be famous. That's what he had told his high school classmates he was going to do when he left his native Alaska in 1963. Early attempts to court the media and begin making a name for himself in the arts and leisure sections of newspapers and magazines were stopped when his then boss, Diller, discovered Simpson was inviting reporters to the Paramount lot and bragging about his exploits. "I put a stop to it at once," Diller would later say. "Simpson, talking to the press? We simply couldn't have it."[6]

So Simpson did the logical thing. He hired a publicist, a sharp New Yorker named Peggy Siegal. Over the next several years Siegal would make Simpson a celebrity.

From the start, Simpson's relationship with Siegal was an anomaly. Producers didn't employ publicists. Studios had their staff of publicity experts, who worked alongside the marketing and distribution departments generating positive coverage for their movies and their stars. The actors themselves often employed personal publicists, as, less often, did directors. Today, of course, even the publicists have publicists. Not in 1983.

In the spring of that year, Siegal got a call from the Simpson-Bruckheimer offices, asking for a meeting. The producers were getting set to release a movie called *Beverly Hills Cop*, but were at a loss for publicity angles. Their star, Eddie Murphy, did not want to do a press tour for the movie—and he was, anyway, not sufficiently celebrated to generate much coverage. (He was rejected for the cover of the premier issue of *Premiere* magazine.) Their director, Marty Brest, was a virtually unknown commodity and was still stinging from press reports of his firing off the feature *WarGames*. Simpson and Bruckheimer had decided they themselves would represent the film, having themselves been stung over the release of *Flashdance*, for which they felt Peter Guber and Jon Peters had claimed—and received in the press—far too much credit for creating. (Not that Guber and Peters felt they'd received proper credit, either. "Thank God I've got bank credit," Guber later complained, "because if I had to depend on screen credit, I'd be in trouble.")[7] Simpson's need for publicity would later drive his *Top Gun* and *Days of Thunder* director, Tony Scott, to hire his own outside publicist, the independent firm of Bumble Ward &

Associates. ("I was hired to represent Tony only because he couldn't get any publicity from Simpson and Bruckheimer," Ward would later say.)

Siegal, who had come to California to work alongside director Steven Spielberg, had already heard about the legendary Simpson and had witnessed him in action. The scene was a birthday party for Paul Schrader, being held in the exclusive upstairs room at the expensive Beverly Hills Chinese restaurant Mr. Chow's. It was, Siegal remembers, "a very hip crowd," a gathering that included Simpson and Bruckheimer, Penny Marshall, producer Kathy Kennedy and others. Drugs were in evidence, if only by the conspicuous, periodic absence of the diners: Schrader and Simpson would suddenly dash off to the men's room together. At the end of the long night, the waiter presented a bill for over $2,000. Simpson grabbed it and began waving his American Express card around. Remembered Siegal, "He was definitely Big Daddy. He was running the show that night and taking everyone to dinner."

At first, Simpson was an ideal client. Siegal recalls setting up lunches with magazine editors—as, one time, she did at New York's Russian Tea Room with the editors from *Esquire*. "They said, 'We'll meet, but we won't guarantee that we'll write anything,'" Siegal recalled. "But Don would be so engaging and so funny that they couldn't take notes fast enough. All we had to do was set up the meetings. Don was young and self-deprecating and funny, and he just charmed everyone." On that New York visit and others, Siegal would throw parties at places like the Canal Bar or 151 Wooster Street. She'd pack the room with New York literati, inviting the then-celebrated novelists Jay McInerney, Bret Easton Ellis, or Richard Price.

(Bruckheimer would say, years later, that the Siegal hiring was "naive." He told an interviewer, "The first thing we did when we went into business together was to hire a publicist. We didn't want somebody else to get credit for what we did. It created a lot of animosity in the press. And you know, Hollywood can be a very back-biting place.")[8]

And Siegal was also saddled with the chore of creating the Simpson-Bruckheimer presence in Aspen—a presence that, within three years, would assume an almost legendary status.

In the fall of 1985 Siegal got a phone call. Simpson said, "I've got good news, and I've got bad news. The good news is we're giving you a Christmas present. We're taking you to Aspen for two weeks, to a house on Red

Mountain, and you're gonna stay with us. The bad news is, you're going to do a party for us. And it's got to be big."[9]

Simpson was a celebutante, and Aspen was to be his coming-out.

Siegal, who had never visited Aspen, panicked. Then she called Michael Douglas, a former client with whom she was friendly. She asked him for ten names of people who were important on the Aspen circuit, and in turn asked each of them for ten names of people who were important on the Aspen circuit. "I got the one hundred most important people," Siegal said. "I got private phone numbers for Ted Kennedy and Jack Nicholson." Siegal ordered invitations printed by Cartier, begging the luminaries' presence for a December 27 event at the house on Red Mountain.

Siegal had already installed extra phone lines and fax lines. She began redecorating, to Simpson and Bruckheimer's specifications. The entire house was first draped in white muslin, reflecting the white motif of Simpson's offices. They installed dozens of small Christmas trees, decorated with tiny white lights. The furniture was wrapped with white muslin, too. And then the RSVPs started coming in. To Siegal's surprise, everyone was saying yes—from the VIPs all the way down to Simpson's personal invites. ("All he wanted was the ski instructors and the bunnies. Don was in charge of the young girls," Siegal said.) Siegal was suddenly sitting on what she called "the hottest holiday party in Aspen." So she called in carpenters, to tent the outside deck, to handle the potential overflow crowd. She rented heaters to warm the deck areas and had the deck hung with white muslin. Then she began hiring security guards because the guest list now included power names like Ted Turner and Barry Diller. Soon it included celebrities, from Goldie Hawn and Sally Field and Cher to directors like Ivan Reitman and Jim Cameron. There were even three U.S. senators—Chris Dodd, Ted Kennedy and future presidential hopeful Bob Kerey.

That night, December 27, 1985, Simpson, Bruckheimer and Siegal stood by the door and greeted more than two hundred guests. Several of the New York papers ran items about the attendees. Don and Jerry were on the Aspen map.

The following year the guest list had grown to three hundred. Simpson decided to create the look of the famed New York nightclub Nell's. The location changed, from the house on Red Mountain to the larger Jerome Hotel. The group from Los Angeles rented bigger houses as well. Simpson rented one Barbra Streisand had occupied. Friends like the ICM agents Jim Wiatt and Jim Berkus got places on Red Mountain. Bruckheimer brought in his girlfriend, and later wife, Linda Balahoutis.

For decoration, Simpson had Siegal order a shipment of overstuffed furniture from the Paramount back lot—at Paramount's expense. Siegal hired production designers to replicate other pieces. For entertainment, Siegal hired Jimmy Buffett—still hot after his 1977 ode to indolence, "Margaritaville." For coverage, many of the New York papers now sent reporters to Aspen to record the season. They covered a whopper, the biggest party in Aspen history, attracting a power list of Hollywood and Washington who's-whos—including, Siegal recalled, a group of "Kennedy cousins, like, twelve of them, who came to the door and demanded to be let in." It was a sensation. "Don had taken over Aspen," Siegal said.

The following year, for the 1988 celebration, the guest list had grown to five hundred. The Jerome Hotel looked like the site of a movie premiere. There were barricades, and security guards on horseback, and camera crews lining the streets outside. The party was to be a jointly hosted event, Simpson sharing the honors with Don Johnson, who after a separation had now returned to Aspen with Melanie Griffith. People began begging Siegal for an invitation as early as Thanksgiving, desperate to attend. There was some fighting, Siegal recalled, over the guest list. "I wanted the senators. Don wanted the girls," she said. In the end, a stellar list was assembled. Guests arrived on foot and by limousine and were corralled into the now-jammed Jerome. "Don had thrown the party with Anthony Yerkovich and Don Johnson, and *everyone* from L.A. was there—in black," recalled actress Greta Blackburn, a friend from the time. "They had spared no expense. There was great food and great champagne." And great drugs. "Every twenty minutes or so someone would disappear for a while."[10]

"All that was missing was a movie," she recalled. "Every wanna-be in America was trying to get into the party. It was like something out of *Day of the Locusts*."

It was expensive, too. Siegal estimated that Simpson had spent $25,000 of his own money to throw the party, some of that on drugs. Unbeknownst to Siegal, Simpson had flown cocaine dealer Rayce Newman in for the affair, to supply the guests with top-grade rocket fuel for the holiday ride. Again, the party was a sensation—but for the wrong reason. Midway through the festivities, Johnson asked for silence and announced his reengagement to Griffith. The press reports the following day did not even mention Simpson.

"He was furious," Siegal said. "He was screaming, 'I spent $25,000 on a fucking engagement party!' "

It was the last Simpson would host there. Though he would return every winter to ski, with friends Yerkovich or Dr. John Korzelius, or with director pals Michael Mann or Rob Cohen, he stopped throwing parties. Nevertheless, he had helped create the mystique that defines the Colorado ski town to this day, and placed it firmly on the map as *the* place to be for the winter social season.

"We did that," Siegal would say later. "We ruined Aspen. Just ruined it."

Simpson might have been excused of some of his megalomania if only because there was so much megalomania around for him to imitate. The 1980s, particularly, saw a dramatic escalation of star salaries and a vast expansion of spoiled star behavior.

Sylvester Stallone asked for and received a Gulfstream jet valued at $12 million, from Carolco Pictures, for his work in the movie *Rambo 3*. Within a short period of time, actors of similar stature were asking for similarly huge paychecks and perks. Within several years, the comic actor Jim Carrey would be asking for, and receiving, $20 million to do Columbia's *The Cable Guy*. Stallone would be promised $20 million per picture, for three pictures, from the upstart—and soon defunct—Savoy Pictures. By taking short money up front in exchange for a huge slice of anticipated profits for the Universal Pictures film *Twins*, Arnold Schwarzenegger would earn an estimated $35 million. Jack Nicholson's deal to play the Joker in Warner Bros. *Batman* netted him an estimated $50 million. For the third installment in that Warner Bros. franchise, Schwarzenegger would earn a reported $25 million in straight salary, for working six weeks in the role of Mr. Freeze. The summer before, Tom Cruise had been paid at least $20 million for his starring role in Paramount Pictures' *Mission: Impossible*. Later that year the Hollywood trade papers would report that Mel Gibson, who had just won an Academy Award for directing the Best Picture winner *Braveheart*, had turned down a $30-million offer from Warner Bros. to star in the fourth installment of the wildly successful *Lethal Weapon* series. Sources said at the time that Warner was considering upping the offer to $35 million. When the deal was finally made, in the summer of 1997, Gibson's guaranteed take-home pay on the movie was reported at $40 million.

As salaries rose, so did the value of the accompanying perks. At the release of the ultimately unsuccessful Steven Spielberg drama *Always*, the principals involved in the film received trendy Mazda Miata coupés as thank-you gifts. When Paramount Pictures' drama *The Firm* cracked the $100-million mark at the box office, the principals received Mercedes coupés valued at $100,000 each. Actors and producers on Warner's *Lethal Weapon* received less expensive but more fashionable Range Rovers.

Sometimes, of course, stars actually bought expensive toys with their own money. According to a June 1997 *Robb Report*, Schwarzenegger spent $38 million on a private Gulfstream. That summer, he and his wife, Maria Shriver, used the jet to fly from Los Angeles to Austria, where a soccer stadium was being named after the actor in his hometown of Graz, in celebration of his fiftieth birthday and as part of the worldwide marketing campaign for his costarring role, as the villainous Mr. Freeze, in the June release *Batman and Robin*.[11] (He was already driving the town's most expensive off-road vehicle, a customized Hummer estimated to have cost over $100,000.) He wasn't the only actor obsessed with expensive cars. Nicolas Cage was reported to have spent $285,000 on a Ferrari.[12] Nor was he the only jet-setter with his own jet. By the mid-1990s they were an important fashion accessory for powerful people—and the size, speed and cost of the jet were very specific measures of the degree of powerful people's power. Las Vegas financier and studio owner Kirk Kerkorian, who'd emerged into power from a successful background in aviation, had long owned a private plane, and that may have set the tone for his predecessors. The Gulfstream was the jet of choice through the end of the 1980s, those players with a Gulfstream III considered more serious than those still flying the Gulfstream II. When the Gulfstream V was introduced in 1997, the company began taking names—and nonrefundable $2-million deposits—for the waiting list. The GV would cost $26 million and, unless he changed his mind and forfeited his deposit, MCA's Edgar Bronfman Jr. would have the first one off the assembly line. David Geffen, who reportedly sold his Gulfstream IV upon partnering up to form DreamWorks, in 1995, with Steven Spielberg and Jeffrey Katzenberg, was also on the list. So was Spielberg. So was Roy Disney, who often flew from Los Angeles to his country home in Ireland, and who would now be able to do so nonstop, on one tank of gas. So was Time Warner, and so were sixty-five other individuals or corporations eager to take advantage of the jet's new flight range (it could make Los Angeles to London or Los Angeles to Tokyo without a refueling stop) and new flight altitude (it cruised at 51,000).[13]

Jets seem to bring out the spoiled baby in other stars as well. When the Planet Hollywood restaurant chain needed cofounders Bruce Willis and Sylvester Stallone to fly to Cancún to support the opening of a Planet Hollywood there, "flying them down on a scheduled airline wasn't even an option," according to one report.[14] The club owners chartered *two* private jets. Stallone flew south with his bodyguard and a Los Angeles golf pro, at a cost of $60,000. Willis and wife Demi Moore flew from New York, at a cost of $80,000.[15]

During the New York segment of the production of *Mary Reilly*, its star, Julia Roberts, had producing company TriStar keep a jet standing by twenty-four hours a day, on the off chance that the actress might suddenly have a crushing need to be in Los Angeles.[16]

John Travolta outdid that. For the Paris-based filming of director Roman Polanksi's *The Double*, Travolta insisted that producing company Mandalay charter *his* private jet to ferry him to France, and then maintain it on twenty-four-hour readiness at an airport near the set. The actor, who was being paid $17 million for his performance, also insisted that Mandalay ship to the set an entourage of more than twelve assistants, among them security guards, chefs, physical trainers and a massage therapist. He also forced Mandalay to ship his own personalized RV to Paris to function as his trailer. Mandalay agreed to do all of this—and then got snubbed when Travolta had "creative disagreements" with Polanksi and walked off the film.[17]

Even commercial airliners, though, aren't immune from star behavior, though some stars show more sensitivity to the *hoi polloi* than others. According to one report, when Mel Gibson needs to fly home to Australia for a visit, he simply books the entire first-class section, so that he and his family can have their required privacy.[18]

Perks often involved petty demands. Sylvester Stallone, for example, arrived in New York to do press interviews in support of the film *Demolition Man*. Upon inspecting the suite in which the interviews were to be conducted, the star balked—at the color of the walls in the room. They were a pale yellow. The actor refused to be photographed against pale yellow. He would only be photographed against peach. The interviews had to be delayed long enough for the entire suite to be repainted.

The actress Demi Moore—so demanding a star that her nickname in Hollywood is Gimme More—was meant to fly from the Idaho home she shares with actor-husband Bruce Willis to New York, in order to attend a premiere and help support the release of *A Few Good Men*, the military courtroom thriller in which she costarred with Tom Cruise and Jack Nicholson. Columbia Pictures arranged to send a jet, owned by corporate parent Sony, to pick Moore up in Idaho. It arrived. The crew waited while Moore made her way to the airport. She arrived late, after the crew had been on the ground for several hours. The crew packed Moore's luggage. Just before takeoff, the star required something she had packed in a bag. Upon inspecting the luggage, Moore demanded that her bags be removed instantly. She was upset that they had been placed on top of each other in the cargo hold, not side by side, and was nervous that some of her things would be wrinkled during the flight. It was pointed out to her that the cargo hold was too small to carry her large collection of luggage any other way, but Moore insisted—and demanded that, if Columbia wanted her in New York, they simply send a larger jet. Columbia capitulated.[19]

On another occasion, while doing voice work for the animated Disney film *The Hunchback of Notre Dame*, Moore balked at the scheduling of a recording session, saying that it conflicted with her plan to attend a PTA meeting at her child's school. The studio offered to arrange Moore's transportation from the Burbank lot to the PTA meeting and agreed to finish Moore's session by the stated hour. When that hour arrived, Moore was horrified to discover the studio had arranged only for a limousine. She had neglected to tell the studio that her PTA meeting was in Idaho.[20] The studio was forced to hire a private jet, at an estimated cost of $4,500 per hour, to get Moore back to the ranch.[21]

According to one report, Moore led the league in prima donna perks, billing the production of *The Scarlet Letter* $877,000 in "entourage costs." Close behind were Julia Roberts, who billed *I Love Trouble* an estimated $841,000, and Melanie Griffith, who billed *Born Yesterday* $589,000.[22] According to the same report, Moore demanded the studio make available two jets and a helicopter, to transport her and her personal entourage of cooks, assistants, trainers, nannies and drivers to an appearance on *The Late Show with David Letterman*.

Another Columbia star from the same period was also famous for preposterous demands—and for having them met. In December 1992 the movie star and *Prince of Tides* film director Barbra Streisand visited Washington, D.C., to attend the inaugural festivities for recently elected President Bill Clinton. She was met at the airport by a limousine, which drove her to her hotel. When shown the suite of rooms that had been reserved for her, Streisand asked whether they were the largest set of rooms in the hotel. She was told they were not; there was one suite, not as nice, that was slightly larger. Streisand demanded to be moved into those rooms but was told they were already occupied. Streisand insisted the current tenants be evicted. She was told that was impossible: The current tenants were the mother and father of the First Lady–elect, Hillary Rodham Clinton. "I don't care," Streisand screamed. "Get them out or I will stay in another hotel." The concierge, to his credit, offered to help Streisand find another hotel.[23]

(Streisand was also furiously protective of her screen credits. Weeks after the opening of *Prince of Tides*, while the diva was vacationing in Aspen, friends from Los Angeles told her that a hedge on Sunset Boulevard was obscuring part of her *Tides* billboard—not the title of the movie or Streisand's name, but her "Directed by" credit at the bottom. A livid Streisand rang a Columbia executive at 7:00 A.M. on New Year's Day and said, "It's Barbra! My name is in the bushes!")[24]

Television stars, too, seemed bent on behavior big enough to suit their reputations. Roseanne Arnold, as she was then known, forced assistants on her hit ABC show, *Roseanne*, to push her around the stage in an overstuffed chair, so she would not have to stand and walk to different parts of the Disney soundstage between takes.[25] The famously abusive Roseanne once axed a member of her writing staff, a young woman who had dared compare a piece of dialogue in a *Roseanne* episode to dialogue in Shakespeare's *The Merchant of Venice*. When the Ivy League–educated writer had finished her comparison, Roseanne snarled at her, "You . . . are . . . so . . . fucking . . . fired." (That same line of dialogue would wind up accompanying Glenn Close's firing of Michael Keaton in the film *The Paper*.)[26] Roseanne had earlier become outraged to discover that her then husband's parking place was occupied by someone else's car. She had her staff learn the identity of the driver. The car belonged to *Seinfeld* star Julia Louis-Dreyfuss. Roseanne wrote an abusive note to the errant Louis-Dreyfuss, addressing it to "Julia Louis-Drycunt," and posted it on the car in question.

Spoiled film stars were not a novelty in Hollywood. From the early days of film, its most celebrated celebrities were well paid, and they spent flamboyantly. In 1920 comedian Roscoe "Fatty" Arbuckle signed a deal with Paramount Pictures worth $3 million a year. He drove a custom-made Pierce-Arrow that cost $25,000.[27] In the late 1920s a star like Gloria Swanson could boast to the public that her annual clothing bill included expenses of $25,000 for fur coats, $50,000 for gowns, $9,000 for stockings, $10,000 for lingerie, $5,000 for purses and $6,000 for perfumes. With other clothing expenses, her total annual layout was $125,000—a large chunk of her $900,000 annual salary.[28] Swanson, quoted in *Hollywood Babylon*, explained, "In those days the public wanted us to live like kings and queens. So we did—and why not? We were making more money than we ever dreamed existed and there was no reason to believe it would ever stop."[29]

Nor was it only the stars who were spoiling themselves or making others spoil for them. Sony's studio head, Peter Guber, for example, built a private stairway from his Stone Canyon home, down the hill to the exclusive Bel Air Hotel, so that room service meals could be delivered more quickly to his residence at 15433 Brownwood Place. Guber spent vast sums of Sony money refurbishing the home until it resembled a Japanese palace, adding touches like a guesthouse, tennis court, four fireplaces, two spas and a projection room. It also included a "flotarium," described in its owner's manual as "the Rolls-Royce of floatation tanks."[30]

Sony had hired Guber in 1989, along with partner Jon Peters, to run its Hollywood studio operations. The vastly overpaid executives—who cost an estimated $1 billion to hire out of their contracts at Warner Bros. and were paid an annual salary of $2.9 million[31]—used vast quantities of Sony money to refurbish the company's Culver City lot. According to documents published by veteran reporters Nancy Griffin and Kim Masters, furniture purchased to decorate the studio included a 1780 French cherry-wood desk that cost $12,400, a $26,000 Chippendale writing table and a $26,000 mahogany linen press.

The two executives also used large sums to amuse themselves. Peters once filled a corporate jet with fresh-cut flowers and flew it to New York to impress a woman he wanted to date—reportedly the international supermodel Vendela.[32] The adventure ended badly. The Sony jet Peters sent to New York had been promised to Bruce Willis, who was intending to use it to visit his wife on the set of the Columbia film *Mortal Thoughts*. The studio had to spend a sudden $50,000 to hire another plane.[33]

Guber spent on his house. As part of a 1992 contract negotiation, Sony agreed to buy the now refurbished Brownwood home from Guber for a reported $5.5 million. The Japanese company later dumped the home, selling it in 1996 for $2 million, for a cash loss of $3.5 million.[34]

In 1989 Guber had purchased a $4.5-million oceanfront home in Malibu and spent heavily to transform the 3,661-foot residence into what was described as a "Japanese showplace."[35] He also bought a twenty-two-acre ranch in Aspen, Colorado, which he transformed into a similarly spectacular showplace, importing llamas and reindeer and airlifting boulders for decoration.[36] His partner, Jon Peters, attempted to spend $22 million to buy a Santa Barbara ranch and hotel.

Nor was it just at home that Guber indulged himself. He spent an unknown sum of money to purchase and outfit *Sea Oz*, a 110-foot yacht that featured a full-time captain and staff of four, with an on-board Jacuzzi and Jet Skis. On holidays Guber would fly pals down to wherever the boat was moored—as he did one Martin Luther King Jr. weekend, when Columbia's Barry Josephson and CAA's Jay Moloney jetted to Puerta Vallarta.[37]

Sometimes the star excess was wildly childlike, as when actor Charlie Sheen spent $6,537 to purchase all 2,615 seats behind the left-field fence at Anaheim Stadium in order to improve his chances of catching a home run ball at an Angels-Tigers game.[38] Sometimes the expenses were petty, as when film director and former child star Ron Howard insisted that his limousine be stocked with chocolate chip cookies and a pitcher of *cold* milk.[39] Sometimes they were outright silly, as when actor Billy Crystal spent his own money to replace a bathroom in his home with an exact replica of an airliner bathroom, complete with the cramped space and amenities like tissues, tampons and barf bags.[40]

Sometimes—as was occasionally the case with Simpson—the expense was more chilling. Simpson once proposed to his friend the private investigator Anthony Pellicano the creation of an "antijournalists fund." Angered by what he thought were unfair accounts in the press, Simpson proposed that he and fourteen other prominent show business personalities pool $1,000 each "to protect ourselves from journalists trying to write shitty stories about us," he explained. The money would be used to hire

Pellicano, or attorney Bert Fields, "to push the envelope and push the limits of litigation and investigation," Simpson said, "to do whatever necessary to cause trouble for whatever reporter is making trouble for us."[41] The "whatever necessary" part could get very personal. In one instance, fearing a story from a crusading reporter, Simpson had Pellicano investigate. He discovered the reporter had once had domestic violence charges brought against him by his wife. Simpson told Pellicano to threaten the reporter with a public exposé of the charges unless he dropped his story about Simpson.

Another similarly targeted reporter had a similarly unpleasant experience. While reporting on the impending Heidi Fleiss scandal and her possible connection to officers at Columbia Pictures, the reporter told a Columbia source, "From now on, when I call, I am going to use the name Ted Williams. Don't speak to anyone who calls using my name. I'll *only* call as Ted Williams." Within days the reporter had a call from Pellicano, who, after making several charges and threats, said, "By the way, that's a stupid name to use. Ted Williams is a stupid name." The reporter was convinced that Pellicano could only have learned his code name by listening in on his telephone calls.[42]

Simpson's lifestyle was an expensive one. When he bought his Stone Canyon home, in 1991, he paid $4 million and immediately began a reported $1.5-million renovation. A previous home had just gone on the market for $7.75 million, but Simpson had already vacated that property. During the renovation, he lived in a third house, rented for a rumored $10,000 a month.[43] Entertainer-entrepreneur Merv Griffin would subsequently achieve a greater sale for his chunk of Bel Air real estate, selling it in 1997 for $8.5 million, the most ever paid for a Southern California home site. It wasn't as much as it might have been, though. The house was up for sale, on and off, for eleven years, and in 1989 had an asking price of $25 million.[44] In that same year, Barbra Streisand bought an 8,000-square-foot, five-bedroom estate on six acres of Beverly Hills property for a reported $5.5 million. The home, built in the 1930s for film director King Vidor, had been occupied over the years by bright lights from the music business, among them singer-songwriters Stephen Stills and Mac Davis and Broadway composer-lyricist Jerry Herman. Streisand bought the home from actor Richard Harris. In June 1997 she sold it to a London-based businessman relocating to Beverly Hills, taking a loss of a reported $4.9 million. (The well-housed Streisand also maintained a large compound in the Santa Monica mountains, and a home in nearby Holmby Hills, valued at $7.5 million.)[45] On the day that Streisand's sale was announced—in a widely read *Los Angeles Times* column known as "Hot Properties"—there was also the news that producer Joel Silver had purchased four acres of open land in Brentwood and that screenwriter Daniel Waters, who'd written Silver's Sylvester Stallone vehicle *Demolition Man* and Silver's Bruce Willis vehicle *Hudson Hawk*, had purchased the home of the late Orson Welles for $1.2 million.[46]

Not all Hollywood luminaries were so lucky in their real estate ventures. Peter Bogdanovich, the Academy Award–winning director of *Paper Moon* and *The Last Picture Show*, filed for bankruptcy in Los Angeles Superior Court, after a jury levied against him a $4.9-million fine for reneging on a $1.9-million purchase of a Mulholland Drive house high above the Hollywood Hills. The plaintiff's attorneys in the case disputed Bogdanovich's claims of poverty, asserting that the director and his wife were driving matching Mercedes-Benz convertibles, that Bogdanovich's wardrobe was worth $67,000 and that he paid $250 every time he got his hair cut. Bogdanovich's attorneys countered with the statement that "a certain standard of living is necessary to be taken seriously as a player in Hollywood"[47]—an assertion that Simpson would certainly have supported.

Simpson could not compete in the renovation arena, either, where the prize for the 1980s went to television impresario Aaron Spelling and his wife, Candy. While framing their $45-million home in Holmby Hills—at 52,500 square feet, it would be Los Angeles' largest residence, and include four bars, three kitchens, a movie theater, a gym, an indoor Olympic-size pool, eight double-car garages, a bowling alley, a wine room, a doll museum and an elevator[48]—Mrs. Spelling wanted to observe the view-to-be from her bedroom window. Spelling's contractors hired a crane and lifted her to approximately the position her bedroom window would ultimately occupy. She was horrified, one contractor later reported, to discover that the view from her window included the green neon sign advertising Beverly Hills' Robinson's department store. Her husband first attempted to get the department store to move or remove the sign; they refused. So the Spelling contractors were ordered to destroy the home's foundation, excavate soil, and lower the entire structure ten feet. The cost of thus improving Mrs. Spelling's view was estimated at $60,000.[49] (Not to be outdone, David Geffen in 1990 spent hideously to acquire the home, property, and belongings once owned by mogul Jack Warner, for a reported $47 million—a price that would hold for almost a decade as the highest amount ever paid for a California residence.)

Simpson was keen enough on his redesign project that he had scale models of the house and grounds built and delivered for inspection. The model was so detailed, in fact, that it contained not just a model swimming pool, and not just a selection of patio furniture surrounding the pool, but also tiny model girls, nude, on display poolside.[50]

Living in the house, once Simpson occupied it, was a costly proposition. Copies of Simpson's household accounts show an annual "flowers and decorations" bill of $12,077.05 for 1989. Dry cleaning bills for the same year totaled $11,886, and for the following year ran to $10,499.85. In 1993, records show Simpson paying a Westside florist a weekly fee of $325 to provide flower arrangements around the house, one each in the bathroom, office, powder room, kitchen and guesthouse, three in the dining room and two in the living room. His annual bill from that florist, for flower arrangements alone, was $11,650 for 1993. Simpson also demanded an array of glossy magazine publications, which he read almost religiously, and which assistants were instructed, very specifically, to arrange in a fan pattern on several coffee tables. One former assistant said that, as part of her duties, she had to drive to the Universal newsstand in Hollywood every morning to pick up magazines. Some mornings she would purchase as many as sixty individual titles and deliver them to Simpson's home.[51]

Other decorations were vastly more expensive. In the late 1980s Simpson began collecting art. Over several years he would pay "far more than was necessary," according to one dealer, for works from Ed Ruscha, Robert Mapplethorpe, David Hockney and others. He was especially fond of the Mapplethorpe photographic portraits of female bodybuilder Lisa Lyons.[52] (The auction house Sotheby's sold paintings from the estate following Simpson's death, fetching $58,075 for four Richard Diebenkorn prints and $69,450 for two works by Eric Fischl. Two other Fischl works, valued at roughly $8,000, did not sell.)[53] Simpson also overspent on automobiles, which he subsequently complained he could not get rid of without taking a loss.[54]

There were also the clothes. Simpson, who had been voted "Best

Dressed" among fellow students in high school, was a dandy who indulged his taste for finery with his customary obsessiveness and a total absence of shame. In 1990 Simpson told a *GQ* interviewer, "I wear boots, Levi's and a T-shirt with a leather jacket or Armani with the collar up or a cashmere six-button double-breasted jacket—blue or black, depending on my mood. That's the uniform." He chronicled his forty pairs of cowboy boots, which he claimed to design himself, boasting that the best were made from deer. He mentioned that when he traveled he always booked a suite with two bedrooms. "One I sleep in, one is my closet," he said. Boasting of the "fourteen-inch difference between my chest and my waist," he said that Giorgio Armani designed a personal Simpson "prototype," for single-breasted and six- and four-button double-breasted suits. "The first time I went through the [Armani] book, I chose fifty-seven suits," he said. "Thirty-one were available, so I bought them." Rising to fantastic heights of delusion and self-importance, Simpson added that Giorgio himself had insisted on designing a special Simpson tuxedo. "He made a six-button with satin peaked lapels," Simpson said. "One of a kind. Equivalent of a Lamborghini. A cross between Adolphe Menjou and Clark Gable." He then confessed to his interviewer that he was even obsessive about his off-the-rack Levi jeans—which he would routinely purchase, wear once and discard. Calling this "my luxury in life—the way I use my vast fortune," Simpson explained: "because I'm a legitimate 29/32, and they shrink about a half inch when you wash them—which makes them a half inch wrong. Also the color drops off just that much. I like black to be what I call technical black. I can afford it. One time only, and they're out. In my house I've got a stack with the tags on them. Got to have the tags on them. Because I don't believe anyone if they say they're new unless they have the tags."[55] (Simpson would subsequently deny ever having said anything about tossing once-worn jeans and insist that the *GQ* reporter had simply invented the story.)

Simpson also spent lavishly on vacationing. A typical week at his be-loved Canyon Ranch could run to $3,350—not counting the cost of personal hikes, massage sessions and other extras—and Simpson often stayed at the ranch for ten or twelve weeks at a time. (He tipped hiking guides a customary $100 a week, according to one ranch employee.)[56]

For vacations, Simpson liked macho activities. Over the ten-year period from 1984 to 1994, he undertook at least seven extended manly holidays with his chums—fishing in Alaska, hiking in Hawaii or river rafting down the mighty Colorado. (Tom Cruise got a bad dunking on one visit, Jeffrey Katzenberg a nasty near-drowning on another.)[57] Photos from the Alaska trip show a burly, bearded and *beaming* Simpson, wearing a fishing vest, and surrounded by pals Bruckheimer and Katzenberg, director Rob Cohen, agent Jim Berkus and studio executive Tom Pollock. (Two guides, not identified, are wearing *Top Gun* gimme-caps.) In no other existing photograph of Simpson does he look happier or more at ease.

Ski trips, too, were minutely planned and very expensive. According to personal memos created by a Simpson assistant, a seventeen-day trip to Aspen that began on December 17, 1993, was nonstop amusement. A selection of Armani suits was packed in one bag, which was accompanied by six more, including a "running bag," containing personal items like prescription drugs, ski wear, money orders, $6,000 in cash and two wristwatches. A town car from a limousine company owned by friend Jeff Welles would arrive to scoot Simpson from his home to Burbank Airport, where he would board a Lear jet (a Lear 4, tail number N664C1) for the one-hour, thirty-seven-minute flight to Aspen. There another car would take him to the Little Nell Hotel, to an executive suite which his assistant had already stocked, according to Simpson's instructions, with "Chivas, Dom Pérignon, Stoli, gin, tequila, Bacardi, Absolut and Molson Light," as well as a Christmas tree, wreath and associated decorations. (On most occasions, according to sources, Simpson rented a house, usually a subdued, five-bedroom, Santa Fe–style "corporate house" on Red Mountain—at a cost of $25,000 a week.)[58] Days one and two were skiing with pal Paul Ruid, an ex-professional skier—at a cost of roughly $200 a day—and dinner at the trendy Chanin's or Abetone's. Every evening included a massage from local therapist Billy Lucchesi, at a cost of $75 for the massage and $25 for the tip. Days three to five were skiing with Ruid and Los Angeles friends Hawk Wolinsky or Dr. John Korzelius. Dinner might be across the table from Jann Wenner, at Mezzaluna, Piñons or Renaissance. Friends in town through the holiday would include partner Bruckheimer and his girlfriend Linda, and the wealthy movie mogul Ted Field, and Simpson's retainers. ("He always had an assistant trailing after him, taking care of his business, and there were always five or six people staying at the house—another assistant, a private chef, and some others," remembered Lucchesi, who gave Simpson massages at home.)[59] The rented car for the period had to be a Jeep Wrangler or Jeep Cherokee, and it had to be black or, failing that, navy. Newspapers had to be delivered daily, from

Explorer Bookstore, and they had to be *USA Today*, the *New York Times* and the Sunday *Los Angeles Times*. The rented skis had to be either Salomon 9E 2S or Equipe 900 rented from Aspen Ski Mart. (The cost of Simpson's locker at Ski Mart was $500.) Christmas night was to be a private party. New Year's Eve was to be spent at billionaire Marvin Davis' traditional bash at Little Nell.

According to massage therapist Lucchesi, Simpson would begin the week hard-charging the slopes, skiing his first several days from 8:30 A.M. to at least 4:00 P.M. "He was totally obsessive and totally committed," Lucchesi said. "When he'd come off the slopes, he'd be in so much pain it was almost impossible to touch him. But he'd be up the following day, and I'd see him again that evening." This regimen typically lasted only a week, though. "He'd always come down with something like 'the flu,' " recalled Lucchesi, who treated Simpson each season for eight or nine years in the late 1980s and early 1990s. "I think it was a combination of the skiing and the nightlife. He partied pretty hard."[60]

If Simpson spent heavily on himself, he was also terribly generous with family and friends, who told story after story of Simpson's unstinting charity. He gave one girlfriend a Bulgari cigarette lighter, when they'd known each other only a week. When he had known her a month, the girlfriend said, "He had someone from Valentino bring the entire collection to his office at Paramount, just to help me pick out a few things." At Christmas there were $400 gift baskets sent to associates and employees past and present.[61] Even casual acquaintances typically received a large freshly cut pine Christmas wreath. (This is an industry where casual gifts are as often meant to humor, or insult, as flatter. Then-CAA head Michael Ovitz, displeased with a recent trade story, sent *Daily Variety* reporter Anita M. Busch a large bottle of MSG, after learning that Busch was deathly allergic to that Asian flavor enhancer.[62] CAA agent Jay Moloney sent a flask of liquor to his friend Barry Josephson, a production executive at Columbia Pictures, to console him for the anticipated poor showing of Columbia's bomb *Last Action Hero*, with a note attached: "You're going to need this."[63]) Former employees recall at least two round-the-world cruises Simpson insisted his father and mother take, in the company of five or six of their friends each time. According to several reports, Simpson sent his brother, Lary, through law school, paid the private school tuition for his niece and nephew and even paid for his sister-in-law's triathlon training costs.[64]

In late 1994 Simpson also spent to acquire that most fashionable of celebrity fashion accessories, co-ownership of a celebrity restaurant. He took an unknown percentage stake in his friend Anthony Yerkovich's Buffalo Club, a Santa Monica bar and restaurant.

Arnold Schwarzenegger had already opened his Schatzi, as had Robert DeNiro his Tribeca. Simpson's pals Steven Spielberg and Jeffrey Katzenberg had opened their splashy Dive! Bruce Willis, Sylvester Stallone, Demi Moore and others had lent their celebrity to the Planet Hollywood chain. Harkening back, perhaps, to a time when some of Hollywood's most powerful names had pooled their money to turn Dominick's Diner—a quiet hangout where you could catch the Lew Wassermans dining—into their own private restaurant, Simpson was helping create a home away from home for himself.

The Buffalo Club was modeled somewhat on the famed 1970s industry watering hole Ma Maison, and outfitted with only the finest appointments—real leather booths and banquettes, antique beveled mirrors, oak wainscoting and brass lamps.[65] Like its predecessor, it was appropriately exclusive. (When chef Patrick Terrail opened Ma Maison, he actually issued a press release to announce that his bistro would have an unlisted telephone number.[66] What is the point of being exclusive, after all, if the hoi polloi don't know they are being excluded?) Yerkovich, the creator of TV's Miami Vice series, played a similar ruse on the rubes. He shared the club's telephone number only with his fellow investors and with industry powers who were natives of the Buffalo, New York, town that gave the restaurant its name—among them Murphy Brown creator Diane English and NYPD Blue cocreator David Milch.[67] Anyone dialing 411 for directory assistance, as late as June 1997, would be given the name of a clothing store with the same Buffalo Club name. (For the record, the correct number is 310-450-8600. The address is 1520 Olympic Boulevard.) With renowned chef Patrick Healy, of St. Germaine, Champagne and Xiomara fame, serving classic American cooking—haute cuisine versions of downhome dishes like pork chops, roast beef, chicken potpie, pot roast and macaroni and cheese—the Buffalo Club was soon among the Westside's trendiest nightspots, and one of the few public places where Simpson felt comfortably at home. And why not? He could see Quentin Tarantino, who'd helped write his Crimson Tide, across the room. He could see his friend Warren Beatty there, too. On other nights he might have seen Kato Kaelin or Heidi Fleiss, who were also occasional diners.[68] His whole world was right there. Whether it returned on his investment, however, was doubtful: By mid-1996, food critics were reporting that the club's exclusive policy was being relaxed and that most nights showed no better than a half-capacity crowd.

Simpson's tendency to excess took many forms, not all of them in the realm of conspicuous consumption. He was, among other things, excessively direct.

The director Steven Soderbergh, in 1989, was the hottest flavor-of-the-month in town. His independent film *sex, lies and videotape* . . . had swept the Sundance Film Festival. Soderbergh was contacted by *Rolling Stone* magazine and asked to submit to an interview for inclusion in their annual "hot" issue. While being interviewed, Soderbergh had received a phone message saying that Simpson and Bruckheimer wanted to meet with him. He scoffed at the message and called the two producers "slime that barely passed for human." The *Rolling Stone* reporter jotted this down and later included it in the Soderbergh profile.

Soderbergh got a call from his agent, who told him that Simpson and Bruckheimer wanted a sit-down. He went, rather nervously, to visit with the producers at their Paramount office. A "very gracious" Simpson, Soderbergh recalled, said to him, "We do not know you. We have not worked with you. If you had worked with us, that would be one thing. But you haven't. So why are you slagging us in the press?" Soderbergh— whose impressions of Simpson and Bruckheimer were based entirely on Lynn Hirschberg's *Esquire* profile of Simpson in 1985—immediately apologized and said, "You're absolutely right. It wasn't fair." For the next thirty minutes the three men talked about movies. The incident was never mentioned again.[69]

Simpson was also excessively competitive. When he took drugs or alcohol with friends, he'd often insist on proving he could take more of both than they could. "He'd be like, 'Two lines? I'm doing *ten* lines, motherfucker," one friend remembered. "If you took a shot of tequila, he'd guzzle half a bottle."[70] On trips to the Grand Canyon, Simpson would insist on footraces from the rim of the canyon to its base two miles below. In the company of friends Jeffrey Katzenberg and actor Tony Danza, Simpson would usually rush into the lead, run until he was out of sight and then sit to rest on a rock. When Katzenberg and Danza caught up,

Simpson would suggest that they, too, sit down for a rest. As soon as they did, he'd dash off again and invariably win. (Danza was also competitive—perhaps too competitive. One of these overheated races landed him in the hospital for a potentially life-threatening case of dehydration.) At Canyon Ranch, where Simpson retreated for detox and physical self-improvement, his behavior on the hiking trials was so competitive that other guests would refuse to hike with him. "He'd always insist on going on the advanced hikes, and he always had to be in the very front, even though he wasn't physically fit enough to do it," recalled a Canyon Ranch regular. "He'd fall back, panting and wheezing, and then rush ahead during the rest breaks. He *had* to be in front. Usually, on a long hike, you hit a point where you mellow out. You lose your tension and your stress, and you shift down. He never shifted down. He never lost this furious, intense desire to win, even on a seven- or eight-hour hike."[71] The Canyon Ranch regulars hated this. "He was the epitome—as a successful man, as a representative of Hollywood, as a male animal—of the kind of person who made your skin crawl," one ranch habitué said.[72] In Aspen, Simpson was a terribly competitive skier, often challenging the ex-Olympians he'd hired as instructors to race him down the slopes—and often winning.[73]

Competitiveness is practically an art form in Hollywood and is practiced there in unusual ways.

The screenwriter and author John Gregory Dunne reported that, during a dinner conversation with Michael Eisner, he mentioned that he, like Eisner, had recently undergone bypass surgery. "Of course, mine was more serious," Eisner shot back.[74]

Once, when I myself had occasion to telephone Michael Ovitz on the day the death of CAA client John Candy was announced, I began by saying how sorry I was. "I got the first call," Ovitz said, apropos of nothing. "I was the first one they called." On another occasion I was first to tell Ovitz that his client Hugh Grant had been arrested the night before, for engaging in an act of public lewdness with a prostitute. "It is not true," Ovitz said, and then asked me to hold. When he came back, he said, "How much more do you know? Was he with a *man?*" (At least he did not have to take the same call, and ask the same question, after Eddie Murphy was caught picking up a transsexual—when the question would have been much more difficult to answer. By then Ovitz had moved from CAA to Disney, and was no longer responsible for clients' misbehavior.)

Competitiveness meant trying to lease the largest yacht at the Cannes

International Film Festival. It meant lying about your movie grosses, in order to trump the competition for the weekend box-office report. In Simpson's case it meant being the most excessive rebel in a town full of excessive rebels—even when winning that competition threatened to undermine his health and his sanity.

Competitiveness also meant an increasing anxiety about box-office performance—as if he and Bruckheimer had set the bar too high, and now had to be concerned, with every release, that they could cross it one more time.

And, early on, Simpson worried about his own excessiveness—even as, in excess, he continued to put his own personal bar ever higher. One source remembers that Simpson was terribly upset at the news of the 1982 death of the legendarily excessive *Saturday Night Live* comedian John Belushi, who died in a room at West Hollywood's Chateau Marmont after taking a massive injection of illegal narcotics. "We were all at a birthday party for Michael Eisner, and it was all Simpson could talk about," a friend and colleague from the time said. "It was almost as if he saw his own death in that."[75]

CHAPTER SEVEN

THE PICTURES GOT SMALL

On January 18, 1991, almost exactly one year after announcing their "visionary alliance" with Paramount Pictures, Simpson and Bruckheimer left the Melrose Avenue lot. Around them, the industry was in flux. The Japanese electronics giant Matsushita was completing its $6.1-billion buyout of MCA, copycatting rival Sony by purchasing a movie and television studio, film libraries, record companies and affiliated businesses, following Sony's move from electronic hardware into the "software" side of the entertainment and information industries. Simpson's former colleague Sid Ganis was leaving his berth at Paramount for a new position under Peter Guber and Jon Peters at Sony's Columbia. At Warner Bros. the ink was drying on deals to bring Mel Gibson to the Warner lot for a *Lethal Weapon* sequel, and to make another *Batman* movie with director Tim Burton. 20th Century-Fox's Macaulay Culkin comedy *Home Alone*, which Warner had declined to make because they thought writer-director-producer John Hughes' budget of $18 million was too high, had been the number one movie in America for twelve straight weeks and had earned over $380 million at North American box offices. The National Association of Theatre Owners, at their annual ShoWest convention in Las Vegas, was preparing to name Hughes Producer of the Year, an honor Simpson and Bruckheimer had themselves enjoyed several times.

Retreating across the Hollywood Hills to Burbank, Simpson and Bruckheimer signed a nonexclusive, five-year deal with Walt Disney Studios and took up residence in the famed Animation Building, where for decades Walt's pen and ink masters had created some of the happiest images in film history.

The Burbank lot was not a happy place. The studio's legendary penury and the iron rule and meddlesome micromanagement practiced by Simpson's former Paramount colleagues Michael Eisner and Jeffrey Katzenberg cramped creativity and made Disney, for many filmmakers, the lot of last resort. It had been that for Simpson and Bruckheimer, whose high-flying style scared off most film executives. 20th Century-Fox, now under the control of Simpson's former Paramount boss Barry Diller, had made a show of interest in bringing the pair to its Pico Boulevard lot, but did not make a serious offer. No other studio seemed willing to foot the duo's overhead or pay for their increasingly expensive movies. But Simpson and Bruckheimer needed a refuge, and a release from their contract at Paramount, and for P.R. reasons they needed it fast. But they may not have been all that happy to make their new home Disney, a studio called, by those who toiled there, Mauschwitz.

The unhappiness at Disney stemmed in part from a growing crisis affecting the entire movie industry. For years, through the 1960s and 1970s, the theatrical motion picture business had been one of diminishing returns. Studios succeeded or failed principally on their ability to produce a steady stream of television product. By the mid-seventies, though, that was changing, as a new audience of baby boomer children began to fuel movie industry growth. The releases of *Billy Jack* in 1971 and *Jaws* in 1975 had taught the industry two new lessons: that a national marketing campaign, even on the grassroots level, could create a hit; and that a huge national release could return immediately on a big investment. Soon the growing teenage audience was making enormous hits out of lowbrow entertainment like *Animal House, Porky's* and *Star Wars*. Eisner and Katzenberg had ridden the wave successfully. After taking over the filmed entertainment divisions at Disney in 1981, when Disney was almost out of the picture business and controlled a feeble 3 percent of the domestic film market share, Eisner and Katzenberg were by 1989 beating all comers, controlling that year an industry-best 14 percent market share. In 1990 that rose to 16 percent. In 1992 it rose again, to 19 percent. The mid-1980s saw Disney churning out, factory style, one high-concept comedy hit after another, from *Down and Out in Beverly Hills* to *Ruthless People* to *Three Men and a Baby* to *Honey, I Shrunk the Kids*. (More serious filmmakers stayed away from the micromanaging Disney, with few exceptions. Martin Scorsese earned reasonably good box-office and critical acclaim for his Paul Newman/Tom Cruise drama *The Color of Money*, a quasi-sequel to Newman's earlier, and more brilliant, *The Hustler*. Director Peter Weir had teamed the wacky comedy of Robin Williams with serious lessons about young adulthood in *Dead Poets Society*. Barry Levinson achieved almost universally good reviews, and earned almost zero box office, for his Baltimore history lesson *Tin Men*. But there the parade of serious filmmakers ended.) Pushing the envelope on animation, Disney had scored brilliantly with the live action/animation mélange *Who Framed Roger Rabbit?* and had broken box-office records turning a sordid small study of a Hollywood prostitute into a preposterously glitzy fairy tale called *Pretty Woman*.

Disney had also, along with the rest of the movie industry, gorged itself on the rising flood of new money being generated by the home video market. In 1980 only 2.4 percent of American households had videocassette recorders in them. By 1991 more than 70 percent of American homes had a VCR. Sales of prerecorded videos rose from 3 million cassettes in 1980 to 269 million in 1991.[1] The rental business had grown accordingly. The major studios, though they had been slow to recognize the future importance of the videocassette side of the business, were making a fortune from this newfound ancillary market. Dozens of new companies had sprung up and grown fat on the new revenue—especially upstart independents like De Laurentiis Entertainment Group, Atlantic Releasing, Yoram Globus and Menachem Golan's Cannon Films, Avenue Pictures, Vestron, Hemdale and others.

In 1986 Simpson had told writer Mark Litwak, in an interview for Litwak's book *Reel Power: The Struggle for Influence and Success in the New Hollywood*, "Hollywood is a boom town at the moment. There's a lot of money to be made, and a lot of action. There's a lot of opportunity. I have never seen it like this."[2]

Against the background of that boom, though, were rising signs of disaster. The costs of making and releasing movies were accelerating at an alarming pace. The average expense for creating a motion picture in 1980 was $9.3 million, and the average cost of marketing and advertising it was $4.3 million. By 1991 the cost of making the movie had almost tripled, to

$26.1 million, as had the cost of marketing it, to $12 million. The inflation of movie theater ticket prices could not keep pace, and the sheer number of tickets being sold was not rising.[3] Hollywood was spending more and more to create a product that, to the consumer, was not increasing in value or appeal. Worse still, there were more and more movies being made. This ceded control of the movie business to the theater owners, who could dump a movie after its first weekend, and replace it with another, if it wasn't, in the parlance of theater owners, "putting butts in the seats." The pressure was on: Studios and producers had to deliver hit movies, movies that would "open" big on their debut weekend, or die. A film, said producer Robert Evans, "is like a parachute jump. If it doesn't open you are dead."[4]

By 1991, as Simpson and Bruckheimer were setting up shop at Disney, the boom was going bust. The video business had flattened. Many of Hollywood's high-flying independents had gone broke. And Eisner and Katzenberg seemed to be losing their edge. Alongside hits like *Pretty Woman* and the animated *The Little Mermaid* were high-concept, fish-out-of-water stiffs like *Big Business, Spaced Invaders, Taking Care of Business, The Marrying Man, Green Card, Gross Anatomy, Oscar* and *One Good Cop* and failed action movies and thrillers like *Shoot to Kill, D.O.A., Firebirds, Run, An Innocent Man, The Rocketeer* and *Deceived.* Having taken a financial bath on *Billy Bathgate,* Disney also tanked with turgid dramas like *Stella, Where the Heart Is, The Good Mother* and *Blaze.*

The losses were expensive. Documents published subsequently show that Disney's 1991 Dustin Hoffman film *Billy Bathgate* cost the studio a stunning $55.9 million in pure losses. *Blame It on the Bellboy* lost $10.8 million. The next year, Disney would lost $18.9 million on *Passed Away* and a remarkable $42.8 million on the musical *Newsies.*[5]

Their competition was struggling as well. Columbia Pictures and its sister, TriStar Pictures, had hits with *City Slickers* and *Terminator 2* and moderate success with *The Prince of Tides* and *Hook* but suffered losses on utterly forgettable titles like *Men of Respect, Mortal Thoughts* and *Return to the Blue Lagoon.* Paramount broke the $100-million barrier with *The Addams Family* but lost big on disappointments like *Frankie and Johnny,* which paired Al Pacino and Michelle Pfeiffer to total audience indifference. 20th Century-Fox's *Sleeping with the Enemy* creaked to $101 million, leaving in its wake substantial losers like *Only the Lonely, Dying Young,*

Dutch and *Naked Lunch,* as well as the expensive failures *For the Boys* and *Grand Canyon.* Universal Pictures' *Backdraft, Cape Fear* and *Fried Green Tomatoes* performed well, as did not the flubs *King Ralph, The Hard Way* and the expensive animated sequel, *An American Tail: Fievel Goes West.* Warner Bros., Disney's chief rival and the industry leader for 1991, had a real hit with *Robin Hood: Prince of Thieves* and moderate success with Oliver Stone's *JFK* but lost on flops like *Switch, Showdown in Little Tokyo, Strictly Business, Born to Ride, If Looks Could Kill, Guilty by Suspicion* and the bizarre John Candy/Dan Ackroyd comedy *Nothing but Trouble*—titles that drained production money and did nothing to enhance Warner's bottom line.

Formulaic filmmaking, at Disney, worked best. The bonehead *Ernest* movies *(Ernest Goes to Camp, Ernest Saves Christmas, Ernest Goes to Jail,* etc.) were steady, low-risk revenue suppliers that would prefigure later dumbbell comedies featuring actors like Pauly Shore. The animated features from Disney's ample library performed well at the box office and drove strong sales and rentals in video, and earned vast revenues from sales of licensed merchandise. And remake rights acquisitions deals for several French comedies, such as *Three Men and a Baby, Three Men and a Little Lady,* and *Three Fugitives,* all based on previous Gallic releases, scored well stateside. (The more ambitious *Paradise,* based on the French film *Le Grand Chemin,* was a notable failure.)

But Eisner and Katzenberg's upward curve was flattening. In 1985 Disney had released only eight films, and two, *Fantasia* and *101 Dalmatians,* were rereleases. By 1990 Disney was releasing seventeen films; a year later, the studio released twenty titles. Their animated movies, new and old, were all strong performers, as Katzenberg and Roy Disney pumped fresh funds into the animation division and scored huge hits with *Beauty and the Beast* and *Aladdin* and the rereleases *The Jungle Book, 101 Dalmatians* again and *Pinocchio.* The live-action films, though, were faltering. Katzenberg's high-concept concept, learned at Simpson's knee, was creating more misses than hits. The 1991 release schedule, as Simpson and Bruckheimer were arriving, included flops like *True Identity, V. I. Warshawski, Scenes from a Mall* and *Wild Hearts Can't Be Broken.* The slate for 1992 looked even worse, riddled with unpromising titles like *Blame It on the Bellboy, Straight Talk, Noises Off, Passed Away, 3 Ninjas, Captain Ron, A Stranger Among Us, Crossing the Bridge, The Gun in Betty Lou's Handbag, Sarafina!* and *Muppet Christmas Carol.* (None was expensive to make, but the average box-office earnings for those films was only $12.7 million.) Movies in production for 1993 included appalling losers like *Aspen Extreme*, *The Cemetery Club*, the Nazi-era musical *Swing Kids*, *Father Hood*, *Money for Nothing* and *A Far Off Place*, none of which would earn enough to cover its marketing costs.

Katzenberg's program was failing—and he knew it. On January 17, 1991, only days before Simpson and Bruckheimer were to join him on the Disney lot, word appeared in *Daily Variety* that Katzenberg had been circulating a "white paper" to top executives. An excerpt of the paper, containing references to Simpson and Bruckheimer, appeared in *Daily Variety* that day. Two weeks later the trade paper printed the entire, remarkable document—a twenty-eight-page memorandum entitled "The World Is Changing: Some Thoughts on Our Business."

It was a cry of alarm. Katzenberg felt that Disney and most of its competitors had lost their way, and, entering an economic downtown, faced serious consequences should they not heed the warning signs. "Since 1984, we have slowly drifted away from our original vision of how to run our movie business," Katzenberg wrote.[6] "Once we had a fairly strict and pretty successful strategy, which was referred to as our 'Singles and Doubles Philosophy' "—a reference to Katzenberg's penchant for hitting solid "base hits" with his movies, rather than overspending in an attempt to hit "home runs." "At some point, we seemed to have replaced it with a strategy that might best be called the 'Yes, But Philosophy' . . . as in, 'Yes, he's expensive, but it's a great opportunity for us' or 'Yes, that's a lot to spend on marketing, but we have too much at stake not to . . .' " Pointing an accusatory finger at his competitors, and repeatedly congratulating himself on previous hits like *Pretty Woman* and *Dead Poets Society*, Katzenberg noted the box-office failures of high-concept, star-driven, can't-miss movies like Universal's *Back to the Future 3* and *Havana*, Paramount's *Another 48 Hrs.*, Warner Bros.' *Bonfire of the Vanities* and Simpson-Bruckheimer's own *Days of Thunder*. These movies, he wrote, were the result of "what happened when the blockbuster mentality got its true test."

But the principal cause of Katzenberg's alarm appeared to be his own recent movie *Dick Tracy*, which had since its release the previous summer earned just over $100 million. Katzenberg, in retrospect, believed making the movie had been a mistake. "By every rational measure, it was a success," he wrote. "It topped $100 million in domestic box office, sold millions of dollars of merchandise, and was by all accounts a cultural event. Nevertheless, having tried and succeeded, we should now look long and hard at the blockbuster business . . . and get out of it."[7]

For Simpson and Bruckheimer this was disaster. Katzenberg's sea change created a climate in which the large-canvas "event" pictures, which had been Simpson and Bruckheimer's signature movies, were off the program—and they had been on the lot less than three weeks. In the instantly controversial memo, Katzenberg named the two producers and defended Disney's new (nonvisionary, it seemed) alliance with them. "Some might think this runs counter to the sentiments being expressed in this memo. Nothing could be further from the truth. Don and Jerry are among the best and most responsible producers in the business. I know that the 'conventional wisdom' holds that they can only make giant big budget movies. As usual, the 'conventional wisdom' is wrong."

This was no palliative for Simpson. "Disney just wasn't in the big movie business," he complained. "That *is* our business."[8] Katzenberg, asked years later about the producers' fallow period, admitted, "The agenda at Disney fluctuated, and these guys got caught in the crunch."[9]

Over the two years that followed, Simpson griped, Katzenberg and Disney would reject as too expensive dozens of projects Simpson and Bruckheimer had first shot at producing—among them such subsequent hits as *Presumed Innocent, Disclosure* and *Apollo 13.*[10]

Katzenberg's penury should not have surprised Simpson. Almost immediately upon arriving at Disney, he and his partner got a taste of the studio's tightfistedness. The producers installed their massive C-shaped desk in their first-floor offices, then asked the studio to install bathrooms on the premises. Unlike most studio buildings, the Animation Building did not include such executive facilities, and Eisner balked at the expense. Simpson had the bathrooms done anyway, in dark marble, and billed the studio. He would often take visitors for a tour. "Jesus, Don," Eisner complained afterward. "Now *everybody* wants bathrooms." "Michael," Simpson reportedly responded, "you just don't understand about bodily functions."[11]

In another sense, Simpson should have been gratified by the Katzenberg memo, for it dramatically resembled a similar white paper he had helped oversee ten years before, as a production executive, at Paramount.

In 1979 and 1980, with assistance from Katzenberg and David Kirkpatrick, who would later briefly rule Paramount after Eisner and Diller left the lot, Simpson crafted a "Paramount Corporate Philosophy" paper. It was designed to chronicle the hard lessons he and his bosses had learned in their years together and to guide the company through the years ahead. The document is perfectly Simpsonian in its bluntness, crafted in the unapologetic, direct language spoken by his superiors, and expressing in stunning clarity the one seldom-spoken truth that is the primal essence of Hollywood.

"The pursuit of making money is the only reason to make movies," the document announced in its opening salvo.[12]

"We have no obligation to make history. We have no obligation to make art. We have no obligation to make a statement. Our obligation is to make money, and to make money, it may be necessary to make *history*. To make money, it may be important to make art, or some significant *statement*. To make money, it may be important to win the Academy Award, for it might mean another ten million dollars at the box office. Our only objective is to make money, but in order to make money, we must always make entertaining movies."

Encapsulating the basics of the high-concept theory developed at Paramount, and demonstrating the degree to which Simpson's cynicism about the picture business had overtaken him, the document continued: "A powerful *idea* is the heart of any successful movie. The creative premise is what first attracts people to the product . . . A good idea is one that seems imaginative, original, and in some way new and unique. The power of the biggest blockbuster movies is that they come from out of nowhere and break new ground. In many cases, a compelling idea may not be strictly original, but it will seem different and exciting for its time. The most distinctive quality of a strong concept is that it does not seem familiar."

The appropriate star or cast is important, too, the document argued, as are the contributions of the film's writer and director. But all concerns are secondary to concept. "A creative writer can also apply his talents to greatly enhance an idea that would have otherwise been only mildly interesting. It is almost never the case, however, that a beautifully written screenplay will be successful if the fundamental premise of the movie is not in some way new and different." Likewise, "In many instances the director can virtually make or break a particular story. A poor director can also destroy what could have been an excellent motion picture. Despite the talents of the director, the success of a movie is still unlikely if the basic concept of the film lacks a spark of uniqueness."[13]

"The memo was all Simpson's work," recalled Tom Wright, a production executive who worked below Simpson at the time. "This was what he'd learned from the movies he made happen—*Trading Places*, *48 Hrs.*, *An Officer and a Gentleman*. If you looked in the studio 'redbook' "—a ledger used to keep track of projects in development and production, where each title was accompanied by the initials of the executive responsible for it—"they're all his. He made the concepts work and he made the movies work. He was the visionary. That's why he was tolerated. Why else would [Paramount] put up with his crap?"[14]

According to sources, Eisner used Simpson's document to complete his own—a forty-page treatise posted November 1, 1982, entitled, after his own initials, "MDE Philosophy." Recasting Simpson's ideas, Eisner wrote, "Every movie we release must have some aspect that distinguishes the project and gives it a 'reason for being.' Without exception, this criteria [sic] must also apply to every project we put into development, and to every negative pick-up we acquire"—this last a reference to movies made elsewhere but purchased for distribution by the studio. "The most important reason for being is the creative premise of the movie. The demand for an interesting and imaginative idea should be the first, second, third, fourth and fifth criteria in deciding to commit to any project. The only way to stay on the road in making successful movies is to do whatever is necessary in each particular case to realize the best creative material."[15]

Eisner went on to pat his studio on the back for taking creative risks with movies like *Ordinary People* and *Reds* and for having faith in Steven Spielberg when his *Raiders of the Lost Ark* looked like an expensive long shot. He also criticized himself and his executives for failing to see "the larger conceptual picture of 'Goldie Hawn Meets the Army,' " as Eisner called it, a high-concept screenplay for the movie Paramount rejected before it turned into the hit *Private Benjamin*. Eisner patted his "Golden Retriever" Katzenberg on the head, applauding his ability to obtain rights to books, novels, plays and magazine articles, through his "consistent contacts with agents, writers, producers, directors and virtually anyone who might have a good idea." But he also added a stricture that Katzenberg might have better heeded during his subsequent days at Disney, when his studio seemed to have been paralyzed by the rising cost of doing business: "Do not make the movie because the deal is good," Eisner wrote. "Don't let a low budget justify the material. A smart creative team will never let a low budget excuse deficiencies in the material. There is no such thing as no risk."

In the recycled version published in 1991, Katzenberg almost *sounded* like Simpson, from whom he had learned so much. "There should be a sympathetic protagonist who goes through some transforming experience with which the audience can relate," Katzenberg wrote—echoing Simpson's screenplay notes on projects like *Flashdance, Top Gun, Days of Thunder* and even the early *An Officer and a Gentleman*. "Despite all the hype and promotional noise, in the end the public will search out the movies it wants to see," Katzenberg continued. "And these films, more often than not, will be primarily based on two elements—a good story, well executed. In the dizzying world of moviemaking, we must not be distracted from one fundamental concept: *the idea is king.*"

This was pure Simpson, though Katzenberg did not credit him. He gave honors instead to his Disney boss, Eisner. "One of the most misunderstood and misused phrases in the Hollywood lexicon is 'high concept,' " he wrote. "The phrase was introduced by Michael for internal use by creative executives at Paramount as a guide for evaluating ideas. It embellishes the concept that 'idea is king.' "

In fact, Katzenberg's new outlook, though lacking focus, was only anticipating a reality to which the entire industry was gradually awakening. "Event" motion pictures, within a decade, would become mandatory and would eventually dwarf—in their expense and their scope and their box-office performance—everything else on the big screen. Audiences, increasingly jaded by the star-driven action movies of the 1980s, would demand increasingly pumped-up entertainment. With producers like Larry Gordon, Joel Silver and Simpson and Bruckheimer setting the industry standards for excitement, a spoiled audience expected more. They had been weaned on Silver's *Commando* and *Predator,* and the Silver-Gordon teamings *48 Hrs.* and *Die Hard,* and the Silver/Richard Donner production of *Lethal Weapon,* and Simpson-Bruckheimer's *Beverly Hills Cop* movies. Audiences demanded big stars—Stallone, Schwarzenegger, Gibson, Willis—and huge action, and they weren't easily satisfied. Several trips to the lucrative action-comedy well came up dry, as Silver learned with Carl Weathers in *Action Jackson,* Patrick Swayze in *Roadhouse,* Andrew "Dice" Clay in *The Adventures of Ford Fairlane,* Bruce Willis in *Hudson*

Hawk and *The Last Boy Scout,* Denzel Washington in *Ricochet,* Sylvester
Stallone in *Demolition Man* and, after teaming Stallone with Antonio
Banderas, *Assassins.* All were disappointments. Others would learn the
same lesson, with movies like Gibson's *Bird on a Wire* and Schwarzenegger's *Last Action Hero.*

Katzenberg, spooked in part by his own big-budget *Dick Tracy,* imper-
fectly understood the problem. He determined that potential high-yield
pictures weren't worth the risk, and determined to concentrate on
midbudget movies—films that cost under $20 million and did not include
big stars at big-star salaries.

Katzenberg's own track record would demonstrate his failure to properly estimate audience desires. Disney over the next few years churned out
record numbers of these midbudget movies, dominating market share but
failing to send any one film into large profitability. Around him, other
executives were squirming, too. Tom Pollock, then the head of Universal
Pictures, determined in 1994 that, as he put it then, "The $20-million John
Hughes comedy is murdering the motion picture business."[16] That filmmaker had brought 20th Century-Fox an enormous hit with the Macaulay
Culkin comedy *Home Alone,* having earlier made profitable movies out of
teen fables like *Pretty in Pink, Ferris Bueller's Day Off* and *Some Kind of
Wonderful.* But then he'd hit a bad patch, grinding out comedies—*The
Great Outdoors, Uncle Buck, Career Opportunities, Dutch, Only the
Lonely, Dennis the Menace* and *Curly Sue* among them—that cost too
much to make and returned too little at the box office. They didn't have
expensive stars, or costly action sequences or special effects, but they had
names (John Belushi, John Candy, etc.) who demanded midrange salaries,
and enough gags to drive the budget north of $20 million. Pollock at the
time predicted a coming schism in motion picture economics: Studios had
to roll the dice on action epics (as he would do with the catastrophic Kevin
Costner movie *Waterworld,* which eventually cost $175 million to make)
because audiences demanded it. But they also had to maintain costs on
smaller pictures to under $10 million, because accounting demanded it.

It would take another half-decade for the creative community to get the
point—and cry out against it. Following a year at the box office and at the
Academy Awards in which big-budget studio entertainments like *Twister*
and *Independence Day* dominated business while low-budget independent
movies like *The English Patient, Secrets & Lies, Shine* and *Slingblade*
dominated the Oscars, filmmaker Steven Spielberg complained, "I think

that we're at DefCon Three now," a reference to the submarine emergency situation made famous by Simpson-Bruckheimer's *Crimson Tide*. "It is getting to the point where only two kinds of movies are being made, the tentpole summer or Christmas hits or the sequels, and the audacious little Gramercy, Fine Line or Miramax films. It's kind of like India, where there's an upper class and a poverty class and no middle class. Right now, we're squeezing the middle class out of Hollywood, and only allowing the $70 million-plus films or the $10 million-minus films. And that is going to spell doom for everyone."[17]

A short time later, Katzenberg's successor, Joe Roth, would almost completely reverse the Katzenberg order, cutting the number of releases by half, eschewing most of the "singles and doubles" low-budget comedies that Katzenberg adored and committing his studio to large budgets on movies like Mel Gibson's *Ransom*, Bruckheimer's *Con Air* and the Bruce Willis vehicle *Armageddon*, from *The Rock* director Michael Bay—at an estimated cost of over $100 million. A *Los Angeles Times* interviewer concluded, "Roth believes Disney can derive its best return on investment by making big, star-driven, adult-oriented movies . . ."[18] Katzenberg was repudiated.

Simpson and Bruckheimer had generally made movies at a cost, avoiding superstar actor salaries, among other things, by declining to hire superstar actors. Tom Cruise was a relatively fresh and inexpensive face when they cast him in *Top Gun*, as had been Eddie Murphy when they hired him for *Beverly Hills Cop*. While at Disney, though they would court Warren Beatty and Brad Pitt for *Crimson Tide*, they would hire Gene Hackman and Denzel Washington for that movie, TV's Will Smith and Martin Lawrence for *Bad Boys* and Sean Connery and Nicolas Cage for *The Rock*. Big names and serious actors, yes. Superstars like Schwarzenegger, Stallone, Willis or Gibson, no.

By 1996 the trend was irreversible, as movies costing in excess of $70 million—*ID4, Twister, Mission: Impossible, Daylight, Cutthroat Island*—became an industry standard. By 1997 the trend appeared to be out of control. The year started with Universal's volcano disaster film *Dante's Peak*, released at a final budget of $115 million. By April, Fox had its own lava epic out, with *Volcano*, at a reported cost of $85 million. The successful Jim Carrey comedy *Liar, Liar* cost $65 million, thanks in part to the $20 million salary paid its star. The action movies *The Saint* and *The*

Devil's Own cost $80 million and $90 million, and resulted in staggering losses. The summer slate included a $70-million *Alien: Resurrection*, a $104-million sequel in *Speed 2: Cruise Control*, a $100-million price tag for *Starship Troopers* and the biggest-budgeted movie ever—the $200-million-plus James Cameron historical action epic, *Titanic*.

Simpson had helped create a monster.

For two years at Disney, Simpson and Bruckheimer struggled and failed as producers: They produced nothing. Despite promising starts on several projects in development—the pair always had between twenty-five and forty projects at various stages of incompletion—they could not convince Disney to pull the trigger and authorize a budget. (Nor could they come to terms with Paramount over *Beverly Hills Cop 3*. The Hollywood trade papers announced on October 7, 1991, that the project was moving forward without Simpson and Bruckheimer on board. It would subsequently be produced by the team of Mace Neufeld and Bob Rehme. Its 1994 release caused scant reaction at the box office.) "At Disney, all of a sudden he's hearing the same mantra he heard at Paramount," said Gary Lucchesi. "Joel Silver and Dick Donner are making these huge *Lethal Weapon* movies at Warner Bros. and getting paid off in Range Rovers. It drove Don crazy."[19] Remembered Bonnie Bruckheimer, Jerry's ex-wife, who also had a deal with her partner, Bette Midler, on the lot, "They were used to a different way of doing business."[20]

As their projects languished, Simpson and Bruckheimer grew restless. For the first time in their ten-year partnership, they sought official representation with a talent agency. (Jake Bloom, their attorney, and their ICM friends Jim Berkus, Jim Wiatt and Jeff Berg had been the partners' unofficial representatives in the past.) Following what were termed "informal conversations" with Creative Artists Agency since late 1990, when their relationship with Paramount was souring, Simpson and Bruckheimer in April announced that they would henceforth be guided by CAA's Robert Bookman and Jack Rapke. (Bookman, the pipe smoker, and Rapke, the cigar smoker, were two of the agency's most senior men, both highly regarded if not as envied or feared as the agency's cofounders and undisputed leaders, Michael Ovitz and Ron Meyer.) Simpson explained the move not as a cry for help but as "a function of Jerry and me expanding our business."[21] They were acquiring material rapidly and expected to begin production soon on any number of films. "We're expecting to get twelve scripts in over the next eight weeks," Simpson said. Among those they intended to make were the Denis Leary black comedy *The Ref* and the Dana Carvey/Jon Lovitz action-comedy *Bad Boys*.

In the summer of 1993 they fulfilled that first promise, as *The Ref* went into production. For *Bad Boys*, they failed—but not without coming close.

Bad Boys was meant to be a raucous, irreverent action-comedy designed for *Saturday Night Live* veteran comedians Lovitz and Carvey. Arguments over salary, however, ended as the actors' window of availability closed. That wasn't all that had upset the deal. Several sources indicated that, in his eagerness to seal Carvey and Lovitz, Simpson arranged for a wild two-day trip to Las Vegas. It is not known what, exactly, occurred, but by the time the weekend was over, the movie was, too. According to one source intimate with Simpson, "Let's just say Don scared the shit out of Dana Carvey, and the deal was off."[22] According to another studio source close to the movie, even before the Vegas weekend, the relationship between star and producer was rocky. "Their personalities are supplementary," the source said. "Carvey is a shy, twerpy little nerd, with a lot of hostility. The only way to deal with him is to sit on a couch and let him take over and start performing. You have to be the audience. Well, Simpson was *never* the audience. He dominated. Carvey felt intimidated by him."

Bad Boys had started life as a script by George Gallo. Simpson's friend James Toback was brought in to rewrite and was paid $120,000 a week for six weeks. Future *NYPD Blue* cocreator David Milch was brought on to rewrite Toback. Salary discussions drove Carvey's fee to $2 million. But for Simpson the end was in sight. He knew that Paramount was planning a sequel to *Wayne's World*, in which Carvey had costarred with his *SNL* partner Mike Myers. Simpson told Toback, "If he decides that *Wayne's World 2* is going to make a lot of money, we're dead." Carvey did, and Simpson was: Carvey left the project before it ever had a completed script.

But Simpson had a second plan. He told Toback, at least two months before Carvey walked, "In the long run, we may end up doing what I did on *Beverly Hills Cop*—and take it black." According to Mark Canton, who was head of Columbia Pictures at the time, it was *he* who conceived, along with his lieutenant, Barry Josephson, the idea of casting black actors in *Bad*

Boys. Canton said he had come to Bruckheimer when it appeared that Carvey and Lovitz were not going to work out, and said to him, "If you can get it out from Disney, we'll make it with you in a more interesting way." Katzenberg got wind of this plan and asked Canton, "Why do you want to buy this? It's a piece of shit."[23] Canton's Columbia colleagues had similar ideas. "We wanted to do something with Will Smith and came up with this idea of pairing him with Martin Lawrence," Canton recalled. "We wanted to keep the cost down and figured it at $22 million. But the geniuses at [Columbia parent company] Sony thought we were insane. They said the movie would gross something like $14 million." Canton and Josephson, with help from Simpson and Bruckheimer, eventually convinced Disney to let the movie go, and the Sony suits to make the budget happen. Smith and Lawrence were cast.

But Disney was eager to get some kind of movie made, any kind of movie, to offset Simpson-Bruckheimer's overhead costs. Weary of *Bad Boys*, Katzenberg demanded the pair concentrate on *The Ref*, which ultimately starred Denis Leary, Kevin Spacey and Judy Davis. It was the kind of job Simpson and Bruckheimer could have done in their sleep—and, in effect, that's how they did it. The wry comedy—about a thief who takes refuge in the home of an argumentative couple and inadvertently becomes prisoner to their marital battles—impressed some critics but attracted few viewers, and sank without making a dent at the box office.

Simpson and Bruckheimer were unconcerned by the failure of *The Ref*. They were more concerned with their own projects—concerned, sometimes, to the point of obsession. One of their obsessions was *Dharma Blue*, an original idea Simpson had concocted, a thriller about the federal government's forty-year cover-up of UFOs. Simpson had bought the rights to *Out There*, a book by former *New York Times* reporter Howard Blum, about the possibility of real UFOs. Pairing those rights and his original idea, Simpson approached the superstar scriptwriting team of John Gregory Dunne and Joan Didion. The pair were growing increasingly frustrated by Disney's inability to come to terms with their script for the movie that would become the Robert Redford/Michelle Pfeiffer drama *Up Close and Personal*. They welcomed a break, and a fresh paycheck, and agreed to meet with Simpson and Bruckheimer, in New York, to discuss the project.

In his nonfiction account of the making of *Up Close and Personal*, a wry look at Hollywood called *Monster*, Dunne writes that in late February

1992, when Simpson and Bruckheimer had been at Disney just a year, the two producers and the two screenwriters met at a lavish five-room suite Simpson had rented at the Regency Hotel. After initial discussions, it was agreed that *Dharma Blue* would be a cross between *All the President's Men* and the political thriller *Z*—"a kind of paranoid extraterrestrial *JFK*," Dunne wrote later.

Dunne found Simpson an agreeable producer. Over the coming months, he supplied his new writers with vast quantities of material on UFOs, through which Didion and Dunne sifted at a suite in the vast, pink Beverly Hills Hotel as they sorted out a story line. Their cast of characters included an "over the hill reporter," "an Edward Teller clone," the clone's daughter, "an organic chemist, and the love interest," "a gay physicist who had lost his security clearance because of his homosexuality—or perhaps had not" and a "genius prodigy scientist who at age sixteen had invented his own argon laser but had turned into a UFO crackpot." The writers consulted with their friend the novelist and screenwriter Michael Crichton about things like "string theory" and "orthogonal dimensions," to make their dialogue sound scientifically informed. They made a short presentation to Simpson and Bruckheimer, who proposed to meet with them again in New York in ten days.

There followed one of Simpson's infamous memos. This one was thirty-eight pages long and included the following paean: "Regardless of the plethora of comments I will make about logic and structure and motivation, Joan and John have done a superb job already as regarding what's implied in terms of 'talent,' 'texture' and 'mise-en-scene.' " ("We were not sure what that meant," Dunne wrote, "if anything.") Didion and Dunne absorbed the thirty-eight pages and met with Simpson and Bruckheimer, again, at Simpson's palatial Regency Hotel rooms. "When the meeting began to run into dinner," Dunne recalled, "Simpson called his secretary in Los Angeles and asked her to delay the reservation we had previously made at a restaurant twenty blocks north of the Regency." Didion and Dunne were regulars at the restaurant, so Didion offered to call the owner herself to make the adjustment. "No," Simpson replied. His secretary, three thousand miles west in Los Angeles, rang the New York restaurant twenty blocks north of her boss's hotel room and changed the reservation.

After their meeting, Didion and Dunne sent Simpson and Bruckheimer a detailed outline of *Dharma Blue*. They received another massive memo from Simpson, this one thirty-seven pages long. Simpson told the writers, "We are on very solid ground when it comes to the majority of our characterizations. And when the problems I've suggested in this memo have been addressed, the relationships between the characters will definitely work, and their actions at each turn will be unassailably logical. Hooray for that!"

Hooray, indeed. As Dunne recalled, at that moment, "Not a page of the script had been written."

Within months a screenplay was written. Simpson "seemed ecstatic," according to Dunne. He wrote, "Let me say for the record that this is one of the best first drafts we have ever received . . . It moves like the wind." Nevertheless, it required rewriting. Didion and Dunne promised a second draft by Christmas 1992 and went back to work.

On December 2, 1992, Didion and Dunne delivered. For a month, there was silence. Shortly after New Year's Day, Simpson's office warned the screenwriters that a new set of Simpson notes was to arrive. It did, in the form of a twenty-three-page memo—"vintage Simpson," according to Dunne—in which the producer predicted *Dharma Blue* would be "a major, major movie" and "one of the biggest movies ever." The notes, though, "appeared to have been dictated while [Simpson] was buzzed on some upper of choice. It seemed to us that Don was demanding the insertion of plot points we thought we had already inserted—in too much top-heavy detail." Vintage Simpson, indeed. The writers responded with a densely detailed memo of their own, answering Simpson's points one by one, which ran to thirty-eight single-spaced typewritten pages. "Almost a parody Simpson memo," Dunne wrote.

Months later, the writers received a call from Bruckheimer. He told them that the filmmakers had read the memo and found it extremely "interesting," and noted that the writers had "made a major contribution to the project" and that they would now be paid in full for their efforts. He added that he would be in New York shortly and that they would all meet for lunch.

Dunne hung up the phone and said to Didion, "We just got fired."

Dharma Blue was later retitled *Zone of Silence*. As late as May 24, 1995, less than eight months before his death, Simpson was still working on the project. He told *The Hollywood Reporter*—in a piece headlined

"Production Tide Is High for Simpson-Bruckheimer"—that novelist Pete Dexter was hard at work even then on a reworking of the Didion-Dunne original script.[24]

Didion and Dunne never spoke to either Simpson or Bruckheimer after they were fired.

The Ref, the first Simpson-Bruckheimer production since 1990's *Days of Thunder*, opened and closed within weeks. Though liked by reviewers, it was ignored by audiences. Simpson, restless in the absence of forward motion, sickened to find himself backwatered at Disney, was sliding once more into drug and alcohol abuse. From the set of *Bad Boys* he had said to an acquaintance who remarked on Simpson's evident health, "I've discovered the secret. It's L.A. I have to stay out of that fucking town. When I'm on the road, I'm fine. When I get home, I start falling back into all that shit."[25]

During the production of *Bad Boys* rumors were rife that Simpson had already fallen. Reporters around town traded tips: Simpson was in rehab again. Simpson was holed up at his house. Simpson was in the hospital. He was not, at least, in jail, or likely to be in court: The 1989 sexual harassment suit filed by former assistant Monica Harmon was dismissed in February 1992, as Judge Patti Kitching ruled it without merit. At the time, Simpson's hard-knuckled attorney, Bert Fields, who had already helped file a $5-million defamation countersuit, said, "Most people pay off such claims to avoid publicity. Don and Jerry refused to do that—they had the courage to fight these claims, and they have been publicly vindicated."[26]

(An executive at the studio at the time shrugged and said, "There was a lot of that [sexual harassment] stuff going around. We'd get these calls from secretaries. They'd all get paid off. It was just easier.")[27]

But the rumors of rehab and drug addiction did not go away. Reached at the Florida *Bad Boys* location and asked about his health by *Los Angeles* magazine columnist Ed Dwyer, Simpson laughed and said, "It's true. I've fallen into a late-night pizza and M&M's pattern."[28] A year later Simpson would tell *New York Times* reporter Bernard Weinraub, "The days of drugs, sex and rock-and-roll are long over. At least they are for us old guys. I'm not going to tell you I've never done drugs. That would be a lie. But I do have one addiction. Unfortunately, it's food."[29]

Simpson was telling the truth and hiding it at the same time. Through the early 1990s he was, in fact, battling his weight. But he was also beginning to experiment with prescription drugs and had not lost his taste for illegal ones. As early as 1990 Simpson was receiving prescriptions written by Dr. Stephen Ammerman, the would-be screenwriter who would turn up dead, in August 1995, in Simpson's pool house. One 1990 prescription was for dextroamphetamine. In 1993 Ammerman arranged for Simpson to get prescription-strength morphine.

And the food addiction was a real one. Sources at the posh Canyon Ranch resort near Tucson, Arizona, to which Simpson would regularly retreat for drying out and pumping up, recalled Simpson's frequent trips "over the wall" for late-night pizza or burgers. On his first trip to the ranch, around 1985, he confided to hiking guide Mark Jablonski his need for unsupervised amusement. The two had been part of a group hike that had winded the out-of-shape Simpson badly. Immediately after, though, he took Jablonski aside. "He wanted me to take him, immediately, without even going back to the ranch, to a titty bar. He said, 'I want some tit and I need some beers!' " (Jablonski did not accompany Simpson. The following day, on the trail, he noticed that Simpson kept disappearing behind cactuses and then reappearing with "powdery shit falling out of his nose." Jablonski told him, "Mr. Simpson, you can't snort *cocaine* on the trail!")[30] At Canyon Ranch, where pizza was forbidden, one of Simpson's massage therapists recalled her client making a major score. "On the last night before he was leaving us, someone from his company sent him a huge Domino's cheese pizza. He said it was like finding a naked blonde in high heels in his bed—only better."[31] Another massage therapist, Nancy Davis, said Simpson was very self-conscious about his weight and would always refer to himself as "the fat boy" when he called to reserve a massage. "He'd say, 'You gotta rub the fat boy,' but he sure loved his junk food. He *loved* pizza and cheeseburgers and beer."[32]

At his recently purchased Stone Canyon home, Simpson had installed two refrigerators, in a second-story closet, for easy midnight access to microwavable frozen foods—among them hamburgers and pizzas. And in his daybook, in the section marked "restaurants," Simpson kept handy the telephone numbers for a half dozen pizza delivery shops.

Simpson's frustration with Disney was intense. As an executive at Paramount, Simpson had answered only to Diller and Eisner. As a producer at Paramount, he and Bruckheimer were a prized pair of filmmakers who could virtually green-light their own pictures. Now, with the changing tides at Disney, they were facing a confusing array of executives. Eisner ran the studio. Katzenberg ran the film divisions. But the film divisions consisted of two competing organizations—Touchstone Pictures, operated by David Hoberman, and Hollywood Pictures, operated by Simpson's former assistant Ricardo Mestres. Each of those executives, in turn, had a phalanx of vice presidents and creative executives whose opinion on upcoming projects was solicited and heard. While Simpson and Bruckheimer had been busy making films, the film business had changed.

Simpson's former boss Barry Diller felt the time of the Simpson-style, or Simpson-sympathetic, executive had passed. "Simpson was a little crazy, which is not a bad thing. He had an over-the-top personality. A *full* personality. A little craziness doesn't hurt. Unless you're a little crazy, you can't make good decisions. The movie business was always better served by these slightly gamy characters—like Simpson, or Robert Evans, or [former Warner Bros. head] Ted Ashley or [former Paramount executive and MGM head] Frank Yablans—than by the current crop of executives, who are dull *and* stupid."[33]

Remarking the influx into the executive ranks of M.B.A.'s and lawyers, Simpson complained in 1986, "The failing of the present-day system is quite simply based on the fact that the studio executives are by and large ex-lawyers, agents, business-oriented people who are fantastic executives and managers who don't have a clue about telling stories."[34]

Bad Boys was released in May 1995 and was greeted by mixed reviews. *Rolling Stone*'s Peter Travers sneered, "You can picture superslick producers Don Simpson and Jerry Bruckheimer behind the camera hollering, 'Work that formula, baby!' " Travers called the picture "special effects noise and nonsense." But others heralded that "formula" as a welcome return to form. "After a dormant period, the Simpson/Bruckheimer machine is back in working order with this ultra-slick combination of expensive action, rude attitude, sassy humor, trendy locations, fast cars, heavy soundtrack and decorous violence," cheered *Variety*. *The Hollywood Reporter* echoed, "The *Beverly Hills Cop* juggernaut may have run its course, but Don Simpson and Jerry Bruckheimer look to have a worthy successor with *Bad Boys*."

Audiences agreed. The $20-million-budget action picture opened at

$15.5 million—very good numbers for a nonholiday, nonsummer movie without huge stars. Simpson and Bruckheimer used the opportunity to begin, for the first time since the *Days of Thunder* debacle, to expose themselves to their larger public, granting interviews to publications like *Time, Entertainment Weekly* and *Newsweek.* Simpson took the opportunity to rehabilitate his bad-boy image, while retaining just enough of it to tantalize. "I would acknowledge that in the past we had a tendency to be 'out there,'" Simpson told *Entertainment Weekly.*[35] "And sometimes the glitz got in the way. It was fun, but it became painful, because people didn't really like us." Simpson, for the *EW* reporter, typified his relationship with Bruckheimer in typically appealing sound-bite fashion: "We have something like a good marriage, except there's no sex, so there's no fighting," he said. While lauding the producers for their newfound success with *Bad Boys* and the anticipated success of *Crimson Tide* and *Dangerous Minds,* the reporter interviewed enough Simpson-Bruckheimer cronies to infuse the article with bad-boy flavor. "When push comes to shove, they don't give a fuck what people think," said Denis Leary of his *The Ref* producers. "They want a project done, and that leaves a lot of dead bodies in their wake. If you get in the way of their finishing a movie their way, they're not the kind of guys who take prisoners." Michael Bay, who directed *Bad Boys,* recounted an incident that took place during production of his movie, at a nightclub, in the middle of the night, as he sat drinking with Simpson and Bruckheimer. "Don's telling this story, and he's perched on this tiny stool, and all of a sudden he rolls over onto his back, knocking over the drinks," Bay said. "And Jerry says, calmly, 'Well, that's one way to clear a table.' He's seen it all before."[36]

Bay later said that days before shooting he was convinced *Bad Boys* would never happen at all—because of Simpson's erratic behavior. "I watched my career go down the toilet the Saturday before shooting began," Bay said. "Don came in with forty pages of dictation, and slammed the script down, and said, 'We're taking our names off this project.' And Jerry just said, 'Don't worry, we'll fix it.'"[37] During production, on a schedule that Bay found terrifyingly short, Bay said, "We would be shooting action sequences that should have taken four days to shoot, and we would have one." Bruckheimer would say, "We can do it," and Simpson would turn to Bay and say, "You and me, Michael, we're realists, but Jerry, he's out of his fucking mind." Nevertheless, Bay said, "We would do it in one day every time."[38]

It's a perfect set of Simpson-Bruckheimer moments. Don's the brilliant cavalier madman; Jerry's the sobering influence; together they're complimentary, interchangeable, indomitable. As *Beverly Hills Cop* director Marty Brest once said of the pair, "Don and Jerry are atomic producers. They're like plutonium—their energy can either drive a city or destroy it," and as one longtime Simpson-Bruckheimer observer said at the time, "It's not 'good cop, bad cop.' It's 'bad cop, *worse* cop.' "

Simpson had worried for years that he had lost his touch. He told a producer friend in 1989, over dinner at Morton's, "I made all these successful movies because I had this great, physical rapport with the audience—and I've lost it. And since I don't know what it is or how I got it in the first place, I don't know how to get it back."[39] Producer Howard Rosenman, a friend for more than a decade, remembered bumping into Simpson at the premiere of *The Ref* in 1994. "He stood in the back of the theater popping pills, he was so nervous," Rosenman recalled.[40]

Now, though, with *Bad Boys* out and two more anticipated hits coming, Simpson could stop worrying. Not only were *Crimson Tide* and *Dangerous Minds* on the way; the Simpson-Bruckheimer development hopper was full. Under the headline "Prod'n Tide Is High for Simpson-Bruckheimer" in May 1995, the producers unveiled a slate of impressive titles working their way to the big screen. There was *Angels of Eden*, a screenplay by Simpson's friend Carol Wolper; *Zone of Silence*, the John Dunne/Joan Didion original now being written by novelist Pete Dexter; a script about the navy SEALs from Dan Gordon, who'd written Warner Bros.' *Passenger 57* and *Wyatt Earp*, called *Rogue Warrior*; a Robert Towne script called *Witness to the Truth*, a true story about the inner workings of the FBI; high-profile projects from celebrated writers like Ron Bass, Lorenzo Semple Jr. and *NYPD Blue* cocreator David Milch.[41] And there was *The Rock*.

The year to come was to be the best in Simpson's entire career. It would also be his last.

CHAPTER EIGHT

DOCTOR'S ORDERS

Around nine-thirty on the night of August 15, 1995, Dr. Stephen Ammerman stumbled from the living room at Don Simpson's house on Stone Canyon Road and made his way shakily across the yard, past the swimming pool and into the pool house. The blond, blue-eyed doctor—an athletic forty-four-year-old who was five-foot-ten and weighed just over two hundred pounds—had been living in the house for the past ten days, since undergoing a hair transplant procedure, and he'd been living high: Every night was a party at Simpson's. From inside the house this night—an unseasonably cool night, with the evening low temperature dipping to almost sixty degrees—came the sounds of rock music, raucous laughter and, by eleven, a loud argument.

Linda, a flight attendant and Ammerman's girlfriend of three months, woke up when Ammerman entered the pool house. She knew he was high, knew he was taking more than the Demerol his doctor had prescribed for his scalp pain, and she was angry. Ammerman had suffered from drug addiction for years, but Linda had been convinced that this time he was sober and intended to stay that way. She and Ammerman argued for a few minutes. Ammerman seemed incoherent and unfocused. He said he was feeling extremely hot and went to take a shower. Still overheated after washing, he walked outside, nude, and dove into Simpson's pool. Linda heard Ammerman swim several laps. He crawled into bed with her shortly after, wet and wrapped in a sodden towel. He was growling and making strange statements, unlike anything Linda had ever heard him say, and she became alarmed.[1] Ammerman refused to tell her whether he had taken anything, or what he had taken, but she had reason to suspect he was using methamphetamines, or perhaps the hot new designer drug GHB—the drug that had helped kill actor River Phoenix. Angry at Ammerman's fall from sobriety, and disgusted by his condition, Linda left the pool house and drove home around 1:30 A.M.[2]

Sometime in the next several hours, Ammerman roused himself from the bed and went into the adjacent bathroom. He injected himself with a dose of prescription-strength morphine—four times the lethal amount.[3] He sat down on the floor and leaned back against the glass shower door and died.

The following morning, at approximately eleven-thirty, Simpson's assistant Michelle McElroy was told to prepare breakfast for her boss. She went out to the pool house to get some sausage links from the freezer and saw Ammerman's body in the bathroom. She called 911. "I need a paramedic at 685 Stone Canyon Road," she said in a low, nervous voice. "I have somebody who's unconscious and I think he's dead. Please hurry."[4]

Paramedics arrived and determined that McElroy was right. They covered Ammerman's body with a white bathrobe and called the cops. An investigator on the scene discovered one 3cc syringe, apparently used, on the bathroom floor near Ammerman's body. In the bedroom he found a pair of shorts; in the pocket was a vial of Valium, prescribed by Ammerman himself, filled on July 26, 1995. The instructions told the patient to "inject 10cc every four to six hours, as needed." The patient's name was Dan Wilson.

Police investigators found more prescription drugs on the premises, as coroners later would inside Ammerman's body. Initial indicators turned up evidence of Xanax, Demerol, Valium, alcohol and, as Linda had expected, GHB. The autopsy revealed that Ammerman had also taken cocaine, morphine, two different kinds of diazepam—a variant of Valium—and Venlafaxine, an antidepressant. In his stomach was a small amount of partially digested food—which the coroner was able to deduce was the remnants of a Granny Smith apple: Ammerman had swallowed the identifying plastic label along with a bite of the apple. Police investigators called the death "accidental," and the cause of death "multiple drug intoxication." And they started wondering: Who was Dr. Nomi Frederick, and why was she writing so many prescriptions?

Dr. Frederick had been treating Simpson for several years. Records show that she was prescribing medications for him as early as October 1993.[5] She was an area psychiatrist known for a very liberal attitude about prescription medications. Patients who wanted them got them. Patients who wanted more got more. Patients who were being prescribed an illegal amount of medication, and who wanted to avoid detection, used pseudonyms. Simpson used the name Dan Wilson as one; others included Dan Simpson, Dawn Simpson, Don Wilson and Dawn Wilson. He was a very, very good customer for Dr. Frederick. During one ten-day period that August, prior to Ammerman's death, Frederick billed Simpson $38,600 for her services. Her time cost $500 an hour, and she billed her clients for each prescription she wrote.

Simpson had been using her services, and the services of other doctors with a similarly liberal willingness to prescribe large amounts of medications, for some time. He knew he had a problem with drugs. As was his habit, he met the problem head-on—in his way, however, and on *his* terms. The prescription medications were an effort to move away from illegal narcotics. Ammerman's presence in the house was Simpson's attempt to take control of his own medical condition by overseeing his own treatment and the doctor who was giving it. Simpson was in control. But as he had done with every other situation in his adult life, here Simpson went to extremes. What in moderation might have been an intelligent plan turned, in excess, to disaster.

In the months that followed Ammerman's death, police investigators were able to piece together some details that helped explain the tragedy.

Ammerman had been a promising young doctor who specialized in emergency room treatment and who had patented several pieces of emergency room equipment that were widely used by his peers. He also had a weakness for drugs and had been in and out of rehab so many times that he could no longer get a decent hospital position to practice his craft. He was reduced to working graveyard shifts in small emergency rooms and was thinking of leaving medicine altogether and reinventing himself as a screenwriter.

Simpson was helping him develop an adventure story set in Alaska. Ammerman was also working on a project he called *Playing God,* a drama about a brilliant emergency room physician tormented by drug addiction and a history of prescription narcotic abuse. Perhaps Simpson had given Ammerman the Hollywood screenwriters' cliché, "Write what you know." Ammerman's family would allege, after his death, that an Ammerman associate stole the *Playing God* script and sold it, under a pseudonym, to Disney's Touchstone Pictures, which did in 1997 release a feature film called *Playing God*, starring TV's *X-Files* lead David Duchovny, about a drug-addicted physician—an allegation the family failed to prove.[6]

Ammerman was helping Simpson detox. Through the spring and summer of 1995 he had been prescribing various medications in an attempt to get Simpson to beat his addiction to illegal drugs. But not only was he failing in this, he himself had started using drugs again, and his behavior had become erratic. Early in 1995, before he had moved into Simpson's house to personally oversee the treatment program, Ammerman had been found naked and growling in the street. A friend, possibly Simpson, had recommended he see Dr. Frederick, who reportedly determined that Ammerman was having a "bad reaction to sleeping pills."[7] She called his behavior "sleepwalking" and undertook a series of treatments. At least one friend, Ammerman's medical school acquaintance Dr. Randy Capri, was worried. Ammerman told him he thought Simpson's detox program would only take five days. Capri told his friend, "You gotta be really careful. You're going to be around drugs, and that could be a problem for *you*."[8] Six weeks later Ammerman was living at Simpson's house and was deep into drug use. Records show that he began prescribing medications for Simpson early that summer. A check dated August 8 shows a $14,000 payment from Simpson to Ammerman for "medical services."[9]

Simpson's personal private investigator, Anthony Pellicano, was, within weeks, already attempting to publicly separate the patient from the dead doctor. "Ammerman was never Don's doctor," Pellicano told the *Los Angeles Times* two months after Ammerman's death. "There was no medical treatment going on for drugs or for anything else. Ammerman was a hanger-on, one of many who just wouldn't leave Don alone. It's unfortunate that this guy committed suicide, but honestly, we wish it would've happened at someone else's house."[10]

Following Ammerman's death, West Los Angeles police detectives began investigating physicians connected to Simpson and Ammerman and their drug use. In addition to Frederick, police wanted to know why her partner, Dr. Robert Gerner, was writing almost as many prescriptions as Frederick. Both physicians were on staff at Santa Monica's St. John's

Hospital and shared offices in West Los Angeles at 11500 West Olympic Boulevard.

According to press reports and interviews with police sources, Frederick and Gerner had a long history of prescription drug abuse. Gerner, a recognized authority in the fields of sleep deprivation and depression, and the author of more than sixty-five research papers widely admired by his peers, had held key positions at both the UCLA and University of California Irvine medical facilities, as well as at the West Los Angeles Wadsworth Veterans Administration Hospital.[11] Frederick, often referred to as Gerner's protégée, had a more colorful background. Born in Puerto Rico, and a graduate of Brooklyn's prestigious Pratt Institute of Design, Frederick worked with famed puppeteer Jim Henson and had a hand in designing his most famous creation, Miss Piggy. In the 1980s, seeking a career change, Frederick entered medical school, ultimately graduating from New York University School of Medicine in 1989 and completing her residency at UCLA, where she met Gerner.[12] She got her medical license in 1990. The two subsequently entered private practice together and allegedly began overprescribing medications. Subsequent reports would raise questions over their involvement with actress Margaux Hemingway, granddaughter of the Nobel Prize–honored novelist, who in June 1996 followed Simpson and Ammerman into death after taking an overdose of prescription barbiturates.[13]

According to LAPD Detective David Miller, "When we reviewed Dr. Nomi Frederick's patient profiles, we found she was dispensing a staggering amount of dope. The frequency and the volume and the strength of the prescriptions were way out of bounds."[14]

Miller is a salty-tongued, well-built, no-nonsense cop who has "been in dope for twenty-five years," he says, working the drug beat "since before Christ was a corporal."[15] Over a cup of coffee in a West Los Angeles coffee shop, wearing blue jeans, running shoes and a wide leather belt with a buckle that says "Coors," the blunt, blue-eyed detective wastes few words and indicates no sympathy for what he calls "rock heads and rock doctors." Asked about Simpson, he says, "I don't know and I don't care. He was just another slug who got caught in the fast lane and couldn't get out." Though he was part of the investigating team on both the Ammerman and the Simpson death scenes, the deaths did not interest him—until Frederick's name turned up in connection with both. "I wasn't going to do anything about this," he says of the twin Simpson-Ammerman deaths.

"No one put a gun to [Simpson's] head and made him take drugs. But when you get two of them dead in the same location, and with so much dope . . ." *That* interested him. In concert with federal officials, he began a seven-month investigation of Westside prescription drug fraud.

He discovered that Frederick had several celebrity clients. One of them was Aileen Getty, granddaughter of oil baron J. Paul Getty. Records show that on one single day, August 15, 1995—the very day that Ammerman overdosed in Simpson's pool house—Frederick wrote for Getty prescriptions for 120 morphine tablets, 200 Percodan tablets, 200 Dexedrine capsules, 90 doses of clonidine, 90 of Xanax, 60 of Klonopin and 60 of Valium.[16] (Eight days earlier, Frederick wrote Simpson a prescription for morphine sulfate.) This was good business for Frederick, Miller says, estimating that Getty's drug bill for one month ran as high as $100,000.

During the course of his investigation, Miller discovered that, by law, pharmacies are required to keep a record of every prescription they fill, and a record of every medication, every doctor and every patient. By cross-referencing physicians by patients, for example, or by tracking prescriptions of specific medications, Miller soon identified Gerner, Frederick and at least nine other area physicians as likely criminals. He found that Frederick had given one local businessman an estimated six-year supply of Dexedrine, for example, in one six-month period. He found that Frederick and other area physicians had prescribed at least 15,000 medications to Simpson, through a network of eight pharmacies and an unknown number of aliases.[17] (He found, upon investigating Simpson's home, that the prescription medicines were kept in a closet, where, he said, "they had to be alphabetized so he could find his drugs.") He also found that, perhaps working in collaboration with Frederick, Ammerman had also been writing prescriptions for Simpson—a shocking amount of prescriptions.

Pharmacy records show that, during the period of July 17 to August 8, 1995, using only one pharmacy, Ammerman prescribed for Simpson doses of the painkillers Vicodin and Toradol, the antidepressants Thorazine and Librium, the anxiety medications Valium and diazepam, as well as prescriptions for Benadryl, Ativan, clonidine, phenobarbital, Lorazepam, Cogentin and dozens of other drugs used to treat the side effects—nausea, drowsiness, dizziness, high blood pressure—caused by the massive amounts of medication he was on and the complications of mixing them. Simpson's bill for this period—for one three-week period, for just one of his doctors, under only his own name, and using only one pharmacy—was

$12,902. Miller's investigation showed that Simpson was using multiple aliases, at least nine doctors and at least eight pharmacies. During the same period, according to one report, Frederick also wrote prescriptions for Simpson for more than eight hundred pills that were filled at three area pharmacies.[18] Miller estimated that Simpson's prescription medication expenses amounted to $75,000 a month.[19]

According to official reports, the illegal sale of prescription drugs is big business. The U.S. Drug Enforcement Agency has estimated that $25 billion in prescription drugs were sold illegally in 1993.[20] (Comparable figures show cocaine sales, for the same period, at roughly $30 billion. For another comparable figure, the U.S. government spends an estimated $14 billion a year in its "war on drugs" campaign.[21]) Prescribing this amount of medication invariably involves breaking several laws. It is illegal to prescribe certain drugs to a known addict. It is illegal to prescribe drugs to anyone known to be using an alias. It is illegal for a patient to fraudulently obtain prescription drugs. It is illegal to knowingly prescribe drugs to a patient who isn't intending to use them himself. (Only the latter statute, evidently, does not apply to Simpson's situation.) Nevertheless, DEA officials insist the problem is pervasive. One estimate indicated that, among twenty drugs measured, the abuse of prescription painkillers, sedatives, stimulants and tranquilizers was responsible over the course of the study for 75 percent of emergency room admissions.[22]

Charges against Drs. Gerner and Frederick were still pending, as through mid-1997 the police investigation continued. Frederick would have other brushes with the law before the police investigation into potential prescription drug abuse was complete. She was arrested November 30, 1996, on suspicion of drunk driving, after colliding with two cars in one four-hour period and then failing a field sobriety test. Frederick's erratic driving was not the result of drinking alcohol, however, and even though police remained convinced that she was driving "under the influence," according to Deputy City Attorney Lawrence Webster, his office had insufficient evidence to prosecute. The case was dropped.[23]

Gerner's difficulties continued as well. The Medical Board of California suspended his license in 1994 after complaints that he had overprescribed drugs to a patient with whom he was having sexual relations. He was placed on probation for a seven-year period for what, press reports said, the Medical Board determined were "gross misconduct, incompetence and gross negligence."[24] It was subsequently revealed that Gerner had paid that patient's husband—whom he was also treating, for depression—$175,000 to settle a resulting lawsuit.[25]

Nor would Frederick and Gerner be alone in their legal difficulties. In March 1997 another doctor who had treated Simpson was charged with illegally and negligently overprescribing medications. Dr. Michael Lawrence Horowitz was hit with a malpractice suit that alleged he overprescribed morphine to Marcia Ann Roth, forty-five, who had had a history of drug and alcohol abuse, and who while under Horowitz' care died from accidental morphine intoxication on April 7, 1996—four days after filling a prescription for morphine written by Horowitz. Then the director of chemical dependency services at Cedars-Sinai Medical Center, Horowitz oversaw a celebrity clientele that included the late rock star Kurt Cobain. Horowitz, who after Roth's death resigned from Cedars-Sinai to practice privately in Colorado, denied any wrongdoing.[26]

Ammerman's death terrified Simpson. He was more resolved than ever to get clean. He had reason to be: Several doctors had told him, after monitoring his heart and examining the variety and volume of illegal and prescription drugs he was taking, that he was at risk for sudden, immediate death. In one last desperate attempt to get sober, Simpson went to Hawaii with Dr. Frederick, in September. When that didn't work, he checked into St. John's Hospital, where Frederick was on staff, for drug-related psychiatric treatment.[27] That didn't work, either. He left the hospital without notifying his doctor or hospital staff and barricaded himself in his home.

Ammerman's death also unnerved Jerry Bruckheimer. Within a month of the doctor's overdose in Simpson's pool house, on the evening of Friday, September 16, 1995, and only one day after Simpson's return from his self-imposed exile in Hawaii, Simpson and his partner of more than a decade met at the nearby Bel Air Hotel to discuss their professional divorce.

According to sources, it was a brief meeting, lasting no more than thirty minutes. Bruckheimer told Simpson he wanted out. There would be weeks of negotiating: What would become of the company assets, and who would take which project into their new company? "They're splitting everything up," an employee said at the time. "Computers, files, their library, paintings, TVs, furniture . . . It's all being divvied up." There was also discussion of divvying up the company employees. It looked likely that

Simpson-Bruckheimer executives Chad Oman and Jennifer Krug would wind up working for Don, while Lucas Foster would stay with Jerry. The two men also agreed to delay any announcement of their divorce for at least several months, in part to avoid creating the public impression that the split was connected to Ammerman's death.[28] But it was over.

There were projects on the Simpson-Bruckheimer development roster that both producers coveted. *Con Air* wasn't one of them. According to one company employee, the airborne action thriller was about to get the official green light from Disney's Touchstone Pictures and would go into production in 1996. Simpson was evidently happy to let Bruckheimer produce it alone. "Don *hates Con Air*," the employee said at the time. *Rogue Warrior*, on the other hand, was a project both men liked. "Neither one wants to give that up," the employee said. "They're probably going to have to do it together." There was also the *Soldier of Fortune* TV series, with which Simpson was obsessed. He might get that for himself, in exchange for releasing his interest in the TV spin-off version of *Dangerous Minds*, a project that had not seriously interested him even as a feature.

Weeks earlier, press reports had suggested that Simpson and Bruckheimer were on the skids as partners. A *Daily Variety* report on August 29, two weeks to the day after Ammerman's death, ran under the headline "Simpson-Bruckheimer Rift Rumored." Inside the piece: "The two are no longer speaking."

Attempting to silence the resulting gossip, Bruckheimer told a writer from *The Hollywood Reporter*, "It's all rumor and innuendo. This relationship is *on*."

But it wasn't. At the near end of a year that had been, professionally, his best ever—filled with the releases of and revenues from *Bad Boys*, *Crimson Tide* and *Dangerous Minds*—Simpson slid further into a depression from which he would not emerge.

Three months after Ammerman's death, in November, Simpson cleared the balance on their professional relationship and sent a check to Ammerman's family for $17,500, for the "balance of professional services."[29]

But the Ammerman family was not finished with Simpson.

Through that fall, with the help of a family friend who was both a physician and an attorney, Ammerman's father, Richard, had been investigating his son's death. On behalf of his grandson, Ammerman's only child, Richard intended to file a lawsuit that would implicate Simpson and several others in a wrongful death civil case. With family friend Dr. Alexander Lampone, a neighbor in the quiet Westside suburb of Pacific Palisades, he spent the fall and winter of 1995 building his case.

It was ultimately filed on August 14, 1996—one year, minus one day, after Ammerman died, and seven months after Simpson's death. And it was a whopper.

Seeking damages of $53 million, Lampone and the senior Ammerman implicated half of Hollywood.

According to the vast claim—several hundred pages in length—Lampone was in essence charging the Don Simpson estate, Don Simpson Inc., Jerry Bruckheimer, Jerry Bruckheimer Inc., Simpson-Bruckheimer Films, Anthony Pellicano, Lary Simpson, the Walt Disney Company and its officers, several physicians—among them Drs. Frederick and Gerner—and several pharmarcies with a conspiracy: The named individuals and corporations had conspired, the suit alleged, to keep Simpson alive by any means necessary, and that those means had included their tacit approval of Simpson's hiring of Ammerman to oversee his detox, and that this involved a "wrongful death" and "willful misconduct and reckless disregard for human life"—for it brought a known drug addict back into contact with a known drug user and thereby threatened his safety. There were further charges (hello, Pellicano) of "spoilation of evidence" and of "conspiracy to perpetrate intentional spoilation of evidence." The massive document alleged that all those accused "knew, or should have known, that their actions related to the illegal home detoxification program for Don Simpson would create a peculiar risk of harm to Dr. Ammerman." The suit further alleged a "cover-up of the illegal home detoxification program of Don Simpson" and stated that each of the accused had "special interests" in keeping Simpson alive and functioning—"of returning Don Simpson to full productivity as a movie producer for the benefit of Jerry Bruckheimer, Simpson-Bruckheimer" and those other accused, no matter the cost to Simpson and with willful disregard for the safety of Dr. Ammerman. Ammerman himself, they insisted, "operated within the scope of the law" while assisting Simpson with his detox program. Those who benefited from it, the lawsuit argued, did not. There would be hell—or $53 million, anyway—to pay.

CHAPTER NINE

REHAB

As late in his life as July 1994, Simpson had checked himself into the famed Menninger Clinic in Topeka, Kansas—where, to his chagrin, he bumped into an acquaintance from Canyon Ranch. He fled the clinic and returned home, but confessed his embarrassment later to a friend. "Don was horrified that someone he knew was there at the same time," a friend of both patients said.[1]

Simpson was not alone on the rehab circuit. Indeed, in the late eighties and into the early nineties, rehab was as much *the* place to be as Spago or Bar One had been five years earlier. Announcing a stay in rehab was a badge of honor and immediately excused any and all misdeeds for actors and others whose addictions had led them astray. Hollywood wanna-bes joked that the best place in town to "network" and make new business connections was the local AA meeting—especially hot ones like the Monday night meeting held at the Improv on Melrose Avenue.

In much of the nation drug and alcohol addiction were still regarded as signs of weakness and moral depravity, and brought shame, along with the treatment, to the sufferer. In Hollywood, which has traditionally been out of step or one step ahead of the rest of the country, there was no shame. Announcing a stay in rehab meant announcing: I was a party animal in the eighties, but the party is over and I'm hip enough to know it and strong enough to admit it.

Besides, movie people are storytellers, and a stay in rehab was good drama—or good comedy. Simpson's friend Robert Evans checked himself into a facility at Scripps Institute, in La Jolla, California—but hedged his bet, telling his driver, "Stay in the neighborhood." After less than twenty-four hours, feeling he'd seen enough of rehab, Evans found a pay phone and called the driver to come rescue him. "I went over the wall in a pair of pajamas," he'd later say, laughing.[2]

At some studios, rehabilitation for ailing executives was scheduled like summer vacation. During one period at Columbia Pictures, for example, top film division officers actually took turns. Michael Nathanson, then head of production, took the cure at Daniel Freeman Marina Hospital's rehab unit in Marina Del Rey. When he got back, his lieutenant, Amy Pascal, had a stay at Betty Ford. On the lot, this was a scheduling nuisance, but nothing more, as producers with projects in motion were told, "Nathanson's in rehab. We can't move on this for at least three weeks."[3]

At another studio a top officer was taken aside just before Christmas. He had crashed his car in three separate under-the-influence situations, and his bosses were worried. "They told me, 'We love you, we need you and you're doing a terrific job, but you have to do this thing for us.' They gave me a bonus, and they gave me a huge raise, but I had to do twenty-eight days at Betty Ford first," the executive said. He did his four-week penance in the desert and was welcomed back at the studio. Within a week he was drinking again, but only at home. Within a month he was drinking discreetly again, but only at select places where his bosses would be unlikely to spot him. Within two months he was doing cocaine again. Late the following year he was asked to return to rehab. He did, and the pattern repeated itself.[4] This was not evidently considered a serious problem. The executive was very good at his job, which meant he contributed to the profitability of the company's product, which meant that as long as he didn't kill anyone he was *always* going to be welcomed back. If he did kill someone, well, arrangements could always be made.

That executive managed to hold on to his job. The executives at Columbia did not—in part because their drug use was dramatically affecting their ability to make motion pictures. As one source close to Columbia during the early 1990s recalled of one executive, "He'd go into the bathroom if the meeting started to bog down, and then come back, all excited, and say,

'I got it. I want a scene here where the guy walks into the room and just blows this bitch's head off! Okay?'" Two of the executives, that source said, used to routinely fall asleep during morning staff meetings. A producer who had a deal on the lot at the time said of one executive, "Between five and seven it was like the witching hour. He'd come back to life like a coyote coming out at twilight. I literally sold him a project because I knew when to hit him on his high. I needed some money fast, and he agreed to option a five-day look at fifty pages from an unproduced, unknown screenwriter, for $25,000. It was a stupid deal. He never would have made it sober."[5]

Hollywood takes itself very seriously. Even though it is an industry cliché to say, "Hey, we're just making movies. We're not curing cancer," many executives and producers behave as though the fate of the free world depended upon their ability to make successful motion pictures. For, whatever their motives, Hollywood people work very, very hard. The typical executive or agent is generally working the phones by 7:30 A.M., whether it is former Paramount and Columbia marketing executive Sid Ganis making phone calls to New York while working out at home with his personal trainer, or United Talent Agent executive Nick Stevens boasting that he is out of his driveway, making calls from his car, getting the jump on his competition. "By 7:45, it's like I got a gun in my hand, and I'm dialing and I'm firing—bang, bang, bang, bang, bang!—and I've shot five guys before I even hit the office."[6] The hours that follow are long and intense. Jeffrey Katzenberg receives and must return so many phone calls every day, he has said, that he keeps a timer going on his desk and allows no phone call to go longer than two minutes.[7] There are meetings after meetings. Millions of dollars are on the line at each of them, and decisions have to be made.

The typical movie studio has an annual overhead of more than $300 million. That means product has to be made and moved constantly. That means you don't eat breakfast unless it is to discuss business with someone. You don't eat lunch unless you're sitting opposite someone you can do business with. At the end of the day, you don't go home. You go to a cocktail reception to work your contacts, meet a director, schmooze an actor or flatter some producer whose deal at a competing studio is running out. Then you go to a screening, for the same reasons, to see and be seen, to show support for someone's movie, to buy a little industry karma that might someday pay off. Then, if you're a real hustler, you arrange a late dinner with someone you're trying to romance—not romantically, of course, but in the business sense. As Simpson himself once said of his time as a Paramount executive, "I worked so hard that I went five years without speaking to my best friend and roommate. Five years I never said a word to him. All I did was my job. It takes that kind of commitment."[8] It was the fierce competition, Simpson reasoned, that drove young executives to push themselves so hard. He saw himself as a lethal part of that competition. "Any time I see someone come into this business who is smart and talented and has all those things and likes to go to lunch and dinner and party, I know he has failed already," Simpson said. "He hasn't got a prayer. Because someone like me is just going to run over him."[9]

It may have been the same competitiveness that drove Simpson and so many others toward drugs, particularly toward cocaine. The drug was socially acceptable. It was a great way to "bond." It gave you self-confidence, made you feel witty, loquacious and articulate. And it kept you going, fueling you with the false energy required to keep up the pace. Besides, it was chic. Cocaine was in the cool clubs. It was even in the cool music. Eric Clapton turned J. J. Cale's song "Cocaine"—"She don't lie, she don't lie, she don't lie . . . *cocaine*"—into a hit song in 1980. Until cocaine turned into a problem, it was Hollywood's drug of choice.

But then, for many users, it did become a problem. And it became passé. By the late 1980s and early 1990s, executives all around town were checking into rehab. They helped turn rehab into a growth industry.

Founded in 1925, the Menninger Clinic is one of America's oldest facilities specializing in substance abuse. More than 178,000 patients have received treatment at the ninety-five-bed clinic, set on a twenty-acre former farm site outside the city of Topeka, Kansas. The Menninger Addictions Recovery Program, established in 1974, is one of the country's foremost, and most forward-thinking, programs of its type, offering the most advanced diagnostic assessment, psychotherapeutic treatment and medical detoxification. The clinic specializes, among other things, in what the rehab industry calls refractory patients, those who, despite drug or alcohol rehabilitation and treatment, continue to have "pervasive and continual problems with self-destructiveness," or "extraordinarily severe, complex and unremitting symptomatology," or who show a "failure to respond to adequate trials of less intensive treatment."[10] These describe Simpson adequately. It was to Menninger, therefore, that he would return repeatedly for one unsuccessful rehabilitation after another.

He also made repeat visits to the Hazelden Center, another of the country's leading recovery centers. Founded in 1949, set on 488 woody acres near Center City, Minnesota, Hazelden is a nonprofit organization whose sole mission is "helping chemically dependent people and their families." They do a brisk business. The first day of treatment costs $1,009. Treatment days two through four cost $814 a day. Additional days cost $412. A typical twenty-eight day stay could run as high, then, as $13,000.[11]

Simpson also made one attempt at rehabilitation at the more famous Betty Ford Center in the desert near Palm Springs—but just one. As Betty Ford media representative John Boop explained, "We're not very tolerant. We *sometimes* give people a second chance. We don't give people a third chance." The Betty Ford Center, among other things, is rendered somewhat exclusive by its size and its popularity. Operating at "full occupancy," according to Boop, the center has "graduated" more than 33,000 patients from its "campus" since its October 1982 opening. A typical month brings 8,000 calls for help, 1,500 of them from people with serious substance abuse problems and serious intentions of treating them. The campus's eighty beds are full, and there is always a one-week to ten-day waiting period for new arrivals to this remarkably famous treatment center. (A recent center survey, according to Boop, showed that 93 percent of Americans polled knew exactly what the center is and does.) Patients typically stay for twenty-five to twenty-eight days. They get all that the center has to offer, Boop said, and simply are not serious about dealing with their addictions if they need a return visit.[12]

The visits were not inexpensive. The average bill for the average twenty-eight day stay at the Betty Ford Center is $11,400. The Menninger Clinic charges up to $1,300 a day for its hospital services and $6,450 a month for its residence program.

That's not as expensive, however, as most addicts' cocaine habit.

Cocaine, in a sense, built the modern rehab industry. As a relatively expensive drug, it attracted relatively affluent users. Those attempting to kick the habit were willing to pay as handsomely for the cure as they had for the addiction. Treatment programs proliferated. According to a National Institute of Drug Abuse report issued January 1995, "The widespread abuse of cocaine has stimulated intensive efforts to develop treatment programs for this type of drug abuse." In 1990, for example, more than 238,000 Americans sought treatment for cocaine abuse—and represented 36 percent of all treatment facility admissions that year.[13] In a 1987 survey the National Drug and Alcohol Treatment Unit Survey found that a staggering 834,077 Americans had received some form of detoxification or rehabilitation within the previous twelve months.[14] By the late 1980s drug treatment facilities could barely keep pace with patient demand. Another NDATUS survey, in 1989, reported a higher than 90 percent capacity at the nation's rehab centers.[15] And, by the late 1980s, rehab was big business. The cost of diagnosing, treating and rehabilitating drug users in 1985, according to one report, was $2.2 billion[16] and rising fast.

The movie industry, meanwhile, was twelve-stepping itself to sobriety. Director Joel Schumacher, a former set designer and addict who had cleaned up and gone on to direct *Batman* sequels and several screen renditions of the novels of John Grisham, was among the most outspoken. He repeatedly credited the twelve-step system with saving his life and his career. Less public in their support of rehab, but entering rehab just the same, was a host of Hollywood bad boys. In one strikingly brief period, everyone seemed to make the news. Action star Jean-Claude Van Damme voluntarily entered himself into Daniel Freeman Memorial Hospital in California's Marina Del Rey.[17] Apparently the treatment didn't take. Just a year after his December 1996 rehab stay, Van Damme was hit with divorce papers by his wife, Darcy LaPier, in which the fashion model alleged "spousal abuse and mood swings resulting from cocaine addiction."[18] Jan-Michael Vincent, a leading man in the 1970s and TV star in the 1980s, whose career was now mostly spent on direct-to-video action movies, was being investigated for driving under the influence of drugs and alcohol after crashing his car into his girlfriend's car, in Mission Viejo, after a stay in rehab.[19] Actor-comedian Martin Lawrence, who had been arrested several times in 1996 for violent or bizarre behavior, was later that year telling friends he'd straightened up after his friends Magic Johnson and rapper M. C. Hammer got him into a rehab facility.[20] Lawrence was charged by his TV costar, Tisha Campbell, with sexual harassment, in a suit that was later settled, and accused of "violent outbursts . . . when under the influence of marijuana" by his then-estranged wife, and in March 1997 was accused of punching a man at an L.A. nightclub.[21] (Lawrence's handlers explained that the actor was suffering from "exhaustion" after news accounts of Lawrence's strange appearance in a San Fernando Valley intersection, naked and waving a pistol. They later said that Lawrence had misunderstood gun control laws when he was caught carrying a loaded pistol onto a commercial airliner, and thought that boarding an airplane headed *out of state*, with a loaded handgun, was not illegal.)[22] Actor James Caan was reported to have entered Exodus Recovery Center in Marina Del Rey, for the second time in two years, for rehab treatment—following incidents in which he was accused of beating up a girlfriend and brandishing a weapon in public.[23] Shortly after, TV's Kelsey Grammer, of the hit show *Frasier*, overturned his automobile and spent the next several weeks in a California facility for the treatment of alcohol and cocaine abuse.[24] Actor Ken Wahl, of TV's *Wiseguy* fame, was sentenced to a live-in alcohol rehabilitation facility as part of a criminal charge complaint.[25] Actor Gary Busey, best known for his portrayal of Buddy Holly in *The Buddy Holly Story*, agreed to undergo outpatient rehabilitation for cocaine addiction as a Malibu judge dropped criminal charges against him.[26] During the same period, Jack Nicholson was charged with assault twice. Once, when he became enraged at another driver on the Sunset Strip, he shattered the driver's windshield with a golf club; later he allegedly beat up a hooker after refusing to pay her.

Actor Christian Slater, who at times appeared to have based his performing chops on Nicholson's, was aping the aging actor in other ways, too. In December 1997, Slater was sentenced to ninety days in jail—and ordered to spend an additional three months in a residential drug treatment program—after getting into a drug-induced brawl when a fellow party guest objected to Slater beating up his girlfriend.[27] Using words that echoed Don Simpson—and might have been useful to both men had either heeded them—Slater said after his sentencing, "I have been acting since the age of 8, and I have been a celebrity a long time. And when you're a celebrity, you start believing you can act off the screen any way you want without consequence. Now I know that that is not the way I wish to live my life, and I'm ready to take responsibility for my actions."[28]

Actor Robert Downey Jr., who had been nominated for a Best Actor Oscar for his portrayal of Charlie Chaplin in the so-titled Sir Richard Attenborough film, continued to enjoy in-and-out rehab privileges as judges allowed him to continue working if he continued sober.[29]

The young Downey was sentenced in November 1996 to undergo three years probation and to add three months to an already-served three months at a court-ordered drug rehab center, where he was being treated for cocaine and heroin addiction. He had been placed under arrest three times the previous summer and now was sentenced additionally to ninety-nine days in jail for drug and weapons violations. Judge Lawrence J. Mira of Malibu, California, told the actor in open court, "If you've ever had a chance to deal with this problem, and maintain your sobriety, this is it. I wish you good luck."[30]

Good luck arrived in the form of a court order. Less than two weeks after his sentencing, Downey was allowed out of rehab to fly to New York and appear as guest host on the late-night comedy show *Saturday Night Live*, where in 1985 and 1986 he had been a cast member. "I did have a really interesting summer," the actor told the *SNL* audience, before presenting a slide show of himself wearing orange prison fatigues. In a subsequent skit, Downey lectured on the evils of drug use, saying, "In my book, if you do drugs, you go to jail and you stay there. You don't go to some cushy rehab center and take a week off to host some comedy show."[31]

(A single headline speaks volumes about Downey's troubles and the film industry's remarkable willingness to forgive them. At the height of Downey's legal difficulties, the *Los Angeles Times* Calendar section bannered an accounting of them under the headline "Will Downey's Difficulties Hurt His Career?" In any other industry, his career would have been *evaporated* by a tenth of his difficulties. Not in Hollywood—or not, at least, before another entire year of bad-boy behavior finally landed him in the clink. On December 8, 1997, having in October lost his probation status when it was discovered he was using drugs again, Downey finally faced an unsympathetic judge. Sentencing him to six months in lockup, during a hearing broadcast on live television, Judge Lawrence Mira told Downey, "I'm going to incarcerate you, and I'm going to incarcerate you in a way that's very unpleasant for you." Downey's half-hearted response: "I have no excuses. I find myself defenseless."[32])

Downey's troubles were far from over. He would eventually fail to appear for mandatory drug tests before his probation officer, who then went before the judge that had sentenced Downey and had his probation revoked. Downey went back into the tank.

Comedian and fellow *SNL* veteran Chevy Chase's name, meanwhile, continued to make the news, as a former assistant and driver, who had been arrested in 1994 on drug charges, insisted he was buying and delivering the drugs for his boss. Fred Moroz, the driver, pleaded innocent to charges of possessing prescription painkillers with intent to distribute them, telling the court Chase had ordered the Percocet tablets from a New York pharmacy and asked Moroz to deliver them. Chase was earlier admitted to California's Betty Ford Center, in 1986, as—like Elizabeth Taylor before him and Michael Jackson after—he fought a self-confessed addiction to painkillers.[33] Actor Don Johnson, according to sources who worked on Johnson's TV show *Nash Bridges*, had repeated difficulty keeping his distance from drugs and alcohol after a publicized stay in rehab. In May 1997 television star Tim Allen, of the ABC hit *Home Improvement*, was arrested in Birmingham, Michigan, after being clocked driving his Ferrari at 70 mph in a 40 mph zone. He failed four sobriety tests and had his blood alcohol level charted well over the legal limit, at .16 percent.[34] This wasn't Allen's first brush with the law: Before finding fame as a stand-up comic and TV and film star, Allen had served time in a federal penitentiary for marijuana sales. Sources near his TV show said that his resistance to controlled substances was a constant worry to his *Home Improvement* staff.[35]

Everyone seemed to be having trouble. Another *SNL* veteran, fat funny man Chris Farley, admitted that he had struggled with drug and alcohol addiction.[36] And tragically, in December 1997, he died after a night of bingeing. Prior to his December 1997 sentencing, Christian Slater was arrested after scuffling with police, trying to grab a cop's gun, and admitting that he was high on heroin. Lab tests subsequently showed Slater had quantities of cocaine in his system, along with three times the legal limit of alcohol.[37] Actor Charlie Sheen seemed to be under the influence of something when, while promoting the release of his movie *Money Talks*, he failed to appear as scheduled for a spot on Jay Leno's *Tonight Show*, and, at a press junket later that week, babbled incoherently to reporters. When asked about the picture, Sheen replied, "You guys don't want to know about this crap. You just want to know about the drugs and whores." He elaborated: "What do you do when you've got studio heads, men that have intense financial and creative power in this town, that won't hire you? They won't hire you, even though you've screwed the same whores and you ate the bullet for it. Yet they pull you aside at a party, ask how you're holding and say that you're their hero for the things you do. It doesn't make any sense." Neither, evidently, did Sheen.[38]

Actors entering rehab became so much a part of the Hollywood fabric that the *New Yorker* lampooned the tradition in a cartoon. A Hollywood producer wearing shorts and sunglasses and cradling a cellular telephone says into the mouthpiece, "Yeah, he's in rehab, but for the right role I can spring him."[39]

Not everyone was saved by rehab. The talented and energetic Creative Artists Agency agent Jay Moloney, a shining star at the agency as top man Michael Ovitz' assistant, and later a power ten-percenter in his own right, was dismissed from CAA after several rehab attempts failed to cure him of his addiction to controlled substances, which reportedly included heroin.[40] But his dismissal from CAA, and multiple stabs at rehab, did not cure him of his addictions. More than six months after he'd been thrown out of the agency business, he was awakened one morning, after a thirty-six-hour cocaine binge, by his friend Barry Josephson. (Josephson, then president of Columbia Pictures, had been a party boy himself. As an assistant to producer Joel Silver, he was officially known as Vice President of Chicks and Clubs.)[41] Stepping into Moloney's bedroom, Josephson said, "The jig is up," and dragged Moloney into his living room—where he was met by a group of his best friends, among them the most powerful men in Hollywood. There was CAA managing director David "Doc" O'Connor, and Warner Bros. executive vice president of production Tom Lassally, and the former CAA potentate Michael Ovitz.[42]

"We all love you, and we want you to get better," Ovitz said. "But you will never see the people in this room again unless you leave this house. And you stop doing drugs."

Moloney was led from the house by Ovitz, who offered the ailing addict one final inducement to stop doing drugs. If Moloney left the hospital to which Ovitz was escorting him before he was off the drugs, Ovitz said, he would personally break both of his legs with a baseball bat.[43]

Even that offer, however, proved insufficient. After the intervention and a marathon stay at Hazelden, Moloney appeared to have begun using cocaine again, permanently scotching his chances of ever returning to the Hollywood power pack.[44]

Rehab was also grossly unsuccessful for Don Simpson, but not for any lack of trying. The available services simply failed to take effect on his deepening addictions.

"I would take him to AA meetings about once every six months," said producer Howard Rosenman, a former cocaine user who had successfully cleaned up more than a decade ago. "It didn't help. As an intellectual, he took ideas from it. But he could never get to that spiritual place where you 'surrender.' "[45] Producer Steve Roth, having survived his own brushes with drug addiction, remembered taking Simpson to a detox center in Pasadena, California, in 1983. "For a while, he was 'hyperdetox,' very healthy," Roth said. "After he got out, we'd go to Morton's, or we'd go to Spago, and he'd be fine. Then after a time he'd start pounding the drinks, and then he'd start smacking the coke again."[46]

It wasn't only to those established rehab centers that Simpson turned. Friends say he also attempted short rehabilitations at St. John's Hospital in Santa Monica—a stay that ended when he slipped out of the hospital without informing doctors—and at the more exclusive Cedars-Sinai Hospital in Beverly Hills.

Moreover, Simpson attempted several assaults on his addictions using less common means. The Canyon Ranch, near Tucson, Arizona, was a frequent retreat. Simpson would stay for weeks at a time, denying himself intoxicants and undergoing an extreme regimen of diet and exercise—hiking up to eight hours a day, bicycling in the gym for four-hour stretches, powerlifting or working out in the swimming pool with an "aqua-therapist." During other periods, Simpson went to Maui, where without professional attention he would hike the Maui mountains, jog on back roads, swim in the sea and maintain a rigorously fat- and drug-free diet until his weight and substance addictions were under control.

On a more spiritual plane, Simpson would retreat to the Ashram, a meditation center north of Los Angeles in the Simi Valley.

Simpson even, at one point, yielded to the well-marketed and then-trendy Church of Scientology. Simpson signed on—at the suggestion of his friend the screenwriter Floyd Mutrux—at the church's Hollywood Celebrity Centre, where before him luminaries like Tom Cruise and Kirstie Alley had enlisted. Mutrux himself had joined the church in the 1970s after reading the writings of founder L. Ron Hubbard. "I thought, this guy's writing is terrific, this might be it," Mutrux said.[47] He was attracted to the clear, "scientific" approach to spiritual and mental well-being and found immediate applications for the church's practices—among them "auditing," a process through which, using a sort of lie detector called an E-meter, the faithful remove negative influences from their thoughts and their lives. Paying hefty fees for these audits—more than $14,000 for the Hubbard Key to Life/Life Orientation Course—Scientologists would sometimes spend years attempting to "go clear," or achieve a nirvana-like state in which their inner negative forces had been entirely exorcised.

(Hubbard's fundamental beliefs, rarely discussed outside the church, read more like science fiction than religious instruction. Hubbard believed that 75 million years ago an alien named Xenu imprisoned enemy aliens inside volcanoes, on earth, and then destroyed them, leaving their "thetan" spirits disembodied and searching for human form. Only a prolonged series of Scientology studies, Hubbard believed, could release the pure spirit of the thetans. The highest rung in the Scientology ladder—in which members receive titles and ranks to go with the military-style uniforms, complete with gold epaulets and ornamental woven braids, worn by church officers and employees—is called Operating Thetan, to indicate a liberated thetan at rest, finally, in fully realized human form. According to the *Basic Dictionary of Dianetics & Scientology*, the E-meter tracks "engrams," each of which is "a mental image picture which is a recording of an experience containing pain, unconsciousness and a real or fancied threat to survival." An Operating Thetan is "a state of beingness" with control "over matter, energy, space, time, form and life.")[48]

Simpson would later claim that he entirely bought the Scientology theories. "I'm chagrined to say I almost went clear—did the E-meter, the whole thing," he told *Premiere* magazine writer John H. Richardson for a Scientology piece Richardson was preparing.[49]

He wasn't alone among Hollywood truth-seekers. In addition to Cruise and Alley, other actors attracted to Scientology were Mimi Rogers, who brought in Cruise when the two were a couple; Brad Pitt, a member while dating Juliette Lewis; Cruise's current wife, Nicole Kidman; Anne Archer; Kelly Preston, who joined with husband John Travolta; Lisa Marie Presley and her mother, Priscilla Presley; and Karen Black. Others who have dabbled in Scientology include actors Jerry Seinfeld and Patrick Swayze. In varying degrees they have hidden or shielded their involvement with the church from the press. Tom Cruise, for example, has bristled repeatedly when asked about his involvement, once telling *Premiere* magazine, "I have no idea why my religion, or anybody's would be the subject of an article in *Premiere*. I shouldn't be subjected to an inquiry on my religion." At a party celebrating his wedding to Nicole Kidman, thrown by his agents at Creative Artists Associates, however, Cruise sat flanked by CAA's powerful head, Michael Ovitz, and David Miscavige, then the most powerful man in the Church of Scientology.[50]

For Simpson, Scientology was potentially a perfect religion. Like the treatments he underwent at Canyon Ranch and the many rehab facilities, Scientology was expensive. Simpson estimated he spent more than $25,000 on Scientology courses—enough, in other words, to command his respect. Simpson felt convinced that if he spent enough money he could conquer anything—his weight problems, his drug addictions, his spiritual loneliness and, later, his physical appearance and, in his experiments with prescription drugs, his moods, sleep patterns and even his heart rate. (Scientology even offers its own brand of detox, a physically demanding series of procedures, designed to cleanse the body, called the Purification Rundown.) Scientology represented a tantalizing offer: Spend the money and you will get well. Simpson spent but did not get well. After months with the organization, Simpson asked a counselor there, "I've almost gone clear, why aren't I happier?" He was told he would be "okay" when he went "through OT3"—or achieved a third-level "Operating Thetan" plateau. "At that point," Simpson told *Premiere*'s Richardson, "I realized it was a con."[51]

Simpson's attempts at rehabilitation did not stop at the spiritual and chemical. He also became obsessed with creating, developing or buying the body he felt he deserved. The English wit Cyril Connolly wrote, famously, that "imprisoned in every fat man [is] a thin one wildly signaling to be let out." In Simpson's case it was rather the other way around. With exercise, medication and surgery he forced his body to become thin, but the fat man within was desperately, persistently fighting for dominance.

Between 1988 and 1994 Simpson underwent at least ten surgical procedures designed to increase his appeal and improve his looks. (He had expressed, in 1990, his horror of growing old and "turning into an aged Inuit of indeterminate gender.")[52] During that period he had collagen injections in his cheeks and chin, to make them more pronounced; a forehead lift and a restructuring of his eyebrow, to give it a sterner definition; liposuction in his belly, to make it flatter; a buttock lift, to make his bottom firmer; collagen injections in his lips, to make them fuller and more sensual; and injections of fat into his penis, to make it wider and more wieldy.

In this, as in all things, Simpson was only anticipating a national trend—and overdoing it.

Between 1992 and 1996, according to documents published by the American Society of Plastic and Reconstructive Surgery, the number of men who submitted themselves to cosmetic surgery rose from 54,845 to 73,921. (California led the nation in most procedures, in 1992 and 1996, when it was the site of more than 25 percent of all breast augmentation surgeries, for example—with almost triple the numbers for any other state.) Over that period the number of buttock lifts quadrupled. (A friend of Simpson's said, "Every time I ever visited his office, he was in there trying on jeans and complaining about his ass. He always thought it looked funny in pants.")[53] The number of cheek implants doubled. The number of collagen injections rose from 34,091 to 41,623. Liposuction treatments—Simpson underwent at least five, according to one former Simpson employee[54]—during the period rose from 47,212 to a remarkable 109,353. In 1992 men accounted for just 12 percent of liposuction patients. In 1996 that number had risen to 15.7 percent. Simpson was, literally and figuratively, on the cutting edge.

And he was spending big money. According to interviews with several prominent plastic surgeons, an average rate for raising or restructuring the eyebrows is $4,000. A face-lift runs to $10,000, a nose job $5,500 and collagen injections $500 each. And, cautions Dr. Ronald Iverson, president of the American Society of Plastic and Reconstructive Surgeons and a twenty-four-year veteran of the craft, "Those figures don't include any accompanying costs," for things like hospital or clinic stays, anesthetics, medications or follow-up visits.[55]

(Plastic surgery had become common enough by 1996 that it allowed this interesting slip of the tongue. Publicist Ronni Chasen, while arguing with a journalist about access to one of her clients, actually said, "Why are you getting so upset? It's only a movie. It's not like we're talking about plastic surgery.")[56]

Dr. Melvyn Rosenstein, in the early 1990s Southern California's pre-eminent practitioner of penile enlargement—he was known as Dr. Dick—was charging patients $5,900 for the dual widening and lengthening procedure know as penile augmentation. (The specific lengthening procedure, according to sources, was originally conceived and designed by a plastic surgeon with the impossibly coincidental name Dr. D. C. Long.)[57] For lengthening, the procedure involved cutting a V-shaped incision just above the pubic bone and then the severing of the suspensory ligament, which attaches the base of the penis to the pubic bone. Severing this ligament releases the part of the patient's penis residing inside his body and allows it to extend outside the body. (Though one report indicates this can add up to 20 percent in new length, it also warned that the procedure "can change the angle of the penis during erection. Instead of pointing upward, it may point out horizontally. It may even point down."[58] It can also result in deformities, as the newly freed length of penis may grow to resemble the pubic patch itself, and grow hair follicles. This has been called the hairy donut problem.[59]) For the widening procedure, known as a girth enhancement, fat is removed by liposuction from the abdomen and injected into the penis. This fifteen-minute surgery cost an additional $2,500.

The American Society of Plastic and Reconstructive Surgeons reported that 21 percent of all cosmetic surgery patients in 1996 were "repeat patients"—those who returned for a repeat procedure—and that 37 percent of those patients underwent multiple surgical procedures during the same visit with their plastic surgeons.

It is not known—and not knowable—whether Simpson had his penis injected with fat liposuctioned out of his abdomen during the same day of surgery, though that would have been a handy bit of recycling.

It is known that Simpson underwent the girth enhancement surgery and, as is not uncommon, that the surgery was a disaster.

According to several cosmetic surgeons, the injection of liposuctioned fat into the penis often leads, as it did in Simpson's case, to infection. There is often swelling, and often discoloration, and often pain. "The fat injection procedure has led to 'bumpy' penises, some of them quite deformed," said Dr. Hunter Wessells, an expert in the area of corrective penile surgery, at the University of Arizona's Tucson medical center. "This can make insertion or penetration difficult, or can make it difficult to keep a condom on, and anyways is not very cosmetically pleasing. And the fat injections tend to resorb quickly anyway. After a year or so there may not be any lasting increase at all."[60]

In Simpson's case the injections became infected. A former employee who spoke strictly on condition of anonymity drove his boss on multiple occasions to visit the Sherman Oaks plastic surgeon who had performed Simpson's girth enhancement. "It had turned all black-and-blue, and it was very painful," said this source. "There was a lot of swelling and fever. In the end they had to take out whatever it was they put in there. You can't believe how pissed Don was."[61]

Iverson and Wessells both said that reversing the process, removing the fat, is far more time-consuming and painful than injecting it, and can lead to additional scarring and discoloration of the penis and surrounding tissue. They also both note that the famed Dr. Dick, Melvyn Rosenstein, was investigated by the California Medical Board and no longer practices penile augmentation medicine. Both physicians also note that, in the case of most patients they have met seeking penile enhancement, the procedure is more about psychology than physical reality.

"We always say that these men who want their penises enlarged ought to have their *other* head examined," Wessells said. "Because it's more a self-esteem issue than one of true size. Most of the people who want this operation, in my experience, had normal penises to begin with."

In Wessells' experience, pornography may be a contributing factor—and a harmful one. He and a colleague, Dr. Peter Lehman, also of the University of Arizona, have studied groups of men to determine from what, exactly, they derive their idea of how relatively small or large their penises are. Their unofficial findings: "We think pornography is a real influence on how men perceive their penises," Wessells said. "Unfortunately, they never have men with small penises in porno films." And Simpson, it is known, surrounded himself with pornographic films and with "sex toys," which included rubber penises also of abnormally large size.[62]

(Given the inordinate amount of time Simpson's penis was on semipublic display, and the vast number of women who observed it, it is curious that no one interviewed for this book noticed any swelling, discoloration or other defect. That might be a result of doctor's orders: Most patients are told to wait one month after the surgery to resume sexual relations.)[63]

A similarly invasive procedure Simpson underwent before the production of *Days of Thunder* had similarly negative results. Eager to increase his sex drive and general energy level, Simpson had testosterone implants placed in his buttocks. Their "time release" function failed, however, flooding his system with very high doses of the aggression-inducing hormone. This may have resulted in a reported exchange between Simpson and Bruckheimer on the *Thunder* set, when, Simpson said, he "literally ripped the door off" one of the production vehicles. "I don't know what you're taking," Bruckheimer reportedly responded. "But whatever it is, stop taking it."[64]

Bruckheimer turned not to liposuction but to diet and exercise. The usually reticent producer told an interviewer from *GQ*, for a 1990 story cheekily called "Beverly Hills Fops," "I really got into it when I started getting love handles. I wondered, 'How can you get rid of these things without plastic surgery?' So I went to Tom [Cruise's] trainer on *Top Gun*.

This guy took Tom and totally transformed his body in three weeks. I said, 'Well, if he can do this to Tom Cruise, it'll take a little longer with me, but maybe he can fix me up.' I'm telling you, my body changed completely."[65]

Male cosmetic surgery was on the rise. Several people have competing theories to explain that.

"These are the guys who grew up in the 1950s, when the men in gray suits were the establishment, and they don't want to be that way," said Dr. Steven Teitelbaum. "They want to be youthful guys in sneakers and baseball caps."

Teitelbaum, who reported that as much as one-third of his West Los Angeles clientele is now men, has performed more than 20,000 face-lifts and more than 10,000 breast augmentation surgeries. He identified several reasons for the increase in his male clientele: "It is far less stigmatizing than it was before. Men used to be afraid of anyone finding out. Now people don't care. Plus, men feel now, for whatever reason, that they need to remain looking attractive."[66]

Simpson insisted this was not an issue for him personally. In 1990, asked if he was worried about losing his physical appeal, Simpson said, "That kind of thing wouldn't concern me." Nor, he said, did anyone's reason for finding him attractive: "I don't care why they come on to me. I never understood why women get upset when men come on to them (a) because they're sexy, (b) because they're well dressed—who gives a shit? The way I look at it is, folks, if you wake up and you're ugly, you know what real pain is. That ain't fun. So I don't want to hear . . . 'I think it's real difficult to be good-looking and be an actress or be smart . . .' Give me a fucking break. The truth is, the more attractive you are, the easier life is. That's just the way it is." Besides, he added, "I'm not attracted to them just because they're good-looking. They have to be extremely smart, extremely funny, ambitious. On the other hand, I don't walk across a room to meet a woman just because she's got a nice personality. Sorry, folks. And if I don't have a good ass, they ain't walking across the room to meet me. That's showbiz, okay? So if somewhere along the curve and trajectory of one's involvement with a member of the opposite gender some of the elements fall off, the way I look at it is, one of the wheels fell off the wagon, so we ain't riding anymore. And if one of the wheels falls off the Don wagon, Don don't deserve to be ridden."[67]

In the midst of that verbiage, Simpson was speaking volumes about his own self-image. Although one woman close to Simpson said that his physical equipment was more than adequate,[68] Simpson obviously felt otherwise.

Like an anorexic who at eighty pounds still feels she is fat, Simpson gradually lost perspective on his physical appearance and continued experimenting with cosmetic surgery until he resembled an inflated ball of Naugahyde. A friend from the Paramount days was surprised when a man he did not recognize stopped at his table in a restaurant, called him by name and sat down. "He said, 'It's Simpson!' " the friend said. "I swear I did not know who it was."[69] Gone, entirely, was any trace of fat. His face was lean, sharp and angular. His lips were full. His brow was severe, and now entirely shaded his eyes, making them, in turn, look darker and more deeply set. His physique, too, had changed. His hips were narrower, and his chest fuller. (One source insisted that Simpson had also undergone collagen injections in his pectoral muscles to increase his new bodybuilder look.) To highlight the new body, Simpson began wearing more tightly fitting clothing—often a black leather vest, with nothing on underneath. As the cosmetic procedures continued, Simpson at last began to resemble nothing so much as the chiseled, cartoon superheroes he'd obsessed over as a teenage comic book fanatic.

But Simpson's loss of perspective affected the way he felt about his physical appearance even when his physical appearance was visibly worsening. He continued to wear sleeveless shirts and tight vests even as his weight, during the summer and fall of 1995, was rising precipitously out of control. Unlike his former Paramount colleague Alan Carr, who hid his ballooning weight under elaborate caftans, Simpson kept dressing like James Dean. During interviews he conducted with the press in support of *Crimson Tide* and *Bad Boys*, Simpson dressed in black leather jeans, black boots with red highlights, collarless dress shirts buttoned close to his neck and a black Armani sports jacket—everything several sizes too small for his expanding girth.[70] His skin was browned—whether by the sun or at a tanning center, which he frequented, is not known—and leathery. He wore sunglasses whenever it was possibly acceptable, even at night, even indoors. Friends and acquaintances who saw him at his last official public appearance—in July, when the reconditioned Beverly Hills Hotel reopened for business—found him bow-tied and bloated in his too-small dinner jacket.[71] Simpson apparently had no idea that his appearance was bordering on the ridiculous.

"Simpson was always going up and down in weight, constantly checking into clinics for a tune-up, a nip here, a tuck there, so that he looked
different every time I saw him," wrote *Premiere*'s Peter Biskind in his
postmortem. "He was an essence in search of an appearance." The last
time the writer and the producer met, Biskind wrote, "His weight was up
dramatically. His neck had disappeared into an aureole of fat that obscured
the planes of his face. His hair, which looked unwashed and greasy, was
long and pulled back into a ponytail. He was wearing a black T-shirt with
the sleeves cut off. His arms were beefy, like sausages . . ."[72]

Simpson's attempts at perfecting his physical form did not stop at either
bodybuilding or plastic surgery. He also experimented with hormone implants, which left him so agitated that, he told his masseuse, he had to
drink twelve bottles of beer just to calm down. He told a different massage
therapist that he had injected his penis with a special formula that made it
possible to remain erect for twelve hours. "That way," the therapist explained, "he could have wild sex for as long as he wanted."[73]

"The key to Simpson was that he wanted to remain nineteen," according to friend James Toback. "Everyone wants the fountain of youth, but
Don was obsessed with it. 'Take these supplements, and your organs will
be thirty years younger.' He was taking speed, downers—all prescribed—
and arcane medical supplements and growth hormones. Stuff from Ger-
many that Don said only he could get—or afford. Don was getting the
hormones through Ammerman."[74]

Toback reasoned that Simpson's life was "an ongoing flight" from his
strict, repressive childhood and saw Simpson's weight fluctuations as an
external expression of his internal struggle. "He would sink to the depths
of self-abuse, then begin a quest for redemption. His weight was a para-
digm: It's the most physical thing, the most personal thing. You wake up
in the morning, you feel fat. You take a shit, there's a gut hanging over
you that shouldn't be there. You can't escape your own body or the
compulsion to inflate it to the point of self-loathing, followed by the
compulsion to deny it so you can get back in shape. And the older you get,
the more difficult it is to restore yourself. Metabolically, it just doesn't
work anymore."[75] The last time he had seen Simpson, Toback said, was in
September, at the Buffalo Club. "He was very fat then—215, 200. 'This is
utterly grotesque,' he told me. But he was a compulsive eater—big jars of
peanut butter every night at two in the morning, and no bread. People ask,
'What did he die from?' Try conspicuous consumption. You're sixty

pounds overweight, and you treat your arteries to a full jar of peanut butter and jelly overnight?"

But that was Simpson. "Anything worth doing is worth *overdoing*," he once said. "It's not enough until it's too much. Because how do you know it's enough *until* it's too much? That's the only way to find out."[76]

CHAPTER TEN

DEATH

Readers of *Daily Variety* and *The Hollywood Reporter* were greeted on the morning of December 20, 1995, with headlines that read, respectively, "Top Gun Producers Go Separate Ways" and "Simpson, Bruckheimer Split." It was official. The Simpson-Bruckheimer partnership, which had begun in 1983, produced ten films, earned revenues in excess of $3 billion and brought the partnership two Oscars and ten Academy Award nominations, was officially over. A jointly released statement, a masterpiece of hollow doublespeak, said, "The decision to form our own individual companies is a direct result of our desires to move in mutually supported directions and produce as many films a year as we individually choose to. We are, and always will remain, close friends and look forward to working together to successfully complete the many projects we currently have in progress."[1] Bruckheimer, who in August had dismissed the idea of a separation as nothing more than "rumor and innuendo," told *Daily Variety*, "We're still close friends. I talk to him every day. There's no animosity. We had a good run together."[2] There was no comment, anywhere in the press, from Simpson.

What Bruckheimer did not say, but what close friends and employees knew, was that he had simply had enough. Since the peak of their high-concept high, in the mid-1980s, Simpson had been on an almost nonstop bender, a perpetual attempt to live his life at the very edge of every extreme. It had worn badly on his health and his ability to function as a producer. It had also worn badly on Bruckheimer's patience.

There had been rumblings of anticipation about the divorce. On August 29 a headline in *Daily Variety* read "Simpson, Bruckheimer Rift Rumored"; the accompanying story said, "The two are no longer speaking." Two days later Bruckheimer—as he had done so many times over the course of their partnership—publicly defended Simpson and shot down the speculation they were to part. "It's all rumors and innuendo," he told *The Hollywood Reporter.* "This relationship is on."

It wasn't. At the urging of his wife, friends said, Bruckheimer was increasingly envisioning a professional life free of Simpson. For more than a decade the shy, reticent Detroit native had operated as Simpson's apologist, explaining away, to friends or to reporters, Simpson's repeated disappearances into drug rehab facilities or, worse, his disappearances *from* them. "You know Don," Bruckheimer would purr into the telephone. "He's in Hawaii, beefing up," or, "He's in Arizona, working on his tan." But their business dealings were growing infrequent. Simpson had been almost totally absent from the late-1995 production of *The Rock,* an action-thriller starring Sean Connery and Nicolas Cage, which Simpson-Bruckheimer was producing under its deal at Disney. He had visited the San Francisco set—on the famed prison island Alcatraz, where much of the movie's action took place—only once, and had been seen on the soundstages at Sony—where the postproduction and interior scenes were being completed—only twice. Though there were many potential new projects at Disney, among them the airborne action movie that would become, in 1996, the Nicolas Cage hit *Con Air,* Simpson was no longer contributing anything to them. Bruckheimer was working alone, with only the baggage of Simpson's reputation, and his anxiety over his longtime associate's health, to remind him that he even had a partner. As the fall wore on, Bruckheimer struggled with the decision to pull the plug. By late fall he had made his decision, and he made his move, telling Simpson, at a brief meeting in the Bel Air Hotel bar, that it was over.

It was a divorce of some moment. Stability and permanence in professional Hollywood relationships are as rare as stability and permanence in Hollywood marriages, and business partners change as often as domestic ones. Tom Pollock had run Universal under Sidney Sheinberg for eons—but with Seagram newly in charge of Universal, both men were out. Eisner and Katzenberg had run Disney for more than a decade, but when Eisner resisted sharing real control of the studio with Katzenberg, Katzenberg had walked. At the major studios only Warner Bros.' Terry Semel and Bob Daly, partners of fifteen years' service at the studio, continued to share longtime responsibilities—but after the merger of Time Warner with Ted Turner's empire, some people believed even *that* partnership was in jeopardy. Among producers of note, there were none who had shared such a beaming limelight, with such success, for as long as Simpson and Bruckheimer. A Hollywood that featured the two men as competitors was almost not imaginable.

Indeed, Simpson and Bruckheimer had indicated previously that they themselves could not envision solo careers. Bruckheimer had once said that he and his partner were "different parts of the same brain. I'm introverted, shy. My partner is extroverted . . . someone who likes to be the center of attention. I'd rather put the process together, then stand back and let the well-greased machine work. He prefers to be on the mantel." (Simpson had replied, "Now that you've said all these derogatory things about me, let me say that it's not an accurate assessment. It's just that I have a particular aptitude for the conceptual and no love of process for the sake of process. I'm an active creative person.")[3]

Some of Simpson's acquaintances kidded him about his newfound solo status. The gossip columnist Liz Smith sent him a note just after Christmas 1995. "Thank you for my beautiful Christmas wreath," she wrote. "Now that you and Gerry [sic] are split I hope I don't get half a wreath next year. Kidding! Love and kisses and happy New Year."[4]

Others felt the separation would have dire consequences—for both producers. "Don can sell but he can't execute. Jerry can execute but he can't sell," Lucas Foster, who was then a Simpson-Bruckheimer executive, said to an acquaintance. "Don needs to be managed. He's not capable of having a self-governed life."[5] An unnamed source told *Daily Variety* at the time, "Don is a creative genius; he is difficult to manage, at war with himself, but he is really talented. But he doesn't have Jerry's organizational skills. Jerry is interested in the details, but not so good with talent. It's going to be hard for them. Each of them needs someone to bounce off. When they did, it was good chemistry, and they made great movies."[6]

An unnamed agent told reporter Jeffrey Wells, then working with *Entertainment Weekly*, "Jerry can probably stand alone, but Don can't." A development executive said, "It's a lot easier for Don to find an efficient, hands-on type like Jerry than for Jerry to find another creative dynamo like Don." The agent noted, with some irony, that "between the two of them they make a great producer."[7] Another S-B executive similarly said, "Jerry will never be able to do it on his own. He'll have to find a creative powerhouse to augment his talent, which is to execute and administrate." On the other hand, the executive said, "A lot of people are saying Don won't make it on his own, and he's been getting really angry when he hears this being said. I think it's going to focus him." That executive reported that Bruckheimer was "bad-mouthing" Simpson to their professional acquaintances, which was making Simpson "furious."[8]

That executive believed that *Con Air* would be produced by Bruckheimer alone—because, among other things, she said, Simpson "hated" the project. She thought the two producers would fight over the feature *Rogue Warrior*, an inside look at the FBI's criminal investigation unit. Simpson would focus on *Soldier of Fortune*, a thirteen-part TV series of adventures taken from the magazine of that name. Bruckheimer would take *Dangerous Minds*—both the potential sequel and the planned TV series.

Whatever the case, and despite Bruckheimer's upbeat attitude about working with Simpson on upcoming projects, people close to the pair believed that Bruckheimer's insistence on the divorce was more of an intervention, designed to frighten Simpson into sobriety, than a strategic business move. Those sources also felt that Bruckheimer's wife, Linda Balahoutis—the former magazine editor with whom Bruckheimer had lived for close to a decade before marrying in 1993—had a great deal to do with the decision. Said one, "Jerry could never have made this big a step on his own. Linda encouraged it."[9] "It's got to be, 'Okay, we're not going down with him,' " one friend of Jerry and Linda said. "They had had it, and it was also their idea of tough love."[10] Another source at the time said, "Don has been this way forever. He makes Howard Hughes look mildly eccentric. But it's not eccentricity. It's self-destruction. My guess is Jerry finally said, 'Enough is enough. This has gone too far.' "[11]

His friend Rob Cohen, the film director, believed Simpson's decline increased markedly as a result of the rift—but believed that the divorce from Bruckheimer was inevitable and might have awakened Simpson to the depth of the trouble he was in. "I think Jerry was convinced that this was the only way he could shock Don into losing fifty pounds, get him to stop drinking like a fish and stop coking and stop whoring," Cohen said.

"He was saying, 'I'm not going to be dragged down by you and your scandals and your lawsuits and all this crap.' But it didn't work."[12]

Whatever the reason, Simpson's decline, physical and mental, through the fall and winter of 1995, had been steep.

Producer Joel Silver recalled visiting Simpson, at home, with ICM agent Bill Block, some months before Simpson's death. As they sat in his study, Simpson picked up the phone, saying, "I gotta call Toback." Once he had the writer-director on the line, he began screaming, "Where are the pages? Send me the fucking pages, you prick! Send them now!" Silver glanced at the phone next to Simpson; there was no line lighted there; Simpson was screaming at no one. Shortly after, Simpson excused himself and said, "Here come the pages from Toback." As he went into the other room to retrieve the pages, Silver went to the kitchen for a glass of water. There he saw script pages being fed into a fax machine. By the time he got back, they had gone through, and Simpson was waving them around.

"He had someone send him these 'pages' from his own fax machine in his own kitchen—to impress who?" Silver said. "To impress me and Bill Block? It was pathetic."[13] (But not a new gag. A hairdresser at the Gadabout Salon at Arizona's Canyon Ranch recalled a similar incident from the early 1990s. "He'd come in to get his hair cut and demand a phone," the hairdresser said. "He'd have these long, loud, really obnoxious phone conversations—except there wasn't anyone on the line. It was all a big show, to let people know he was a big shot.")[14]

Simpson may have been similarly delusional about relaunching his producing career. In late December of 1995, less than a month before he died, he told *Vanity Fair*'s Kim Masters that, despondent though he was over losing his partner, he wasn't losing his producing chops. "I've got several little psychological, darker pictures which I'm anxious to make with newcomers," he said. "I'm definitely going to get another partner," he added, someone to do "the mule work" and "the fighting with the studios."[15] He said that the divorce from Bruckheimer was a blow, but not a serious one. "I would be lying if I said I'm sitting here destroyed, because I'm not. It opens up a lot of opportunity for me." Simpson was, in part, relieved of the limitations of Bruckheimer's imagination and ambition. Simpson had not wanted, for example, to make the movie *Bad Boys*. "I said, 'There's nothing in it for me. It's a programmer.' But Jerry loves doing that. He's a worker bee." Simpson felt he was more of an artist, and more of an entrepreneur. "Jerry's very penurious," he said. "I'm the type of guy that will put a million dollars of my own money into a movie. Jerry's never wanted to do that. Jerry is basically a big-studio filmmaker, and I always think more like an artist."

But Masters found him morose, and daunted by the work that lay ahead. "I hadn't planned on starting over at this stage of my life," he told her. "But that's what I've got to do."[16] Meeting with Simpson in December 1995, Masters said Simpson seemed alternatingly despondent and upbeat. "He started to ruminate about the difficulty of breaking old habits, of learning to change," Masters wrote.

Simpson had an additional reason to feel morose, though he did not share it with Masters. He had been informed in early 1995 that he was a father. Simpson, who "found the entire idea of family abhorrent,"[17] had a daughter. And her mother, Victoria Fulton Vicuna, was pressing Simpson to recognize his paternity and act accordingly by supporting his child.

Simpson had been introduced to Vicuna in 1987 by the novelist Jay McInerney, when he and Bruckheimer had traveled to New York to discuss optioning McInerney's *Bright Lights, Big City* for the movies. Simpson and Vicuna, a Manhattan socialite with an appetite for the high life, saw each other sporadically for the next two years. Simpson flew Vicuna and a friend to Aspen for one of the legendary parties—the one at which Don Johnson and Melanie Griffith announced their "reengagement"—and saw her whenever he came to New York on business. Vicuna said she was never in love with Simpson, that the relationship was "a bicoastal thing, more of a flirtation than a romance." But the flirtation included unprotected sex, on several occasions.[18]

The daughter was born in 1992 and dubbed Alexandra. At the time of her birth, and for the next three years, Vicuna was in a monagamous relationship that she hoped would turn into a marriage. It didn't. Broke and facing what she felt was the real threat of homelessness, Vicuna began sending Simpson photographs of their daughter, begging for financial support. Simpson did not reply. Soon Vicuna was pressing Simpson's brother, Lary, and attempting to contact Simpson's parents. According to several friends, Vicuna's pleas depressed Simpson terribly—though not enough to make him begin supporting his daughter—and perhaps forced him to ruminate on his own early years.

Simpson said to Masters, in a flash of clarity and self-awareness, "People live their childhood until they're too old to do anything else," and complained that Hollywood encouraged that. "Too much money, too much freedom," he said. "It's a town that allows you as much eccentricity as you like—as long as you're productive."[19]

On paper, Simpson still looked productive. *The Rock* was finishing production, and already it was expected to be a hit. Less than a year before, after the long fallow period at Disney, he and Bruckheimer had returned to the box office with their powerhouse triple play, releasing *Bad Boys, Crimson Tide* and *Dangerous Minds*. Now they had paired Nicolas Cage with Sean Connery and teamed them against the brilliant character actor Ed Harris, in an action-thriller set on San Francisco's Alcatraz Island. In their story a renegade soldier captures the island in the name of lost soldiers and holds the city of San Francisco hostage with chemical weapons, threatening to annihilate Baghdad by the Bay if the U.S. government does not make reparations to the lost marines. Cage is a chemical weapons scientist; Connery is a former British intelligence officer who, imprisoned on false charges at Alcatraz, and held there under a veil of total secrecy, is the only man to ever escape the Rock.

Simpson was almost solely responsible for conceiving the character Harris would play.

According to screenwriter Jonathan Hensleigh, hired by Simpson and Bruckheimer to rewrite *The Rock* in May of 1995, Simpson took charge of the Harris character and guided Hensleigh through his rewrite. Which was substantial. "The original script was silly," Hensleigh said. "It wasn't adult. The plot was ludicrous. At first, I refused to do it, because the whole story was so unreal."[20]

Among Hensleigh's problems: The Connery and Cage characters take over the heavily armed and defended Alcatraz in an unassisted assault, with a single rubber boat; the Connery character has no secret service background, but is simply an ex-con who escaped from Alcatraz.

"I talked to Don extensively," Hensleigh said. "I asked him, 'How can a guy escape from Alcatraz [in the movie] when everyone knows that *no one* ever escaped from Alcatraz? And if he escaped from Alcatraz, how come no one knows about it?' Don had the answer: No one knew he was there *in the first place*. He was a secret prisoner."

That solved one problem. Another persisted. The Ed Harris character was thoroughly one-dimensional and thoroughly unsympathetic. Simpson and Hensleigh had marathon late-night phone conversations, more than a dozen of them in a one-month period. Simpson would get on the phone at 8:00 or 9:00 P.M., Los Angeles time, and start talking. Hensleigh, working in New York, would sometimes be on the phone four or five hours, until 3:00 or 4:00 A.M., as he and Simpson wandered around the problems in the script. Hensleigh found his producer "a lunatic, but very funny, and full of life." After an hour or so on the phone, Hensleigh would say, "It's getting late. I'm going to make a drink." Simpson would say, "I'll join you." The two men would drink, and talk, and drink some more, usually until Simpson said, "Let's take a break. I'm getting kind of fucked up here. Let's pick it up tomorrow."

Simpson had just read the memoirs of Colonel David H. Hackworth, a much-decorated Vietnam field commander who in April 1995 published an assault on American military mismanagement of its long Southeast Asian campaign.[21] Simpson had also seen a recent *60 Minutes* investigation of marines who had done covert, unlawful Southeast Asian operations for the Pentagon, which promptly abandoned the marines' families if the soldiers were killed. Simpson combined elements of both and gave Ed Harris' character an honorable mission, and a sympathetic reason to take over Alcatraz and hold the city of San Francisco hostage. He was going to stand his ground until the Pentagon made itself accountable to the men who had died serving their country.

"Simpson's contribution was in creating a really compelling villain," Hensleigh said. "A soldier with a noble end, but, unfortunately, psychotic means."

That contribution had come during preproduction on *The Rock.* With the movie actually being filmed, Simpson was scarce. Hensleigh, who was on-set every day of filming, did not remember seeing Simpson once during the San Francisco phase. Once production shifted to Los Angeles, sets were built on Sony Pictures' famed Stage 30 on the Culver City lot—the same stage where MGM's *The Wizard of Oz* was shot. While Bruckheimer oversaw the actual production, Simpson would drop by periodically. To Hensleigh, Simpson was visibly deteriorating. "He was still the ironclad guy, impregnable as always, but he looked *bad.* He looked sick. He was very overweight. He was pasty. He was full of energy, but he looked like a dying man."

Simpson wasn't acting like a dying man. Outwardly, he was attempting to rebuild his career as a producer, going solo as a filmmaker for the first time in his life. Among his immediate requirements: staff. Through the summer of 1995 he had a secretary advertise for a personal assistant, seeking an aide to work with him in his Stone Canyon house. Applicants were exclusively female, exclusively young, and to be interviewed only at night. An appointment sheet indicates more than twelve applicants scheduled to be seen in one evening, at fifteen-minute intervals, between the hours of seven-thirty and ten.

Karen Kawabata, then twenty-two, was one applicant. She arrived at the Stone Canyon residence one evening, having set up an appointment after hearing from a friend that Simpson was hiring. Met at the door by Simpson's assistant Todd Marrero, she was ushered into the living room and asked several questions. "What have you heard about Mr. Simpson?" "What are your career goals?" "What do you want to do with your life?" After thirty minutes she was led into Simpson's back office.[22]

She found the producer seated behind a desk, wearing a smoking jacket. She found him "overweight, but with great hair, and handsome." But she found his behavior odd. Simpson would first ask reasonable questions, about salary requirements, for example, but then he'd shift to more personal matters. He asked Kawabata, who had come to the meeting dressed in a conservative business suit, about her sexual interests and sexual history. He indicated that any assistant of his would have to be very liberal. "He said, 'There are lots of crazy parties here, and lots of prostitutes. Someone like Emilio Estevez might be here, and I'd need to know that you wouldn't talk to the press about that.' " Kawabata responded, "What you do in your personal life is not my business." This was not satisfactory.

After an hour or so, Simpson took Kawabata into his bedroom. He showed her his clothes closet. He told her about old girlfriends and how he was planning to go to Hawaii soon, "to detox and lose weight and get some exercise." He told her that, among her other duties, she would periodically be expected to perform that rather macabre task of "staying up with me all night, just to make sure I'm not dead." Simpson explained this was one of the things his current assistant, Jeannelle Trepanier, often did for him.

(He did not say anything else about Trepanier, though it might have interested his job applicant. Trepanier had been familiar with one of Simpson's drug dealers and met him, Trepanier said, on a drug deal. Simpson had found her bright and ambitious and encouraged her to do something more interesting with her life. Eventually, he helped her do that: He hired her and moved her into his house. "He taught me everything about the business," Trepanier said later. "I was enlightened and educated on a daily basis. I owe my whole career to him."[23] Subsequent to Simpson's death, Trepanier—who carries on her key chain Simpson's laminated Paramount security pass—moved on. By mid-1997 she was working as an executive for another Hollywood bad boy, Charlie Sheen.)

Simpson then slipped into a bathroom. When he emerged he was excited, but after he and Kawabata had sat in the office again, his energy was gone. "He was snorting coke, or something," Kawabata remembered. "He would be excited and talking, then he would doze off for a minute. Then he'd leave the room again."

The meeting went on. Simpson improved the job offer. Kawabata could live in his guesthouse. His assistant would take her shopping for clothes. The salary would be immense. "I was very intimidated by him," Kawabata said. "He was promising me this great job, but I was terrified. He had me in this back room, and it was dark, and it was late. I was afraid to make him angry. He finally said to me, 'I might need you in the middle of the night. I might need you to have sex with me.' " At that, Kawabata decided to leave.

"I said, 'Well, I am not here to do any sexual favors.' I gave him my résumé and got up to go." A disgusted Simpson, Kawabata said, threw her résumé into the garbage. Sneering, he said, "You'd better go on home now, *good little girl.*"

By early January, Simpson's schedule was limited almost exclusively to medical appointments. As the new year opened, Simpson had simply stopped going out and would tell friends that he felt too unwell to join them for dinners or premieres.

Simpson's appointment book for the last month of his life is a bleak expanse of emptiness. For the week of January 15, Simpson was scheduled for daily, hour-long visits to Dr. James Grotstein, a Westwood-based psychiatrist. On January 17 he had a "cut and color" hair appointment with a stylist named Diane, who came to the house and who would probably work on Simpson's newly grown beard and mustache.[24] On January 18, aside from his usual visit to Grotstein, he would see his brother, Lary, and his attorney, Jake Bloom. He visited *The Rock* set on Sony's soundstages in Culver City, making brief, scheduled appearances on January 8 and January 9. Through the early part of the month, according to the sheets faxed to Simpson every morning by his Simpson-Bruckheimer Films assistant Karla Kempf, Simpson had also seen or had appointments to see five different doctors.

By November of 1995 Simpson had become deeply alarmed at both his drug intake and his ballooning weight. Bingeing between highs on junk food—he kept a refrigerator in a hallway outside his second-floor bedroom stocked with frozen pizza, frozen cheeseburgers and tubs of the peanut butter he liked to eat straight from the jar—had sent his weight up by at least fifty pounds. His five-foot-seven-inch frame was now carrying 230 pounds. He was so ashamed of his obesity that he rarely left his home and had not been seen at a public Hollywood function since the June 3, 1995, gala reopening of the Beverly Hills Hotel. (A longtime colleague, Sid Ganis, would later say, "He looked desperately ill, and was so out of it he could barely speak.") Earlier in the year, Simpson had made the acquaintance of a physical trainer who had once taught Jane Fonda aerobics. This flimsy connection provided a bridge between Simpson-Bruckheimer and Fonda's husband, Ted Turner, and led in time to a meeting between Simpson, Bruckheimer and Turner's man in Los Angeles, executive Scott Sassa. The two men visited Sassa at his Century City offices, Simpson dressed head to toe in a too-tight Armani outfit that, Sassa thought, made him look "like the Michelin man." Worse, Sassa said, Simpson "made zero sense." The meeting ended cordially but hurriedly. In the hall outside Sassa's office, Simpson ran into producer Charles Roven and his wife, Dawn Steel—who fifteen years earlier had been Simpson's protégée and a close ally, when Simpson was riding high at Paramount. Steel told Sassa, "My God! I didn't even recognize him."[25]

Through the fall Simpson had been consulting regularly with a West Los Angeles physician named John O'Dea. An Irish native with a pleasantly burring brogue, O'Dea specialized in the hormonal treatment of psychological or psychiatric mood disorders. He thought Simpson was hyperactive by nature and suffered from severe testosterone imbalances and, possibly, adult attention deficit disorder. He also thought Simpson was in immediate danger of sudden heart failure and told him so. After conducting cardiology tests on Simpson and conferring with a colleague, Dr. William P. Stuppy, Simpson was told his heart might stop at any moment, most probably "either at the dinner table, on the can, or when waking up," Stuppy said. The conclusion was certain. Stuppy later said,

"What I read from Simpson's chart was like a singing telegram: *You are going to die.*" Simpson, though initially frightened by their findings, O'Dea says, rejected them. He had his heart monitored by Dr. Lester Tarr at UCLA Medical Center—but told Tarr nothing of O'Dea and Stuppy's findings, and nothing of the vast amount of pharmaceuticals he was taking. After a routine cardiac check, Simpson was told he had nothing to fear. He broke off contact with Stuppy and O'Dea.[26]

There are several indications that, despite his doctors' warnings, Simpson was attempting to rebuild his life. He was certainly attempting to rehabilitate himself physically. Had he not expired on January 19, Simpson in the following days would have met with a Sherman Oaks diet expert, Dr. Morton Maxwell, on January 23. He would have had his teeth cleaned by a Dr. Roger Lewis, on January 25. He would have seen Dr. Grotstein again that afternoon and met with a physical therapist at the Beverly Hills Therapy sports medicine center. The following week he would have begun a series of meetings with Sid Tessler, a Westside certified public accountant, presumably with a view to setting up the finances for his new solo company.[27]

Simpson's schedule for the two days following his death, January 20 and 21, reflects the emptiness in which he lived his final hours. According to the daily sheet faxed to him by Kempf, that Saturday and Sunday were marked, simply, "Open."

On the afternoon of January 18, Simpson met for several hours at the Stone Canyon house with his brother, Lary, his attorney, Jake Bloom, and his agent and close friend, Jim Wiatt—who would later report that Simpson seemed optimistic and full of plans for his immediate future. That afternoon, following their departure, Simpson had a five-thirty session with Dr. Grotstein.[28]

Wiatt left Simpson near dark. Some hours later, Simpson received a call from an old friend, the producer Tova Laiter. A soft-spoken Israeli-born Sabra, Laiter had known Simpson since 1972, and Simpson had been a friend, a mentor, a confidant and a teacher—once telling her, when she was considering taking a studio job, "When you wake up in the morning, put on your battle fatigues. Put a gun in your right pocket, and put a gun in your left pocket, and go to work. That's how you survive at the studio." Now, changing jobs and worried about her career, Laiter had heard Simpson was feeling low as well. She called to commiserate and found Simpson oddly hyper and excited. "He had just talked to Wiatt, and he sounded upbeat," Laiter recalled. "He said, 'Jerry and I are going to do a couple of things together, and then I'm going solo.'" Laiter suggested they get together but, as he often had recently, Simpson groaned and begged off, saying, "I can't go out. I have to lose some weight first." Laiter laughed, and chided Simpson about his eating habits, drug habits and other bad habits. She said, "You told me you were going to be a bad boy until you were fifty, and then you were going to become a holy man. So, are you ready for the holy man part?" Simpson laughed and said, "No! Not for another twenty-five years!"

Simpson had reason to feel upbeat, despite the calamity of his physical health. He and Wiatt had discussed, among other things, finding Simpson a production deal, a studio home at which to base his new solo career. Wiatt would later say that Simpson "was in great spirits. He wanted to produce movies and be a director. He was looking forward to the rest of his life. For the first time in months I saw Don really excited."[29]

But finding a new home was problematic. Every studio executive in town knew about Simpson's drug problems and erratic behavior. Friends who might have been counted on to overlook that, and invest instead in Simpson's well-earned reputation as a visionary, creative genius, either were not in a position to help or had decided the only help Simpson deserved was none at all. Two of his oldest and closest friends were David Geffen and Jeffrey Katzenberg. Geffen had ended his long relationship with Warner Bros., and Katzenberg had acrimoniously ended a ten-year stint at Disney—during which time he brought Simpson and Bruckheimer to the studio—to create their own company, with Steven Spielberg, called DreamWorks. A deal there would have been natural, but Geffen and Katzenberg were in league with Bruckheimer and his new "tough love" approach to Simpson's persistent drug addictions. (Katzenberg had attempted an intervention to force Simpson into treatment, according to another old friend, the writer-director James Toback. Simpson told Toback that Katzenberg had said, "As someone who loves you and admires you and has learned everything he knows from you, you must completely turn over your life to me, for the next six months." Simpson had refused.)[30] Disney was probably out, because Bruckheimer's deal and production offices were there. Paramount, for whom Simpson and Bruckheimer made five hit movies, was out, because the relationship had ended badly. Simpson had no friends at 20th Century-Fox. MGM-UA had been put on the auction block and was unstable, as were the Sony-owned studios TriStar and Columbia, where Simpson-Bruckheimer's *Bad Boys* had been made.

That left Universal. Though it was also in flux, having been recently sold by the Japanese electronics giant Matsushita to the Canadian beverage giant Seagram, Simpson had an ally there in Casey Silver, the head of film production. Silver had begun his Hollywood career making dry-ice smoke on director Adrian Lyne's American debut, *Foxes*, and had worked as Lyne's assistant on his first American hit, the Simpson-Bruckheimer smash *Flashdance*. He had subsequently gone to work for Simpson-Bruckheimer, ultimately rising to run their development operations. He could be counted upon.

But had Casey called? Wiatt wanted to know. Had Casey spoken to Jake Bloom? Conversations over the last several weeks indicated Silver was willing to talk, maybe willing to offer Simpson a home—out of affection, loyalty and respect, and the hope that Simpson would straighten out and bring some of his signature big-ticket action movies to a studio that had recently suffered the indignity of the big-budget disaster *Waterworld* and was starved for hits.

Silver had not called. He was planning to, but had not entirely made up his mind. "I wanted to make sure I was ready to dance," Silver said later.

Hours later Toback called from New York. Getting no answer, he left a message at the Stone Canyon house. Simpson called back minutes later and growled, "I hope you're calling about *Harvard Man*."

Harvard Man was a movie Toback had written and hoped to direct. Simpson hoped to produce it and to star in it. A dark, twisted drama about a Harvard basketball team guard who takes a $50,000 Mafia bribe to throw the Harvard-Yale game, *Harvard Man* had a part in it—a renegade FBI agent with bizarre sexual perversions—that had obsessed Simpson. That night he told Toback, "Do you know how exciting this is going to be for me? This is going to be great." Toback said Simpson "had no doubts about striking out on his own. He was confident and exuberant." Simpson planned to take *Harvard Man* to Disney's Joe Roth, for whom he and Bruckheimer had made the hits *Dangerous Minds* and *Crimson Tide*, and he *knew* Roth would cut a deal. For his part, he promised to lose some weight for his FBI agent role. Toback had last seen Simpson in September, almost four months before, at West Los Angeles' trendy restaurant Buffalo Club, and had been shocked at Simpson's appearance. (Simpson called himself "grotesque" that night on the telephone.) But now Simpson said, "I understand I have to be naked in this movie, and I know the FBI has rules about fat, and I'm going to adhere to them." He was planning an extended stay at Canyon Ranch, where in the past he had successfully beefed up and shed pounds. He promised Toback, "It's going to change when you next see me. I'll call you as soon as I get out of Joe Roth's office. Be ready to come out."

It was a three-hour conversation, lasting past midnight, before Simpson hung up. Toback said Simpson's energy and attention span had begun to fade near the end of the call: Simpson had been drinking wine and guzzling peanut butter. And it was late. Toback hung up the phone confident about Simpson's state of mind and *Harvard Man*'s future.

Simpson did not go directly to bed. He left his second-floor bedroom for his office on the first floor and left a telephone message for his assistant Todd Marrero. Sometime later he went into the bathroom, wearing a bathrobe and his reading glasses. In his hands was a copy of James Riordan's just-published biography of filmmaker Oliver Stone, aptly titled *Stone: The Controversies, Excesses, and Exploits of a Radical Filmmaker.*

Simpson sat down on the toilet, and he died. Sometime around one o'clock, on the morning of January 19, 1996, Simpson's heart simply stopped beating. He fell to the bathroom tiles, clutching his glasses, as the Stone biography dashed down beside him.

Simpson's body was found the following afternoon by a maid, who immediately notified Marrero. Marrero made several telephone calls—at least one to Simpson's friend the private investigator Anthony Pellicano. Alerting the authorities, a shaky-sounding Marrero called 911: "Hi. I need an ambulance, please. Uh, someone has passed out." When asked if the person was still breathing, Marrero said, "It does not look like it. It looks like he's dead. I can't tell."[31]

In Burbank, Jerry Bruckheimer was just setting off for a meeting with several Disney TV executives, to discuss their upcoming production, for ABC, of a TV series based on the successful Simpson-Bruckheimer feature *Dangerous Minds.* The movie had starred Michelle Pfeiffer; the TV show would star Annie Potts. Bruckheimer's assistant called Disney's David Kissinger on the telephone and asked to reschedule the meeting for the following week. "Something has come up," the assistant said. Across the

Disney lot, Michael Eisner got the call informing him of Simpson's death. He said, "I've been waiting for this call for twenty years." Someone from the Simpson-Bruckheimer offices rang ABC executive Stuart Bloomberg, regarding the *Dangerous Minds* project. "Don't worry," Bloomberg was told. "This Simpson thing won't slow us down."

"This Simpson thing" was Simpson's death. By late Friday afternoon the word was getting out—first that Simpson had overdosed, then that he was in a hospital, then, by evening, that he was gone.

He may have been attempting, in the last hours of his life, to begin rebuilding his image. Sometime during the week before his death, Simpson had an assistant track down *Vanity Fair* writer Maureen Orth, who in 1978 had put Simpson on the map with her *New West* article "The Baby Moguls." Though they had not seen each other in more than ten years, Orth was not that surprised to hear from Simpson, for they had been in contact by telephone and always had lively conversations. Orth was a little surprised, though, at Simpson's persistence. She was on the road, covering a story, and began receiving repeated messages from Simpson's office. Simpson wanted to speak to her *at once*. Orth said she was too busy, but that she'd be in Los Angeles by the end of the week. "I said, 'I'll be at the Four Seasons on Friday, and I'll call when I get in,' " Orth recalled. "I said that maybe we could have lunch on Saturday, and his secretary said, 'Oh, that would be great!' But then she said, 'No, actually let's set up something on the phone.' " Simpson, evidently, was still not ready to make any public appearances.

When Orth arrived at the Four Seasons, there were several messages from Simpson and his secretary, including one confirming a phone conversation scheduled for two-thirty the following afternoon. Orth did not return the calls Friday. Saturday morning, she remembered, "I picked up the paper and there it was. He was dead."[32]

In Bel Air, at the Stone Canyon house, on the answering machine in his downstairs office, there was a telephone greeting from Universal's Casey Silver. He'd decided to offer Simpson a production deal, after all, and wanted to talk terms. His phone call had come in around four o'clock that Friday afternoon. Simpson's body was discovered about an hour later.

That night, private investigator Anthony Pellicano said to an acquaintance, "Jeez. I always thought he'd go out with more of a bang than that."[33]

Emergency crews were on the scene within fifteen minutes, but someone had gotten there first—perhaps before Marrero made the 911 call. According to press reports, Simpson's attorneys Robert Chapman and Brian Edwards were at the house before the police were.[34] Police reports indicate "the scene had been sanitized," a reference to efforts to hide or remove evidence of drug use. The recording officer also noted Ammerman's death at the same residence—"male dead in bed with a drug background"—and noted "investigators' immediate impression the scene had been sanitized. At scene police suspect the same in this case, the decedent said to have histories of PCP and cocaine abuse, possibly marijuana."[35]

Dr. Charles Kivowitz, a Beverly Hills physician who had treated Simpson sporadically for "insomnia and depression," according to police documents, was also called to the scene—but upon his arrival refused to sign documents pronouncing Simpson dead. He instead requested a coroner's investigation and left the house. Paramedics signed the death certificate. The Los Angeles Police Department officer overseeing the immediate investigation discovered no suicide note and no "obvious trauma." He duly noted Simpson's eye color (hazel), hair color (brown), height and weight (67 inches, 200 pounds), the presence of a beard and mustache and the facts that Simpson's teeth appeared to be his own and that his complexion was "fair/jaundiced?" He listed Larry (sic) Simpson as next of kin and indicated that he was notified of his brother's death at the scene. Simpson's parents, Russell and June Simpson of Rogers, Arkansas, were also notified, according to the same report. The officer stamped the report "ACC," indicating death by natural causes, and typed the words "drug background" under the Special Circumstances field. At 9:15 P.M., the officer noted, Simpson's body was transported away from 685 Stone Canyon Road. The following day Simpson's parents arrived in Los Angeles. On January 23 they consigned their son's body to the mortuary.

Life in Hollywood went on. Simpson's death was duly noted in the daily press. The Los Angeles Times obituary—coauthored by Eric Malnic and Chuck Philips, who would later do excellent reporting on the Simpson-related investigation of prescription drug abuse—cited police sources and said, "The fifty-two-year-old Oscar nominee's death appeared to be from natural causes." Bruckheimer was quoted as saying he was "in a state of shock," and said, "I have had the privilege to know and work with one of the most gifted and talented men in our industry. Don was a true original. There will never be another one like him."[36] Simpson's obituary ran under the headline "Don Simpson, Producer of Action Films, Found Dead" and was decorated with a photograph of a handsome Simpson, with a head shot apparently taken around his *Days of Thunder* period. (Two months later, announcing the result of autopsy reports in the same newspaper, Philips and Malnic's headline read, "Autopsy Finds Don Simpson Died of Overdose." The accompanying photograph was a more recent one, in which a bloated, unshaven Simpson leered into the lens.)[37] Though the *Times* obit included references to Simpson's stellar career—calling him and his partner "the quintessential action producers of the last decade"—it was also sprinkled with references to Simpson's seamy lifestyle. A coroner's spokesman was asked about drugs and drug paraphernalia; an investigation was said to be under way; Ammerman's death was recounted; and Ammerman's father was quoted on the subject of Simpson's drug addictions. Two "business associates said Friday that Simpson had appeared 'very depressed' recently," the article said. "Friends of the producer also told of similar stories of his drug use, and he was portrayed as a frequent drug user in *You'll Never Eat Lunch in This Town Again*, a book by Julia Phillips about the wild side of Hollywood."

The *New York Times* obituary was more circumspect. Simpson's successes were enumerated at length, but his excesses were not highlighted. Simpson and Bruckheimer here were "the archetypal Hollywood producers of the 1980s . . ." Simpson "was popular and well respected [and] considered a brilliant developer and analyst of scripts, with a knack for zeroing in on a flaw in a screenplay." There was only one reference to the shadows over Simpson's life. "His clothes were casual, his speech was quick and his moods were volatile," the *Times'* Eric Pace wrote. "He fought a weight problem with repeated slimming programs. Over the years, he acquired a reputation for high living and personal excesses. He loved parties, and in Julia Phillips' 1990 book about Hollywood, *You'll Never Eat Lunch in This Town Again*, he was depicted as using drugs."[38]

Hollywood did not pause to mark the moment. Simpson's old friend Penny Marshall ended her production deal at Columbia Pictures and replaced it with one at Universal—where, had he survived, Simpson, at the invitation of his former assistant Casey Silver, would have joined her. Demi Moore, who had enjoyed a similar deal at Columbia, also moved to Universal. Viacom's Sumner Redstone parted company with his fiercely able lieutenant, Frank Biondi, who would also find his way to Universal. Edgar Bronfman Jr., the Seagram heir who had recently become Universal's owner and chief officer, announced "Talent as Priority" at a meeting with television executives and station owners. Disney's Michael Eisner and Michael Ovitz—now known around the lot as "M.E. and M.O."—visited top Wall Street investors to encourage support for their company. Sandra Bullock agreed to star in a sequel to *Speed*. Clint Eastwood agreed to make *Absolute Power* his next picture, as did Harrison Ford *Air Force One*. Uma Thurman was officially announced as Poison Ivy in the upcoming sequel *Batman and Robin*. That film's star, George Clooney, was cast opposite Michelle Pfeiffer in Simpson's old friend Lynda Obst's comedy *One Fine Day*. Paramount Pictures, where Simpson served as an executive and where he made his most winning movies, announced a new "five-year plan" to make movies with Simpson's most successful leading man, Tom Cruise. *From Dusk Till Dawn* was briefly the most popular movie in America.

Within two months, though, Simpson was back in the headlines, as the results of his January 23, 1996, autopsy were revealed. The *Los Angeles Times'* Malnic and Philips' report on March 27 led with the paragraph, "An autopsy shows that top movie producer Don Simpson—whose reckless appetite for drugs and women made him a legend in Hollywood—died in January of heart failure caused by a massive overdose of cocaine and prescription medications" found in Simpson's home. They quoted coroner's office spokesman Scott Carrier: "This is like a medicine case of drugs." They quoted Los Angeles Police Department Detective Brad Roberts: "The place looked like a pharmaceutical supply house." The writers noted that, at the time of his death, police sources had said no drugs or drug paraphernalia had been found at the scene. "The discrepancies between the first and second police reports have not been made clear," they wrote. They quoted attorney Alexander Lampone, who would later file the $53-million wrongful death civil action against the Simpson estate for the death of Stephen Ammerman: "Two people died of drugs in that house in less than six months. They both died due to overdoses of prescription drugs, obtained through licensed practitioners, and we are seeking to find out how it happened." According to the *Times*, the drugs found in Simpson's body included "cocaine, a stimulant, and a variety of drugs used in the treatment of depression, anxiety and sleeplessness—Unisom, Atarax, Vistaril, Librium, Valium, Compazine, Xanax, Desyrel and Tigan."

A report appearing the same day in *Daily Variety* quoted LAPD Detective David Miller, who had begun his investigation into prescription drug abuse after Simpson's death, as saying, "There were more than 2,000 individual pills and capsules found at Simpson's house," and listed the same collection of pharmaceuticals listed in the *Times*.

The actual autopsy report is a thoroughly depressing document, deadening in its hollow, scientific tone and, to the untrained reader, chilling in its clinical attention to physical detail. Having determined the cause of death as "combined effects of multiple drug intake," Christopher Rogers, M.D., chief of the Forensic Medicine Division for the Los Angeles County Department of Coroner—witnessed by one Russell Grimble, and in consultation with a Dr. Fishbein from Cedars-Sinai Medical Center—filed his report March 27, after conducting his initial autopsy January 23.

Rogers' "external examination" said that "the body is that of an unembalmed Caucasian middle-age male who appears the stated age of 52 years. The body is identified by toe tags. The body weighs 200 pounds, measures 67 inches in length and is moderately obese. No tattoos are present. The head, which is normo-cephalic, is covered with brown hair. There are no scars of the chest or abdomen. The abdomen is flat. The genitalia are those of a circumcised adult. There is no anal or genital trauma. There are no needle tracks."

Rogers' "initial incision" revealed nothing out of the ordinary. There were no fractures; there was no hemorrhage. The lungs were "well-expanded." After further, deeper incisions, Rogers made several discoveries. Simpson's heart showed evidence of myocardial fibrosis, a thickening of the heart's muscle walls. In his summing-up, Rogers wrote, "Cocaine use, in the presence of myocardial fibrosis, may induce fatal arrhythmia"—exactly the diagnosis Simpson had received, and ignored, from Drs. John O'Dea and William Stuppy the previous fall.

Rogers then invited the reader to peruse the accompanying toxicology report, conducted in consultation with the coroner's office's Joseph Moto. Analysis of Simpson's bile indicated substantial evidence of cocaine use, as did analysis of his urine. Blood testing showed levels of chlordiazepoxide, desmethydiazepam, diazepam, doxylamine, hydroxine, norchlorcyclizine, prochlorperazine, trazodone and trimethobenzamide. Liver analysis confirmed those findings and showed additional levels of clonazepam.

The death was ruled "accidental." The paperwork on autopsy report 96-00611 was filed. Simpson's body was released to Pierce Brothers Mortuary in Westwood, where it was subsequently cremated.

Several weeks later Jerry Bruckheimer and a few key Simpson allies flew with the ashes to Aspen and scattered him into the wind.

The *Los Angeles Times* writers closed their report on the autopsy with these words: "Simpson's excesses were as famous as his loud, large movies. His raucous lifestyle got him some juicy paragraphs in a couple of Hollywood tell-alls, including the recently released memoir of four self-described call girls, *You'll Never Make Love in This Town Again.* In the book, one of the girls details what she claims were her sexual exploits with the producer. Not to be outdone, former Hollywood madam Heidi Fleiss, convicted on pandering and money-laundering charges in connection with her prostitution business, told a reporter that Simpson was 'not just a customer, but a close friend.' "[39]

This was the end of the end. Simpson was dead. His personal habits and excesses were on display, and the physical details of his demise were a matter of public record. The Simpson legend—not the one he wanted, not the one he attempted to create, but the one his weaknesses, sexual predilections and substance addictions created for him—was struck.

CHAPTER ELEVEN

AFTERMATH

Word began to spread, on the afternoon of Friday, January 19, 1996, that Simpson was in trouble. "He OD'd," one source reported. "He's in the hospital or something," said another. By evening the news was worsening. "I think he's dead," the first source called to add.[1] By six o'clock the rumors became real. Private investigator Anthony Pellicano, a close Simpson associate, said, "Yeah, it's true." He said that Simpson had died "of a heart attack, sitting on the toilet." As was his wont, Pellicano began the spin campaign to direct attention from the true cause of death, a campaign he would continue for some weeks. "The funny thing is, it wasn't an overdose, but everyone will say it is," Pellicano said.[2] Pellicano added that Simpson, though he was desperately overweight, had undergone a physical checkup recently and had seemed well. "He'd never been so 'up' in his life," Pellicano said.

By nighttime the news was general. Jeff Berg, the powerful head of ICM and a twenty-year Simpson associate, said, "What can I say? He was a totally unique guy—one of a kind."[3] Reached at his Disney office by Simpson's attorney, Jake Bloom, Simpson's former boss and mentor Michael Eisner said, "I've been waiting for this call for twenty years."[4] Jonathan Hensleigh, a writer on *The Rock*, was in a water tank supervising underwater scenes when word hit the set, on a Culver City soundstage. He recalled *Rock* costar Sean Connery's reaction. "Sean said to me, 'I have to say, I'm not *that* surprised.' "[5] A glum Rob Cohen, a film director who had been a Simpson crony for more than a decade, said, "Don was a guy who spoke very, very highly about a man he really loathed. Which was himself,"[6] and added, "He succeeded at everything he ever tried to do, and he'd been trying to do this for a long time."[7] After receiving a phone call from Frank Pesce, the actor who had originally introduced her to Simpson more than a decade before, Bonnie Bradigan said, "It's got to be the booze and the pills. He took 'em like M&M's." She and Pesce, apparently attempting a reconciliation between Bradigan and Simpson, had been planning to meet that Friday night at Pesce's house and then pay Simpson a social visit. They never got there.[8]

Simpson's associates immediately began organizing their late friend's memorial services. There were to be two—first an informal gathering of his closest friends, who would meet at Simpson's house and dine at his Buffalo Club restaurant in Santa Monica, and then another for his industry contacts, who would meet at the industry's most famous watering hole, Morton's.

To the first event were invited old friends like Craig Baumgarten, Shep Gordon, Warren Beatty, Mark Canton, Jim Berkus, Jake Bloom, Tony Danza, Don Johnson, Barry Josephson, Michael Mann, Jack Rapke, Paul Schrader, Steve Tisch, James Toback, Jim Wiatt, Hawk Wolinsky and the Buffalo Club's owner, Anthony Yerkovich. (That part of the list read like an informal membership roster of a different kind of Buffalo club, a collection of free-ranging, carnivorous and endangered species of predatory American male.) There were also business associates like Jeffrey Katzenberg, attorney Bert Fields, Tom Pollock, Dawn Steel, Joe Roth, Robert Towne, Michael Eisner, David Friendly, Martin Brest, agent Bob Bookman and producer Dan Melnick. Actors Tom Cruise, Jon Lovitz, Sean Penn, Richard Dreyfuss and Nick Nolte were invited, as were Simpson-Bruckheimer directors Tony Scott and Michael Bay. Beatty's wife, Annette Bening, was on the list, as were Tina Sinatra and Alana Stewart. So were old girlfriends Susan Lentini and Priscilla Nedd, now married to David Friendly, and old friend Melissa Prophet, now married to Craig Baumgarten. Personal assistants Todd Marrero and Michelle McElroy were there, as was Simpson stalwart Anthony Pellicano—who had just been quoted, continuing his spin control campaign on his friend's behalf, as saying of Dr. Stephen Ammerman's death, "I've had a lot of clients who've had people die in their homes. What's the big deal?"[9]

Notes obtained through Simpson's office indicate a strong turnout. Tony Danza's representatives said he had to be in Las Vegas but would "be there in spirit." Sean Penn's said he was "out of the country until Friday night" but would attend the Morton's event the following Monday. Jack Rapke was also out of town. Directors Paul Schrader and Marty Brest couldn't make it but would try for Monday. *Rolling Stone* founder Jann Wenner, an old friend from Simpson's Aspen winters, had just lost his mother-in-law and was trying to make it from Sun Valley to Los Angeles in time for the event. Tony Scott, out of town shooting his Robert De Niro/Wesley Snipes thriller *The Fan*," might not make it either. Simpson's brother, Lary, and his wife, Sally, and Simpson's parents, Russ and June, would certainly attend. So would Casey Silver, a late addition to the invite list. So, of course, would Jerry and Linda Bruckheimer.[10]

It would be a private affair—no press, no photographers. The Buffalo Club was closed for the night, and no one who wasn't on the list would get inside. Simpson acquaintances who rang his office angling for an invitation were told they *might* be added to the Morton's list.[11]

At the Buffalo Club, underneath a burned-out neon sign reading "Olympic Club," guests drank champagne, made toasts and shared memories of their late friend. It was, several attendees said, a very quiet and sentimental evening. Simpson, no sentimentalist, "would have gotten bored and split after half an hour," one guest said.[12]

The following Monday night, at Simpson's closed-door memorial reception at Morton's, photographers noted many Hollywood luminaries hobnobbing over wine and cheese. Steve Tisch hugged Jeffrey Katzenberg. Jim Berkus stood chatting with Joe Roth. Howard Rosenman was photographed with Berkus, director Michael Mann and a sour-faced Anthony Pellicano. Richard Dreyfuss shared a word with Simpson's former protégée Dawn Steel.[13] Outwardly, it looked like any night at Morton's: One source who attended described the evening as "grotesque," a standard Hollywood gathering full of the standard "schmoozing and bullshit."[14]

Former girlfriend Lentini sat quietly in a corner, watching the video monitors, next to Priscilla Nedd. Across the room was Bonnie Bruckheimer, Jerry's ex-wife. "It was a terrible tragedy, and very sad," Bruckheimer said. "There was a lot of talk about the old days, because even the people there didn't respect him anymore, didn't respect what he had become. They respected who he had been, but there was a great feeling of pity in the room, that night, about what he had turned into."[15] "I was crazy about him," Nedd-Friendly said, but added, "The Don he became is not the Don I knew."[16] There was silence, as the video reel ran, and then there were stories from the old days and a bit of networking. Some of the people in the room, like Bonnie Bruckheimer, hadn't seen some of Simpson's friends in years—especially in the last, dark years when Simpson himself was increasingly scarce. There were some reunions. Was there an inappropriate amount of "schmoozing" going on? "This is Hollywood," Bruckheimer said. "No one ever misses an opportunity to do a little business."

There was also some grieving. Lentini said, "Don always told me he struggled with the demons of depression and the thought of maybe checking out. He struggled with it every day. Once he said to me, 'None of us get out of here alive anyway.' "[17] Heidi Fleiss, without pretense or self-protection, told reporters exactly how she felt about her late friend and customer. "I loved him dearly," Fleiss said the day after Simpson's death. "I used to call him my little Eskimo."[18]

Over the next several months, Simpson's younger brother, Lary, oversaw the sanitizing of the Stone Canyon house. He cleaned out Simpson's bedroom and office and threw out box after box of Simpson memorabilia— the framed photocopies of Simpson's paychecks, the framed "visionary alliance" announcement, personal letters and dozens of pairs of Simpson's favorite Calvin Klein underwear.[19] By the summer Lary surprised many of Simpson's friends by moving himself and his wife and two children into the house where his brother, and his brother's physician, had died. He began telling acquaintances that he was leaving the law practice his brother had arranged for him and would become a movie producer.[20] He intended to take over all of Simpson's developing projects and turn them into movies. Among them would be a drama called *Blood of the Lamb*, about a scientist and a priest who attempt to clone the body of Jesus Christ, using the Shroud of Turin for their basic DNA material.[21]

Bruckheimer, solo, announced just before the release of *Con Air* that Disney had extended his producing deal for an additional five years. He subsequently announced his intention to reunite with Eddie Murphy and Paramount Pictures to make a fourth *Beverly Hills Cop* film[22] and his plans to reteam his *Top Gun, Days of Thunder* and *Crimson Tide* director, Tony Scott, with his *Bad Boys* actor Will Smith.[23] Smith, he said, would appear in his *Enemy of the State*, a Capitol Hill–based thriller. He would also go into production soon on *Armageddon*, a production Bruckheimer described as "a *Dirty Dozen* in outer space," starring Bruce Willis.[24]

Disney, meanwhile, was sued by a San Francisco writer who said the studio stole the idea for *Crimson Tide* from his screenplay *Launch Sequence*.[25] *Playing God*, the script that Stephen Ammerman's family alleged in court documents was stolen from the late doctor's private papers, went into production as a planned Disney release, starring *X-Files* sensation David Duchovny.

Smith's *Bad Boys* costar, Martin Lawrence, continued to court disaster. He was accused in April 1997 of punching a man in a nightclub, having been arrested the previous May for carrying a loaded handgun onto an airplane, and, earlier that month, having been hospitalized for "exhaustion" after authorities found him standing in a San Fernando Valley intersection "shouting incoherently in traffic and struggling with police."[26] His inconsistencies were making Hollywood nervous to the extent that one source close to the story said, Columbia Pictures would probably not hire him to appear in *Bad Boys 2*.[27]

The original Beverly Hills Cop, Eddie Murphy, had his own troubles. The actor was stopped by police on a West Hollywood street, around four o'clock in the morning, after Murphy allegedly stopped his Toyota Land Cruiser to pick up a transsexual prostitute. Murphy's spokesman, Paul Bloch, of the public relations firm Rogers & Cowan, issued the astonishing explanation that his client was "simply trying to be a Good Samaritan. He saw a person on the street and was concerned. He stopped to ask if the person needed help and the person asked for a ride home." Bloch, who had also done professional damage control in the past for Simpson, Bruckheimer and action stars Bruce Willis and Sylvester Stallone, added that Murphy frequently came to the aid of homeless people[28]—perhaps, if he could be credited with such foresight, creating a permanently effective explanation: Should his client find himself in a similarly embarrassing situation in the future, Bloch might simply say, "Like I told you before, he's just a Good Samaritan."

Actor Charlie Sheen, who had shared Simpson's habit of using Hollywood madam Heidi Fleiss to arrange his sexual liaisons, was similarly in and out of the news for more bad behavior. In December he was arrested on battery charges after allegedly beating his twenty-four-year-old actress-girlfriend in his Agoura Hills home.[29] The following June, after pleading no contest to the charges, Sheen was sentenced to a suspended one-year jail term, placed on two years probation and fined $2,800.[30] Two months later, meeting members of the press to promote his upcoming comedy *Money Talks,* Sheen appeared to be entirely out of control. When asked about the film, Sheen said, "It's simple. Papa Bear is Baby Bear. Baby Bear is Papa Bear. But Mama Bear is always Mama Bear."[31] His publicist immediately ended the interview.

Months earlier, veteran bad boy Jack Nicholson faced charges similar to those brought against Sheen. An assault and battery lawsuit was filed in November 1996 by a woman who alleged that Nicholson had invited her and another woman to his home and offered each woman $1,000 to have sex with him. He subsequently refused to pay and became violent, one of the women charged.[32]

Also that spring, in a stunning coincidence, it was announced on the very same day that actress-singer Madonna had given birth to a healthy six-pound baby while being attended by Heidi Fleiss' father, the pediatrician Paul Fleiss, *and* that Fleiss had the previous May been placed on probation by the Medical Board of California because of his recent convictions on conspiracy and money-laundering charges. Fleiss had served nine months house arrest after pleading guilty to tax evasion charges stemming from his daughter's pimping and prostitution arrest.[33]

The "wrongful death" lawsuit brought by the late Dr. Stephen Ammerman's family against the Simpson estate, and the other alleged conspirators, wandered its way through the legal system. In mid-1997 a judge threw out the bulk of the suit, on the grounds that Ammerman's family had no evidence to support their contention of a conspiracy to keep Simpson alive, by any means necessary, at the risk of killing his personal physician. Removed at once from the lawsuit were the names Lary Simpson, Jerry Bruckheimer and Anthony Pellicano. A reworked version of the lawsuit, it was promised, would be filed, and the Ammerman family promised an appeal of the judge's decision to remove the Simpson associates from their suit.[34]

Investigations by the Medical Board of California into physician abuse of pharmaceutical drugs continued. In July 1997 investigators issued subpoenas for the medical records of fifteen physicians who treated Simpson during the last year of his life. They also subpoenaed Anthony Pellicano, a pharmacy owner and more than a dozen others to determine details of the private drug rehab program Dr. Ammerman was conducting on Simpson at his home in the months prior to his death.[35]

Bruckheimer himself was conspicuously absent from most of the press accounts that chronicled his late partner's decline and fall, himself declining to submit statements or sit for interviews. He told one reporter, simply, "I'm just too emotional and too raw and too sad. I'm going to protect him in death as I protected him in life."[36]

Bruckheimer's ability to protect Simpson proved, however, somewhat limited. In the months that followed his death, extended accounts of Simpson's difficulties and demise appeared in *Vanity Fair, Premiere, Entertainment Weekly, Playboy,* the *Los Angeles Times,* the *New York Times* and elsewhere. They spoke eloquently of his generosity and genius, but also of his demons and his despair. Long-lost accounts of his abusive behavior and tantrums were repeated. Veteran Simpson cronies Jim Wiatt, Rob Cohen, Steve Tisch, James Toback, Robert Towne, Anthony Yerkovich, Tom Pollock and others spoke lovingly of their late friend. (Very conspicuously absent from these articles were Simpson's stars. Tom Cruise's voice was not heard. Nor was there any statement to the press, or the public, from Eddie Murphy, Richard Gere, Will Smith, Jennifer Beals or Val Kilmer— all of whom, it could be argued, owed their film careers to Simpson and Bruckheimer.) Many of the friends who did grant interviews regretted it, as they read the published tales of Simpson's sexual and narcotic excesses.

But at least Simpson was spared, as they were not, the indignity of *Once More with Feeling,* Dove Books' 1996 sequel to its outrageous 1995 tell-all *You'll Never Make Love in This Town Again.* As if personally offended at Simpson's excesses, the prostitutes who had served him in the early 1990s strode forth to tell their stories. "Michelle" recalled a cocaine- and SM-filled 1992 evening in which she and "perhaps a dozen women" attempted to service the Don. The prostitute collected $1,500 for her efforts—"I must have sucked that hard-core Hollywood dick for an hour, but he never came," Michelle graciously wrote, only to find Simpson still wanting more. "You're not on a fucking time clock," he growled at her when she said she had to leave.[37] On a subsequent evening, though repulsed by what she'd seen the first time, Michelle returned to the Stone Canyon home to collect another $1,500, this time for participating in a three-way sexual situation that ended with Simpson urinating and then ejaculating over Michelle and her partner.[38]

Once More with Feeling rounded up the usual suspects—movie magnate Ted Field, rocker Don Henley, actors Jack Nicholson, Warren Beatty, Dennis Hopper and Charlie Sheen, financier Adnan Kashoggi—and added some new names. Perhaps due to threats of litigation growing out of its predecessor's confessions, though, the sequel was curiously delicate about identifying several Hollywood titans. Producer Robert Evans, eviscerated in the first book for his scatological obsessions, is here transformed into "Alan Smithee"—the pseudonym the Directors Guild of America allows a director to use when he wants to remove his name from a piece of work. Smithee is readily identifiable on several accounts: His best friends appear to be Nicholson and Beatty; his friend and sometime attorney Robert Shapiro is named; his house is described in great detail; and highlights of his career are mentioned.[39] A film producer and former studio president identified as "Mike Mogul" gets the same treatment, but his identify is even less thinly disguised. The book doesn't name him, but its authors deposit clues only the blind could fail to follow. Mike Mogul had "been around Hollywood a long time and served briefly as president at both MGM and Paramount," Michelle writes, narrowing the list of candidates to a handful. She then adds, "Like his friend, the late Don Simpson, this man is a successful and prolific producer of well-known films, whose credits *may* include [italics mine] such films as *That's Entertainment, All That Jazz, Altered States* and more recently *L.A. Story* and *Universal Soldier.*[40] Of those films, only *Universal Soldier* was not produced by former MGM and Paramount studio boss Daniel Melnick.

Life after Simpson, for Bruckheimer, appeared to be an improvement. In June 1996 Bruckheimer presided over the release of *The Rock*, the last movie he and Simpson developed together. The film opened strong on the weekend of June 7 and earned a staggering $25 million in its first three days of release, ultimately earning $134 million in American movie theaters alone.[41] Reviewers were not impressed by the Nicolas Cage/Sean Connery pairing, and many seemed eager to remind their readers that they disapproved of the entire body of Simpson-Bruckheimer films. The *Los Angeles Times'* Kenneth Turan opened his review by writing, "The closing credits for *The Rock* include a dedication 'in loving memory to Don

Simpson,' but this last film from the late producer and his partner Jerry Bruckheimer so perfectly encapsulates everything the pair have stood for that the actual words are superfluous." He continued: "A picture that believes that bigger and louder are better, that success goes to whatever makes the most noise and does the most damage, this story of a nasty hostage situation on Alcatraz epitomizes trends in Hollywood filmmaking that have made many people very rich while impoverishing audiences around the world. Slick and forceful, largely unconcerned with character, eager for any opportunity to pump up the volume both literally and metaphorically, *The Rock* is the kind of efficient entertainment that is hard to take pleasure in. It's this year's model of a dangerous sports car or designer knife: You don't know whether to admire it or run for cover when it approaches."[42]

The *New Yorker*'s Terrence Rafferty said, "The producers of *The Rock* are Don Simpson (who died suddenly last January) and Jerry Bruckheimer, whose approach to filmmaking has always been to pound the captive viewer into submission. With the passage of time, the oppressiveness of their high-grossing pictures . . . could become as legendary as that of Alcatraz; and *The Rock* demonstrates conclusively that even the most resourceful of actors can't escape from the maximum-security concept of a Simpson-Bruckheimer production." Rafferty dismissed director Michael Bay's work as "non-stop action . . . in a manic style that suggests the influence of Simpson and Bruckheimer's pet auteur, Tony Scott"—who helmed *Top Gun, Beverly Hills Cop 2, Crimson Tide* and *Days of Thunder,* though Rafferty neglected to mention Scott's work on that last film. The critic called Connery "just another wisecracking daredevil of the *Die Hard* variety," and said Cage's performance was limited to "glazed expressions and the slowed-down speech of pure stupefaction." He closed his review by writing, "There's nothing inherently wrong with pitching a movie to an adolescent sensibility. *The Rock,* however, is aimed at the least interesting and most dangerous teenagers—not at the rebels but at the bullies. In the movie's most revealing scene, [Cage], just before going into battle, assures [Connery], 'I'll do my best,' and the older man turns on him. 'Losers always whine about doing their best,' [Connery] says. 'Winners go home and fuck the prom queen.'

"Words to live by," Rafferty concluded. "It's the Simpson-Bruckheimer-Bay philosophy in a nutshell."[43]

At the end of 1996 the National Association of Theater Owners gave

The Rock their Best Picture award, presented in February at their annual ShoWest convention. Bruckheimer and director Michael Bay were on hand to accept. Following a rousing screening of the film's highlights, Bruckheimer took the stage and said, "I want to dedicate this to my partner. We lost him on this movie. God bless you, wherever you are." Bay, who was honored with NATO's Best Director award, followed Bruckheimer to the podium. He thanked the many people who had made his movie possible and closed with a tip of the hat to Simpson, "who's not here anymore. God bless you."

Simpson's high-concept legacy was intact. Audiences raved for *The Rock,* apparently immune from what critic Rafferty called "the oppressiveness of [Simpson and Bruckheimer's] high-grossing pictures." Simpson, wherever he was, had partners praying for him in Las Vegas. The theater owners were praying for another hit like *The Rock.* Critics were praying over the death of the intelligent American movie. As the Simpson legacy continued beyond his death, the critics would find their prayer unanswered.

After the success of *The Rock,* there was 1997's *Con Air.* Seen by some as a *Rock* sequel, and by others as a variation on the already-tired "Die Hard on an Airplane" mode—a genre that already included *Die Hard 2,* which *was* on a plane, as well as the thrillers *Passenger 57* and *Air Force One*—*Con Air* attempted to tell the story of Cameron Poe, a good man who has done wrong and paid his debt to society, and who is leaving prison to return to his family. Played by Nicolas Cage, Poe is being transported cross-country in a jet known as *Con Air,* because its principal function is to ferry dangerous cons from one prison to another. In this instance it is ferrying "the worst of the worst" to a new maximum security prison. Poe's copassengers include the brilliant mass murderer Cyrus "the Virus" Grissom, played by John Malkovich; the Hannibal Lector–style killer Garland Greene, played by Steve Buscemi; and the black liberation terrorist Diamond Dog, played by Ving Rhames. "Makes the Manson family look like the Partridge Family," Poe remarks of his fellow passengers.

Con Air marked the first film that Bruckheimer produced without Simpson since they made *Flashdance* together in 1983, and his first film without a partner in his entire career. (Bruckheimer was a producer, but not *the* producer, of earlier efforts like *Cat People, American Gigolo,*

Farewell, My Lovely and *The Culpepper Cattle Company.)* Flying high, and solo, may have gone to his head. According to one source near the marketing of *Con Air*, an evidently insecure Bruckheimer attempted to take *all* the credit, if not all the credits, for making the movie. "We were preparing the production notes and press releases. On the first page of the production notes [as prepared by Bruckheimer's office] it actually said, 'The notable producer Jerry Bruckheimer' and 'the eminent producer Jerry Bruckheimer' and 'the distinguished producer Jerry Bruckheimer,' " the source said. "All on one page! It was like he created, wrote, directed, produced and distributed *Con Air* all on his own. Simon West [the film's director] was livid."[44]

The nation's film critics seemed to take special pleasure in savaging the movie, and few resisted the temptation to take a shot at the late Simpson. In one especially vicious Owen Gleiberman review that appeared in *Entertainment Weekly*, the critic identified *Con Air* as "the first movie to be produced by Jerry Bruckheimer without his partner, Don Simpson, the pioneer of adrenaline-fueled high-concept trash who died of a drug overdose in 1996 after too many years of bad movies and bad living."[45] Gleiberman then called the film "a headache in the form of a movie" and "a homage to everything Simpson stood for as a producer: noise, testosterone, the glory of wretched excess." "It's a drug designed for people who've done every drug and now want to be jet-propelled into numbness," he wrote, concluding, *"Con Air* may be the closest thing yet to pure action-thriller pornography. Ultimately, there's nothing to it but thrust."

Anthony Lane, at the *New Yorker*, liked the film no better but couched his complaints more archly.[46] After assassinating the movie, he wrote, "All this is a way of saying that *Con Air* was produced by Jerry Bruckheimer. With his late partner, Don Simpson, Bruckheimer was responsible for *Top Gun, Beverly Hills Cop, Crimson Tide* and a host of other quiet, Bergmanish delvings into the agony of a godless world. To watch those movies was to have your brains tossed like salad, but anyone who claimed to be wholly impervious to the bright crunch of the Bruckheimer style was either lying or dead. I would be more than happy to welcome *Con Air* into the fold, but it is not one of Bruckheimer's best." Indeed. Lane, finished with Bruckheimer, then assails *Con Air* director Simon West—listing *Con Air*'s cast members Nicolas Cage, John Malkovich, Steve Buscemi and John Cusack, and asking, "How can you make a bad film with a cast like that? Well, it's a tall order, but somehow West pulls it off." Lane lauded only

Cage's performance and concludes his review by writing, "[Cage's] is a valiant quest for irony in a movie that wants only to whack us into oblivion, and in his low-lidded eyes we see a reflection of our own ever-growing predicament: there is nothing so boring in life, let alone in cinema, as the boredom of being excited all the time." *New York*'s David Denby found more to like, though his review read like an apology. "Low and violent as it is, *Con Air* has some life to it," he wrote. "The movie is very nasty fun." But he then went on to criticize the film's producer—unusual, as critics usually hold writers and directors responsible for movies they don't like. Attacking one pointedly emotional scene between Cage and his daughter—and probably taking his cues from Bruckheimer's own self-aggrandizing comments in the production notes—Denby wrote, "That's the Jerry Bruckheimer touch—a bit of 'heart' that allegedly makes the hero appealing. My guess is that a good part of the audience will ridicule the cynicism of 'heart' for the outrageous cornball crap that it is. *Con Air* has about as much heart as an F-16. It does fly, though, a lot higher and faster than anyone would have expected."[47]

(The television critics Gene Siskel and Roger Ebert gave *Con Air* their trademark "two thumbs up." Two weeks later, however, they gave the same top marks to *Speed 2: Cruise Control*.)[48]

Bruckheimer himself said in production notes that he intended something larger than a simple action movie, saying of the original script by writer Scott Rosenberg, "It was certainly great writing, but I instantly surmised that the script needed more heart. It had to be more character driven, which is a common theme through all my films, no matter what the action content might be."

This boast drove David Ansen, of *Newsweek*, to remark in his review, "Maybe I missed something (the thunderous noise level makes it hard to catch all the character-driven subtleties of the script), but it did seem to be the 'action content' that was grabbing the crowd." Ansen continued, "The saving grace of *Con Air* is its sense of its own absurdity. Rosenberg and director Simon West seem to know just how preposterous their story is: the 'heartfelt' moments between Cage and his family are as over the top as the macho 'grand guignol' of a planeload of raving psychopaths." Ansen quoted Bruckheimer as saying, "This film is a story about redemption," and closed his review, "Let's hope he's pulling our legs. If you can't take *Con Air* as a big, noisy joke, why would you want to take it at all?"[49]

"On the contrary," one former Simpson-Bruckheimer employee, the producer Michael London, protested. "*Con Air* is an incredibly visceral experience, and a new level of insulting the audience. It's Jerry, without the humanity of Don, who wouldn't have accepted something so empty and cold."[50]

Con Air nevertheless opened strong. It debuted on Friday, June 6, 1996, competing in a crowded marketplace already dominated by Steven Spielberg's fiercesome box-office monster *The Lost World*. By Monday morning, estimates said the movie had made $25 million and stolen the number one box-office spot from Spielberg's *World*.[51] The opening-weekend numbers were slightly lower than Bruckheimer had enjoyed a year earlier with *The Rock*, but they were powerful. Analysts immediately predicted *Con Air* would go to $100 million at the box office.[52] By the second weekend, despite the arrival of *Speed 2: Cruise Control*, *Con Air* had earned a healthy $49 million. In its third week of release, competing against the huge *Batman and Robin*, *Con Air* held on to third place at the box office, as its earnings rose to $67 million.[53] By summer's end it was nosing $90 million.

And the press, still, had not finished with Simpson. In interview after interview, as he did promotion for *Con Air*, Bruckheimer suffered through questions about his late partner and about the experience of working without him. Irritated, finally, Bruckheimer grew whiny. "You know how Don was," he said, when asked about Simpson's "reported battles with the bottle and with drugs," and his "public struggle with his weight, his bombastic personality, his admitted yearning to be a movie star." Bruckheimer said that he was "tired of people assuming that he was Don Simpson's double," the reporter wrote, quoting a grumpy Bruckheimer: "I was the opposite of my partner. I'm not flamboyant or outgoing like that. But you're painted with the same brush"[54]—a preposterous complaint, since no one had *ever* written about the producing partners without explicitly pointing out the extreme, almost yin-and-yang polarity of their personalities and lifestyles.

In the summing-up over the weeks and months that followed, theories proliferated—about the real cause of Simpson's death, about the real source of his drug addictions, about who and what, after all, Simpson really was. His friend Craig Baumgarten said, "You know something? I think we'll all analyze Don for the rest of our lives."[55]

Others had done their analyses and reached conclusions. His friend Anthony Yerkovich believed Simpson's death was an inevitable result of his inability to find moderation—in anything. "Don had two speeds, both in his business and his life: full throttle, and crash and burn."[56] "Did he have darkness? Sure he had darkness," said his friend Rob Cohen. "Who doesn't? He just wasn't hypocritical about it, or ashamed of it."[57] His excesses, according to his longtime professional associate and former employee Lucas Foster, were sufficiently legendary to have achieved the quality of myth—to the degree, perhaps, that no one could even see the real Don Simpson anymore. "Don has become the poster child for what everybody says is right and wrong about Hollywood," Foster said.[58] More succinctly, speaking at Simpson's memorial service, a former Disney colleague said, "He defined the 1980s. It's the end of an era."[59]

Larry Ferguson, the screenwriter who had helped craft *Beverly Hills Cop*, summed up what he saw as Hollywood's betrayal of his late friend. "It's a very hard thing to ask a person—to dump a wild animal into the middle of the food chain and say, 'Now, discipline yourself.' It's not fair, and it didn't work."[60] Former studio head Tom Pollock, who was Simpson's friend, and had been his attorney, told a friend, "Don pushed the envelope always, and the envelope pushed back."[61]

The Hollywood that Simpson left behind was provincial, incestuous and almost hermeneutic in its isolation from the outside world and ordinary human reality. Money and power provided the isolation. Ambition and the obsession with money, power and movies provided the incest, and united many of the industry's key players in an invisible web of ever-changing loyalties, where personal and professional relationships become impossible to distinguish, and their longevity impossible to predict. Players might move in and out of power, and in and out of favor with each other, but still the players swirl unceasingly about in a kind of circle of sleaziness.

Robert Evans dates Denise Brown, whose sister is later murdered by O. J. Simpson, whose attorney is Robert Shapiro, who is a frequent guest at Evans' house, having represented him on a cocaine possession charge. The drug dealer named J.R. claims to have sold cocaine and other drugs to O.J. and to Nicole Brown *and* to Faye Resnick, years before those three ever met, and years before their whole ugly world would be open to worldwide scrutiny. Faye Resnick later writes of her relationship with

Nicole, in a book published by Dove Audio, which also published *You'll Never Make Love in This Town Again*, which claimed to chronicle Evans' sexual peculiarities. Evans threatens to sue Dove. Dove subsequently makes a deal with Evans to publish the audiotape version of his autobiography, *The Kid Stays in the Picture*. Charlie Sheen, who also appeared in *You'll Never*, is called to testify at Heidi Fleiss' trial. Years earlier, he had been featured on the cover of *Penthouse* magazine, photographed with Pet of the Year Julie Strain, the woman Don Simpson insisted—over Strain's protestations—was a high-end call girl whom he'd paid $5,000 for a night of sex. After Simpson's death, his house assistant Jeannelle Trepanier, who said she loved Simpson and owed her entire career to him, makes a career move and becomes an employee at Sheen's production company.

Investigator Anthony Pellicano, who had been Simpson's black bag man for almost a decade, was a member of the team representing entertainer Michael Jackson on charges that he sexually molested a young boy. A year after Simpson's death and long after the O. J. Simpson murder trial had concluded, Pellicano suddenly pops up in the press as a spokesman for Mark Fuhrman, the Los Angeles Police Department investigator who claimed to have found the infamous "bloody glove" at O.J.'s Brentwood estate, and whose reported racist comments disgraced him and his department and may have contributed to O.J.'s subsequent "not guilty" verdict.[62]

Ivan Nagy, who along with Don Simpson and Robert Evans was a client of Madam Alex Adams, and who later partnered with Heidi Fleiss, had business dealings with Columbia Pictures, when it was cochaired by Jon Peters, another Adams and Fleiss client, and when the movie division was run by Michael Nathanson, who on the advice of his attorney, Howard Weitzman, announced to the world that he'd never known Fleiss or been her client—before anyone in the world ever accused him publicly of those things. Attorney Anthony Brooklier, making a career of it, represents Heidi Fleiss on her pimping and prostitution case, having earlier represented Madam Alex Adams on *her* prostitution case. Weitzman, who was also part of the O. J. Simpson defense team and of the Michael Jackson defense team, *and* part of the group that unsuccessfully defended boxer Mike Tyson on rape charges, *and*, with Pellicano, helped defend accused cocaine trafficker John DeLorean, leaves his law firm and becomes a top officer of MCA Universal, where he works alongside ex-CAA agent Ron Meyer, who replaced Tom Pollock, who had been Don Simpson's attorney, and who had hired Casey Silver, who had been Simpson's assistant. Meyer's first action as head of Universal is to make a rich, three-picture deal with Sylvester Stallone, who was supposed to have been the original Beverly Hills Cop. Calls to confirm details of Stallone's life or career are returned by publicist Paul Bloch, who does similar damage control for Bruce Willis and Jerry Bruckheimer. After Eddie Murphy's brush with disaster, when he was suspected of having picked up and paid ten dollars to a transsexual for the purpose of having sex, Bloch is suddenly in the news speaking for *him*, too.

In late 1996 there was one single, stunning example of Hollywood cross-pollination. Writer Joe Eszterhas, whose first big break had been his rewrite of Simpson and Bruckheimer's *Flashdance*, crafted a screenplay for a movie to be called *An Alan Smithee Film*. It told the story of a movie director who wants to take his name off a production gone bad. (The Directors Guild of America won't allow that, but does let directors place the pseudonym "Alan Smithee" over films with which their directors don't want to be associated. Previous uses of the pseudonym included Richard Sarafian, who had his name removed from the hit *Starfire;* Don Siegel, who similarly divorced himself from *Death of a Gunfighter;* and, coincidentally, Jerrold Freedman, who distanced himself from the 1995 telefilm *The O. J. Simpson Story.*)[63] This fictional Alan Smithee becomes so enraged at the studio for ruining his film that he kidnaps the only copy of it, and comic situations, as they will, ensue. Through the end of 1996, Eszterhas and his director, Arthur Hiller, and their producers announced an amazing cast of actors and nonactors. Eric Idle would play the director. Appearing alongside him, playing cameo roles as themselves, would be Sylvester Stallone, Whoopi Goldberg, Richard Gere, Jackie Chan, Ryan O'Neal, twin filmmakers Allen and Albert Hughes, action screenwriter Shane Black, talk show host Larry King, rap singers Chuck D and Coolio— who'd contributed to Simpson and Bruckheimer's *Dangerous Minds* sound track—and attorney Robert Shapiro, investigator Anthony Pellicano and producer Robert Evans, who, with Eszterhas, had made the failed film *Sliver*, which starred Sharon Stone, who was dating Evans' former partner Bill McDonald, whose wife was Naomi, who left McDonald when she found out about the affair, and who subsequently married Eszterhas.

Then, in a development that was widely assumed to be a publicity stunt, Eszterhas and Hiller disagreed about the final cut of *An Alan Smithee*

Film, and Hiller demanded his name be removed. *An Alan Smithee Film* now, officially, was an Alan Smithee film.

Vanity Fair's Maureen Orth, on the day after Simpson's death, stood in the eye of the circle of sleaze. Shocked though she was to read the Saturday morning headlines recalling the "Baby Mogul's" demise, that Saturday evening she attended a party at Robert Evans' house. "It was quite amazing," Orth said later. "I walked into this party and the first person I see is Robert Shapiro. Standing next to him is Robert Evans. Standing next to *him* is Jon Peters. Next to Michael Viner. Next to Geraldo Rivera."[64]

Bloch, Shapiro, Pellicano, Weitzman, Brooklier and, to a degree, Nagy, Adams and Fleiss, all made careers for themselves as part of the protective web surrounding Hollywood's leading stars, directors and producers, keeping their names out of the news, sanitizing their images, saving them from their own excesses.

Simpson believed that he had something extra, some intangible connection, that would save him, too. "I've always been able to kind of teeter on the precipice," Simpson told friend Toback while being interviewed for Toback's 1990 film *The Big Bang.* "And a sense of whatever—self-survival, drive, desire—is a kind of celestial cord that pulls me back, that reels me back in."[65]

The celestial cord snapped. Not all the handlers, lawyers, black bag men, publicists and spin control experts in the world could save Simpson from himself. But they had an entire industry to service.

INTRODUCTION

1 Author interview with Eszterhas.
2 Mark Litwak, *Reel Power* (Silman-James Press, 1986), p. 145.
3 Ibid., pp. 94–95.
4 All medical details from *Physician's Desk Reference*, 1997.
5 *GQ*, June 1990.
6 Author interview with Eszterhas.

CHAPTER ONE
THE BABY MOGUL

1 Author interview with *Hollywood Reporter* source.
2 Author interviews with Sylbert and Tisch.
3 "Don Simpson on Don Simpson," Debby Bull, *Smart*, May 1990.
4 Author interview with Ganis.
5 Author interview with Julia Phillips.
6 *Premiere*, April 1996.
7 Ibid.

8 Ibid.
9 Author interview with Cannon.
10 Author interview with Rasnick.
11 Author interview with Julia Phillips.
12 *Smart* and others.
13 Author interview with Bart.
14 Author interview with Obst.
15 Author interview with Towne.
16 Ibid.
17 "The Demons That Drove Don Simpson," *Playboy*, June 1996.
18 *Daily Variety*, Oct. 29, 1943.
19 Author interview with Merle Butchar Millar.
20 Author interview with Bowen.
21 Author interview with Joe Eszterhas.
22 "On Thunder Road with Tom Cruise," *Rolling Stone*, July 12, 1990.
23 *Smart*, May 1990.
24 Ibid.
25 Ibid.
26 B. Weinraub, "The Demons That Drove Don Simpson," *Playboy*, June 1996.
27 James Toback, *The Big Bang*, 1990.
28 Ibid.

29 Ibid.

30 *Smart*, May 1990.

31 "An Interview with Paramount's Top Guns," *Los Angeles Times*, Mar. 18, 1990.

32 Author interview with Oregon State University officials.

33 "Gone Hollywood," *Esquire*, Sept. 1985.

34 James Toback, *The Big Bang*, 1990.

35 Author interview with Simpson.

36 *Smart*, June 1990.

37 *Los Angeles Times*, March 18, 1990.

38 Author interview with Millar.

39 Author interview with assistant.

40 *Smart*, June 1990.

41 Author interview with Simpson.

42 *Smart*, June 1990.

43 Ibid.

44 Margot Dougherty, "1 + 1 = $935 Million: Two Top-Gun Producers See Eye-to-Eye and Make Back-to-Back Megahits," *Life*, April 1987.

45 "David Geffen: Still Hungry," *New York Times*, May 2, 1993.

46 "Hollywood's Terrible Twosome," *Newsweek*, Apr. 24, 1995.

47 *Smart*, June 1990.

48 *Variety*, May 29, 1992, and June 8, 1992.

49 Author interview with Orth.

50 Author interview with Brown.

51 Leonard Louis Levinson, *The Left Handed Dictionary* (Collier Books, 1963), p. 184.

52 Author interview with Kosberg.

53 Nik Cohn, "Saturday Night's Big Bang," *New York*, Dec. 8, 1997.

54 From documents obtained by author.

55 Author interview with Diller.

56 *Esquire*, Sept. 1985.

57 Author interview with Diller.

58 Author interview with Wright.

59 *Premiere*, Apr. 1996.

60 Author interview with Wright.

61 *Daily Variety*, Apr. 1, 1981.

62 Author interview with Paramount source.

63 From documents obtained by author.

64 Author interview with Taylor Hackford.

65 Author interviews with Simpson, Wright, Hackford.

66 "Casting Glances," *Movieline*, June 1997.

67 Author interview with Hackford.

68 *Premiere*, Apr. 1996.

69 Author interview with Tom Wright.

70 Ibid.

71 Ibid.

72 Ibid.

73 "Hollywood's Hottest Stars," *New York*, July 30, 1984.

74 Ibid.

75 Ibid.

76 Author interview with Diller.

77 *Premiere*, Apr. 1996.

78 Author interview with Simpson.

79 Author interview with Bonnie Bruckheimer.

80 *Los Angeles Times*, Mar. 18, 1990.

81 Ibid.

82 From screenplay draft.

83 Author interview with Eszterhas.

84 Author interview with London.

85 Author interview with Phillips.

86 *Premiere*, May 1990; author interview with Jacobson.

87 From script notes obtained by author.

88 Ibid.

89 *Los Angeles Times*, Mar. 18, 1990.

90 Lynda Obst, *Hello, He Lied* (Little, Brown, 1996), p. 64.

91 Author interview with Eszterhas.

92 Ibid.

93 Author interview with Boswell.

94 Author interview with Tom Wright.

95 Author interview with Taylor Hackford.

96 Author interview with Eszterhas.

CHAPTER TWO

BEVERLY HILLS COP

1 Author interview with Bach.

2 Ibid.

3 *Los Angeles Times*, Nov. 18, 1984.

4 Author interview with Proser.

[5] Author interview with Silver.
[6] Author interview with source.
[7] "Sons of Hollywood's Hottest Stars," *New York*, Oct. 8, 1984.
[8] Author interview with Pesce.
[9] Numbers courtesy of National Association of Theater Owners.
[10] *Los Angeles Times*, Nov. 18, 1984.
[11] Ibid., Mar. 18, 1990.
[12] Author interview with Silver.
[13] *Life*, June 1990.
[14] Author interview with Kizyma.
[15] Author interview with assistant.
[16] Author interview with Proser.
[17] Author interview with Ferguson.
[18] Ibid.
[19] Author interview with Mann.
[20] Author interview with Pesce.
[21] *GQ*, Sept. 1991.
[22] "Shooting with the Stars," *Outdoor Life*, Jan. 1992.
[23] Author interview with Proser.
[24] Ibid.
[25] Ibid.
[26] Ibid.
[27] Ibid.
[28] Author interview with assistant.
[29] Author interview with Tanen.
[30] Ibid.
[31] Author interview with Pettigrew.
[32] Author interview with assistant.
[33] Author interview with Pettigrew.
[34] Details courtesy of National Association of Theater Owners.
[35] Author interview with assistant.
[36] *Interview*, May 1985.
[37] Author interview with Stewart.
[38] Author interview with Pettigrew.
[39] Author interviews with assistants.
[40] Ibid.
[41] *Premiere*, Mar. 1996.
[42] "Gone Hollywood," *Esquire*, May 1985.
[43] Author interview with reporter.
[44] *Vanity Fair*, Mar. 1996.
[45] Author interview with Siegal.
[46] Author interview with Mancuso.

CHAPTER THREE

BAD BOY

[1] Alex Adams and William Stadiem, *Madam 90210: My Life as Madam to the Rich and Famous* (Villard, 1993), p. 22.
[2] Ibid., pp. 23–32.
[3] Author interviews with Adams employees and clients.
[4] Author interview with Panetz.
[5] James Toback, *The Big Bang*, 1990.
[6] Author interview with Bowen.
[7] Robin, Liza, Linda and Tiffany, *You'll Never Make Love in This Town Again* (Dove Books, 1995), p. xv.
[8] Author interview with Obst.
[9] Author interview with Eszterhas.
[10] Author interview with Silver.
[11] Author interview with Alex Adams source.
[12] Author interview with Simpson.
[13] Author interview with John H. Richardson.
[14] Mark Litwak, *Reel Power* (Silman-James Press, 1986), p. 280.
[15] Author interview with Silver.
[16] Author interview with London.
[17] Author interview with Pesce.
[18] Author interview with Eszterhas.
[19] Ibid.
[20] Author interviews with Blackburn and Woods.
[21] Author interview with Richardson.
[22] Author interview with Schwartz.
[23] Author interview with "Julie."
[24] Author interview with Obst.
[25] *Premiere*, Mar. 1996.
[26] Author interviews with Fleiss, Nagy and police sources.
[27] Author interview with Roth.
[28] Ibid.
[29] Author interview with Mann.
[30] *Premiere*, Mar. 1996.
[31] Author interview with source.
[32] Author interview with Nagy.
[33] Nick Broomfield, *Heidi Fleiss, Hollywood Madam*, 1996.

34 Ibid.
35 Author interview with Wakefield.
36 Author interview with Nagy.
37 Adams and Stadiem, *Madam 90210,* p. 147.
38 Author interview with Greer.
39 Author interview with Fleiss.
40 Author interview with Clapp.
41 Reuters, Aug. 12, 1982.
42 Ibid.
43 Author interviews with Clapp, Wakefield and others.
44 Author interview with Wakefield.
45 *Hollywood Vice,* ITV, September Films, executive producer David Green, 1990.
46 Tom Hedley, "Don Juan in Turnaround," *Esquire,* Sept. 1996.
47 Ibid.
48 Author interview with Pellicano.
49 Ibid.
50 Rod Lurie, "Now They're Playing Dirty," *Los Angeles Magazine,* Feb. 1992.
51 Shawn Hubler and James Bates, "Streetwise Gumshoe to the Stars," *Los Angeles Times,* Sept. 11, 1993.
52 Ibid.
53 Author interview with Pellicano.
54 Broomfield, *Heidi Fleiss.*
55 Author interview with Nagy.
56 Author interview with St. George.
57 Details supplied by Prophet.
58 Author interview with Datig.
59 Robin et al., *You'll Never Make Love,* pp. 220–23.
60 Ibid., p. 223.
61 Author interview with Datig.
62 Author interview with Bradigan.
63 Ibid.
64 Author interview with Clapp.
65 *Playgirl,* May 1985.
66 *Spy,* Mar. 1990
67 Author interview with Clapp.
68 "How the Great Seducer Became Dr. Devil," *Daily Mail,* London, Mar. 15, 1997.
69 Author interview with Greer.
70 Author interview with Datig.
71 Author interview with Ferguson.

CHAPTER FOUR

HOLLYWOOD HIGH

1 Arnold M. Washton and Mark S. Gold, *Cocaine: A Clinicians Handbook* (The Guilford Press, 1987), p. 87.
2 Ibid.
3 Author interview with McInerney.
4 Author interview with Silver.
5 Author interview with Woods.
6 Author interview with McInerney.
7 Author interview with J.R.
8 Author interview with Simpson friend.
9 Rayce Newman, *The Hollywood Connection: The Drug Supplier to the Stars Tells All* (SPI Books, 1994), pp. 28–30.
10 Ibid., pp. 34–36.
11 Author interview with Newman.
12 Ibid.
13 Newman, *Hollywood Connection,* p. 75.
14 Ibid., p. 86.
15 Author interview with Newman.
16 Ibid.
17 Newman, *Hollywood Connection,* pp. 74–77.
18 Author interview with Newman.
19 Author interview with J.R.
20 Author interview with Roth.
21 Author interview with Schrader.
22 Author interview with Obst.
23 David Freeman, *A Hollywood Education: Tales of Movie Dreams and Easy Money* (Dell, 1986), pp. 135–45.
24 Author interview with Cook.
25 Author interview with assistant.
26 Author interview with Cook.
27 *Playboy,* Aug. 1982.
28 Ibid., Aug. 1986.
29 Newman, *Hollywood Connection,* p. 111.
30 Ibid.
31 "Gone Hollywood," *Esquire,* Sept. 1985.
32 Author interview with Baumgarten source.
33 "Gone Hollywood."

34 Author interviews with St. George and Fabian.

35 *Los Angeles Times,* Nov. 18, 1986.

36 Ibid.

37 *Newsday,* Sept. 14, 1989.

38 Author interview with St. George.

39 Author interviews with Steve Roth, St. George and others.

40 "Scotto Unfree," *New York,* Nov. 20, 1995.

41 Ibid.

42 *Playboy,* Aug. 1986.

43 Author interview with Burnham.

44 *Los Angeles Times,* Dec. 13, 1993.

45 Author interview with Nagy.

46 Author interview with Clapp.

47 Ibid.

48 Author interview with Manni and others.

49 Author interview with Richardson.

50 John H. Richardson, *The Vipers' Club* (Morrow, 1996), p. 133.

51 Author interview with Richardson.

52 Author interview with Silver.

53 Richardson, *Vipers' Club,* p. 160.

54 *Daily Variety,* Mar. 2, 1993.

55 *Los Angeles,* Jan. 1993.

56 Author interview with Eller.

57 Author interview with Simpson.

58 Author interview with "Sarah."

59 From documents obtained by author.

60 Author interview with Laiter.

61 Author interview with "Sarah."

CHAPTER FIVE

DAYS OF PLUNDER

1 Author interview with Young.

2 Author interview with Simpson.

3 Author interview with assistant.

4 Ibid.

5 Author interview with editor Billy Weber.

6 *Time,* Jun. 9, 1997.

7 *Premiere,* Apr. 1996.

8 Author interview with Billy Weber.

9 Author interview with John H. Richardson.

10 Author interview with Bonnie Bruckheimer.

11 Author interview with Schiff.

12 "Hollywood's Terrible Twosome," *Newsweek,* Apr. 24, 1995.

13 Author interview with source.

14 Author interview with Young.

15 Author interview with assistant.

16 Author interview with assistant.

17 Author interview with Peggy Siegal; see also *Premiere,* Mar. 1996.

18 Author interview with assistant.

19 Ibid.

20 *Premiere,* Mar. 1996.

21 Author interview with assistant.

22 Author interview with Siegal.

23 Author interview with assistant.

24 *Spy,* Mar. 1990.

25 Author interview with Simpson source.

26 Author interview with Mancuso.

27 Author interview with London.

28 Author interview with Eddy.

29 Author interview with Mancuso.

30 Author interview with Lucchesi.

31 Author interview with Simpson.

32 Author interview with Young.

33 Ben Stein, "Obituary," *New York* magazine.

34 *Los Angeles Times,* Nov. 18, 1984.

CHAPTER SIX

WRETCHED EXCESS

1 Author interview with Simpson acquaintance.

2 Author interview with Paramount source.

3 Author interview with Simpson friend.

4 Author interview with Garfinkle.

5 Author encounter with Geffen.

6 Author interview with Diller.

7 Nancy Griffin and Kim Masters, *Hit and Run: How Jon Peters and Peter Guber Took Sony for a Ride in Hollywood* (Simon & Schuster, 1996), p. 115.

8 *New York Times,* Jan. 26, 1997.

9 Author interview with Siegal.

10 Author interview with Blackburn.

11 Reuters, June 20, 1997.
12 *Robb Report*, June 1997.
13 "Hollywood Vertigo," *Vanity Fair*, Feb. 1997.
14 *Cosmopolitan*, Mar. 1, 1994.
15 Ibid.
16 Author interview with *Mary Reilly* source.
17 *Daily Variety*, June 24, 1997.
18 *Cosmopolitan*, Mar. 1, 1994.
19 Author interview with Columbia source.
20 Author interview with Disney source.
21 *Daily Variety*, June 24, 1997.
22 Ibid.
23 Author interview with Columbia source.
24 Griffen and Masters, *Hit and Run*, p. 327.
25 Author interview with Disney source.
26 Ibid.
27 Kenneth Anger, *Hollywood Babylon* (Dell, 1975), pp. 30–33.
28 Ibid., p. 109.
29 Ibid., p. 101.
30 *Los Angeles Times*, Sept. 3, 1996.
31 Griffin and Masters, *Hit and Run*, p. 235.
32 *New York Daily News*, Apr. 26, 1990.
33 Ibid.
34 *Los Angeles Times*, Sept. 3, 1996.
35 Griffin and Masters, *Hit and Run*, p. 264.
36 Ibid.
37 Ibid., p. 429.
38 *Premiere*, May 1996.
39 *Cosmopolitan*, Mar. 1, 1994.
40 Author interview with Crystal source.
41 Author interview with Simpson.
42 Author interview with reporter.
43 *Los Angeles Times*, Aug. 18, 1991.
44 *Los Angeles Times*, June 1, 1997.
45 Ibid., June 15, 1997.
46 Ibid.
47 *Daily Variety*, June 10, 1997.
48 *People*, Apr. 4, 1988.
49 Author interview with contractor.
50 Author interview with Simpson employee.
51 Author interview with assistant.

52 Author interview with gallery owner.
53 Dollar amounts courtesy of Sotheby's.
54 Author interview with Simpson.
55 *GQ*, June 1990.
56 Rates courtesy of Canyon Ranch.
57 Author interviews with Simpson friends.
58 Author interview with massage therapist Billy Lucchesi.
59 Ibid.
60 Ibid.
61 Author interview with casting agent Laura Lee Kasten and others.
62 Author interview with *Daily Variety* sources.
63 *Premiere*, July 1997.
64 *Life*, Apr. 1987.
65 *Los Angeles Times Magazine*, Mar. 16, 1996.
66 *Los Angeles*, June 1995.
67 Ibid.
68 Author interview with restaurant writer Merrill Shindler.
69 Author interview with Soderbergh.
70 Author interviews with Paul Rosenfeld and Steve Roth.
71 Author interview with Canyon Ranch resident.
72 Author interview with Canyon Ranch regular.
73 Author interviews with Aspen sources.
74 John Gregory Dunne, *Monster* (Random House, 1997), p. 156.
75 Author interview with Simpson colleague.

CHAPTER SEVEN
THE PICTURES GOT SMALL

1 Numbers courtesy of Motion Picture Association of America.
2 Mark Litwak, *Reel Power* (Silman-James Press, 1986), p. 92.
3 Numbers courtesy of Motion Picture Association of America.
4 Litwak, *Reel Power*, p. 84.
5 John Horn, "Ex-Exec, Disney Wrangle in Lawsuit," Associated Press, June 29, 1997.

6 *Daily Variety,* Jan. 31, 1991.

7 Ibid.

8 "Hollywood's Terrible Twosome," *Newsweek,* Apr. 24, 1995.

9 Ibid.

10 Ibid.

11 *Buzz,* Mar. 1997.

12 From author's copy of "Corporate Philosophy."

13 Ibid.

14 Author interview with Wright.

15 From document obtained by author.

16 Author interview with Pollock.

17 Peter Briskand, "A World Apart," *Premiere,* May 1997.

18 *Los Angeles Times,* June 10, 1997.

19 Author interview with Lucchesi.

20 Author interview with Bonnie Bruckheimer.

21 *Daily Variety,* Apr. 6, 1993.

22 Author interviews with Disney sources.

23 Author interview with Canton.

24 *The Hollywood Reporter,* May 24, 1995.

25 Author interview with Simpson.

26 *Daily Variety,* Feb. 12, 1992.

27 Author interview with source.

28 *Los Angeles,* Jan. 1993.

29 *New York Times,* Mar. 14, 1994.

30 Author interview with Jablonski.

31 Author interview with Canyon Ranch employee.

32 Author interview with Davis.

33 Author interview with Diller.

34 Litwak, *Reel Power,* p. 55.

35 *Entertainment Weekly,* May 19, 1995.

36 Ibid.

37 Ibid., Feb. 2, 1996.

38 Ibid., May 19, 1995.

39 Author interview with Michael Cieply.

40 Author interview with Rosenman.

41 *The Hollywood Reporter,* May 24, 1995.

CHAPTER EIGHT

DOCTOR'S ORDERS

1 Michael Fleeman, "The Doctor, the Movie Producer and the Big Sleep," Associated Press, Sept. 8, 1996.

2 According to police, coroner and autopsy reports.

3 *Los Angeles Times,* Aug. 18, 1996.

4 Associated Press, Sept. 8, 1996.

5 Ibid., Aug. 17, 1996.

6 From Ammerman lawsuit against Simpson estate et al.

7 *Prime Time Live,* March 27, 1997.

8 Ibid.

9 *Los Angeles Times,* Feb. 6, 1996.

10 Ibid., Oct. 26, 1995.

11 Ibid., Aug. 28, 1996.

12 Ibid.

13 *Chicago Tribune,* Aug. 21, 1996.

14 *Los Angeles Times,* Aug. 28, 1996.

15 Author interview with Miller.

16 *Los Angeles Times,* Aug. 28, 1996.

17 Ibid.

18 *Los Angeles Times,* Aug. 17, 1996.

19 Author interview with Miller.

20 *Los Angeles Times,* Aug. 18, 1996.

21 Ibid., Aug. 23, 1996.

22 Ibid., Aug. 18, 1996.

23 Ibid., Dec. 3, 1996.

24 Ibid., Aug. 17, 1996.

25 Ibid., Aug. 28, 1996.

26 Ibid., Mar. 26, 1997.

27 Ibid., Aug. 18, 1996.

28 Author interviews with Simpson-Bruckheimer sources.

29 *Los Angeles Times,* Feb. 6, 1996.

CHAPTER NINE

REHAB

1 Author interview with Canyon Ranch massage therapist Nancy Davis.

2 Author interview with Evans.

3 Author interview with Columbia source.

4 Author interview with executive.

5 Author interviews with Columbia sources.

6 Author interviews with Ganis and Stevens.

7 Author interview with Katzenberg.

8 Mark Litwak, *Reel Power* (Silman-James Press, 1986), p. 120.

9 Ibid.

10 Details supplied by Menninger literature.

11 Details supplied by Hazelden literature.

12 Author interviews with Ford officers.

13 "Cocaine Abuse," NIDA, pp. 2–4.

14 "Drugs, Crime and the Justice System," Bureau of Justice Statistics, p. 109.

15 Ibid.

16 Ibid., p. 132.

17 Reuters, Dec. 12, 1996.

18 "Monitor," *Entertainment Weekly*, Dec. 12, 1997.

19 *Los Angeles Times*, Aug. 28, 1996.

20 *National Enquirer*, Aug. 27, 1996.

21 *People*, June 9, 1997.

22 *Chicago Tribune*, Jan. 17, 1997.

23 *National Enquirer*, Aug. 27, 1996.

24 *Chicago Tribune*, Jan. 17, 1997.

25 Reuters, Mar. 18, 1997.

26 *Los Angeles Times*, Aug. 24, 1996.

27 "Morning Report," *Los Angeles Times*, Dec. 10, 1997.

28 "Morning Report," *Los Angeles Times*, Dec. 11, 1997.

29 *The Hollywood Reporter*, Aug. 26, 1996.

30 *Los Angeles Times*, Nov. 7, 1996.

31 Ibid., Nov. 18, 1996.

32 Jeff Wilson, "Actor Robert Downey Sent to Jail," Associated Press, Dec. 8, 1997.

33 *USA Today*, Aug. 24, 1994; *Los Angeles Times*, Nov. 23, 1996.

34 Reuters, May 30, 1997.

35 Author interview with former Disney executive.

36 "Chris Farley: On the Edge of Disaster," *US*, Sept. 1997.

37 *Los Angeles Times*, Aug. 12, 1997.

38 *Buzz*, Aug. 14, 1997.

39 *New Yorker*, Aug. 19, 1996.

40 John Brodie, "Talent Agents Now Flying Tsuris Class," *Variety*.

41 Author interview with Silver.

42 "Agent Under the Influence," *Premiere*, July 1997.

43 Ibid.

44 Ibid.

45 Author interview with Rosenman.

46 Author interview with Roth.

47 *Premiere*, Sept. 1993.

48 "A Cruise in Outer Space," *California*, June 1991.

49 *Premiere*, Sept. 1993.

50 Ibid.

51 Ibid.

52 James Toback, *The Big Bang*, 1990.

53 Author interview with Paramount source.

54 Author interview with employee.

55 Author interview with Iverson.

56 Author experience with Chasen.

57 Author interviews with Iverson and Wessells.

58 "The Long Hard Days of Dr. Dick," *Esquire*, Sept. 1995.

59 Author interview with Wessells.

60 Ibid.

61 Author interview with employee.

62 Author interviews with Alexandra Datig and others.

63 Author interview with Wessells.

64 "Days of Thunder, Nights of Despair," *Vanity Fair*, Apr. 1996. (Curiously, Simpson told the author the incident was a bad reaction to Prozac.)

65 *GQ*, June 1990.

66 Author interview with Teitelbaum.

67 *GQ*, June 1990.

68 Author interview with Alexandra Datig.

69 Author interview with former Paramount executive.

70 Author interview with Simpson.

71 Author interviews with Sid Ganis and Max Alexander.

72 *Premiere*, Apr. 1996.

73 Author interview with Canyon Ranch massage therapist Keith McDaniel.

74 "From Dusk till Don," *Los Angeles*, Apr. 1996.

75 Ibid.

76 Author interview with Simpson.

CHAPTER TEN

DEATH

1 *The Hollywood Reporter*, Dec. 20, 1995.

2 *Daily Variety*, Dec. 20, 1995.

3 "An Interview with Paramount's Top Guns," *Los Angeles Times*, Mar. 18, 1990.

4 From copy of note obtained by author.

5 Author interview with Simpson-Bruckheimer sources.

6 *Daily Variety*, Dec. 20, 1995.

7 Interview notes courtesy of Jeffrey Wells.

8 Author interview with Simpson-Bruckheimer source.

9 Author interview with Simpson source.

10 "The Demons That Drove Don Simpson," *Playboy*, June 1996.

11 Author interview with Simpson source.

12 "Good Night, Dark Prince," *Premiere*, Apr. 1996.

13 Author interview with Silver.

14 Author interview with Joe Ascuitto.

15 "Days of Thunder, Nights of Despair," *Vanity Fair*, Apr. 1996.

16 Ibid.

17 Author interview with James Toback.

18 Author interview with Vicuna.

19 "Days of Thunder, Nights of Despair."

20 Author interview with Hensleigh.

21 "Terms of Forgiveness," *Newsweek*, Apr. 24, 1995.

22 Author interview with "Kawabata," an alias chosen to protect source.

23 Author interview with Trepanier.

24 See coroner's report.

25 Author interview with Sassa.

26 "Amorality Tale," *Los Angeles*, Mar. 1996.

27 All above from Simpson's personal papers obtained by author.

28 Ibid.

29 *Los Angeles Times*, Jan. 21, 1996.

30 Author interview with Toback.

31 911 recording courtesy of ABC and *Prime Time Live*.

32 Author interview with Orth.

33 Author interview with Pellicano.

34 Associated Press, Sept. 8, 1996.

35 Details from police reports obtained by author.

36 *Los Angeles Times*, Jan. 21, 1996.

37 Ibid. Mar. 27, 1996.

38 *New York Times*, Jan. 21, 1996.

39 *Los Angeles Times*, Mar. 27, 1996.

CHAPTER ELEVEN

AFTERMATH

1 Author interview with sources.

2 Author interview with Pellicano.

3 Author interview with Berg.

4 "The Demons That Drove Don Simpson," *Playboy*, June 1996.

5 Author interview with Hensleigh.

6 "Good Night, Dark Prince," *Premiere*, Apr. 1996.

7 Ibid.

8 Author interviews with Bradigan and Pesce.

9 *Movieline*, May 1996.

10 From documents obtained by author.

11 Author interviews with sources.

12 Author interview with guest.

13 Photos from *Premiere*, Apr. 1996, p. 100.

14 Author interview with source.

15 Author interview with Bonnie Bruckheimer.

16 "The Demons That Drove Don Simpson," *Playboy*, June 1996.

17 Ibid.

18 *Los Angeles Times*, Jan. 21, 1996.

19 Author interviews with memorabilia collectors.

20 Author interviews with Simpson sources.

21 *Los Angeles Times*, Mar. 28, 1997.

22 *Daily Variety*, Mar. 14, 1997.

23 Ibid., Apr. 24, 1997.

24 *New York Times*, June 26, 1997.

25 Associated Press, Aug. 20, 1996.

26 Reuters, Apr. 24, 1997.

27 Author interview with *Bad Boys* screenwriter Larry Ferguson.

28 *Los Angeles Times*, May 3, 1997.

29 Reuters, Dec. 22, 1996.

30 *Los Angeles Times*, June 7, 1997.

31 Author interview with junket attendees.

32 *Entertainment Weekly*, Nov. 22, 1996.

33 *Los Angeles Times*, Oct. 15, 1996.

34 Ibid., July 4, 1997.

35 Ibid., July 31, 1997.

36 "Days of Thunder, Nights of Despair," *Vanity Fair*, Apr. 1996.

37 Lisa, Michelle, Sophie et al., *Once More with Feeling* (Dove Books, 1996), p. 33.

38 Ibid., p. 34.

39 Ibid., p. 35.

40 Ibid., p. 43.

41 Figures courtesy of Reel Source Inc.

42 *Los Angeles Times*, June 7, 1996.

43 *New Yorker*, Jun. 17, 1996.

44 Author interview with *Con Air* source.

45 *Entertainment Weekly*, June 13, 1997.

46 *New Yorker*, June 9, 1997.

47 *New York*, June 16, 1997.

48 *Los Angeles Times* advertisement, June 20, 1997.

49 *Newsweek*, June 9, 1997.

50 Author interview with London.

51 *Los Angeles Times*, June 9, 1997.

52 Reel Source Inc. estimate, June 8, 1997.

53 Figures courtesy of Reel Source Inc.

54 *New York Times*, June 26, 1997.

55 "The Demons That Drove Don Simpson," *Playboy*, June 1996.

56 "Amorality Tale: The Last Days of Don Simpson," *Los Angeles*, April, 1996,

57 Author interview with Cohen.

58 "Amorality Tale."

59 *The Hollywood Reporter*, Jan. 22, 1996.

60 Author interview with Ferguson.

61 Author interview with source.

62 *Los Angeles Times*, Jan. 28, 1997.

63 Credits courtesy of Lone Eagle Press, *Film Directors: A Complete Guide*, 1997, compiled and edited by Michael Singer, p. 30.

64 Author interview with Orth.

65 *Vanity Fair*, Apr. 1996.

Ackerman, Glenn, 93
"Action-comedy" genre, 58
Adams, Elizabeth (Madam Alex), 79–80,
    89–91, 92–93, 95, 98, 100, 103, 106,
    132, 273, 275
Alan Smithee Film, An, 274–75
Allen, Ginger, 106
Allen, Marcus, 106, 118
Allen, Tim, 225
Allman Brothers band, 115
Ammerman, Richard, 215–16
Ammerman, Stephen, 203, 207–10, 212,
    235
Ansen, David, 270
Armani, Giorgio, 153, 177
Aspen parties, 164–67
Auteur theory, 44
Axelrod, Jonathan, 116

Baby Moguls (Hollywood), 25–27
Bach, Danilo, 53–55
Bach, Pamela, 107
Bad Boys, 3, 130, 155, 196, 198–99, 202,
    204–5, 215, 241, 243
Bart, Peter, 18, 30
Bartel, Paul, 16
Bass, Ron, 206
Baumgarten, Craig, 17, 75, 87, 88, 96, 126,
    260, 271
Bay, Michael, 205, 260, 267, 268
Beaches, 141–42
Beals, Jennifer, 36, 44

Beatty, Warren, 2, 75–76, 103, 106, 142,
    180, 196, 260, 266
Beckerman, Barry, 130
Belushi, John, 183
Bening, Annette, 260
Berg, Jeff, 2, 75, 197, 259
Berkus, Jim, 41, 87, 166, 178, 197, 260,
    261
Betty Ford Center, 221
Beverly Hills Cop, 3, 36, 44, 53–60, 77,
    163
Beverly Hills Cop 2, 58, 61, 62, 63, 104,
    130
Beverly Hills Cop 3, 58, 155–57, 158–59,
    197
Beverly Hills Gun Club, 63
Big Bang, The, 22, 62, 275
Biskind, Peter, 235
Black, Cathy and Joe, 93
Blackboard Jungle, 24
Blackburn, Greta, 84–85, 166
Bloch, Paul, 263, 274, 275
Block, Bill, 241
Bloom, Jake, 3, 56, 197, 248, 259, 260
Bloomberg, Stuart, 252
Blum, Howard, 199
Bogdanovich, Peter, 175
Bonnie Beats Mary, 96, 153–54
Bookman, Robert, 54, 197, 260
Boop, John, 221
Boswell, John, 50–51
Bowen, Naomi, 20, 81

Bradigan, Bonnie, 96, 102–6, 108–9, 260
Brady, Carl, Jr., 141
Brest, Martin, 56, 57, 61, 163, 206, 260, 261
Bronfman, Edgar, Jr., 168
Brooklier, Anthony, 273, 275
Broomfield, Nick, 90
Brown, Bobby, 118
Brown, Denise, 272
Brown, J. V., 27–28
Brownstone, Mr. (heroin dealer), 9
Bruckheimer, Bonnie, 42–43, 141–42, 197, 261–62
Bruckheimer, Jerry, 3, 4, 6, 15, 49, 50, 63, 83, 84, 104, 118, 124, 126, 131, 164, 178, 201, 216, 232–33, 244, 247, 249, 251, 254, 257, 261, 265, 274
  background, 43
  Days of Thunder, 140, 148, 149, 157
  solo career, 239–40, 262–63, 268–71
  Top Gun, 60, 68, 69–70, 71, 72, 74–75
  See also Simpson-Bruckheimer partnership
Bruckheimer, Linda, 4, 166, 240, 261
Buffalo Club restaurant, 180–81
Buffett, Jimmy, 166
Bull, Debby, 21
Bumble Ward & Associates, 163–64
Burnham, John, 129
"Burning Porsche, The" (Freeman), 122–24, 131
Buscemi, Steve, 268
Busch, Anita M., 179
Busey, Gary, 106, 107, 223

Caan, James, 106, 107, 223
Cage, Nicolas, 168, 196, 238, 243, 266, 267, 268, 269–70
Cahn, Beth and Debbie, 74
Campbell, Tisha, 222
Canby, Vincent, 77
Candy, John, 182
Cannon, Peter, 16, 17
Cannonball, 16
Canton, Mark, 27, 198–99, 260
Capri, Randy, 210
Cara, Irene, 45
Carrey, Jim, 167
Carrier, Scott, 255
Carvey, Dana, 198
Cash, Jim, 63, 64, 66, 70, 71
"Casting couch" myth, 82
Chapman, Robert, 253
Chase, Chevy, 224–25
Chasen, Ronni, 230
Cieply, Michael, 151
Clapp, Fred, 92–93, 103, 106, 129–30
Cleese, John, 156
Cobain, Kurt, 214
Cocaine, 111–12, 220, 221–22
Cocker, Joe, 38

Cohen, Rob, 167, 178, 240–41, 260, 265, 272
Cohn, Nik, 30
Colombo, Patricia, 97, 99–100, 101, 102
Colombo crime family, 128
Columbia Pictures, 218–19
Con Air, 215, 238, 240, 268–71
Connery, Sean, 196, 243, 260, 266, 267
Conti, Vince, 129–30
Cook, Rusty, 124, 125
Cosmetic surgery industry, 229–33
Costner, Kevin, 35, 95
Cotton Club, The, 87, 96
Crichton, Michael, 200
Crimson Tide, 3, 180, 196, 206, 215, 243, 263
Crosby, David, 106, 107
Cruise, Tom, 3, 129, 141, 167, 178, 196, 227, 228, 232–33, 260
  Days of Thunder, 137, 140, 142, 144, 145, 146, 147, 148, 149
  Top Gun, 70–71, 74, 76
Crystal, Billy, 173

Daly, Robert, 2, 239
Dangerous Minds, 206, 215, 240, 243, 251
Daniel, Sean, 25, 27, 121
Danza, Tony, 181–82, 260, 261
Datig, Alexandra (Tiffany), 96, 97–102, 106–7, 108
Davis, John, 103
Davis, Judy, 199
Davis, Martin S., 39, 57, 139, 151, 155
Davis, Marvin, 179
Davis, Nancy, 203
Days of Thunder, 3, 44, 65, 137–38, 139–51, 155, 157
DeLorean, John, 2, 95
Denby, David, 77, 149, 270
Denver, John, 35
De Palma, Brian, 17
De Souza, Steven, 157, 158
Dexter, Peter, 202
Dharma Blue, 199–202
Diamond, Neil, 38
Dick Tracy, 142, 150, 190–91
Didion, Joan, 199, 200–201
Diller, Barry, 1, 13, 14, 15, 17–18, 28–29, 30, 31, 39, 40–41, 57, 121, 138, 162, 163, 165, 186, 204
Dillon, Matt, 106
Directors Guild of America, 32–33, 274
Disney, Roy, 168–69, 189
Douglas, Michael, 90, 118, 165
Downey, Robert, Jr., 117, 223–24
Dreyfuss, Richard, 2, 260, 261
Drug dealing business, 113–21
Dunne, John Gregory, 182, 199–201
Duvall, Robert, 65, 137, 142, 143
Dwyer, Ed, 202

Ebert, Roger, 270
Eddy, Michael Alan, 156, 157
Edwards, Anthony, 73
Edwards, Brian, 253
Eisner, Michael, 1, 3, 13, 14, 28–29, 30,
     32–33, 36, 37–39, 40, 41, 42, 51, 53,
     54, 57, 58–59, 69, 76, 104, 138, 158,
     162, 182, 186, 188, 191, 193–94, 204,
     238–39, 252, 259, 260
Elfand, Marty, 35, 36, 37, 38
Eller, Claudia, 133, 134
Ellis, Bret Easton, 164
Elwes, Cary, 143
English, Diane, 180
Epps, Jack, 63, 64, 66, 70, 71
Esquire magazine, 76, 126, 164
Estevez, Emilio, 63, 142
Eszterhas, Joe, 3, 11, 44, 45–46, 48–49, 50,
     51–52, 81–82, 83–84, 274–75
Evans, Robert, 17, 40–41, 87, 93, 94, 96,
     103, 106–7, 108, 118, 129, 188, 204,
     218, 266, 272, 273, 274, 275

Fabian, Ava, 125–26, 127, 128–29, 130
Farley, Chris, 225
Ferguson, Larry, 61–62, 109, 272
Field, Syd, 122
Field, Ted, 117, 178, 266
Fields, Bert, 154, 174, 202, 260
Flannery, Janice, 93
Flashdance, 3, 36, 42, 43, 44–52, 58–59,
     77, 103, 163
Fleiss, Heidi, 86–87, 89–92, 93–94, 96, 100,
     106, 107, 180, 257, 262, 273, 275
Fleiss, Paul, 90, 264
Fleming, Charles, 85–86, 182
48 Hrs., 31, 59–60
Foster, Lucas, 215, 239, 272
Frank (drug dealer), 113, 114
Frederick, Nomi, 209, 210–13, 214, 216
Freeman, David, 47–48, 122–24, 131
Frey, Glenn, 106
Friendly, David, 260
Fuhrman, Mark, 273

Gallo, George, 198
Ganis, Sid, 15–16, 147–48, 149, 185, 219,
     247
Garfinkle, Louis, 162
Gaye, Marvin, Jr., 117
Geffen, David, 1, 6, 25, 38, 75, 121, 162–
     63, 168, 176, 249
Gere, Richard, 35–36, 41–42
Gerner, Robert, 210–11, 212–14, 216
Getty, Aileen, 212
Gibson, Mel, 58, 167–68, 169, 185
Giovanni, Angela, 105
Gleiberman, Owen, 269
Godfather 3, 33–34
Goldberg, Whoopi, 58, 107
Goldman, Ronald, 108, 119

Goldman, William, 6
Gordon, Dan, 206
Gordon, Larry, 59, 75, 131, 153, 194
Gordon, Shep, 103, 260
Gossett, Lou, Jr., 36, 65
Gottleib, Hildy, 59
Grammer, Kelsey, 115, 223
Grant, Hugh, 182
Grease 2, 38–39
Greatest Show on Earth, The, 24, 26
Greer, Liza, 91, 106–8
Greer, Robin, 106
Griffin, Merv, 174
Griffin, Nancy, 172
Griffith, Melanie, 16, 118–19, 166–67, 170
Grimble, Russell, 256
Grotstein, James, 246, 248
Guber, Peter, 45, 87, 163, 172–73, 185
Gulfstream jets, 168–69
Guns, popularity in Hollywood, 63
Guns N' Roses, 115

Hackford, Taylor, 35–38, 41–42
Hackman, Gene, 4, 196
Hackworth, David H., 244
Hamilton, George, 118
Hammond, Linda, 106
Hancock, Herbie, 119
Harmon, Monica, 95, 104, 151–52, 154,
     202
Harris, Ed, 243
Harrison, George, 106
Hart, Lauralei, 93
Harvard Man, 250–51
Hazelden Center, 221
Healy, Patrick, 180
Hedley, Tom, 42, 45–46, 47
Heidi Fleiss, Hollywood Madam, 90
Hemingway, Margaux, 211
Henley, Don, 106, 108, 117, 118, 266
Hensleigh, Jonathan, 243–44, 259–60
Henson, Jim, 211
Hertz, Enid, 87
High-concept movies, 7, 14, 29, 122, 192,
     194, 268
Hill, Walter, 32, 59
Hiller, Arthur, 274–75
Hines, Gregory, 59
Hinson, Hal, 149, 150
Hirsch, Barry, 54
Hirschberg, Lynn, 75–76, 126, 181
Hoberman, David, 204
Hollywood Connection, The (Newman),
     119
Hopper, Dennis, 106, 266
Horowitz, Michael Lawrence, 214
Howard, Ron, 17, 173
Huang, George, 132
Hubbard, L. Ron, 227–28
Hughes, Eric, 147
Hughes, John, 185, 195

Hutton, Timothy, 106

Idol, Billy, 106, 115
Iverson, Ronald, 230, 231–32

Jablonski, Mark, 203
Jackson, Michael, 95, 273
Jacobson, Tom, 45
James, Rick, 118, 119
Jasmine, Paul, 87, 121
Jaws, 29
Jennings, Will, 38
Johnson, Don, 2, 106, 118–19, 166–67,
     225, 260
Josephson, Barry, 173, 179, 198, 199, 226,
     260
J.R. (cocaine dealer), 113–15, 116, 118,
     119–21, 272

Kael, Pauline, 50–51
Kaelin, Kato, 120, 121, 180
Kashoggi, Adnan, 96, 106, 130, 266
Katzenberg, Jeffrey, 1, 4, 13, 14, 27, 31,
     33, 39, 40, 57, 59, 69, 75, 76, 142,
     158, 162, 168, 178, 181, 186, 188, 189,
     190–91, 193, 194, 195, 199, 204, 219,
     239, 249, 260, 261
Katzenberg, Marilyn, 4, 76
Kaufman, Phil, 18
Kawabata, Karen, 245–46
Kempf, Karla, 247, 248
Kennedy, Kathy, 164
Kennedy, Ted, 165
Kidder, Margot, 17
Kidman, Nicole, 137, 142, 143
Kilmer, Val, 72
Kirkpatrick, David, 36, 191
Kissinger, David, 251
Kitching, Patti, 202
Kivowitz, Charles, 253
Kizyma, Adrian, 60–61
Kornfeld, Bernie, 90
Korzelius, John, 167, 178
Kosberg, Robert, 29
Krug, Jennifer, 215

Laiter, Tova, 135, 248–49
Lampone, Alexander, 216, 255–56
Landis, John, 158
Lane, Anthony, 269–70
Lansing, Sherry, 2
LaPier, Darcy, 222
La Rocca, John, 103
Lassally, Tom, 226
Lawrence, Martin, 196, 199, 222–23, 263
Leach, Robin, 126
Leary, Denis, 198, 199, 205
Lebenzon, Chris, 153
Lehman, Peter, 232
Lennon, Julian, 117, 118
Lentini, Susan, 87, 260, 261, 262

Lewis, Roger, 248
Litwak, Mark, 187
Loc, Tone, 140
London, Barry, 45, 50, 148, 155
London, Michael, 83, 139, 156, 271
Long, D. C., 230
Los Angeles Police Department (LAPD),
     92, 93
Louis-Dreyfuss, Julia, 171
"(Love Lift Us Up) Where We Belong," 38
Lovitz, Jon, 198, 260
Lowe, Rob, 118
Lucchesi, Billy, 178, 179
Lucchesi, Gary, 35, 144, 148, 149, 150,
     151, 155, 157, 197
Lyne, Adrian, 45–46, 47–48, 49, 84, 250

Mafia, 68, 105, 128–29
Malkovich, John, 268
Malnic, Eric, 253–54, 255
Maltin, Leonard, 78
Mancuso, Frank, 57, 69–70, 77, 147, 151,
     155, 157–58
Mann, Michael, 75, 125, 167, 260, 261
Mann, Ted, 62, 88
Manni, Vic, 130
Marrero, Todd, 98, 99–100, 245, 251, 260
Marshall, Garry, 142
Marshall, Penny, 164
Maslin, Janet, 149
Masters, Kim, 172, 241–42
Matthews, Jack, 149
Maxwell, Morton, 248
Mayfield, Les, 3
Mazursky, Paul, 17
McCarthy, Jack, 149–50
McElroy, Michelle, 208, 260
McGillis, Kelly, 71, 72, 74
McInerney, Jay, 10, 112–13, 164, 242
McKee, Robert, 122
McQueen, Chad, 117
"MDE Philosophy," 30, 193–94
Melnick, Daniel, 103, 260, 266
Menninger Clinic, 217, 220, 221
Mestres, Ricardo, 36, 204
Meyer, Ron, 197, 274–75
Michelle (prostitute), 100–102
Milch, David, 180, 198, 206
Milius, John, 17
Millar, Merle Butchar, 23
Miller, David, 211–12, 213, 256
Minnelli, Liza, 17
Mira, Lawrence J., 224
Miscavige, David, 228
Moloney, Jay, 173, 179, 226
Monash, Paul, 89
Monster (Dunne), 199–201
Moore, Demi, 36, 103, 169, 170
Morodor, Giorgio, 76
Moroz, Fred, 224
Moto, Joseph, 256

Mount, Thom, 25, 26, 27, 121
Movie business, 5–8, 14, 28–30, 161–62, 185–97, 219–20
MTV, 45
Murphy, Eddie, 3, 57, 59, 63, 118, 156, 157, 158, 163, 182, 196, 262, 263, 274
Music in movies, 38, 44–45, 50
Mutrux, Floyd, 227

Nagy, Ivan, 87, 88–92, 93–94, 95–97, 129, 273, 275
Nathanson, Michael, 218, 273
Nedd, Priscilla, 87, 260, 261, 262
Neil, Vince, 115
Neufeld, Mace, 158, 197
Newman, Rayce, 107, 116–19, 126, 166
Newsweek magazine, 73
Nicholson, Jack, 106, 107, 108, 117–18, 165, 167, 223, 264, 266
Nielsen, Brigitte, 63, 74
Nolte, Nick, 2, 59, 260
Nugent, Ted, 63

Obst, Lynda, 2, 18–19, 42, 45, 47, 81, 86, 122
O'Connor, David "Doc," 226
O'Dea, John, 247–48
Officer and a Gentleman, An, 33, 34–38, 39, 65
Oman, Chad, 215
Once More with Feeling (book), 265–66
Orth, Maureen, 25–27, 252, 275
Ovitz, Michael S., 1, 71, 121, 179, 182, 197, 226, 228

Pace, Eric, 254
Panetz, Susan, 80
"Paramount Corporate Philosophy" (Simpson), 191–92
Paramount Pictures, 13, 43, 44
  corporate culture, 17–18, 28–29, 30
  management changes, 57
  1990 season, 150
  Simpson-Bruckheimer partnership, deal with, 44, 73, 138–39, 150–51, 157–58
  Simpson's tenure with, 14, 15, 17, 18–19, 30, 31–42, 51–52
Pascal, Amy, 218
Pasdar, Adrian, 73
Patinkin, Mandy, 36
Patrick, Vincent, 55–56
Pellicano, Anthony, 2, 94–95, 131–32, 154, 173–74, 210, 216, 251, 252, 259, 260–61, 265, 273, 274, 275
Penile augmentation, 230–32
Penn, Sean, 63, 260, 261
Performance, 15
Perry, Richard, 116
Persico family, 128
Pesce, Frank, 27, 57, 62–63, 83, 103, 105, 260

Peters, Jon, 45, 87, 96, 103, 163, 172–73, 185, 273
Petrie, Daniel, Jr., 56
Pettigrew, Pete, 70–72, 74
Pfeiffer, Michelle, 2, 3, 103, 251
Philips, Chuck, 253–54, 255
Phillips, Julia, 16, 17, 41, 45, 254
Phillips, Michael, 17
Phoenix, River, 9, 115–16, 208
Photo agencies, 130
Pitt, Brad, 196
Playing God, 209–10, 263
Polanski, Roman, 169
Pollock, Tom, 178, 195, 260, 265, 272
Prescription drug fraud, 210–14, 264–65
Price, Richard, 164
Prophet, Melissa, 87–88, 96, 125, 126, 127, 130, 260
Proser, Chip, 56, 61, 63–64, 66–69, 71
Prostitution business, 79–80, 81–82, 88–94, 95–97, 106–8, 109, 265–66
Puzo, Mario, 33

Quaid, Dennis, 35
Quaid, Randy, 143

Radin, Roy, 87
Rafferty, Terrence, 267, 268
Rainer, Peter, 58
Rapke, Jack, 197, 260, 261
Rasnick, Steve, 16–17
Rawls, Lou, Jr., 117
Real estate ventures, 174–76
Rebel Without a Cause, 24
Reel Power (Litwak), 187
Ref, The, 198, 199, 202
Rehab efforts by Hollywood luminaries, 222–26
Rehab industry, 217–22
Rehme, Bob, 158, 197
Reiser, Paul, 156
Resnick, Faye, 97, 119–20, 272–73
Ressner, Jeffrey, 21, 146
Rhames, Ving, 268
Richardson, John H., 76, 85, 131–33, 228, 229
Ritter, John, 106
Robbins, Tim, 72–73
Roberts, Brad, 255
Roberts, Eric, 35
Roberts, Julia, 169, 170
Robertson, Dave, 74, 140, 154
Rock, The, 3, 196, 206, 238, 243–44, 266–68
Rogers, Christopher, 256
Rogue Warrior, 215, 240
Rooker, Michael, 142
Roseanne, 95, 171
Rosenberg, Mark, 25, 27, 121
Rosenberg, Scott, 270
Rosenfeld, Paul, 96

Rosenman, Howard, 121, 206, 226, 261
Rosenstein, Melvyn, 230, 231–32
Ross, Katharine, 17
Rossovich, Rick, 73
Roth, Joe, 1, 196, 250, 260, 261
Roth, Marcia Ann, 214
Roth, Steve, 75, 87, 104, 112, 121, 126, 226
Rourke, Mickey, 56, 63, 118
Roven, Charles, 247
Rubin, Rick, 108
Ruid, Paul, 178
Ryan, Meg, 72

St. George, Cathy, 96, 125–28, 129–31
S&M bondage games, 97–102, 153–54
Santo Pietro, George, 106
Sassa, Scott, 247
Saturday Night Fever, 30
Scarfiotti, Ferdinando, 121
Schiff, Paul, 142
Schrader, Paul, 17, 87, 121–22, 164, 260, 261
Schumacher, Joel, 222
Schwartz, Tony, 85
Schwarzenegger, Arnold, 58, 140, 167, 168
Scientology, Church of, 227–29
Scorsese, Martin, 17
Scott, Tony, 68–69, 70, 72, 74, 77, 96, 104, 105, 137, 140, 141, 145, 149, 163–64, 260, 261, 263
Scotto, John, 128–29
Sellers, Victoria, 91
Sembello, Michael, 45
Semel, Terry, 239
Semple, Lorenzo, Jr., 206
Shapiro, Robert, 2, 266, 272, 274, 275
Sheen, Charlie, 63, 106, 107, 115, 117, 173, 225, 246, 263–64, 266, 273
Shepard, Jewel, 88
"She's a Maniac," 45
Siegal, Peggy, 76, 153, 163, 164–67
Sill, Joel, 38
Silver, Casey, 50, 250, 252, 261, 274
Silver, Joel, 56, 59–60, 82, 96, 112, 131–32, 158, 175, 194, 226, 241
Simon, Carly, 17
Simpson, Don
    acting by, 141–42, 145–46
    "antijournalists fund," 173–74
    art collection, 176
    automobile antics, 124–28
    background, 19–25, 26–27, 80–81
    clothing collection, 176–77
    competitiveness, 16–17, 27–28, 35, 159, 181–83
    contradictions, 4–5
    cosmetic surgery, 141, 229–35
    daughter of, 10, 242
    death, 106, 251–57, 259–60, 271–72
    directorial ambitions, 74, 105, 138–39
    drug abuse, 9, 39, 40, 41, 68–69, 112–13, 116, 117, 121–24, 202, 255–57. *See also* prescription drug abuse *below*
    extortion incident, 128
    generosity, 179
    gun ownership, 60–63
    high-concept movie, creation of, 122
    as Hollywood fixture, 5, 6–8
    hormone implants, 232, 235
    household accounts, 176
    inferiority complex, 162
    last months, 246–51
    literary portraits of, 122–24, 131–33
    media attention, 73, 75–76, 163–64, 205, 265
    memorial services for, 1–4, 8, 260–62
    memos by, 31, 122
    movie career, decision on, 24
    moviemaking, approach to, 19, 31–32, 44–45, 122–24, 191–92
    outrageous behavior, 14, 39–40, 152–53
    as Paramount executive, 14, 15, 17, 18–19, 30, 31–42, 52
    paranoia, 68–69, 105, 131
    "personal ads" in newspapers, 133–35
    philosophy of, 4, 236
    prescription drug abuse, 8–9, 203, 208, 209, 210, 212–13, 255–57
    producing career, start of, 42
    rehab treatments, 217, 220–21, 226–29
    rejection, fear of, 83
    restaurant venture, 180–81
    Scientology involvement, 227–29
    self-concept, 19, 25, 233–34, 241–42
    sex, attitudes about, 133
    sex life, 16, 79, 80–82, 97–102, 153–54, 265–66
    sexual harassment suit against, 151–52, 154, 202
    solo career, plans for, 241–42, 244–46, 248, 249–51
    start in movie business, 15–17
    storytelling talent, 24
    vacations, 177–79
    voice of, 131
    wealth, 161, 162
    weight problem, 17, 202–3, 234–36, 247, 250–51
    women, views on, 76, 82–88, 233
    work ethic, 26, 140, 220
    wrongful death civil suit against, 215–16, 264
    See also Simpson-Bruckheimer partnership
Simpson, June Hazel Clark, 19, 20–21, 23, 51–52, 253
Simpson, Lary, 10, 20, 27–28, 179, 216, 242, 246, 248, 262
Simpson, Nicole Brown, 108, 118, 119
Simpson, O. J., 2, 106, 118, 119–21, 272, 273

Simpson, Russell J., 19, 20–21, 23, 253
Simpson-Bruckheimer partnership
  awards for, 77, 237, 267–68
  C-shaped desk, 60
  Disney, deal with, 158, 186, 190–91
  dissolution of, 214–15, 237–41
  formation of, 42–43
  Paramount, deal with, 44, 73, 138–39,
    150–51, 157–58
  personal and professional differences, 10,
    43, 140, 205–6
  public image, 73–74
  superstar actors, avoidance of, 196
  talent agency representation, 197–98
Sinatra, Tina, 2, 260
Sirico, Tony, 62
Siskel, Gene, 270
Skaaren, Warren, 61, 68, 71, 147
Skerritt, Tom, 73
Slater, Christian, 223, 225
Sleep with Me, 77–78
Smith, Liz, 239
Smith, Will, 2, 196, 199, 263
Soderbergh, Steven, 181
Soldier of Fortune TV series, 215, 240
Spacey, Kevin, 199
Spelling, Aaron and Candy, 175–76
Spielberg, Steven, 1, 75, 168, 195–96, 249
Stallone, Sylvester, 56–57, 58, 63, 118,
  167, 169–70, 274
Star salaries and spoiled behavior, 167–73
Steel, Dawn, 2, 13, 22, 39, 42, 47, 49–50,
  66–67, 247, 260, 261
Stephanie, Princess of Monaco, 118
Stern, Bill, 16
Stevens, Nick, 219
Stewart, Alana, 2, 260
Stewart, Donald, 146
Stewart, Douglas Day, 34–35, 37, 38, 74,
  75, 147
Stewart, Rod, 106, 117
Stills, Stephen, 117
Stoeffel, William, 125
Strain, Julie, 85, 86, 273
Streisand, Barbra, 170–71, 174–75
Stuppy, William P., 247–48
Summer blockbusters, 29
Swanson, Gloria, 172
Swimming with Sharks, 132
Sylbert, Richard, 15, 17–18, 29, 30, 39, 44–
  45

"Take My Breath Away," 76–77
Tanen, Ned, 51–52, 69–70, 146, 147, 158
Tarantino, Quentin, 78, 180
Tarr, Lester, 248
Teitelbaum, Steven, 233
Television business, 28, 30
Terrail, Patrick, 180
Tessler, Sid, 248
Thief of Hearts, 75

Thorne, Dave, 74, 140, 154
Tienken, Richard, 151
Tisch, Steve, 4, 15, 25, 75, 87, 104, 260,
  261, 265
Toback, James, 22, 62, 198, 235–36, 241,
  249, 250–51, 260, 265, 275
Top Gun, 3, 60, 63–75, 76–78, 129, 130
Towne, Robert, 19, 137, 140, 141, 143–44,
  145, 147, 148, 260, 265
Townsend, Claire, 25, 27
Travers, Peter, 204
Travolta, John, 34, 35, 169
Trepanier, Jeannelle, 245–46, 273
Turan, Kenneth, 266–67
Turner, Ted, 165, 247

Umamoto, Don, 73

Van Damme, Jean-Claude, 118, 222
Van Halen band, 115
Vicuña, Victoria Fulton, 10, 242
Videocassette market, 187
Vincent, Jan-Michael, 222
Vipers' Club, The (Richardson), 131–33

Wagner, Paula, 71, 147
Wahl, Ken, 223
Wakefield, Jim, 90, 91, 93
Walt Disney Studios, 1, 57, 158, 186–87,
  188, 189–91, 203–4, 216
Walters, Barbara, 120
Warner Bros., 15–16
Warnes, Jennifer, 38
Washington, Denzel, 4, 196
Waters, Daniel, 175
Weber, Billy, 145, 146, 148, 153
Webster, Lawrence, 213
Weinberg, Marc, 77
Weinraub, Bernard, 202
Weinstein, Paula, 25, 27, 121
Weintraub, Jerry, 35
Weitzman, Howard, 2, 273, 275
Welles, Jeff, 178
Wells, Jeffrey, 239
Wenner, Jann, 178, 261
Wessells, Hunter, 231–32
West, Simon, 269, 270
"What a Feeling," 45
White Dog, 32, 33
Whitlock, Tom, 76
Wiatt, Jim, 3, 41, 48, 75, 87, 104–5, 158,
  166, 197, 248, 249, 260, 265
Willis, Bruce, 58, 169, 172–73, 274
Wilmington, Michael, 57–58
Wilson, Donna, 141
Winberg, Patrick, 154
Wing, Leslie, 36
Winger, Debra, 36, 37
Wittliff, William, 55
Wolinsky, Hawk, 178, 260
Wolper, Carol, 206

Woods, Gary, 84, 112
"World Is Changing, The" (Katzenberg), 190–91, 194
Wright, Tom, 31, 193

Yerkovich, Anthony, 166, 167, 180, 260, 265, 272
You'll Never Eat Lunch in This Town Again (Phillips), 41, 254

You'll Never Make Love in This Town Again (book), 81, 97, 103, 106–7, 108, 257, 273
Young, Lance, 138–40, 143–45, 147, 158
Young Guns, 142

Zaloom, George, 3
Zone of Silence, 201–2, 206
Zslomsowitch, Keith, 108